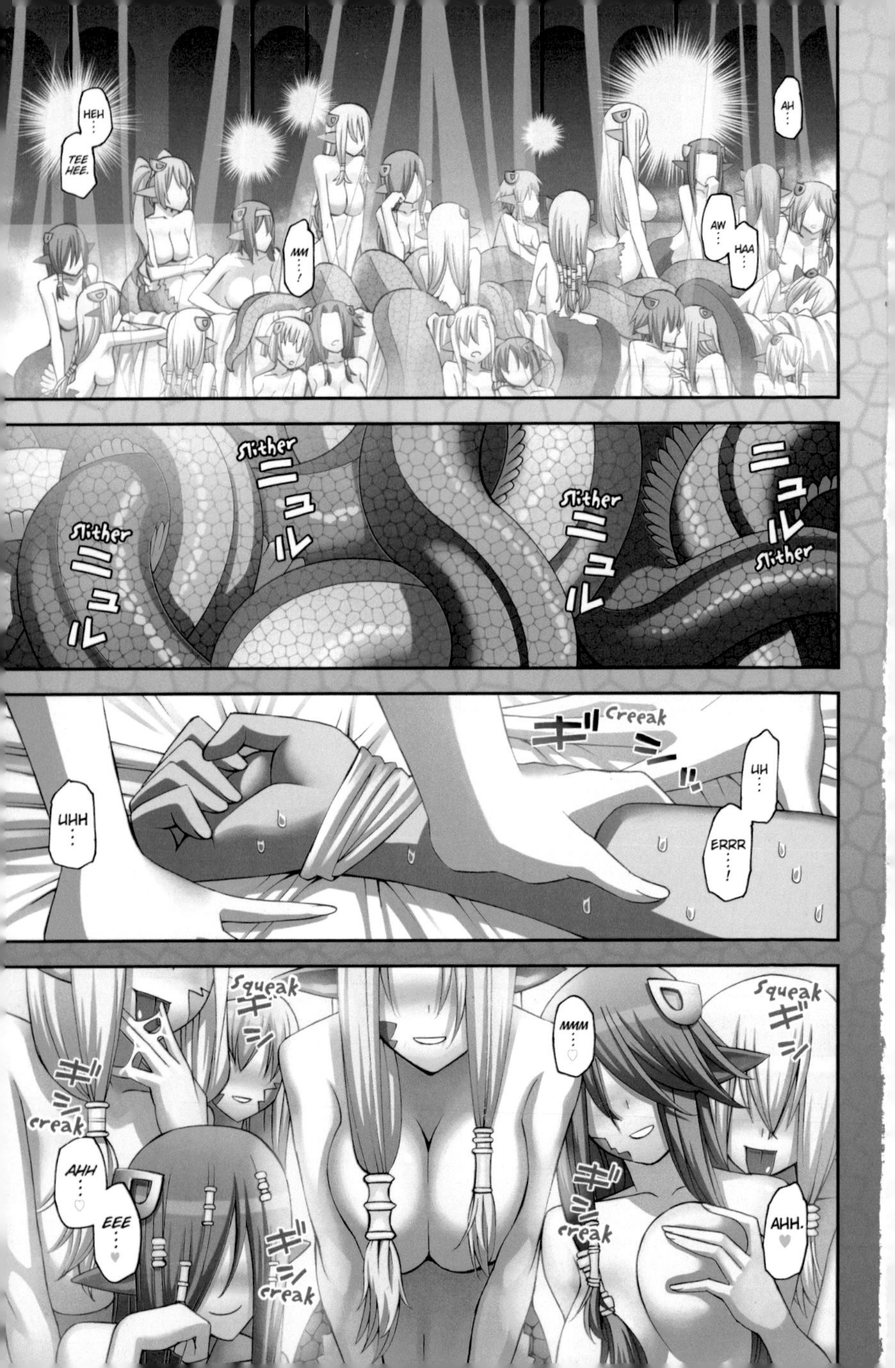
AH...
AW... HAA...
MM...!
HEH... TEE HEE.
ニュル Slither
Slither ニュル
Slither ニュル
Slither ニュル
Creeak ギシッ
UH... ERRR...!
UHH...
Squeak ギシ
MMM...♡
ギシ creak
AHH.♡
Squeak ギシ
ギシ creak
AHH...♡
EEE...♥
ギシ creak

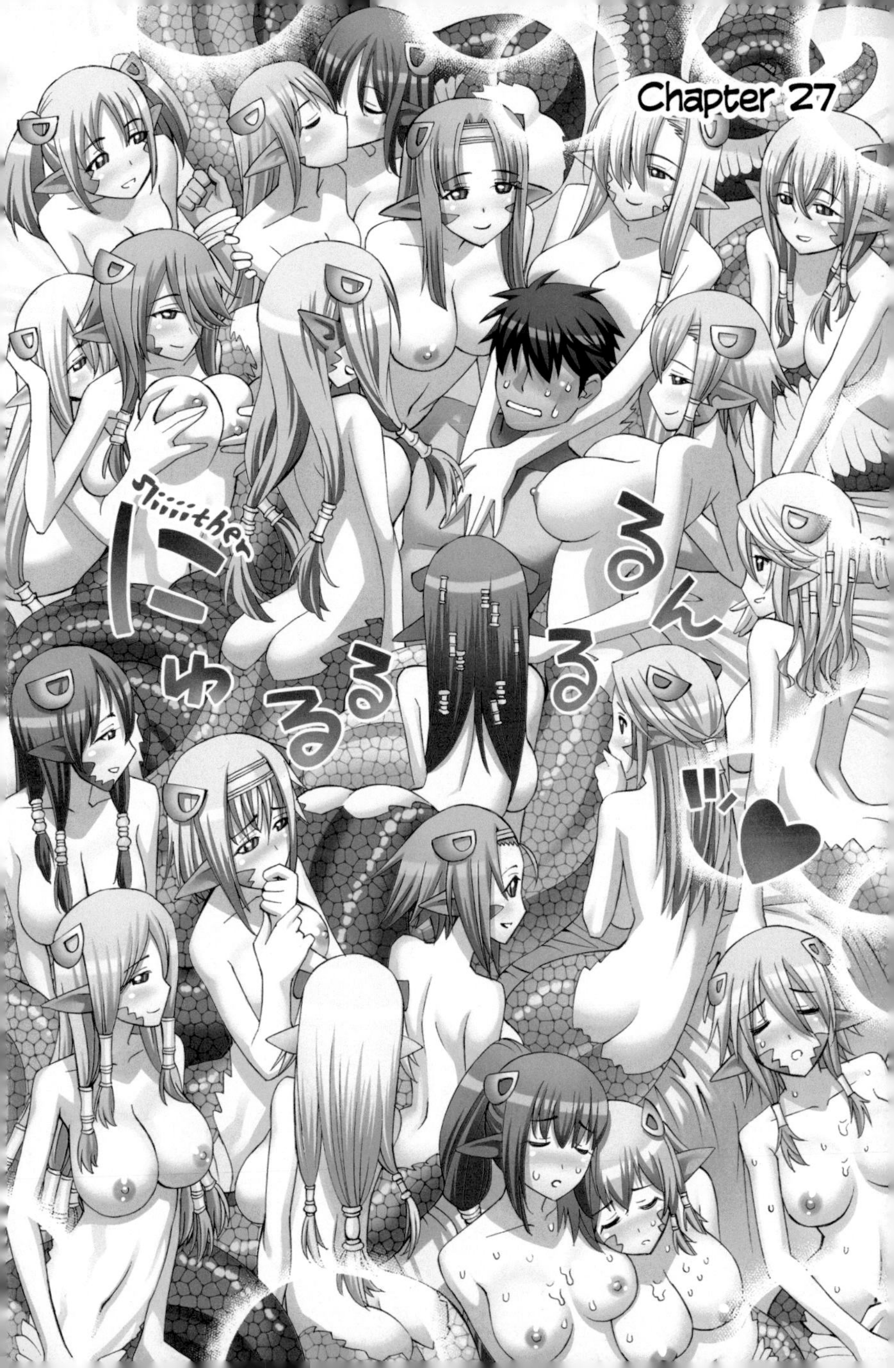
Chapter 27
にゅるるるるん゛♥
Sliiiither

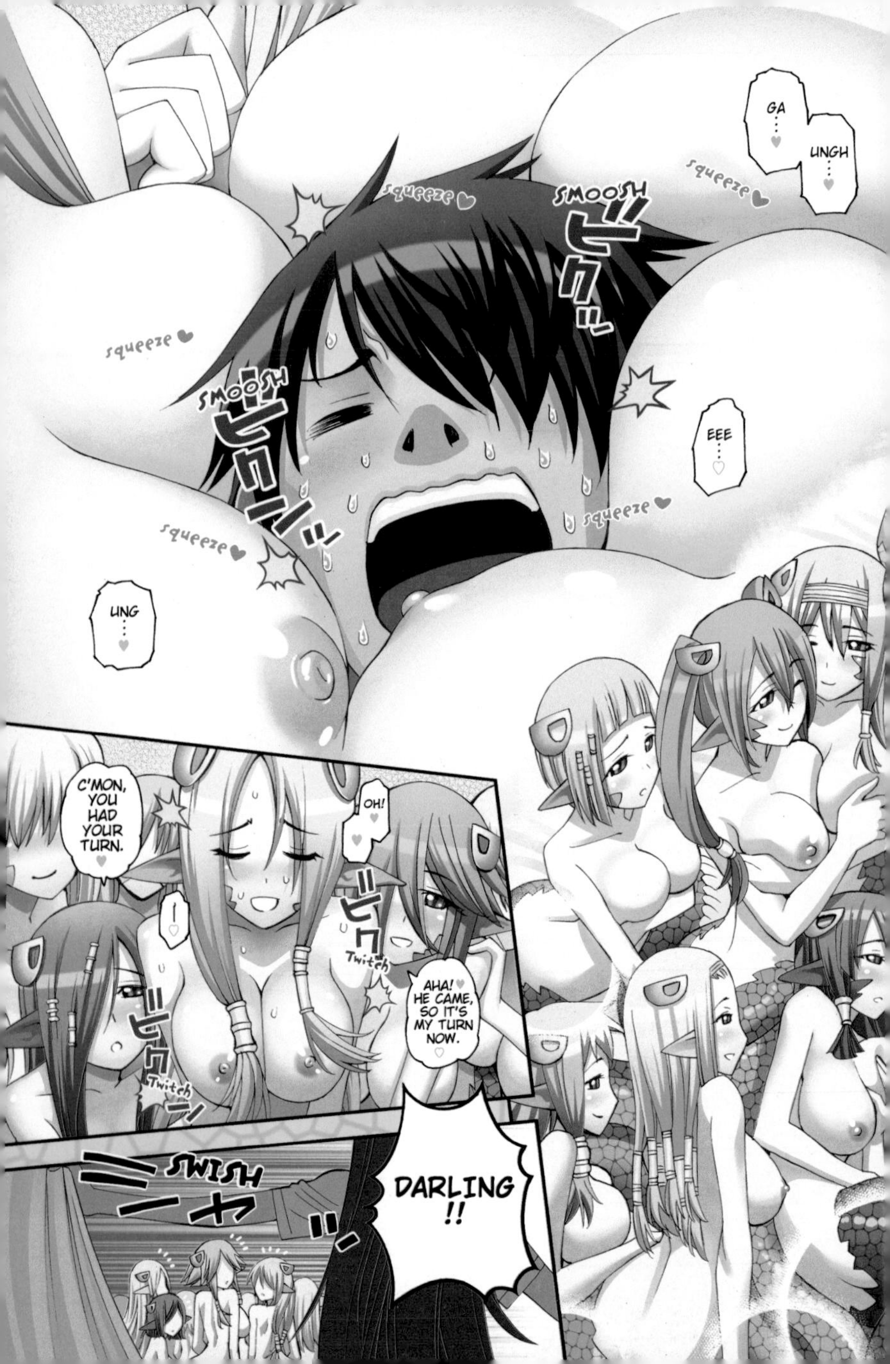
GA... UNGH...
squeeze
SMOOSH
squeeze
EEE...
squeeze
SMOOSH
squeeze
squeeze
UNG...
AHA! HE CAME, SO IT'S MY TURN NOW.
Twitch
OH!
!
C'MON, YOU HAD YOUR TURN.
Twitch
DARLING!!
SWISH

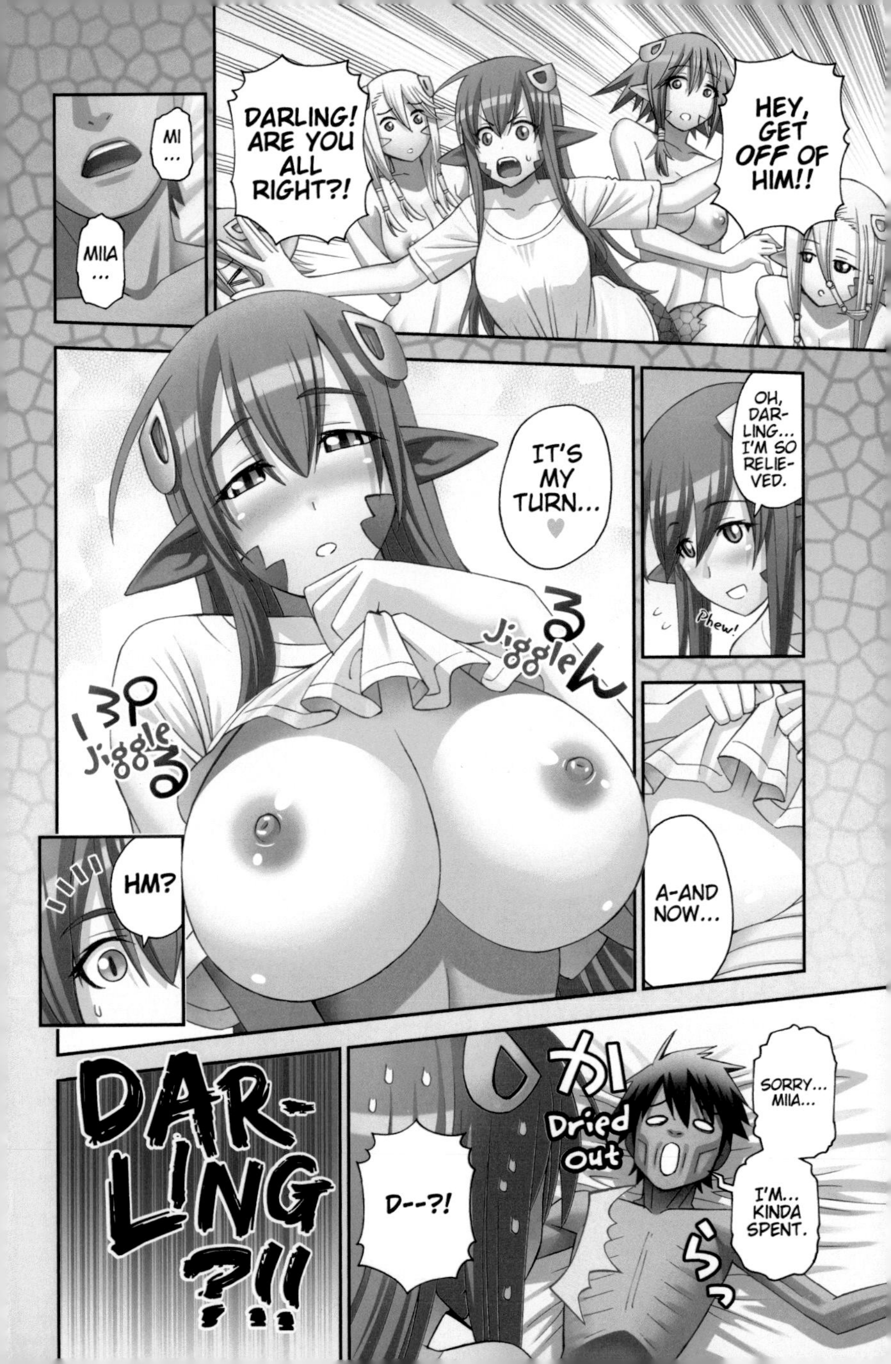
HEY, GET OFF OF HIM!!
DARLING! ARE YOU ALL RIGHT?!
MI ...
MIIA ...
OH, DAR-LING... I'M SO RELIE-VED.
Phew!
A-AND NOW...
IT'S MY TURN... ♥
るん
Jiggle
ぷる
Jiggle
HM?
SORRY... MIIA...
I'M... KINDA SPENT.
かー
Dried out
らっ
D--?!
DAR-LING?!!

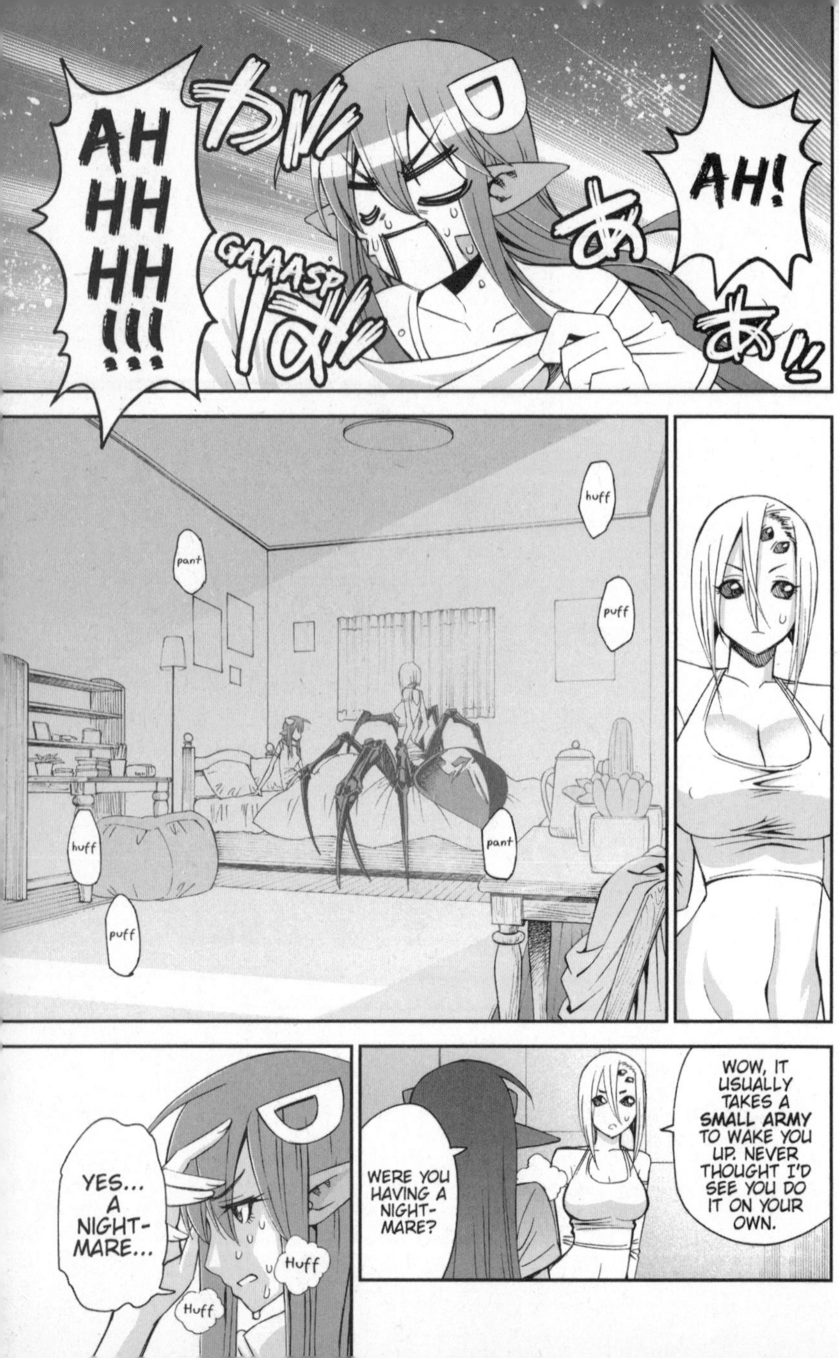
AH!
あ
あ!!
AHHHHHH!!!
GAAASP
huff
puff
pant
huff
puff
pant
WOW, IT USUALLY TAKES A SMALL ARMY TO WAKE YOU UP. NEVER THOUGHT I'D SEE YOU DO IT ON YOUR OWN.
WERE YOU HAVING A NIGHT-MARE?
YES... A NIGHT-MARE...
Huff
Huff

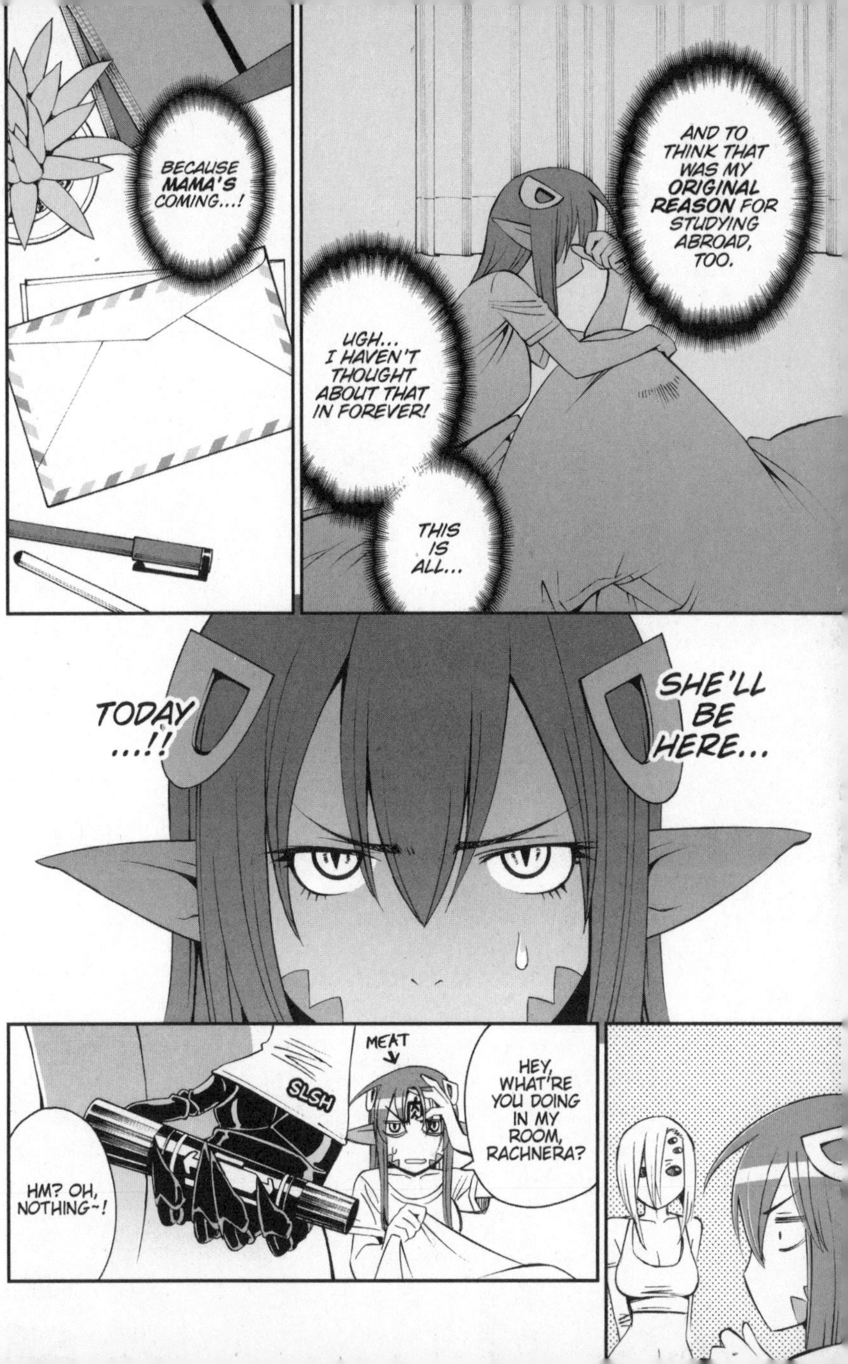
AND TO THINK THAT WAS MY ORIGINAL REASON FOR STUDYING ABROAD, TOO.
UGH... I HAVEN'T THOUGHT ABOUT THAT IN FOREVER!
THIS IS ALL...
BECAUSE MAMA'S COMING...!
SHE'LL BE HERE...
TODAY ...!!
MEAT
HEY, WHAT'RE YOU DOING IN MY ROOM, RACHNERA?
SLSH
HM? OH, NOTHING~!

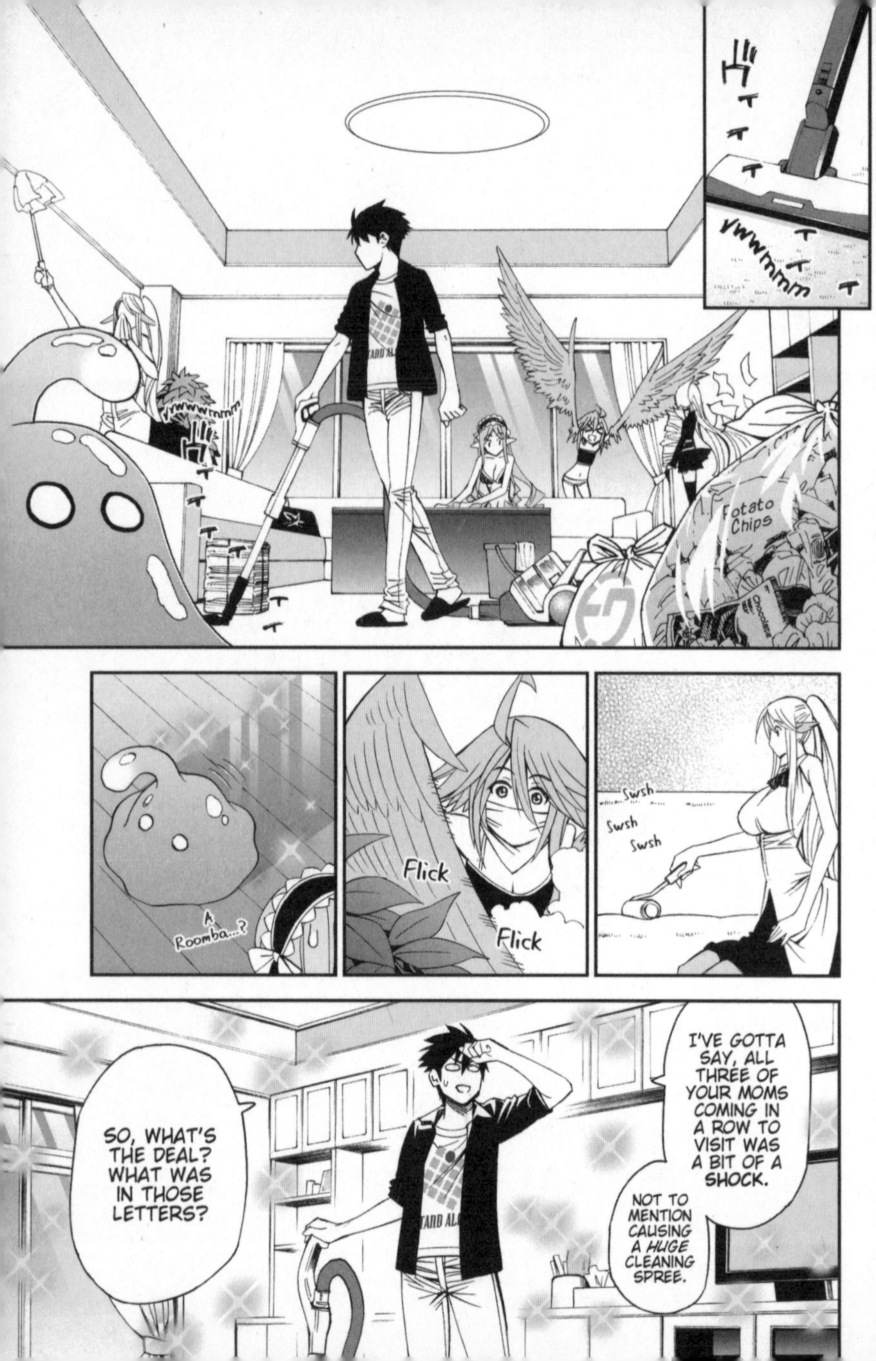

Vwwmmm
Vwwwwmmm
Potato Chips
Chocolate
Swsh
Swsh
Swsh
Flick
Flick
A Roomba...?
I'VE GOTTA SAY, ALL THREE OF YOUR MOMS COMING IN A ROW TO VISIT WAS A BIT OF A SHOCK.
NOT TO MENTION CAUSING A *HUGE* CLEANING SPREE.
SO, WHAT'S THE DEAL? WHAT WAS IN THOSE LETTERS?

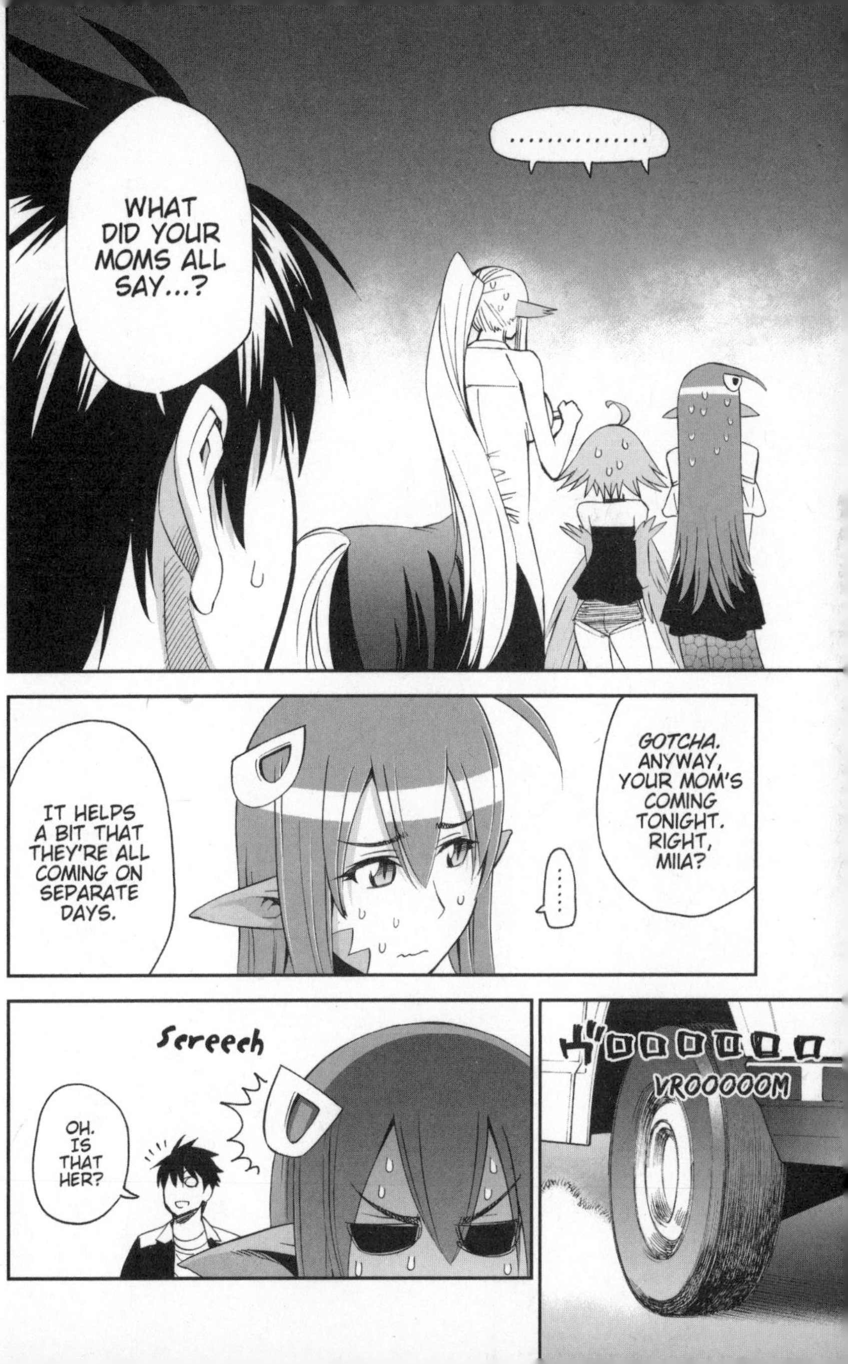
WHAT DID YOUR MOMS ALL SAY...?
....
GOTCHA. ANYWAY, YOUR MOM'S COMING TONIGHT. RIGHT, MIIA?
......
IT HELPS A BIT THAT THEY'RE ALL COMING ON SEPARATE DAYS.
VROOOOOM
Screech
OH. IS THAT HER?

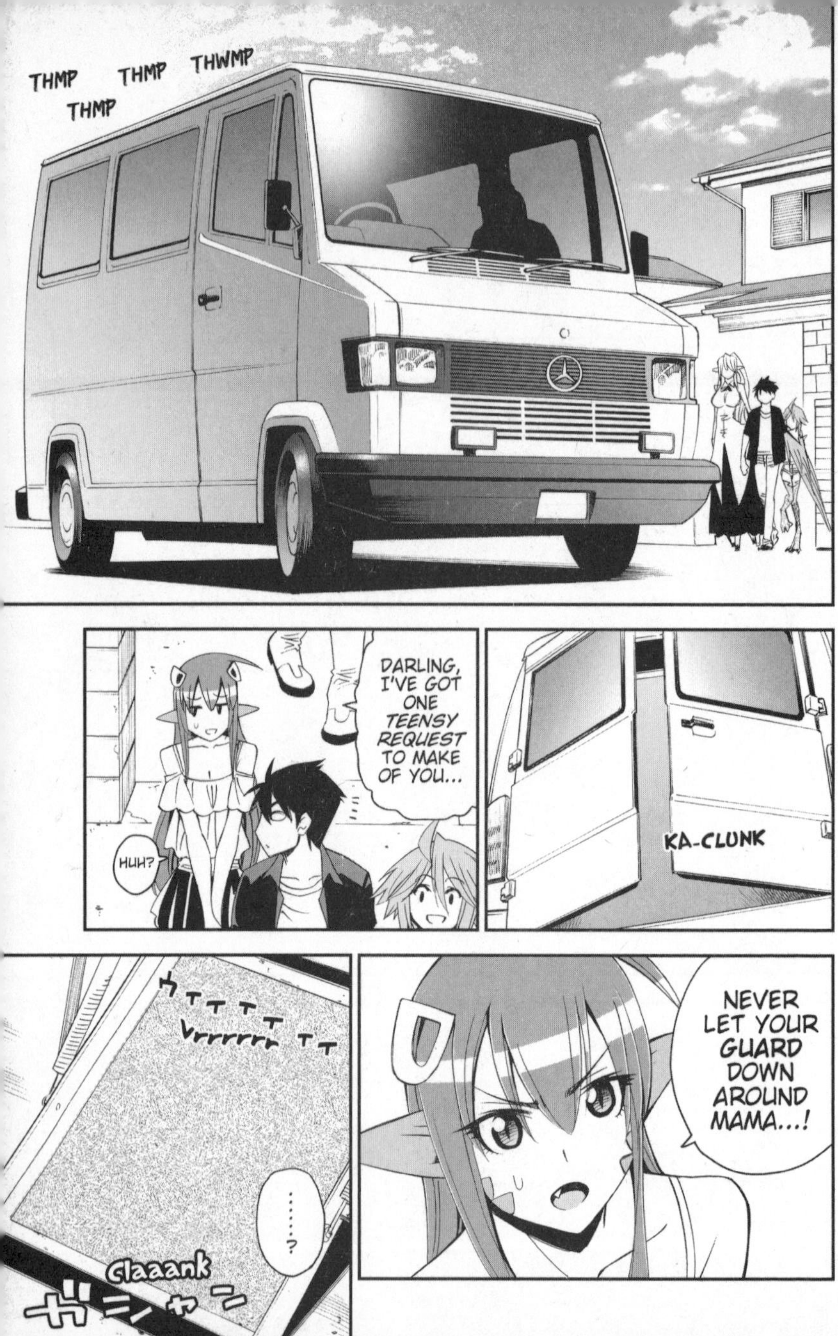
THMP THMP THWMP
THMP
KA-CLUNK
DARLING, I'VE GOT ONE TEENSY REQUEST TO MAKE OF YOU...
HUH?
NEVER LET YOUR GUARD DOWN AROUND MAMA...!
Vrrrrrr
......?
Claaank

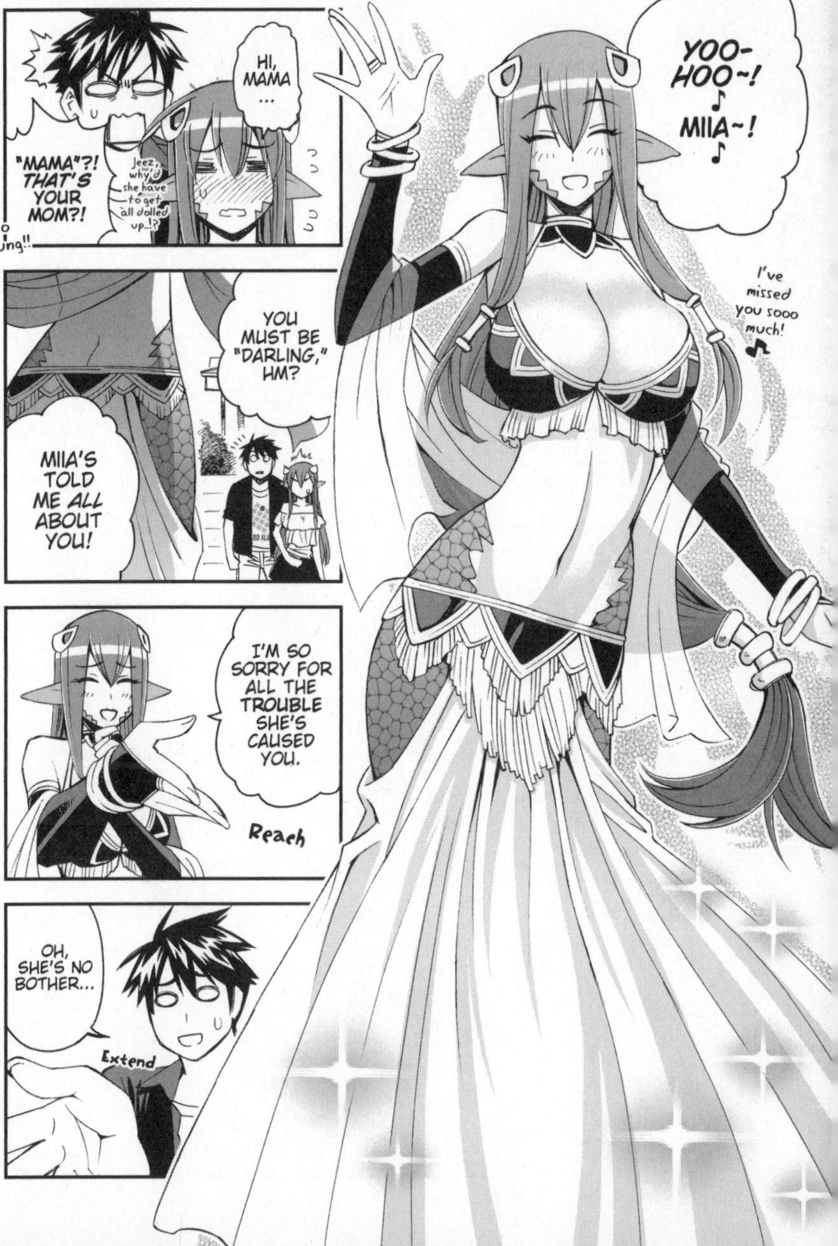
YOO-HOO~! ♪ MIIA~! ♪
I've missed you sooo much!
HI, MAMA ...
Jeez, why'd she have to get all dolled up...!?
"MAMA"?! THAT'S YOUR MOM?!
So young!!
YOU MUST BE "DARLING," HM?
MIIA'S TOLD ME ALL ABOUT YOU!
I'M SO SORRY FOR ALL THE TROUBLE SHE'S CAUSED YOU.
Reach
OH, SHE'S NO BOTHER...
Extend

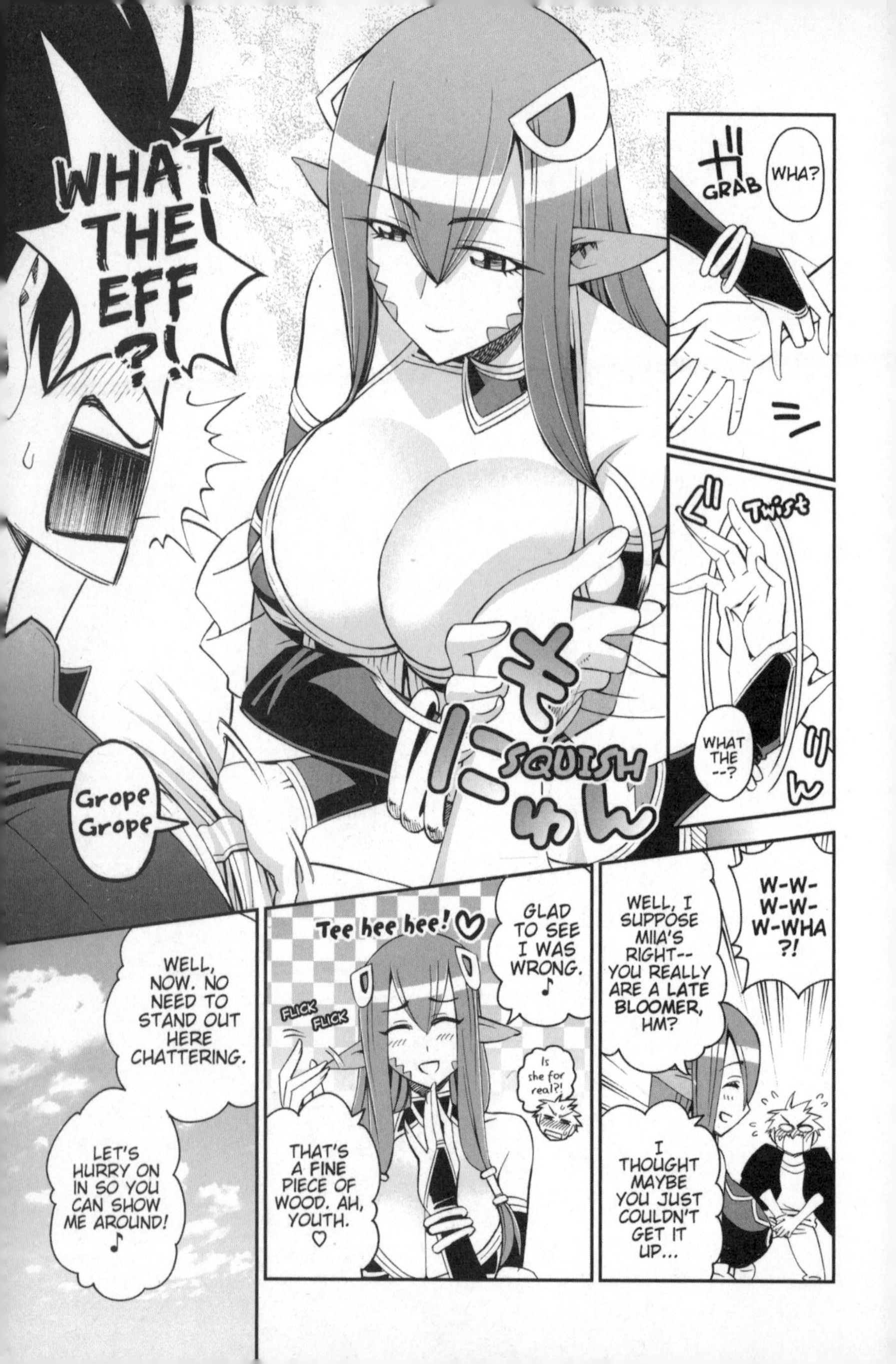
GRAB
WHA?
Twist
WHAT THE --?
WHAT THE EFF ?!
SQUISH
Grope Grope
W-W-W-W-W-WHA ?!
WELL, I SUPPOSE MIIA'S RIGHT-- YOU REALLY ARE A LATE BLOOMER, HM?
I THOUGHT MAYBE YOU JUST COULDN'T GET IT UP...
GLAD TO SEE I WAS WRONG. ♪
Tee hee hee! ♡
FLICK FLICK
Is she for real?!
THAT'S A FINE PIECE OF WOOD. AH, YOUTH. ♡
WELL, NOW. NO NEED TO STAND OUT HERE CHATTERING.
LET'S HURRY ON IN SO YOU CAN SHOW ME AROUND! ♪

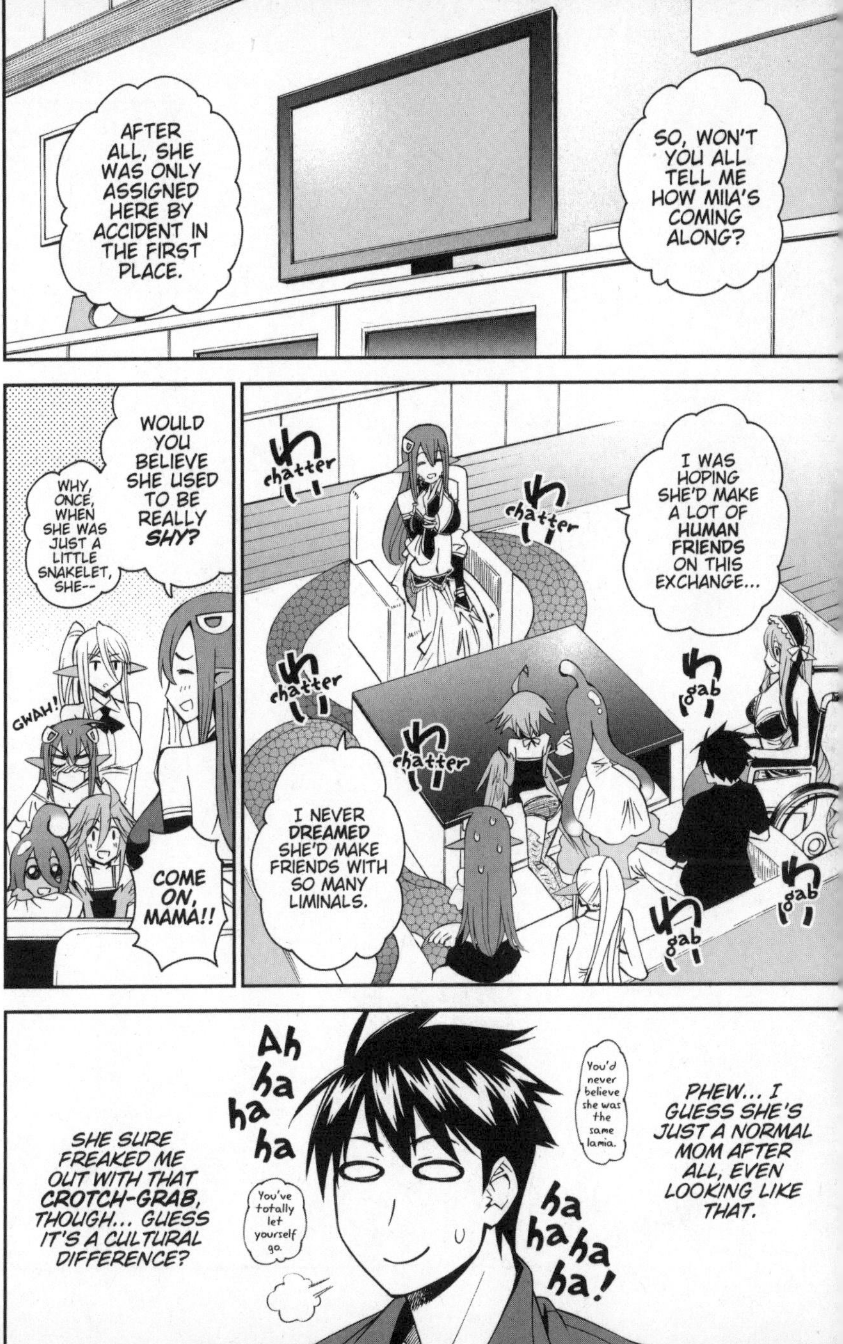
SO, WON'T YOU ALL TELL ME HOW MIIA'S COMING ALONG?
AFTER ALL, SHE WAS ONLY ASSIGNED HERE BY ACCIDENT IN THE FIRST PLACE.
I WAS HOPING SHE'D MAKE A LOT OF HUMAN FRIENDS ON THIS EXCHANGE...
chatter
chatter
gab
gab
I NEVER DREAMED SHE'D MAKE FRIENDS WITH SO MANY LIMINALS.
chatter
chatter
gab
WOULD YOU BELIEVE SHE USED TO BE REALLY SHY?
WHY, ONCE, WHEN SHE WAS JUST A LITTLE SNAKELET, SHE--
GWAH!
COME ON, MAMA!!
PHEW... I GUESS SHE'S JUST A NORMAL MOM AFTER ALL, EVEN LOOKING LIKE THAT.
You'd never believe she was the same lamia.
Ah ha ha ha ha
ha ha ha ha ha!
SHE SURE FREAKED ME OUT WITH THAT CROTCH-GRAB, THOUGH... GUESS IT'S A CULTURAL DIFFERENCE?
You've totally let yourself go.

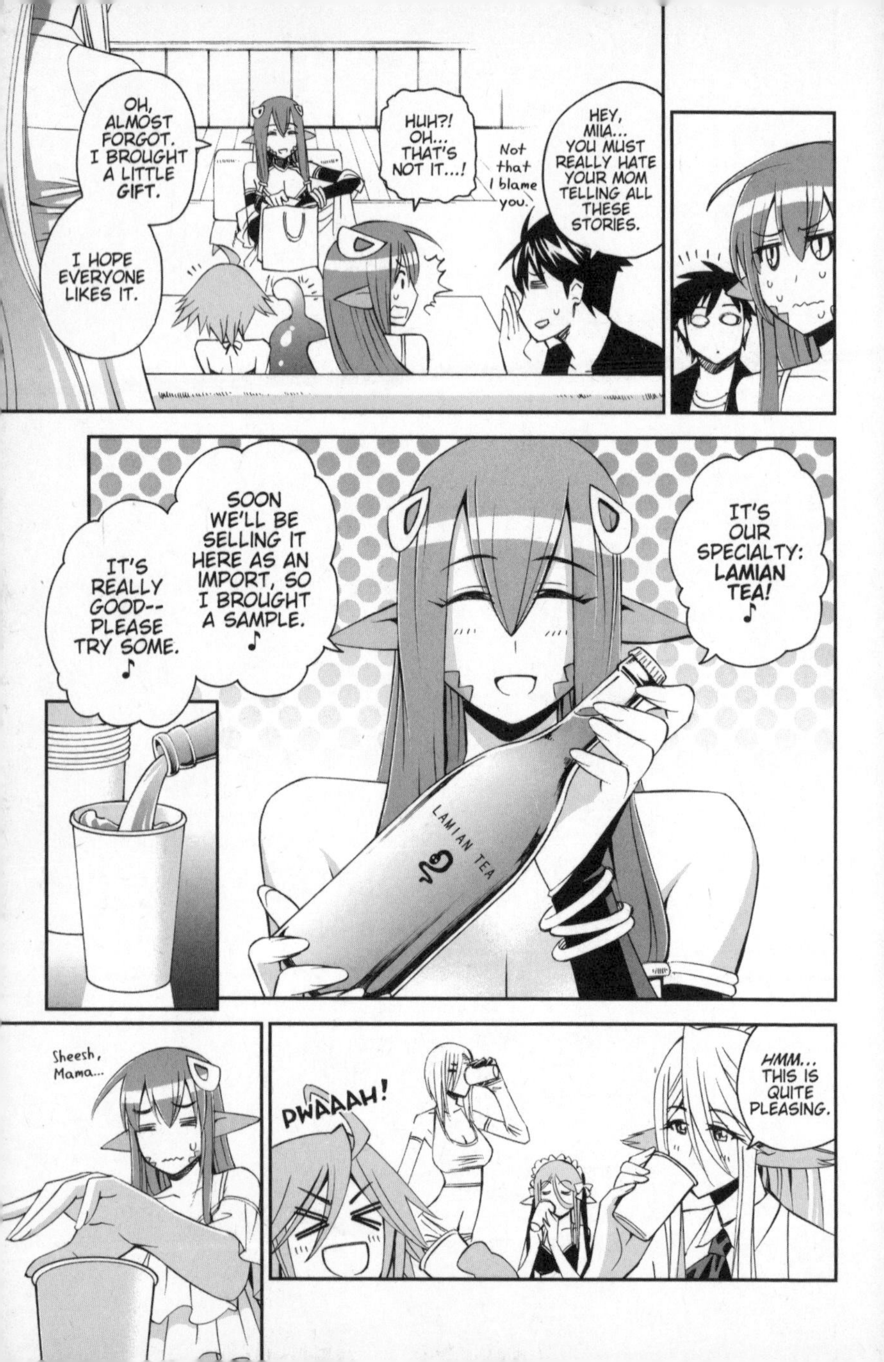
HEY, MIIA... YOU MUST REALLY HATE YOUR MOM TELLING ALL THESE STORIES.
Not that I blame you.
HUH?! OH... THAT'S NOT IT...!
OH, ALMOST FORGOT. I BROUGHT A LITTLE GIFT.
I HOPE EVERYONE LIKES IT.
IT'S OUR SPECIALTY: LAMIAN TEA! ♪
SOON WE'LL BE SELLING IT HERE AS AN IMPORT, SO I BROUGHT A SAMPLE. ♪
IT'S REALLY GOOD-- PLEASE TRY SOME. ♪
LAMIAN TEA
HMM... THIS IS QUITE PLEASING.
PWAAAH!
Sheesh, Mama...

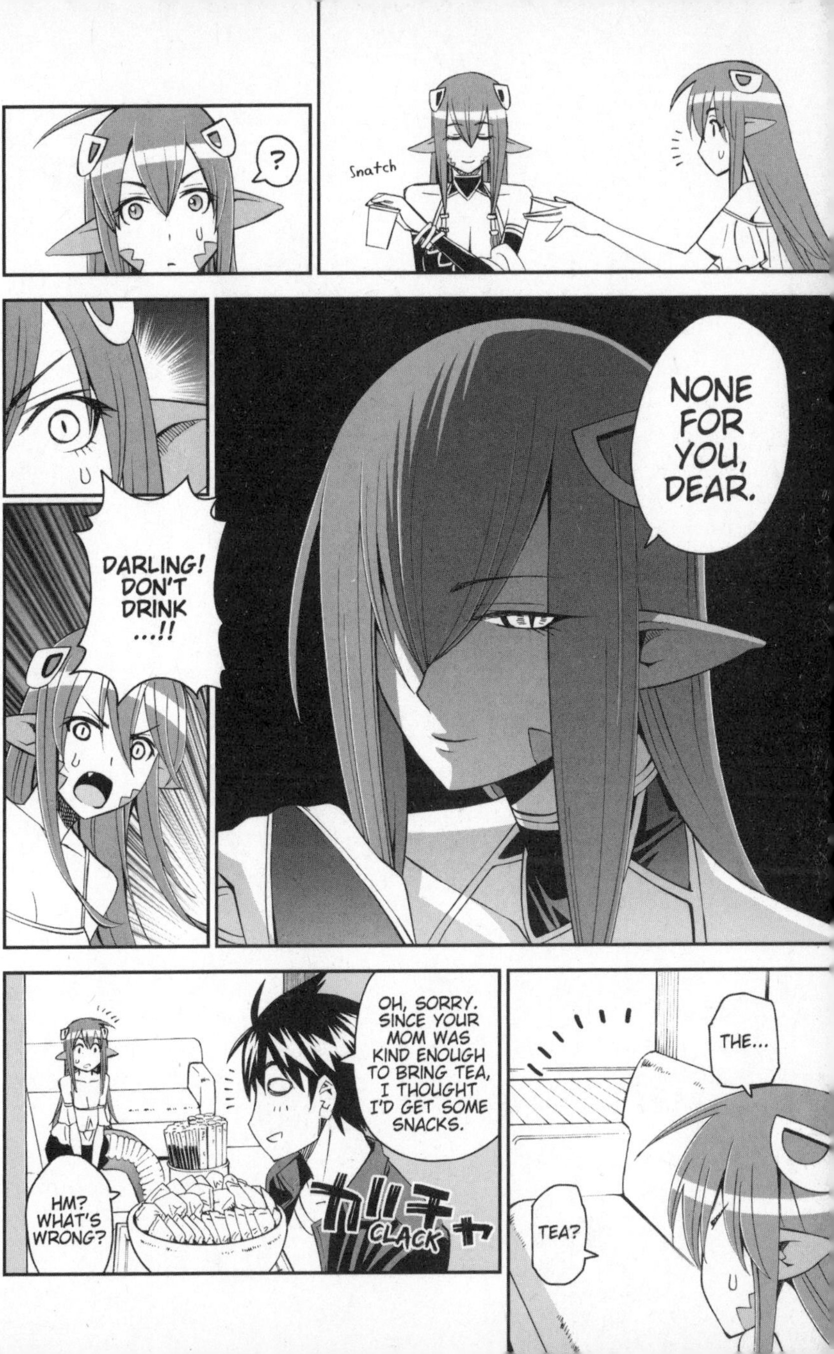
Snatch
?
NONE FOR YOU, DEAR.
DARLING! DON'T DRINK ...!!
THE...
TEA?
OH, SORRY. SINCE YOUR MOM WAS KIND ENOUGH TO BRING TEA, I THOUGHT I'D GET SOME SNACKS.
カチャ
CLACK
HM? WHAT'S WRONG?

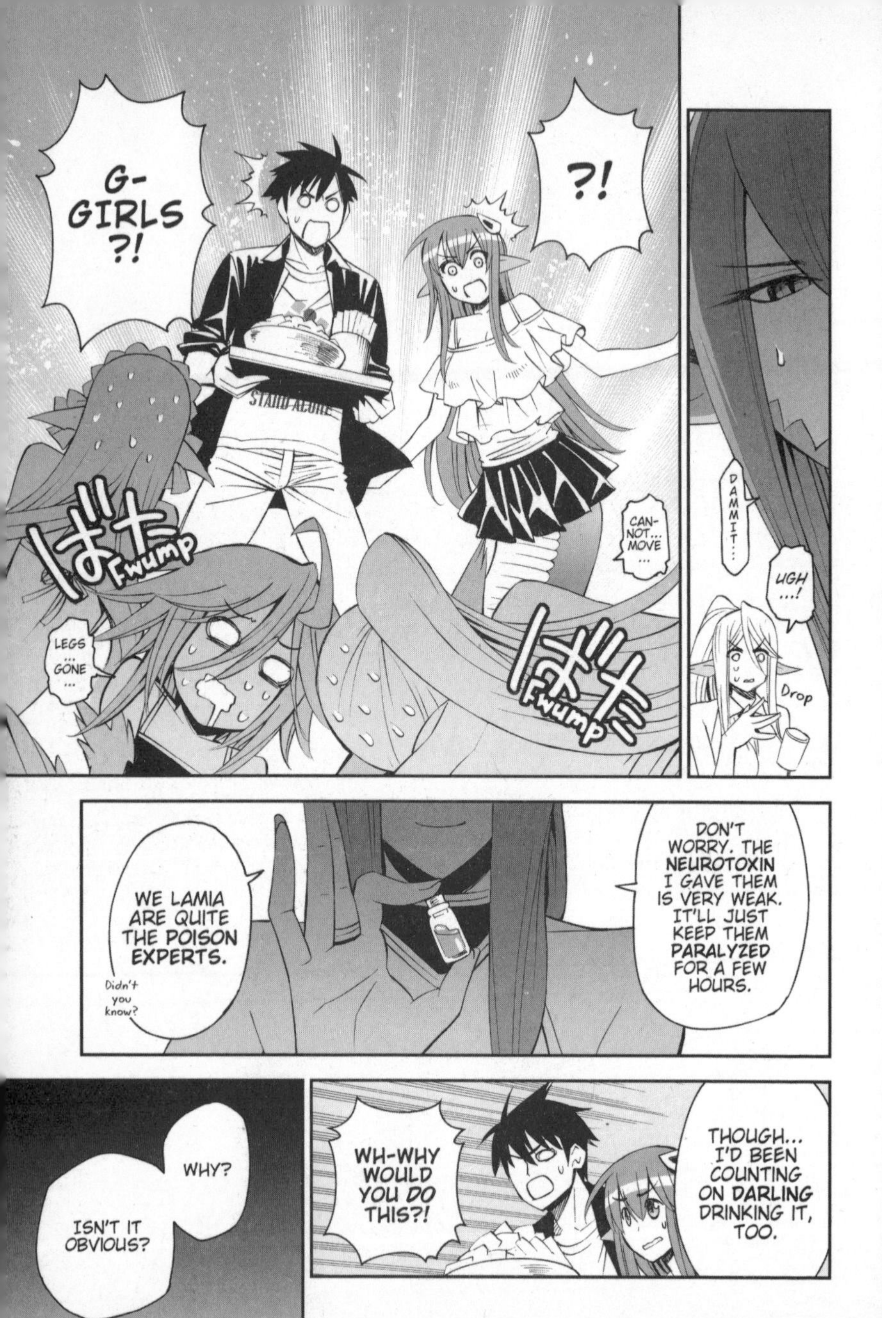
DAMMIT…
UGH …!
Drop
?!
G-GIRLS ?!
CAN-NOT… MOVE …
ばた Fwump
ばた Fwump
LEGS … GONE …
DON'T WORRY. THE NEUROTOXIN I GAVE THEM IS VERY WEAK. IT'LL JUST KEEP THEM PARALYZED FOR A FEW HOURS.
WE LAMIA ARE QUITE THE POISON EXPERTS.
Didn't you know?
THOUGH… I'D BEEN COUNTING ON DARLING DRINKING IT, TOO.
WH-WHY WOULD YOU DO THIS?!
WHY?
ISN'T IT OBVIOUS?

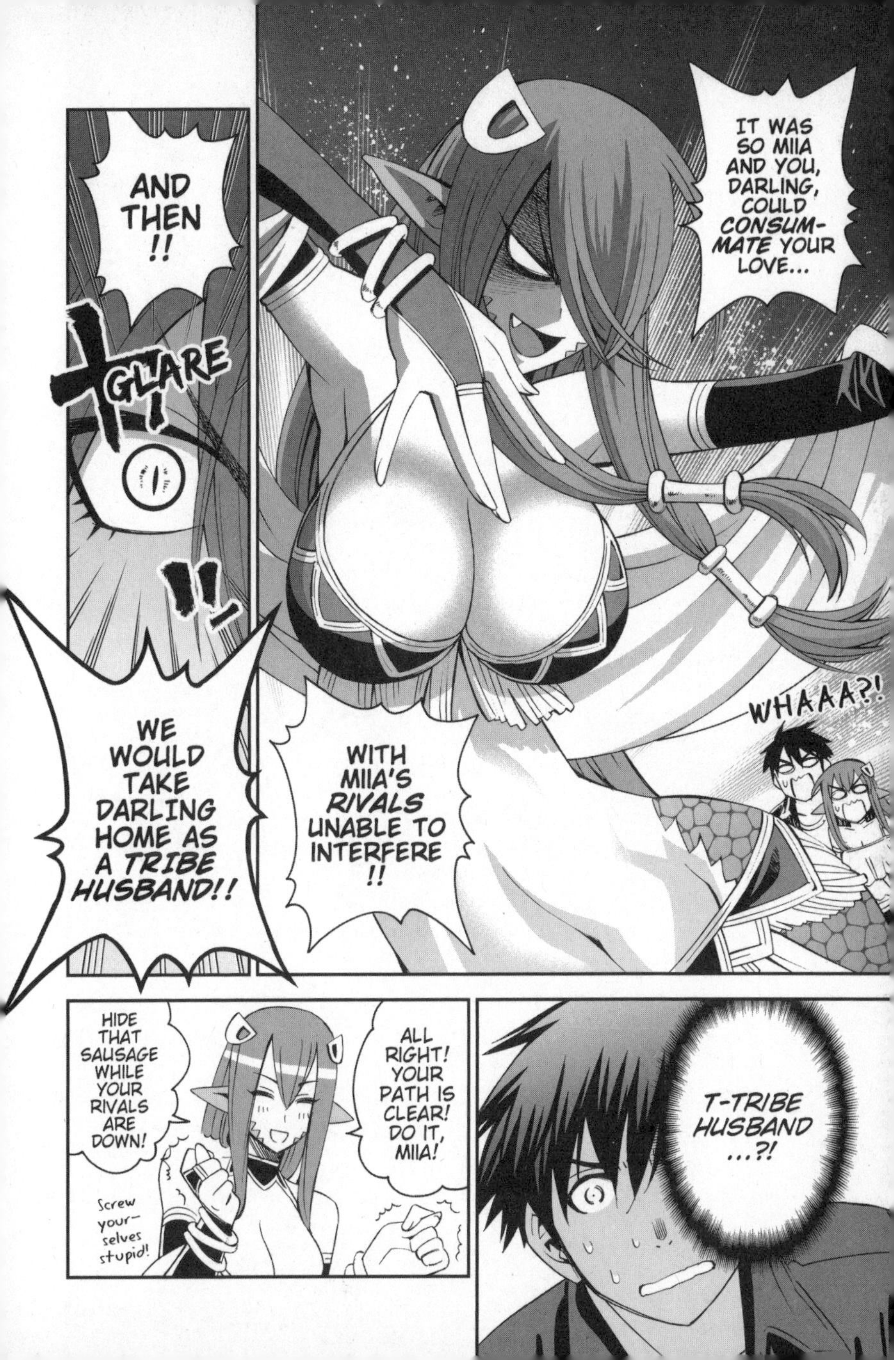
IT WAS SO MIIA AND YOU, DARLING, COULD CONSUMMATE YOUR LOVE...
WITH MIIA'S RIVALS UNABLE TO INTERFERE !!
AND THEN !!
GLARE
!!
WE WOULD TAKE DARLING HOME AS A TRIBE HUSBAND!!
WHAAA?!
T-TRIBE HUSBAND ...?!
ALL RIGHT! YOUR PATH IS CLEAR! DO IT, MIIA!
HIDE THAT SAUSAGE WHILE YOUR RIVALS ARE DOWN!
Screw yourselves stupid!

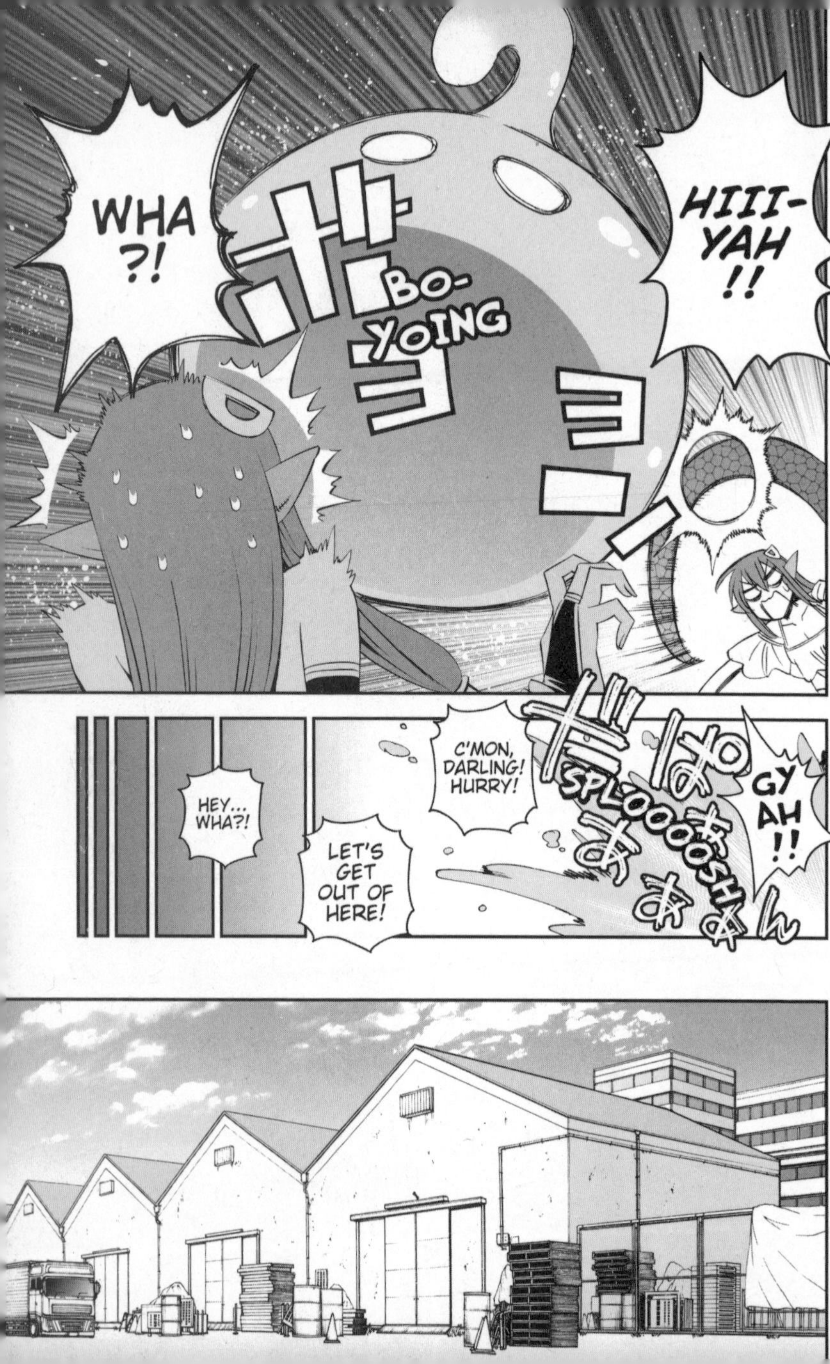
HIIII-YAH!!
WHA?!
BO-YOING
GYAH!!
SPLOOOOSH
C'MON, DARLING! HURRY!
LET'S GET OUT OF HERE!
HEY... WHA?!

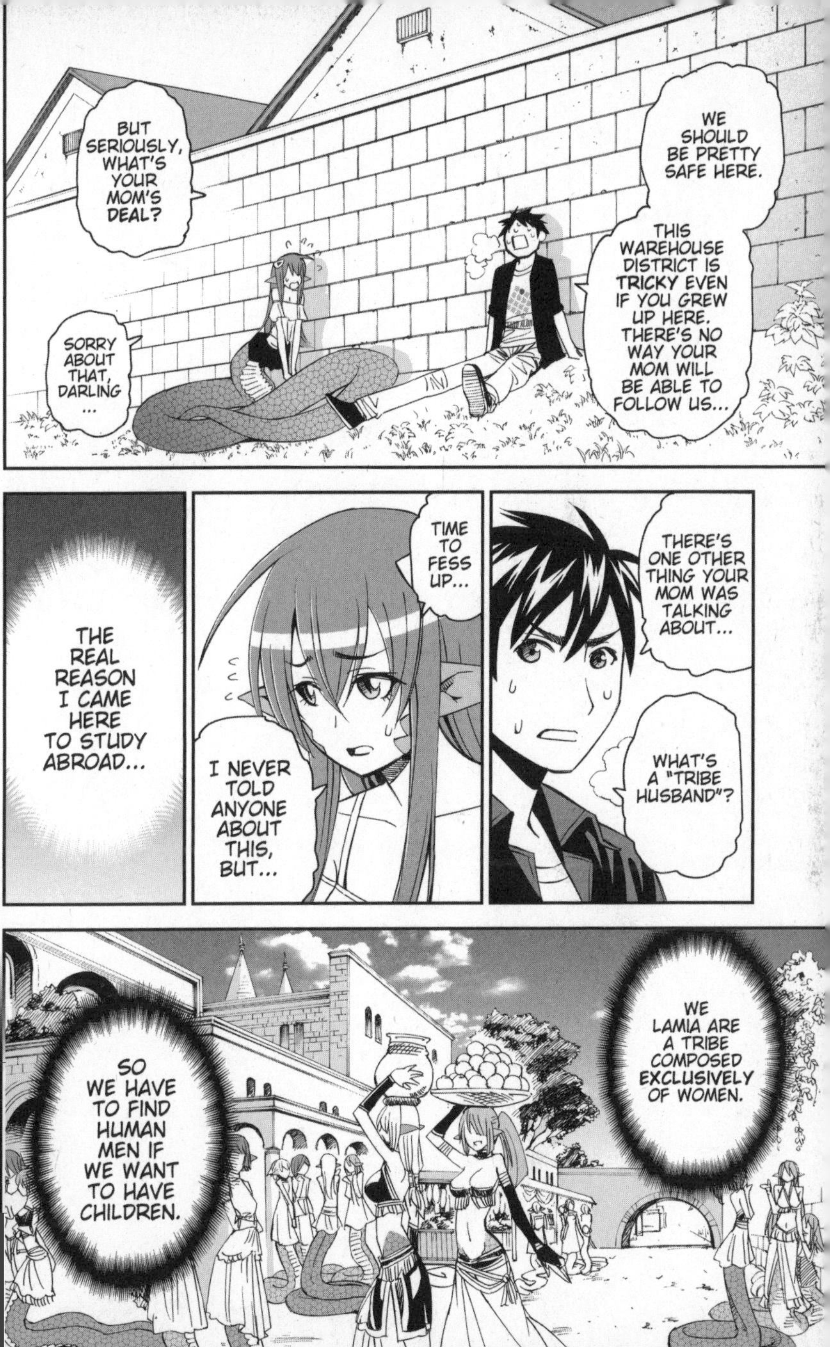
WE SHOULD BE PRETTY SAFE HERE.
THIS WAREHOUSE DISTRICT IS TRICKY EVEN IF YOU GREW UP HERE. THERE'S NO WAY YOUR MOM WILL BE ABLE TO FOLLOW US...
BUT SERIOUSLY, WHAT'S YOUR MOM'S DEAL?
SORRY ABOUT THAT, DARLING...
THERE'S ONE OTHER THING YOUR MOM WAS TALKING ABOUT...
WHAT'S A "TRIBE HUSBAND"?
TIME TO FESS UP...
I NEVER TOLD ANYONE ABOUT THIS, BUT...
THE REAL REASON I CAME HERE TO STUDY ABROAD...
WE LAMIA ARE A TRIBE COMPOSED EXCLUSIVELY OF WOMEN.
SO WE HAVE TO FIND HUMAN MEN IF WE WANT TO HAVE CHILDREN.

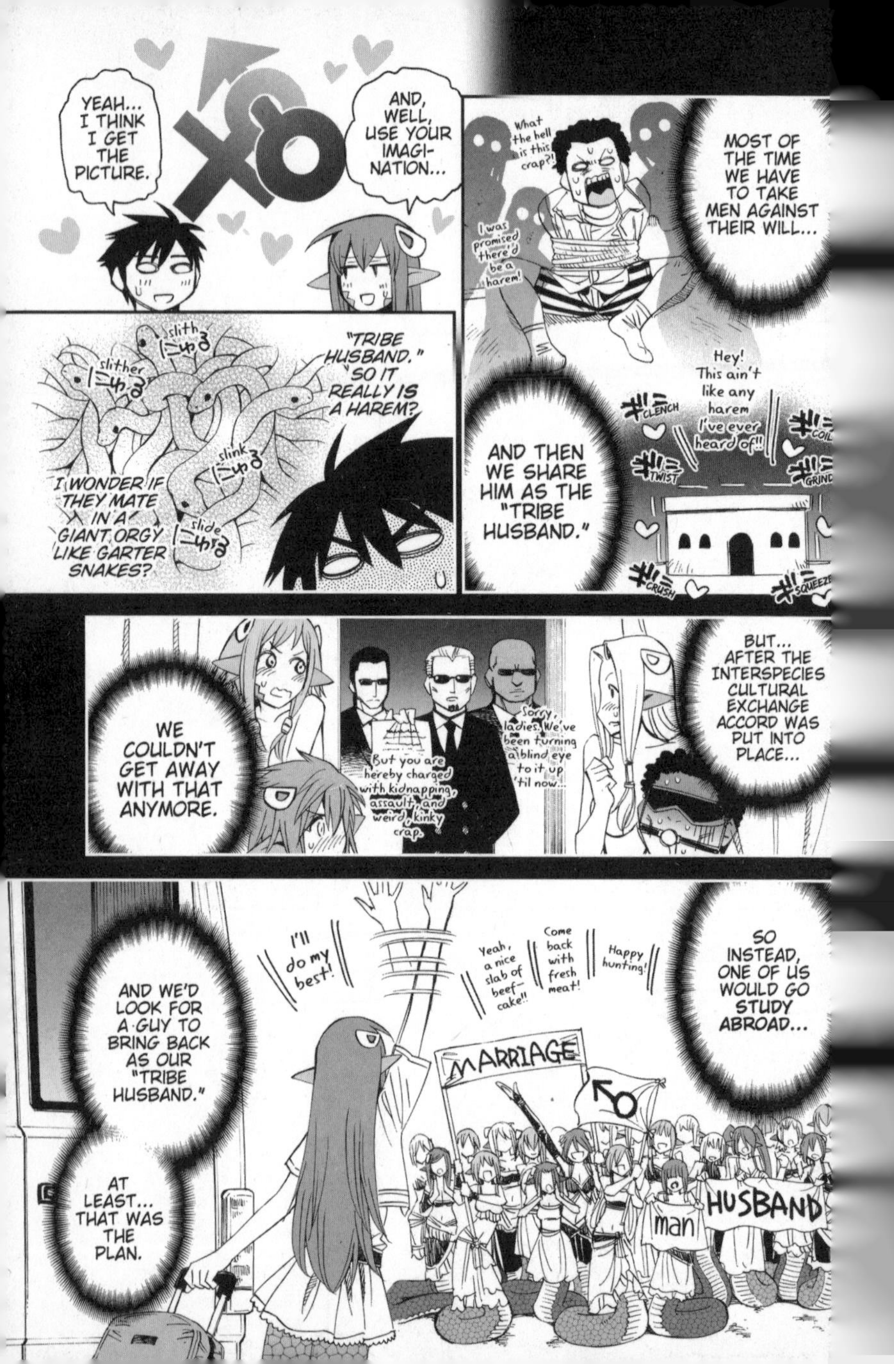
MOST OF THE TIME WE HAVE TO TAKE MEN AGAINST THEIR WILL...
What the hell is this crap?!
I was promised there'd be a harem!
AND, WELL, USE YOUR IMAGI-NATION...
YEAH... I THINK I GET THE PICTURE.
AND THEN WE SHARE HIM AS THE "TRIBE HUSBAND."
Hey! This ain't like any harem I've ever heard of!!
CLENCH
COIL
TWIST
GRIND
CRUSH
SQUEEZE
"TRIBE HUSBAND." SO IT REALLY IS A HAREM?
slith にゅる
slither にゅる
slink にゅる
slide にゅる
I WONDER IF THEY MATE IN A GIANT ORGY LIKE GARTER SNAKES?
BUT... AFTER THE INTERSPECIES CULTURAL EXCHANGE ACCORD WAS PUT INTO PLACE...
Sorry, ladies. We've been turning a blind eye to it up 'til now...
But you are hereby charged with kidnapping, assault, and weird, kinky crap.
WE COULDN'T GET AWAY WITH THAT ANYMORE.
SO INSTEAD, ONE OF US WOULD GO STUDY ABROAD...
Happy hunting!
Come back with fresh meat!
Yeah, a nice slab of beef-cake!!
I'll do my best!
MARRIAGE
HUSBAND
man
AND WE'D LOOK FOR A GUY TO BRING BACK AS OUR "TRIBE HUSBAND."
AT LEAST... THAT WAS THE PLAN.

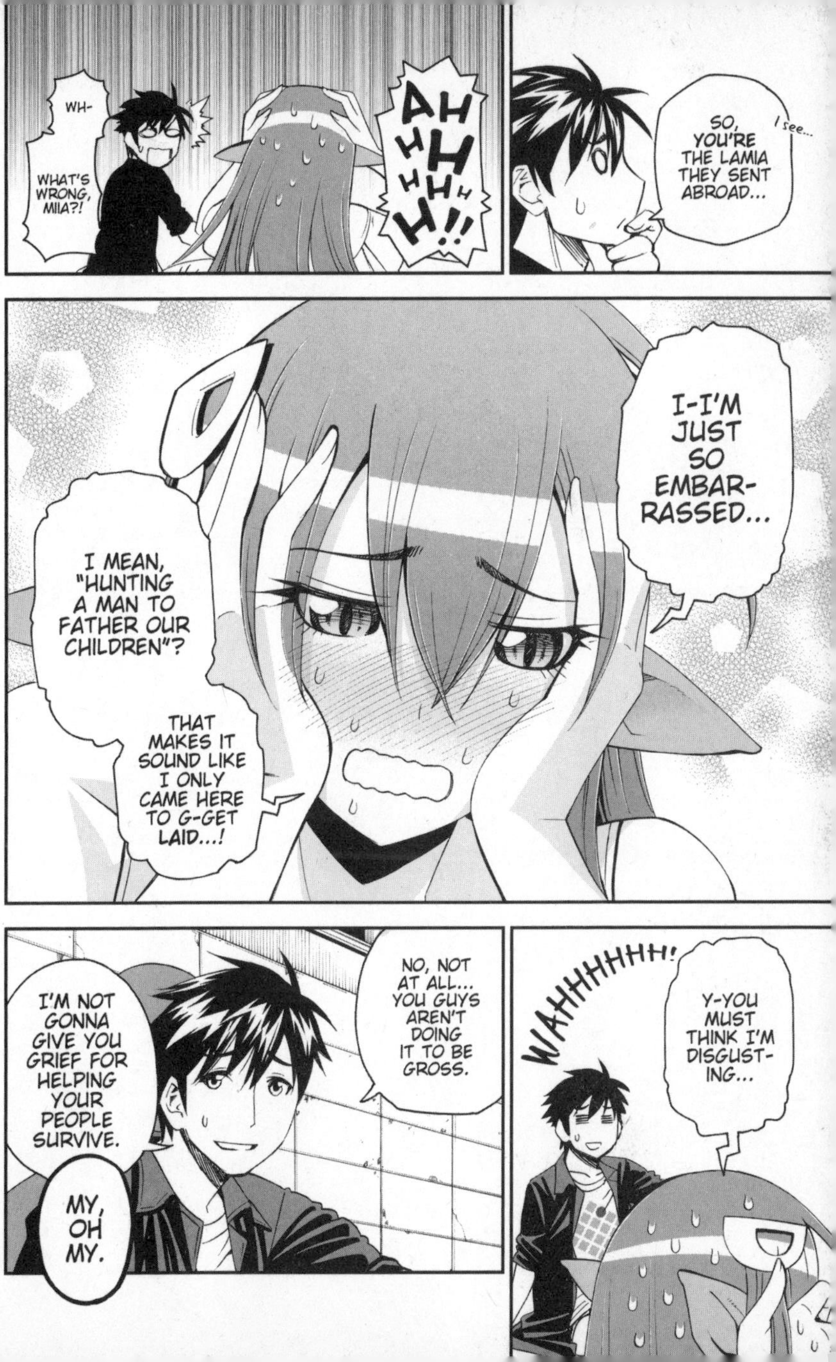
I see...
SO, YOU'RE THE LAMIA THEY SENT ABROAD...
AHHHHHHH!!
WH-
WHAT'S WRONG, MIIA?!
I-I'M JUST SO EMBARRASSED...
I MEAN, "HUNTING A MAN TO FATHER OUR CHILDREN"?
THAT MAKES IT SOUND LIKE I ONLY CAME HERE TO G-GET LAID...!
WAHHHHHHH!
Y-YOU MUST THINK I'M DISGUSTING...
NO, NOT AT ALL... YOU GUYS AREN'T DOING IT TO BE GROSS.
I'M NOT GONNA GIVE YOU GRIEF FOR HELPING YOUR PEOPLE SURVIVE.
MY, OH MY.

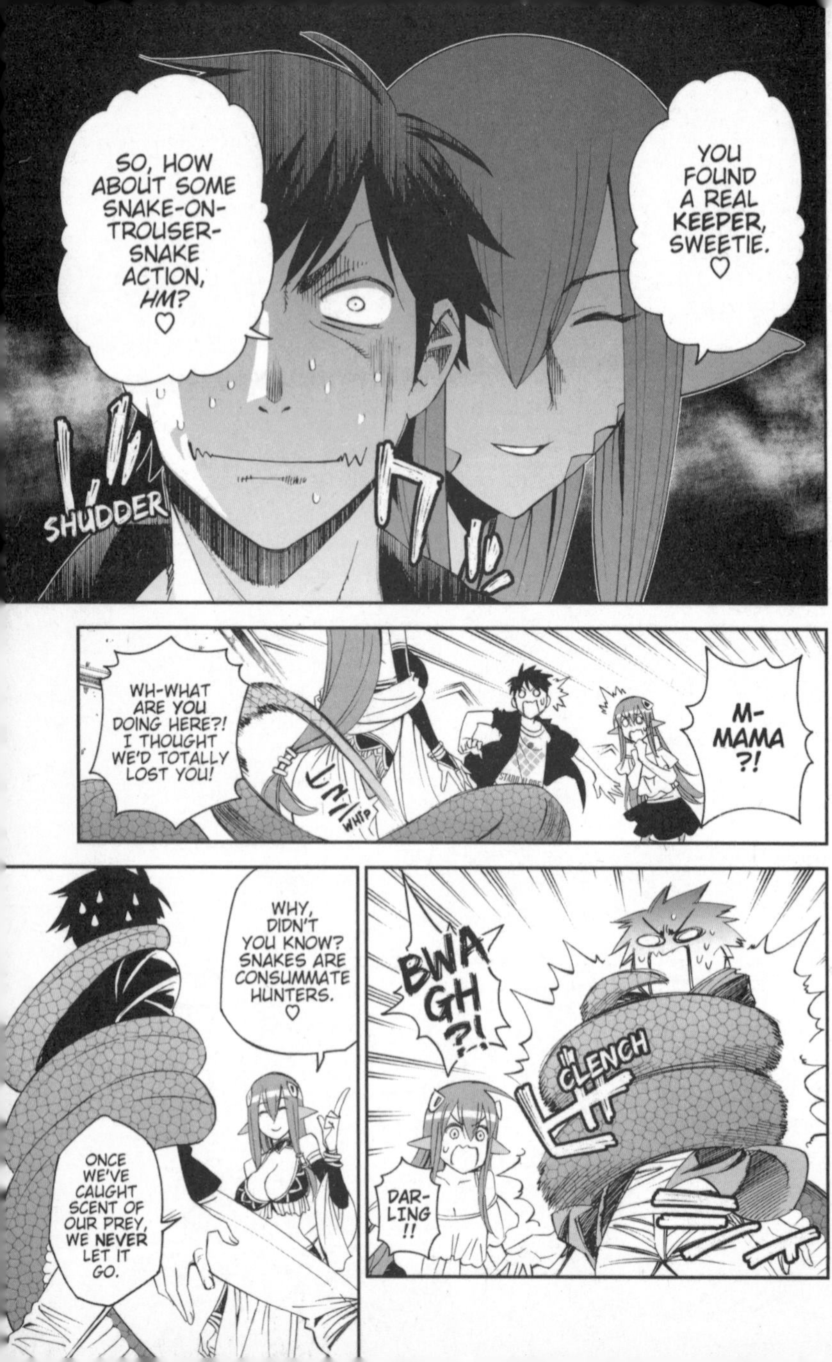
YOU FOUND A REAL KEEPER, SWEETIE. ♡
SO, HOW ABOUT SOME SNAKE-ON-TROUSER-SNAKE ACTION, HM? ♡
SHUDDER
M-MAMA?!
WH-WHAT ARE YOU DOING HERE?! I THOUGHT WE'D TOTALLY LOST YOU!
WHIP
BWAGH?!
CLENCH
DARLING!!
WHY, DIDN'T YOU KNOW? SNAKES ARE CONSUMMATE HUNTERS. ♡
ONCE WE'VE CAUGHT SCENT OF OUR PREY, WE NEVER LET IT GO.

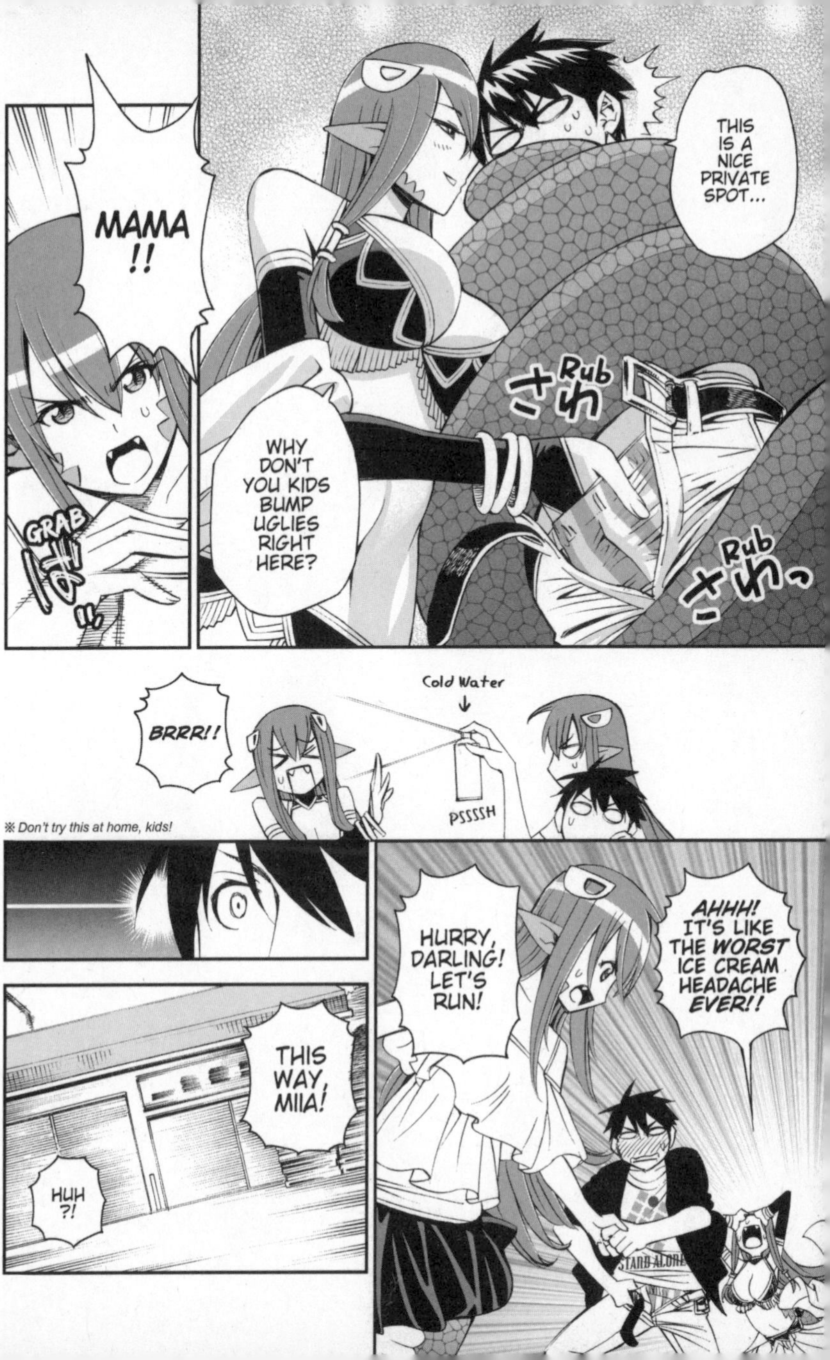
THIS IS A NICE PRIVATE SPOT...
Rub さわ
WHY DON'T YOU KIDS BUMP UGLIES RIGHT HERE?
Rub さわっ
MAMA!!
GRAB
Cold Water
BRRR!!
PSSSSH
AHHH! IT'S LIKE THE WORST ICE CREAM HEADACHE EVER!!
HURRY, DARLING! LET'S RUN!
THIS WAY, MIIA!
HUH?!
STAND ALONE
※ Don't try this at home, kids!

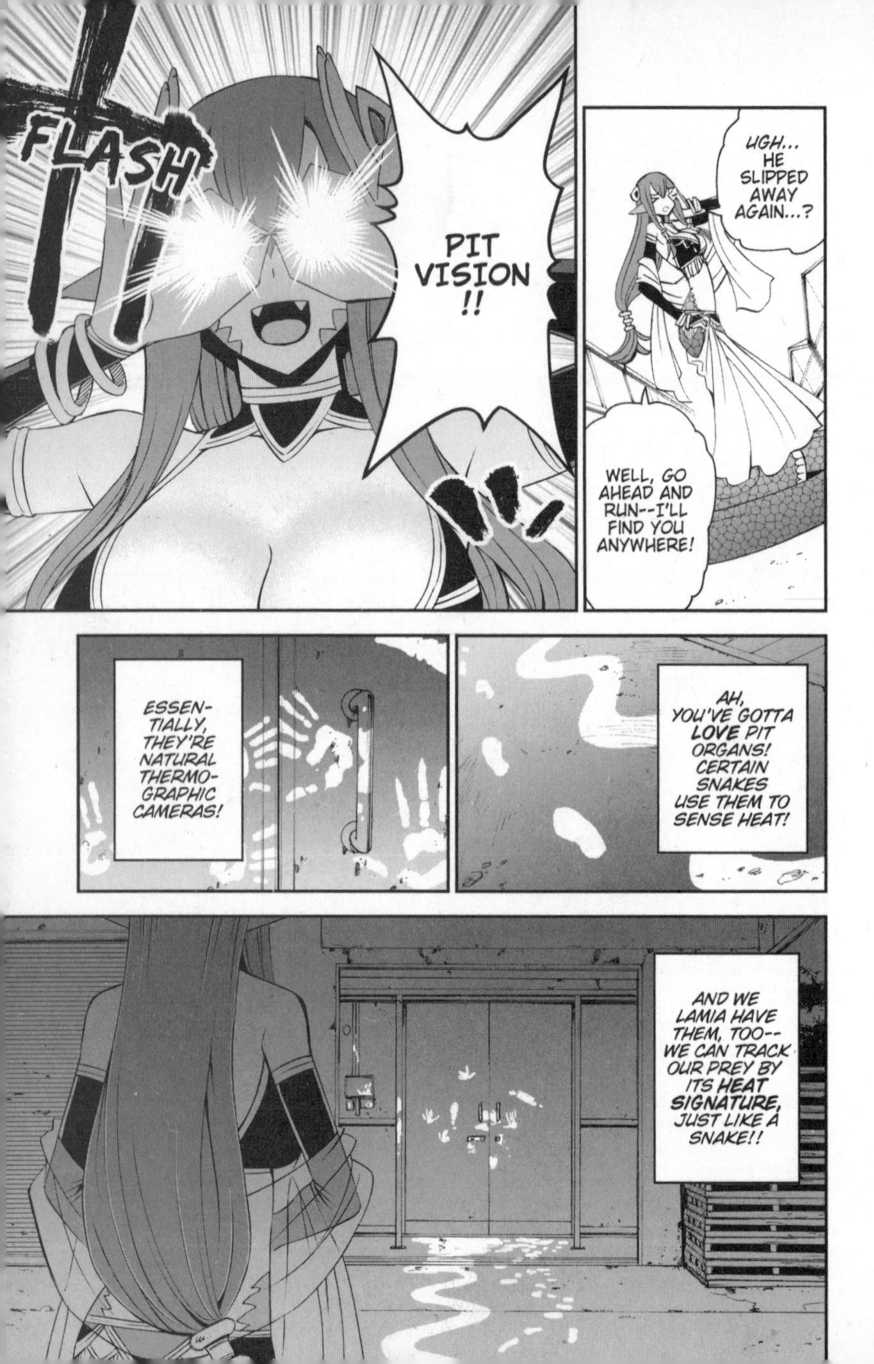
UGH... HE SLIPPED AWAY AGAIN...?
WELL, GO AHEAD AND RUN--I'LL FIND YOU ANYWHERE!
FLASH
PIT VISION !!
AH, YOU'VE GOTTA **LOVE** PIT ORGANS! CERTAIN SNAKES USE THEM TO SENSE HEAT!
ESSEN-TIALLY, THEY'RE NATURAL THERMO-GRAPHIC CAMERAS!
AND WE LAMIA HAVE THEM, TOO-- WE CAN TRACK OUR PREY BY ITS **HEAT SIGNATURE**, JUST LIKE A SNAKE!!

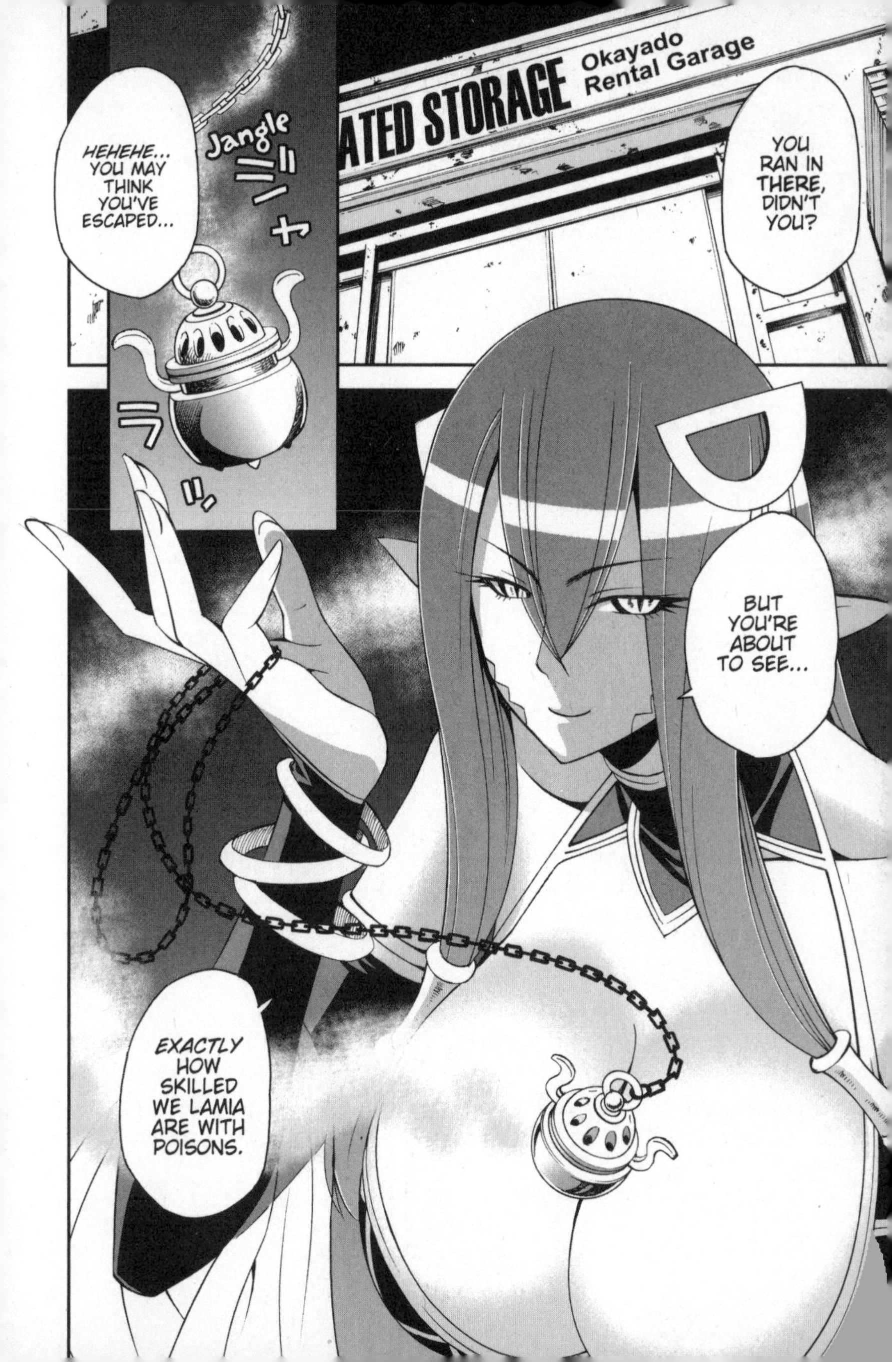

...ATED STORAGE
Okayado Rental Garage
YOU RAN IN THERE, DIDN'T YOU?
HEHEHE... YOU MAY THINK YOU'VE ESCAPED...
Jangle
ジャラッ
BUT YOU'RE ABOUT TO SEE...
EXACTLY HOW SKILLED WE LAMIA ARE WITH POISONS.

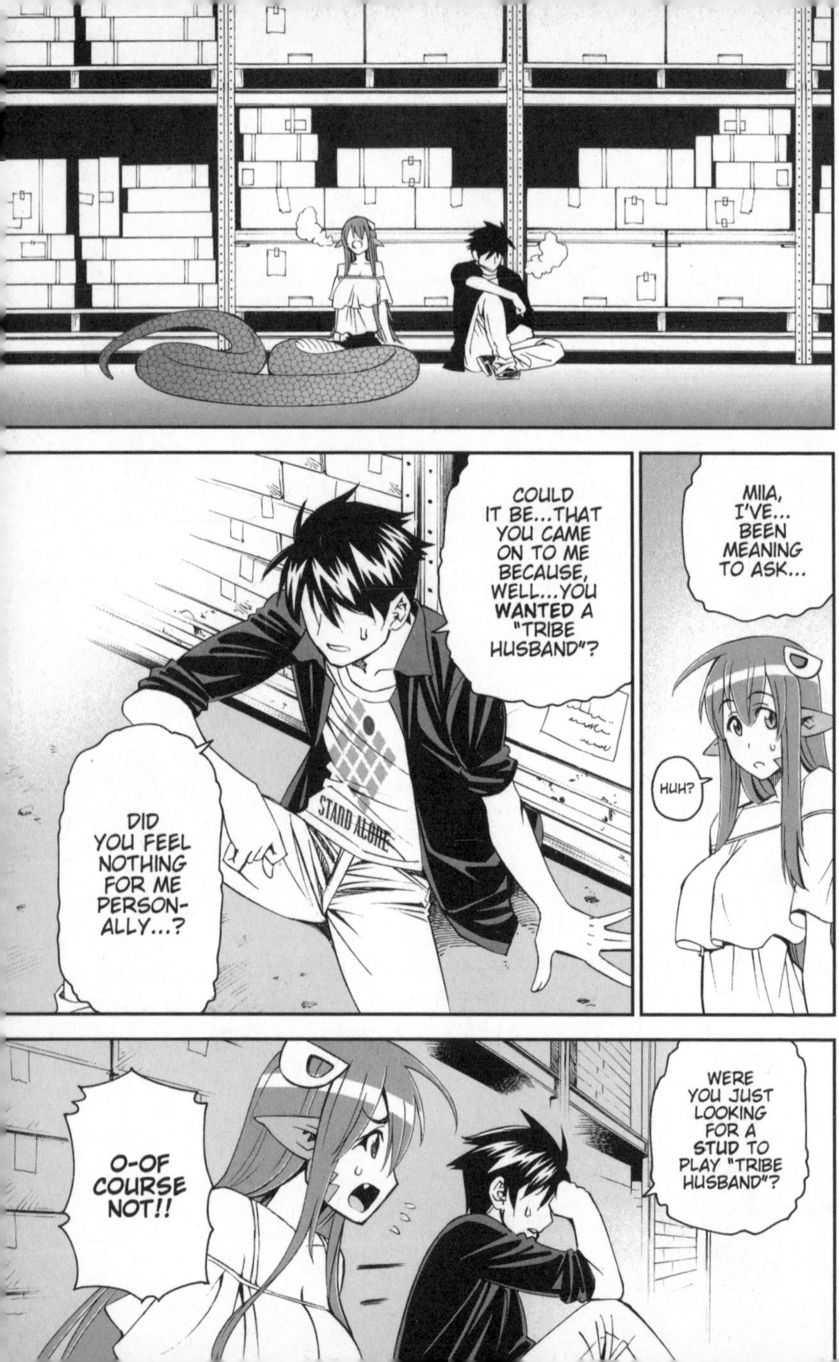
MIIA, I'VE... BEEN MEANING TO ASK...
HUH?
COULD IT BE...THAT YOU CAME ON TO ME BECAUSE, WELL...YOU WANTED A "TRIBE HUSBAND"?
STAND ALONE
DID YOU FEEL NOTHING FOR ME PERSON-ALLY...?
WERE YOU JUST LOOKING FOR A STUD TO PLAY "TRIBE HUSBAND"?
O-OF COURSE NOT!!

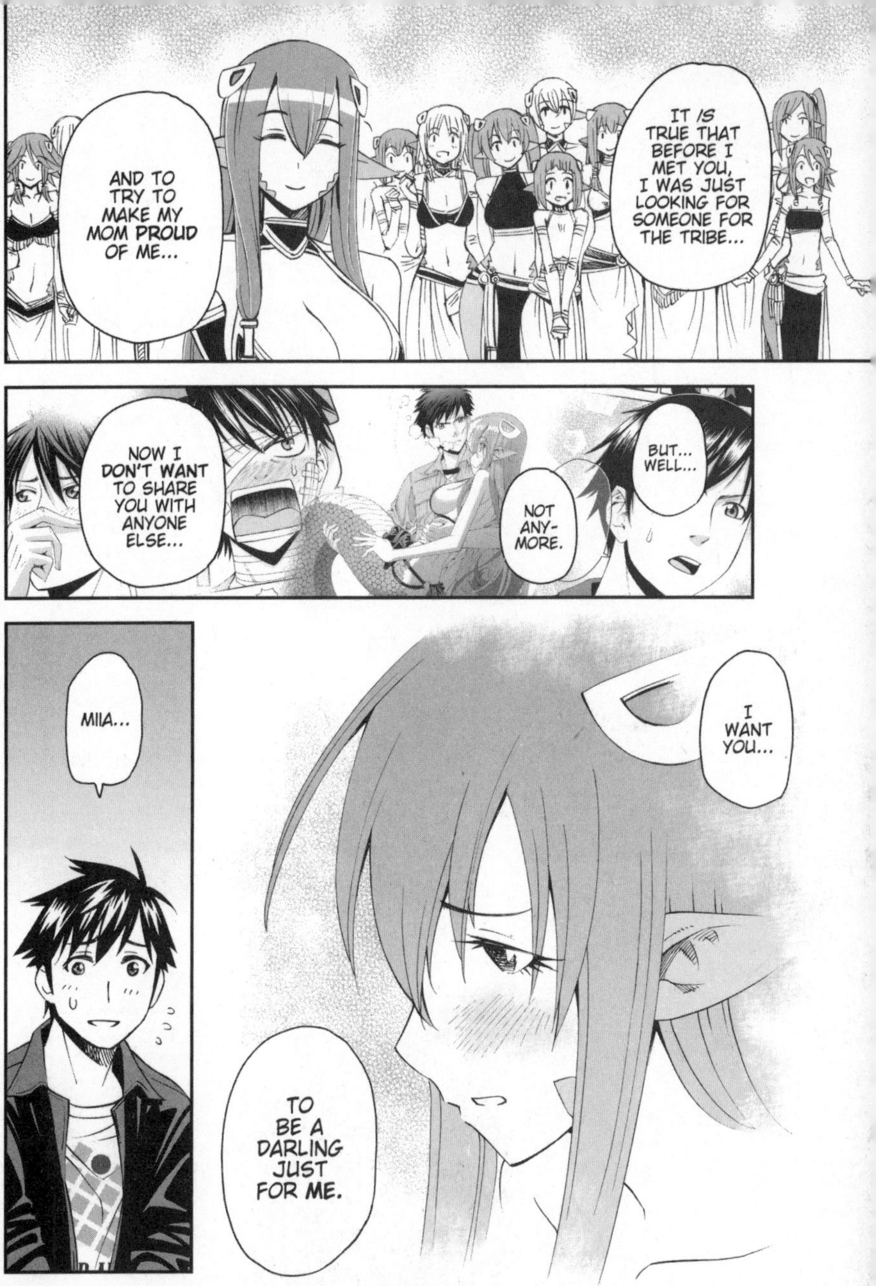
IT IS TRUE THAT BEFORE I MET YOU, I WAS JUST LOOKING FOR SOMEONE FOR THE TRIBE...
AND TO TRY TO MAKE MY MOM PROUD OF ME...
BUT... WELL...
NOT ANYMORE.
NOW I DON'T WANT TO SHARE YOU WITH ANYONE ELSE...
I WANT YOU...
TO BE A DARLING JUST FOR ME.
MIIA...

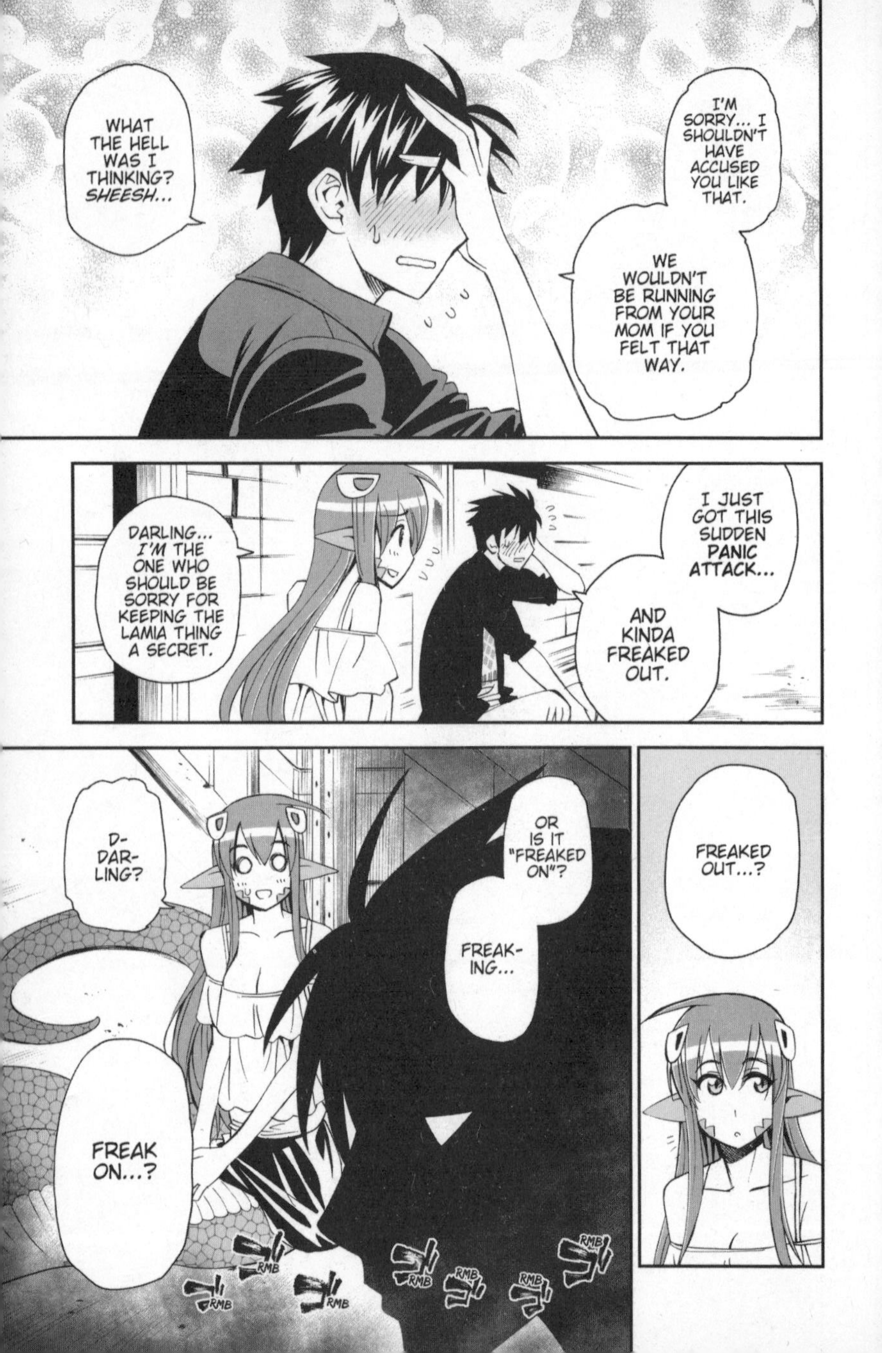
I'M SORRY... I SHOULDN'T HAVE ACCUSED YOU LIKE THAT.
WE WOULDN'T BE RUNNING FROM YOUR MOM IF YOU FELT THAT WAY.
WHAT THE HELL WAS I THINKING? *SHEESH...*
I JUST GOT THIS SUDDEN **PANIC ATTACK...**
AND KINDA FREAKED OUT.
DARLING... *I'M* THE ONE WHO SHOULD BE SORRY FOR KEEPING THE LAMIA THING A SECRET.
FREAKED OUT...?
OR IS IT "FREAKED ON"?
FREAK-ING...
D-DAR-LING?
FREAK ON...?
RMB
RMB
RMB
RMB
RMB
RMB
RMB
RMB

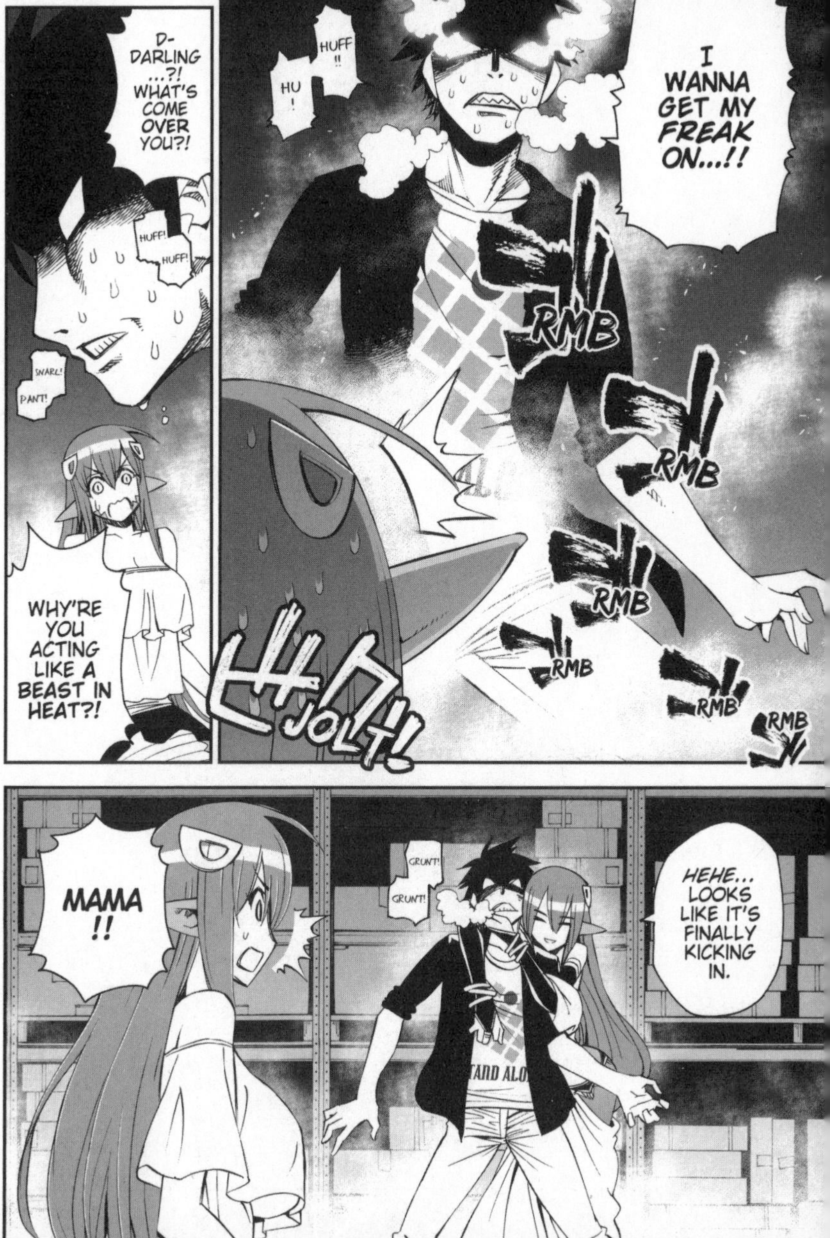
I WANNA GET MY FREAK ON...!!
HUFF!!
HU!
RMB
RMB
RMB
RMB
RMB
RMB
JOLT!
D-DARLING...?! WHAT'S COME OVER YOU?!
HUFF!
HUFF!
SNARL!
PANT!
WHY'RE YOU ACTING LIKE A BEAST IN HEAT?!
HEHE... LOOKS LIKE IT'S FINALLY KICKING IN.
GRUNT!
GRUNT!
MAMA!!

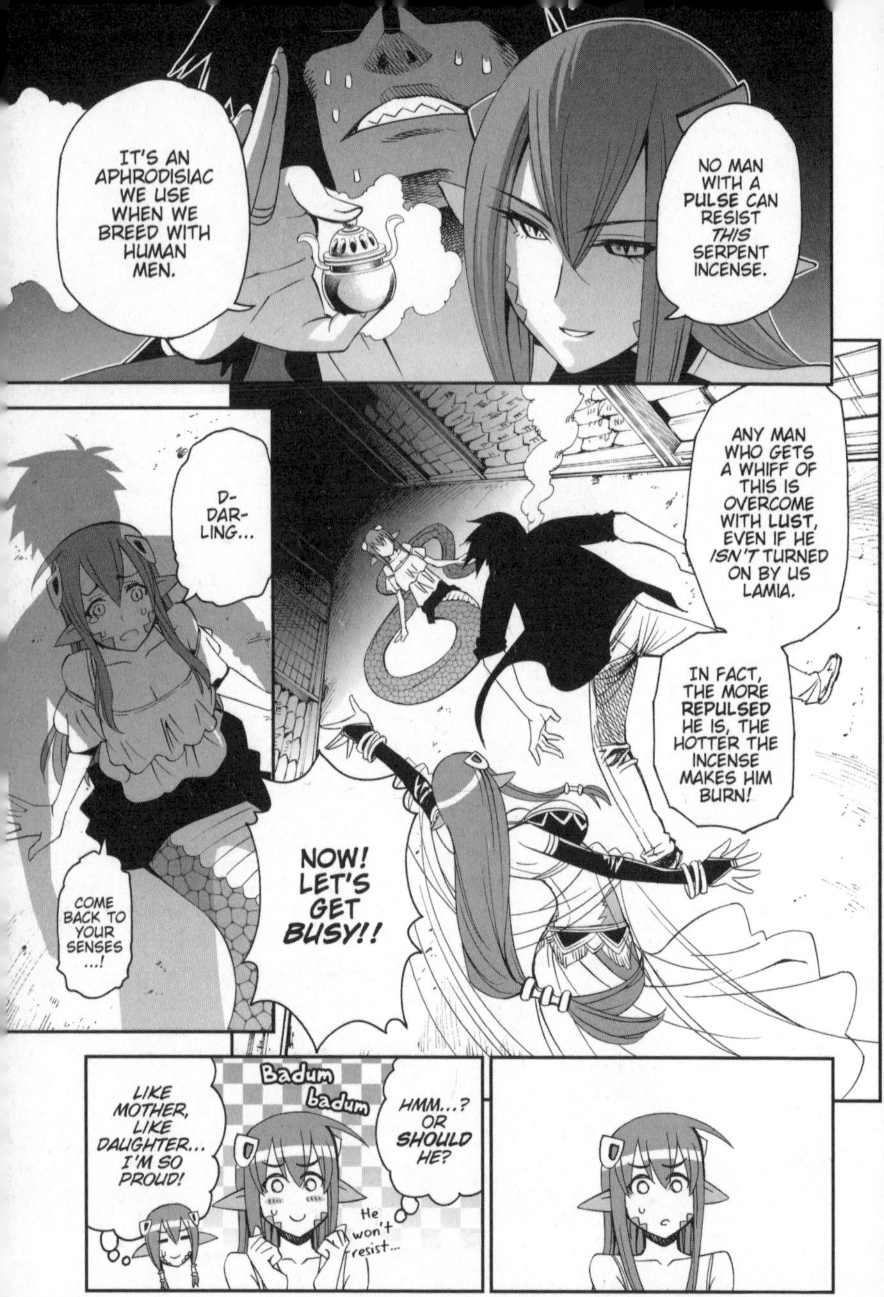
NO MAN WITH A PULSE CAN RESIST *THIS* SERPENT INCENSE.
IT'S AN APHRODISIAC WE USE WHEN WE BREED WITH HUMAN MEN.
ANY MAN WHO GETS A WHIFF OF THIS IS OVERCOME WITH **LUST**, EVEN IF HE *ISN'T* TURNED ON BY US LAMIA.
IN FACT, THE MORE **REPULSED** HE IS, THE HOTTER THE INCENSE MAKES HIM BURN!
NOW! LET'S GET *BUSY!!*
D-DARLING...
COME BACK TO YOUR SENSES...!
Badum badum
HMM...? OR **SHOULD** HE?
LIKE MOTHER, LIKE DAUGHTER... I'M SO PROUD!
He won't resist...

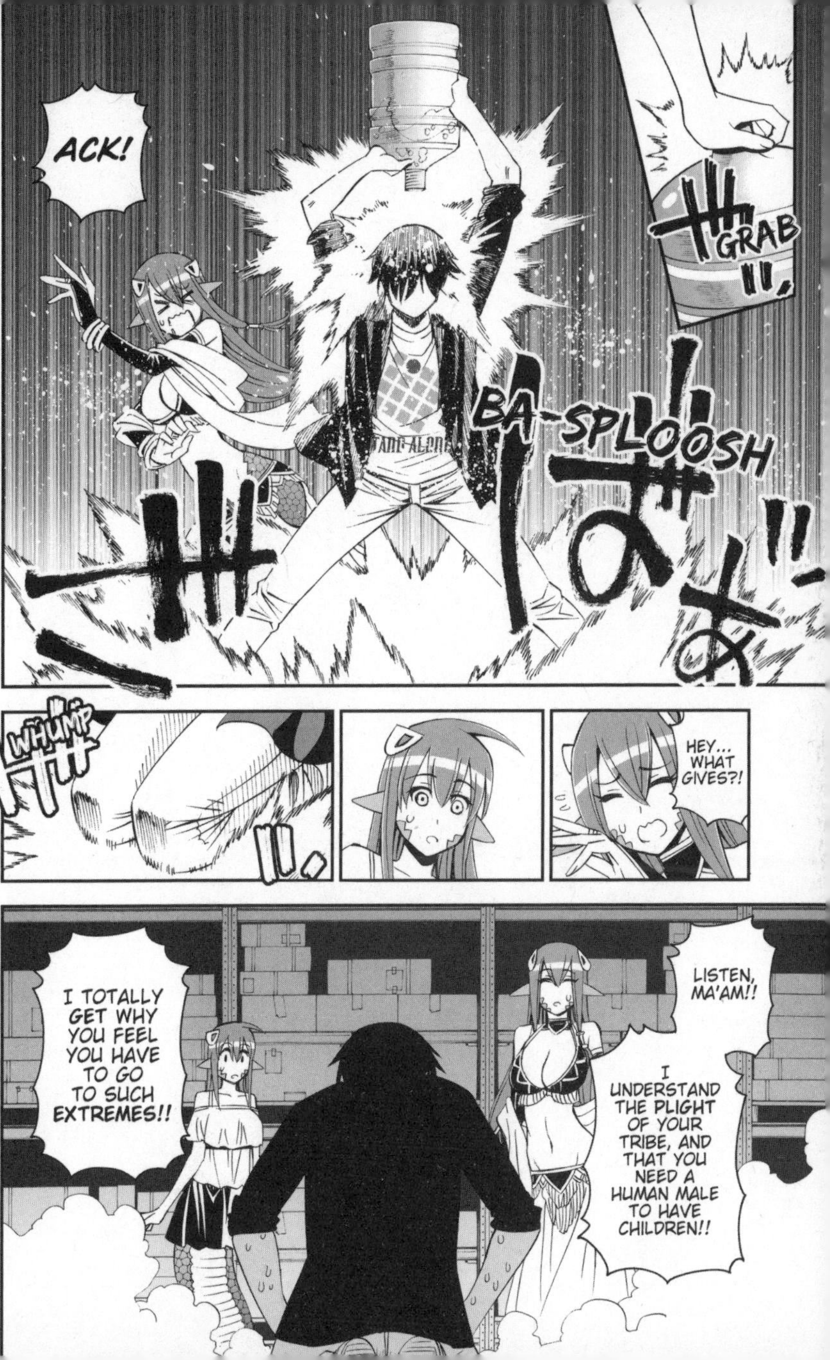
GRAB
BA-SPLOOSH
ACK!
HEY... WHAT GIVES?!
WHUMP
LISTEN, MA'AM!!
I UNDERSTAND THE PLIGHT OF YOUR TRIBE, AND THAT YOU NEED A HUMAN MALE TO HAVE CHILDREN!!
I TOTALLY GET WHY YOU FEEL YOU HAVE TO GO TO SUCH EXTREMES!!

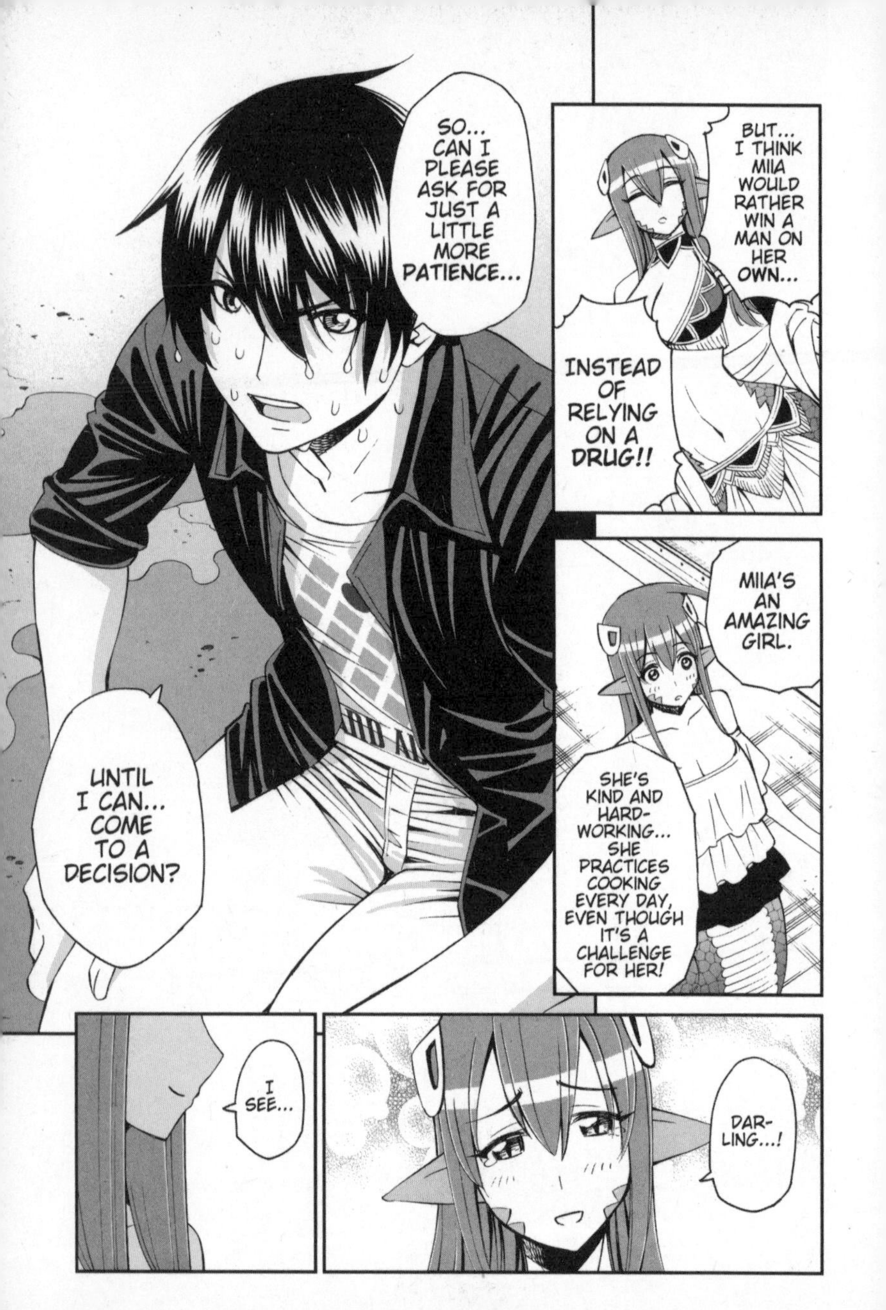
BUT... I THINK MIIA WOULD RATHER WIN A MAN ON HER OWN...
INSTEAD OF RELYING ON A DRUG!!
MIIA'S AN AMAZING GIRL.
SHE'S KIND AND HARD-WORKING... SHE PRACTICES COOKING EVERY DAY, EVEN THOUGH IT'S A CHALLENGE FOR HER!
SO... CAN I PLEASE ASK FOR JUST A LITTLE MORE PATIENCE...
UNTIL I CAN... COME TO A DECISION?
DAR-LING...!
I SEE...

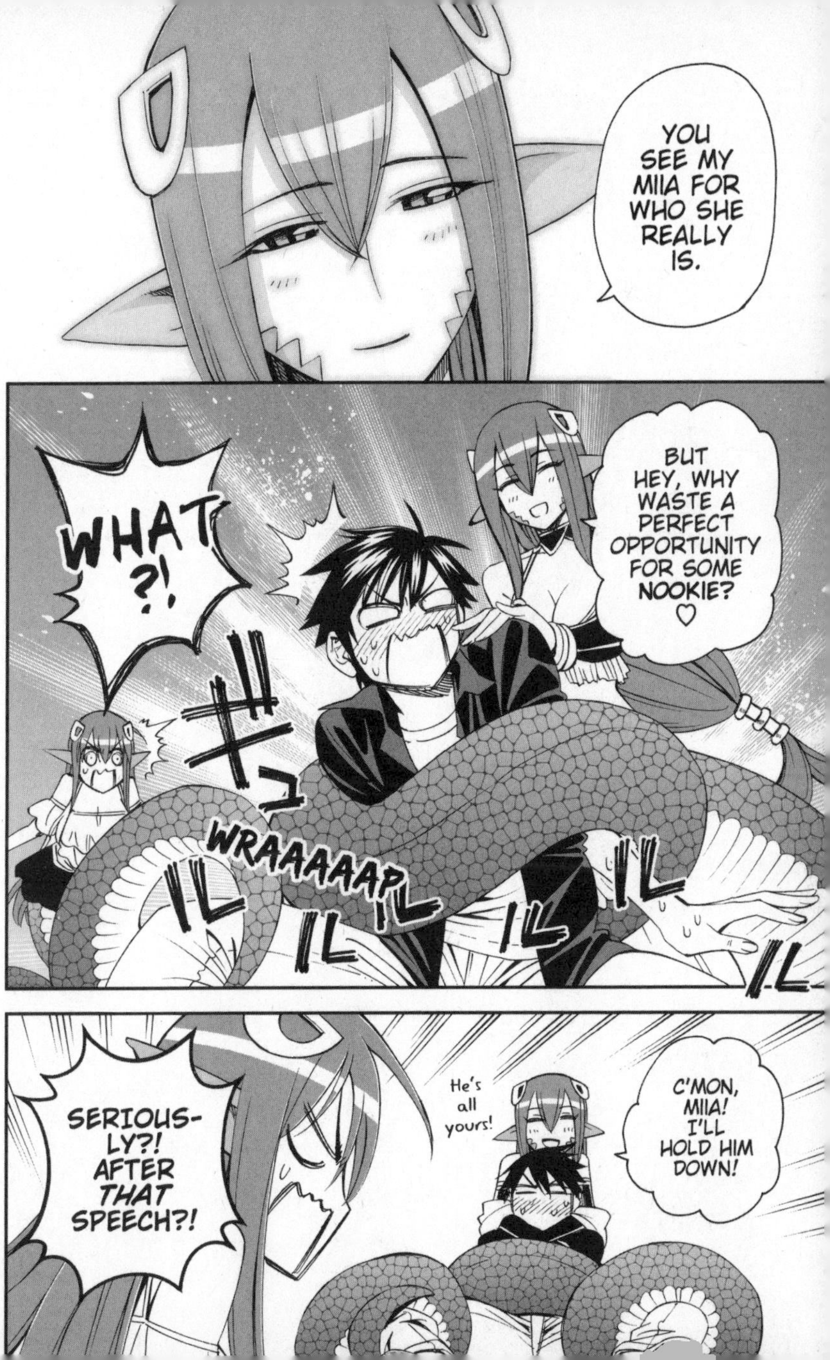
YOU SEE MY MIIA FOR WHO SHE REALLY IS.
BUT HEY, WHY WASTE A PERFECT OPPORTUNITY FOR SOME NOOKIE? ♡
WHAT ?!
WRAAAAAAP
C'MON, MIIA! I'LL HOLD HIM DOWN!
He's all yours!
SERIOUS-LY?! AFTER *THAT* SPEECH?!

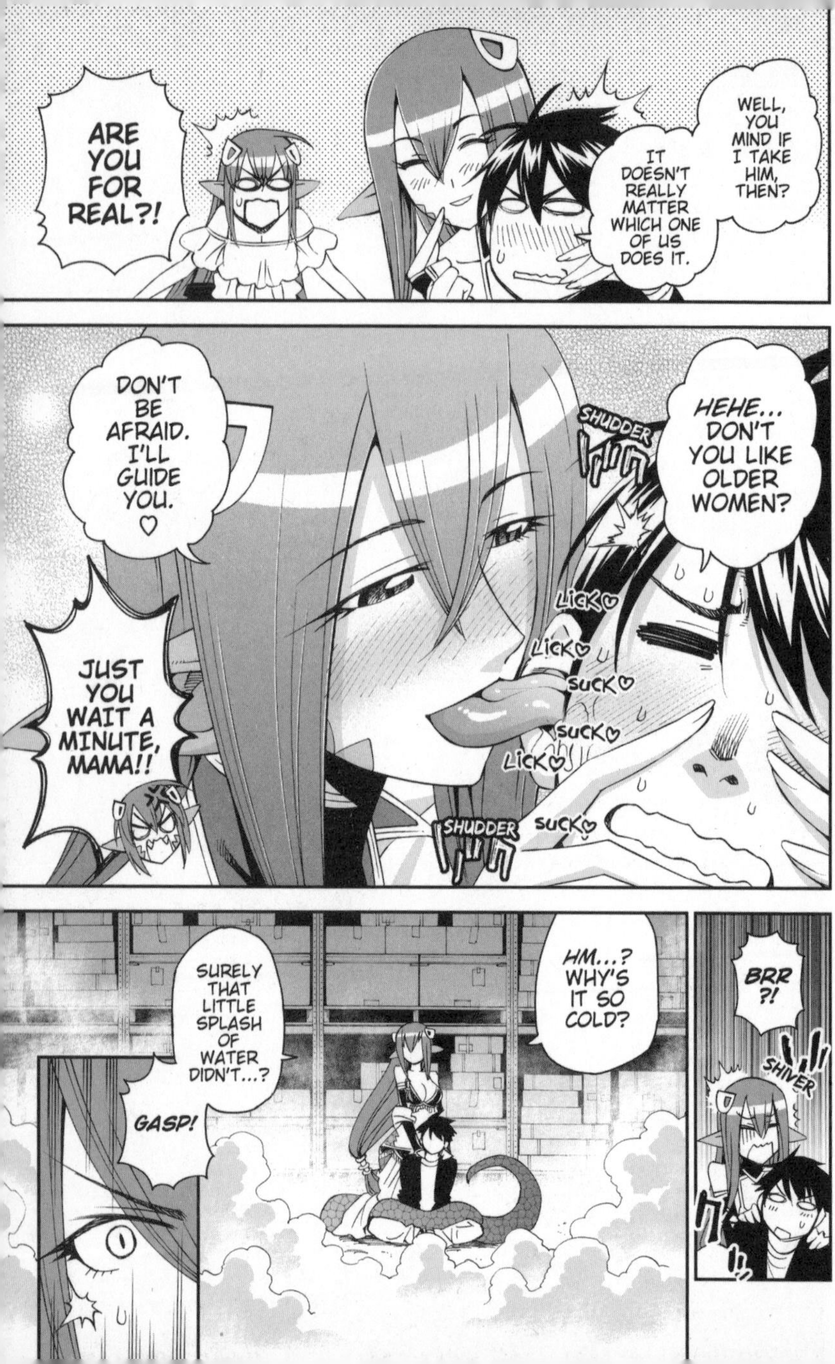
WELL, YOU MIND IF I TAKE HIM, THEN?
IT DOESN'T REALLY MATTER WHICH ONE OF US DOES IT.
ARE YOU FOR REAL?!
HEHE... DON'T YOU LIKE OLDER WOMEN?
SHUDDER
DON'T BE AFRAID. I'LL GUIDE YOU. ♡
LICK♡
LICK♡
SUCK♡
SUCK♡
LICK♡
SUCK♡
SHUDDER
JUST YOU WAIT A MINUTE, MAMA!!
BRR?!
SHIVER
HM...? WHY'S IT SO COLD?
SURELY THAT LITTLE SPLASH OF WATER DIDN'T...?
GASP!

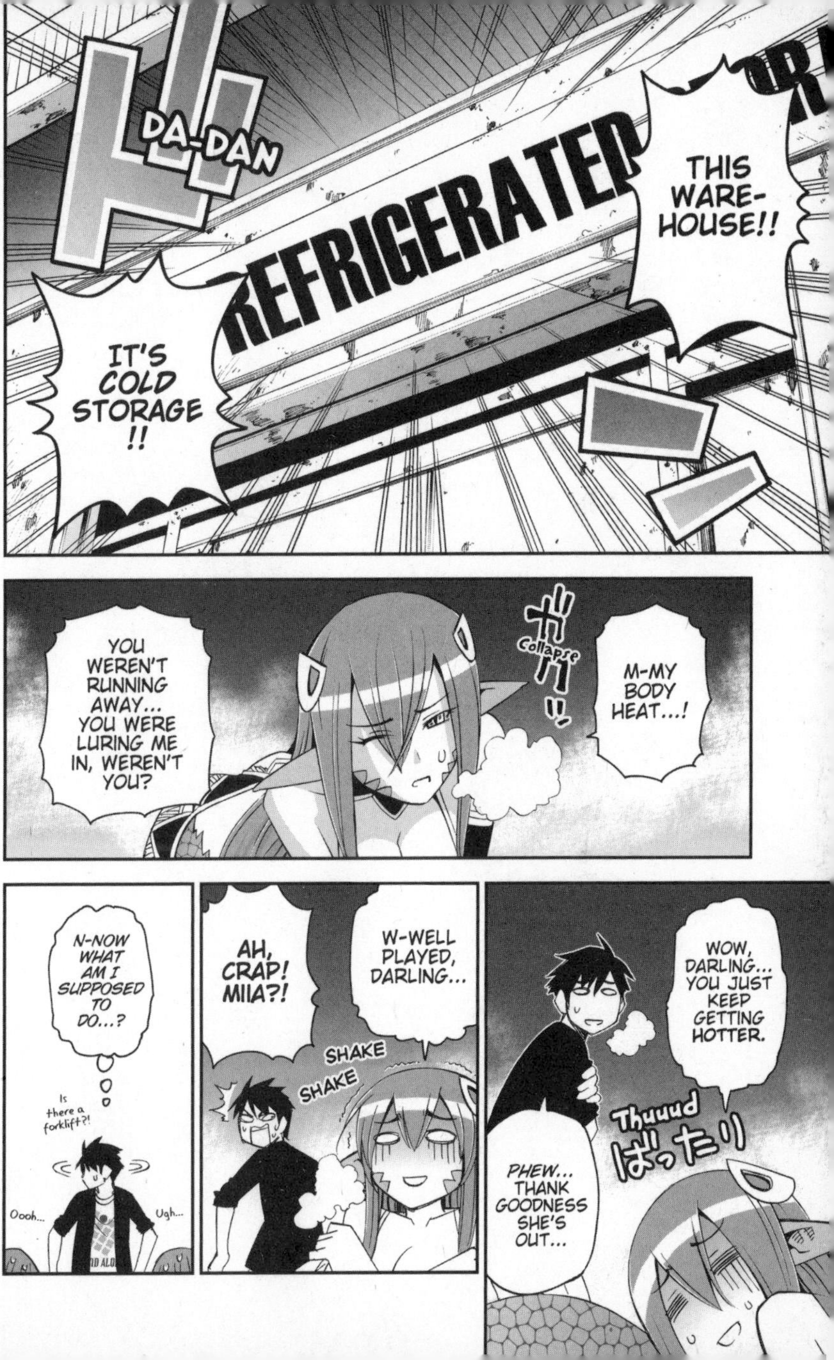
THIS WARE-HOUSE!!
REFRIGERATED
DA-DAN
IT'S COLD STORAGE!!
M-MY BODY HEAT...!
Collapse
YOU WEREN'T RUNNING AWAY... YOU WERE LURING ME IN, WEREN'T YOU?
WOW, DARLING... YOU JUST KEEP GETTING HOTTER.
Thuuud
ばったり
PHEW... THANK GOODNESS SHE'S OUT...
W-WELL PLAYED, DARLING...
AH, CRAP! MIIA?!
SHAKE
SHAKE
N-NOW WHAT AM I SUPPOSED TO DO...?
Is there a forklift?!
Ugh...
Oooh...

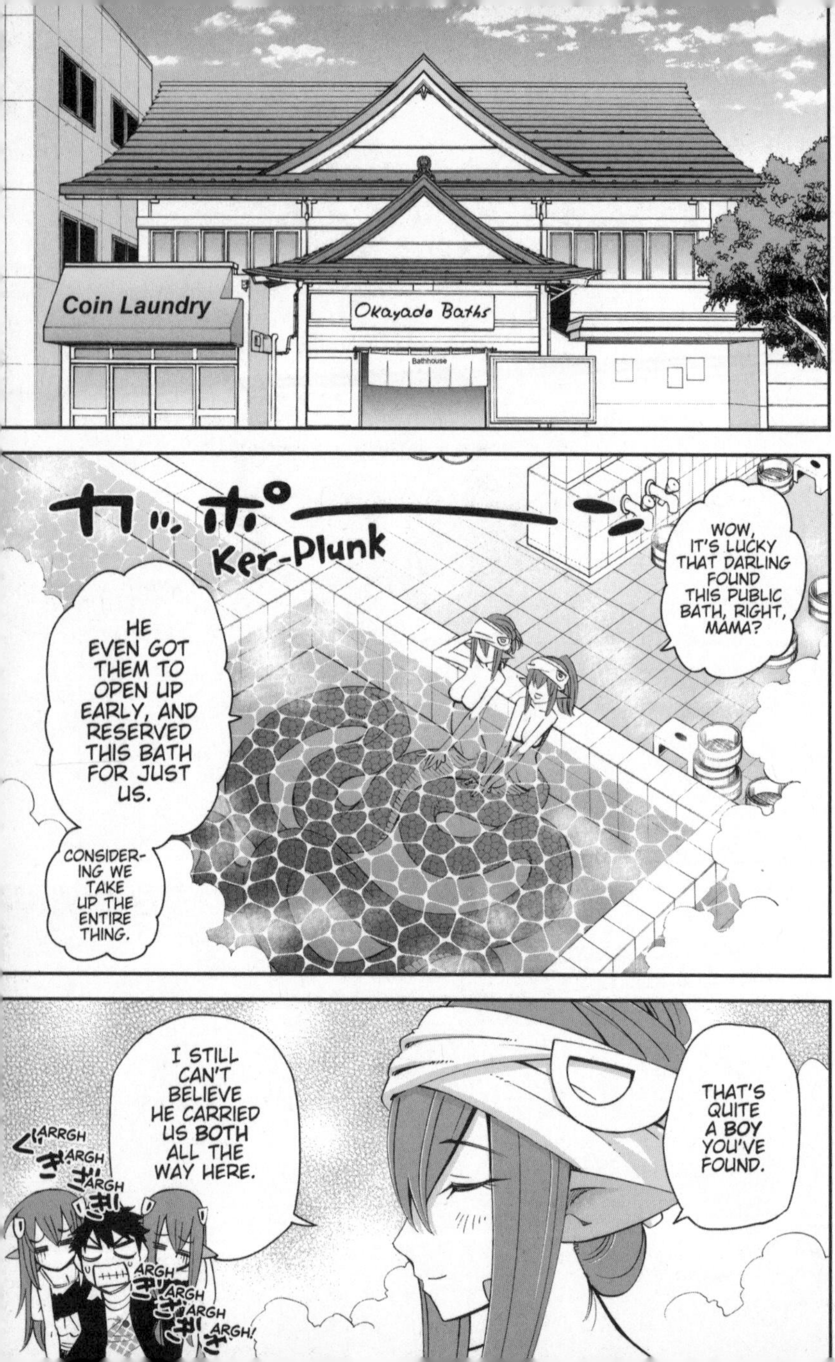
Coin Laundry
Okayado Baths
Bathhouse
WOW, IT'S LUCKY THAT DARLING FOUND THIS PUBLIC BATH, RIGHT, MAMA?
Ker-Plunk
HE EVEN GOT THEM TO OPEN UP EARLY, AND RESERVED THIS BATH FOR JUST US.
CONSIDERING WE TAKE UP THE ENTIRE THING.
THAT'S QUITE A BOY YOU'VE FOUND.
I STILL CAN'T BELIEVE HE CARRIED US BOTH ALL THE WAY HERE.
ARRGH
ARGH
ARGH
ARGH
ARGH
ARGH
ARGH!

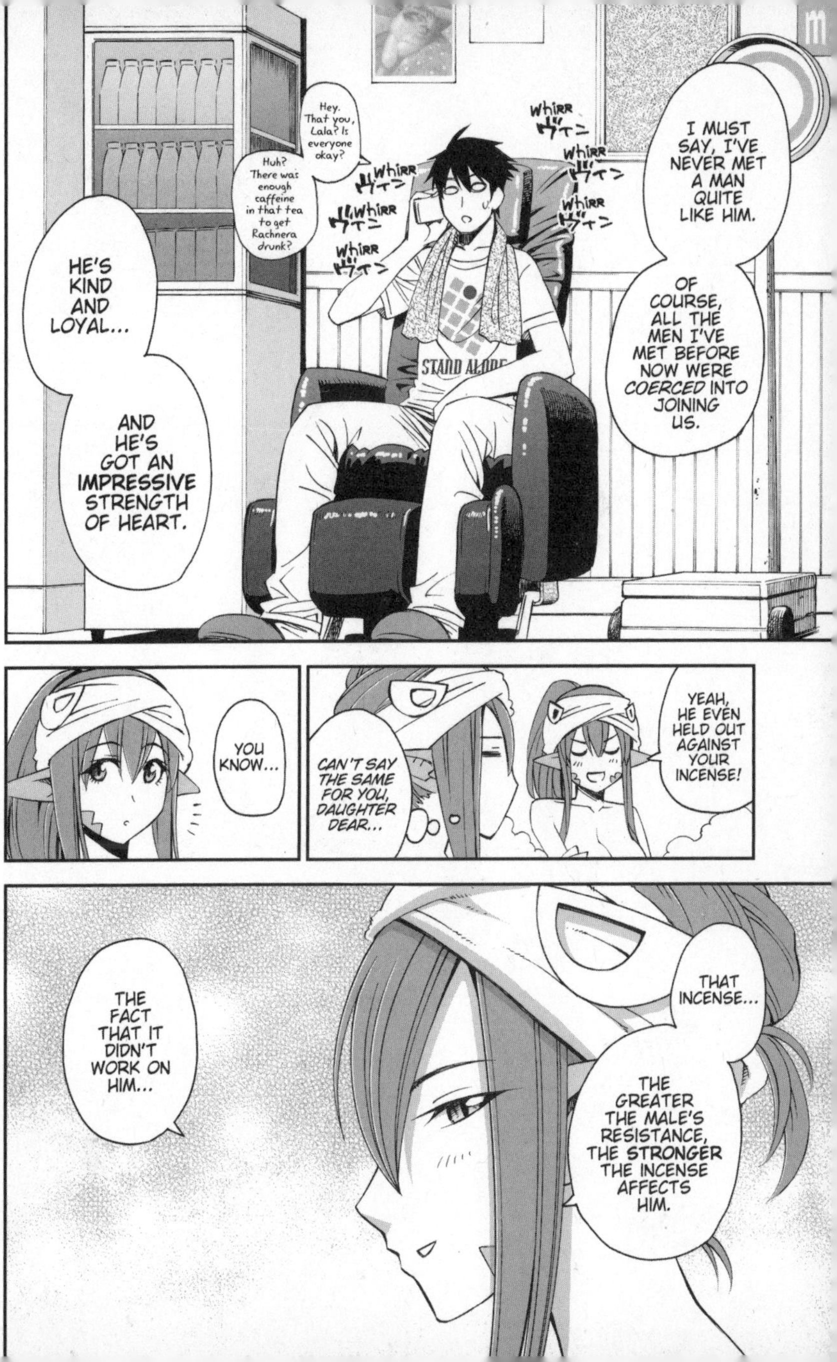
I MUST SAY, I'VE NEVER MET A MAN QUITE LIKE HIM.
OF COURSE, ALL THE MEN I'VE MET BEFORE NOW WERE COERCED INTO JOINING US.
Whirr
Whirr
Whirr
Hey. That you, Lala? Is everyone okay?
Huh? There was enough caffeine in that tea to get Rachnera drunk?
Whirr
Whirr
Whirr
HE'S KIND AND LOYAL...
AND HE'S GOT AN IMPRESSIVE STRENGTH OF HEART.
YEAH, HE EVEN HELD OUT AGAINST YOUR INCENSE!
CAN'T SAY THE SAME FOR YOU, DAUGHTER DEAR...
YOU KNOW...
THAT INCENSE...
THE GREATER THE MALE'S RESISTANCE, THE STRONGER THE INCENSE AFFECTS HIM.
THE FACT THAT IT DIDN'T WORK ON HIM...

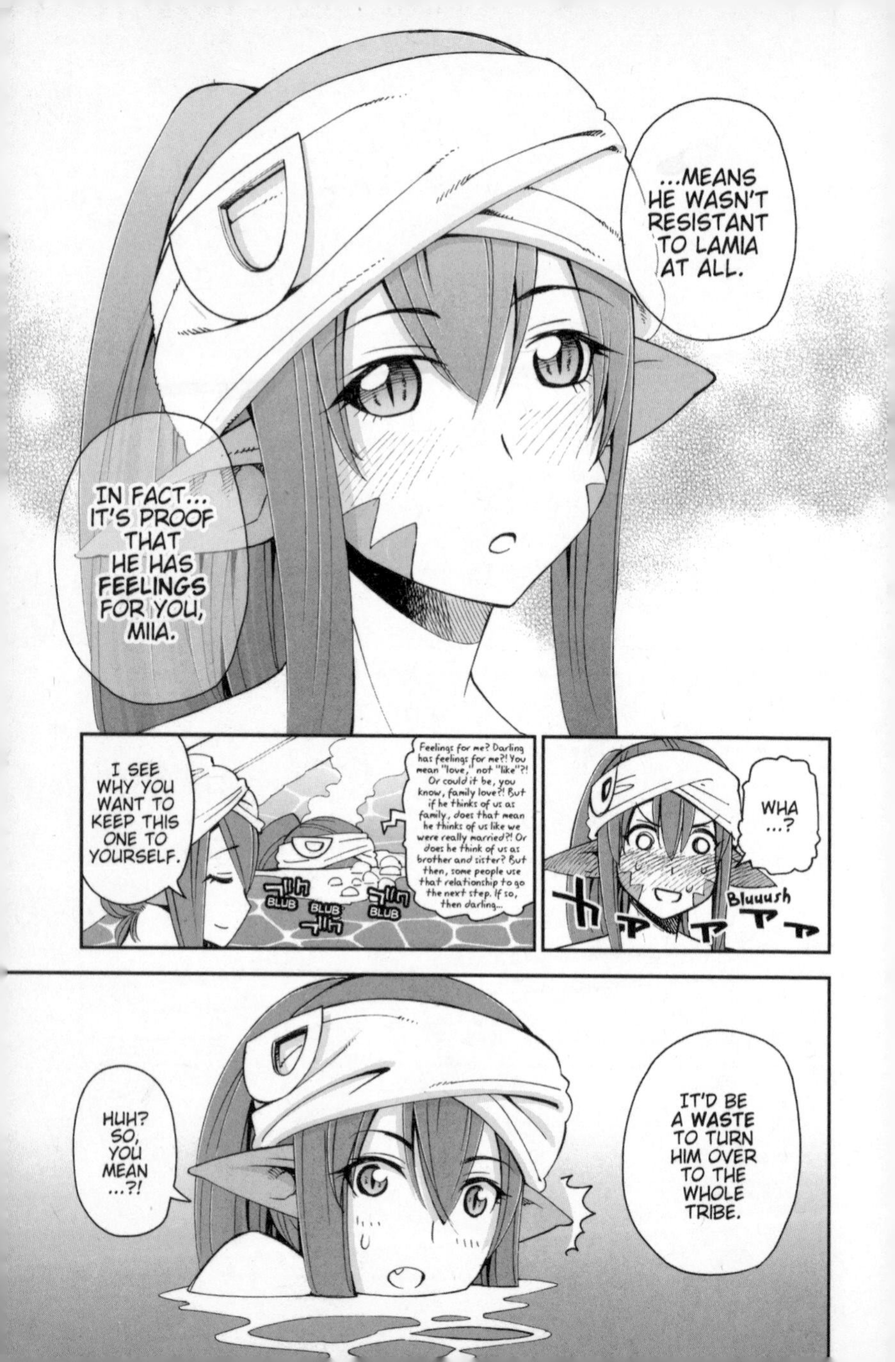
...MEANS HE WASN'T RESISTANT TO LAMIA AT ALL.
IN FACT... IT'S PROOF THAT HE HAS FEELINGS FOR YOU, MIIA.
WHA ...?
Bluuush
Feelings for me? Darling has feelings for me?! You mean "love," not "like"?! Or could it be, you know, family love?! But if he thinks of us as family, does that mean he thinks of us like we were really married?! Or does he think of us as brother and sister? But then, some people use that relationship to go the next step. If so, then darling...
I SEE WHY YOU WANT TO KEEP THIS ONE TO YOURSELF.
BLUB BLUB BLUB
IT'D BE A WASTE TO TURN HIM OVER TO THE WHOLE TRIBE.
HUH? SO, YOU MEAN ...?!

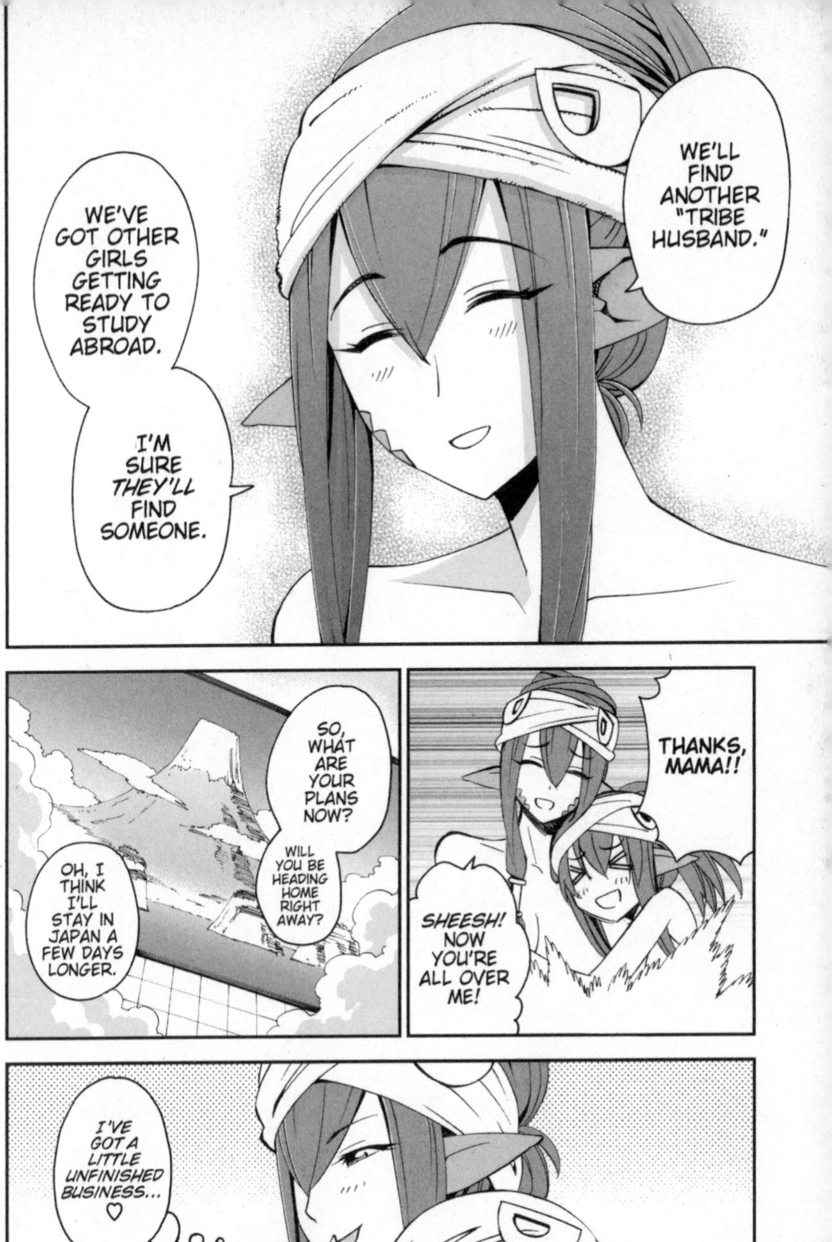
WE'LL FIND ANOTHER "TRIBE HUSBAND."
WE'VE GOT OTHER GIRLS GETTING READY TO STUDY ABROAD.
I'M SURE *THEY'LL* FIND SOMEONE.
THANKS, MAMA!!
SHEESH! NOW YOU'RE ALL OVER ME!
SO, WHAT ARE YOUR PLANS NOW?
WILL YOU BE HEADING HOME RIGHT AWAY?
OH, I THINK I'LL STAY IN JAPAN A FEW DAYS LONGER.
I'VE GOT A LITTLE UNFINISHED BUSINESS... ♡

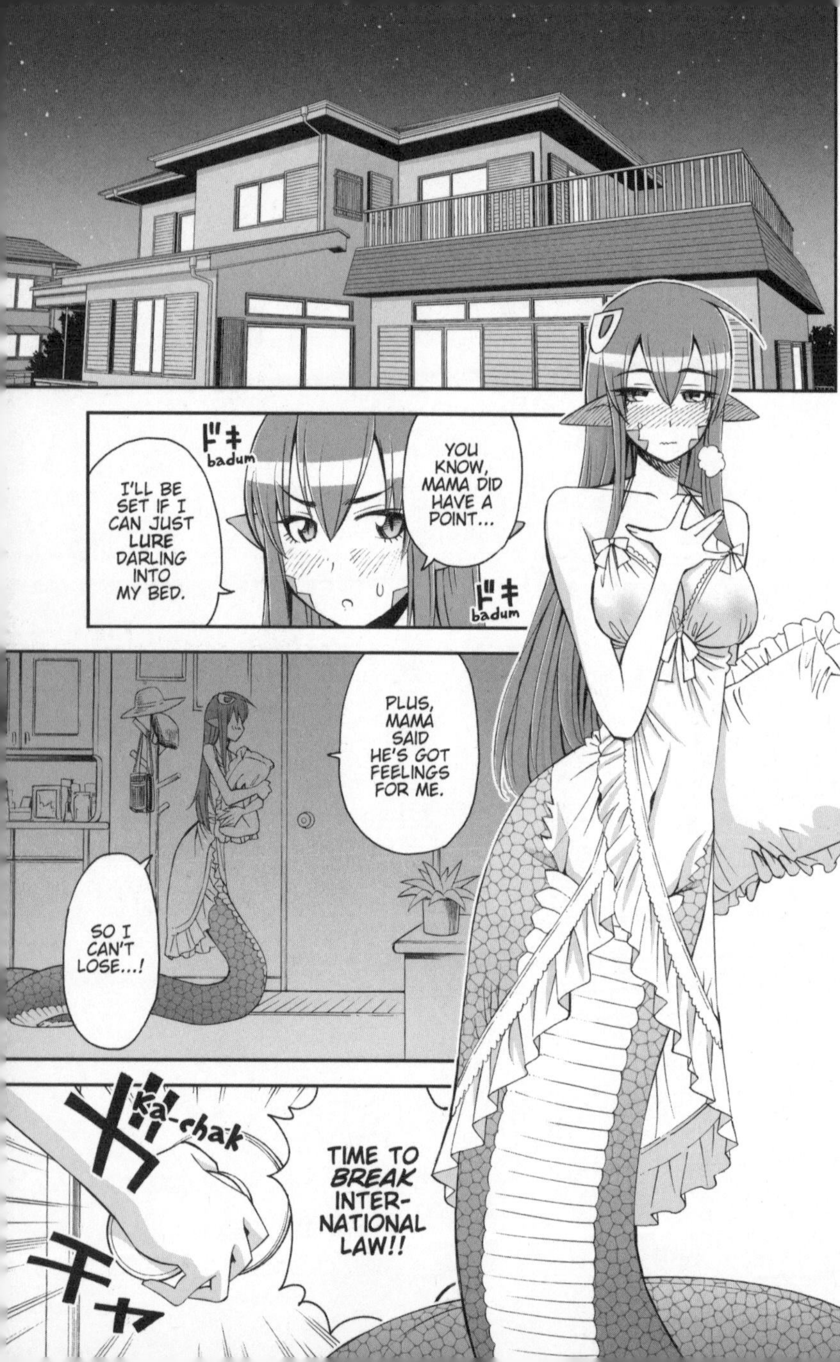
ドキ
badum
YOU KNOW, MAMA DID HAVE A POINT...
ドキ
badum
I'LL BE SET IF I CAN JUST LURE DARLING INTO MY BED.
PLUS, MAMA SAID HE'S GOT FEELINGS FOR ME.
SO I CAN'T LOSE...!
TIME TO *BREAK* INTER-NATIONAL LAW!!
ka-chak

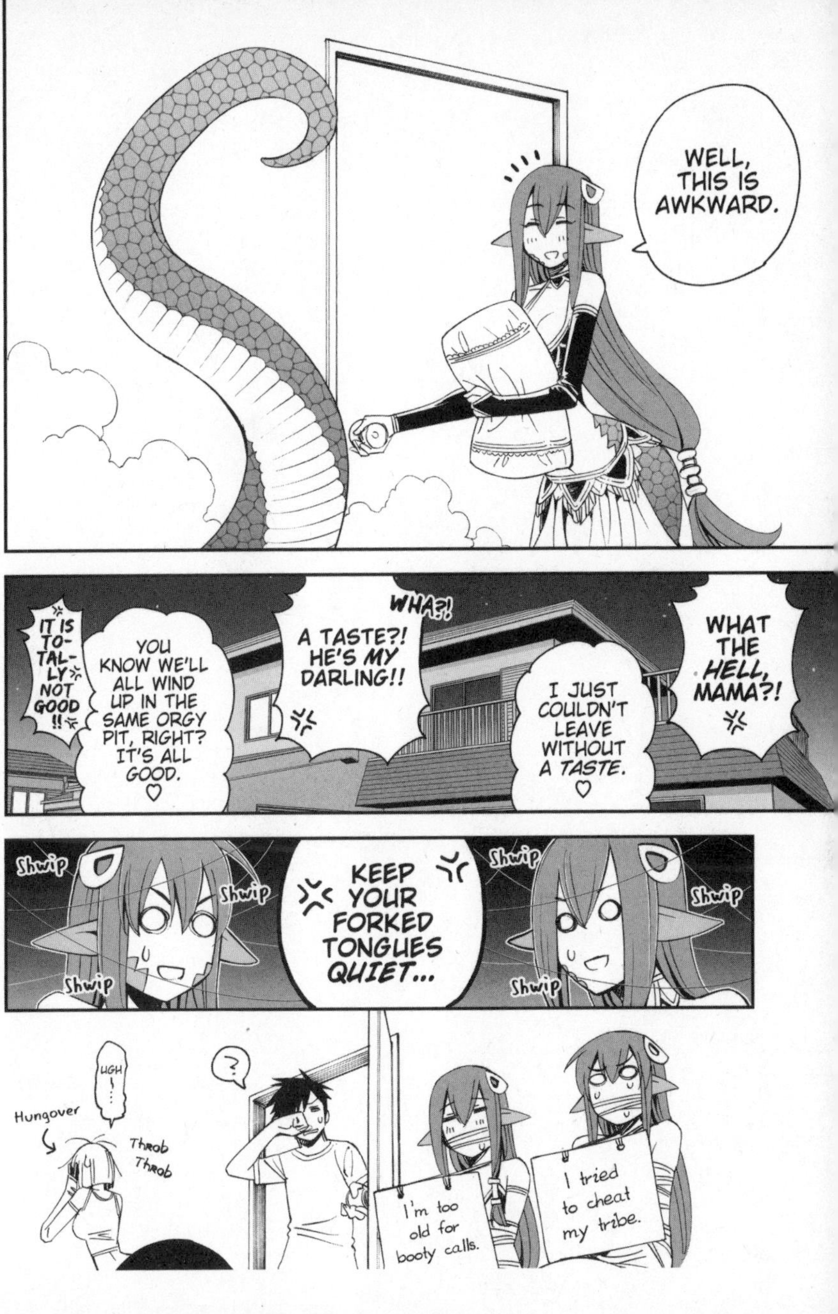
WELL, THIS IS AWKWARD.
WHAT THE HELL, MAMA?!
I JUST COULDN'T LEAVE WITHOUT A TASTE. ♡
WHA?!
A TASTE?! HE'S MY DARLING!!
YOU KNOW WE'LL ALL WIND UP IN THE SAME ORGY PIT, RIGHT? IT'S ALL GOOD. ♡
IT IS TO-TAL-LY NOT GOOD!!
Shwip
Shwip
Shwip
Shwip
KEEP YOUR FORKED TONGUES QUIET...
Shwip
Shwip
Shwip
Shwip
I tried to cheat my tribe.
I'm too old for booty calls.
?
UGH...
Throb Throb
Hungover

Monster Musume

Everyday Life with Monster Girls

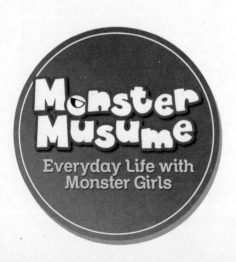

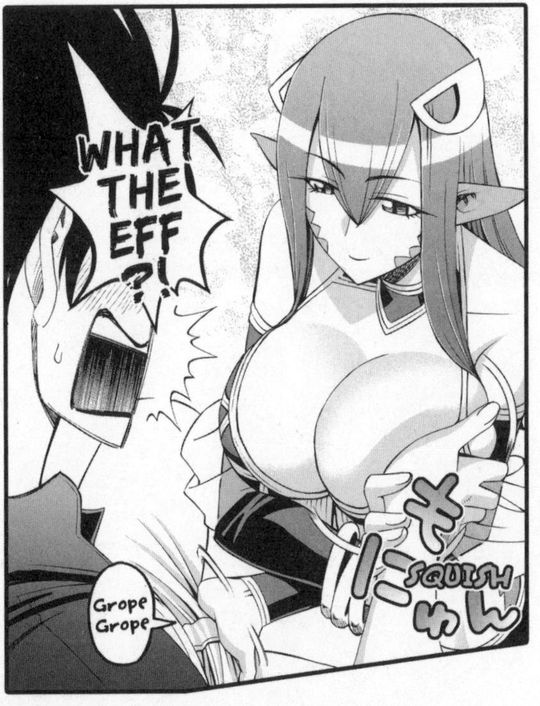
WHAT THE EFF?!
SQUISH
Grope Grope

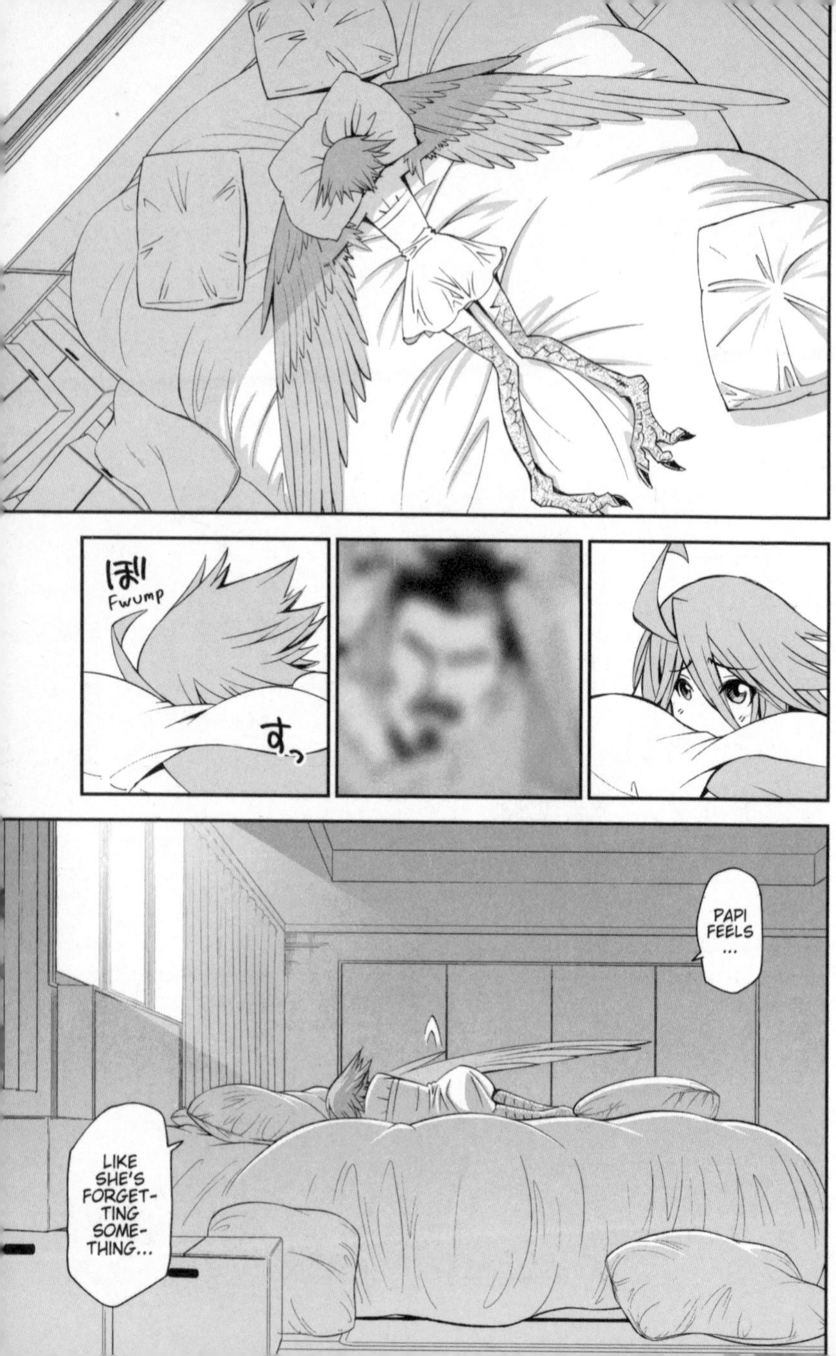
Fwump
すっ
PAPI FEELS ...
LIKE SHE'S FORGET-TING SOME-THING...

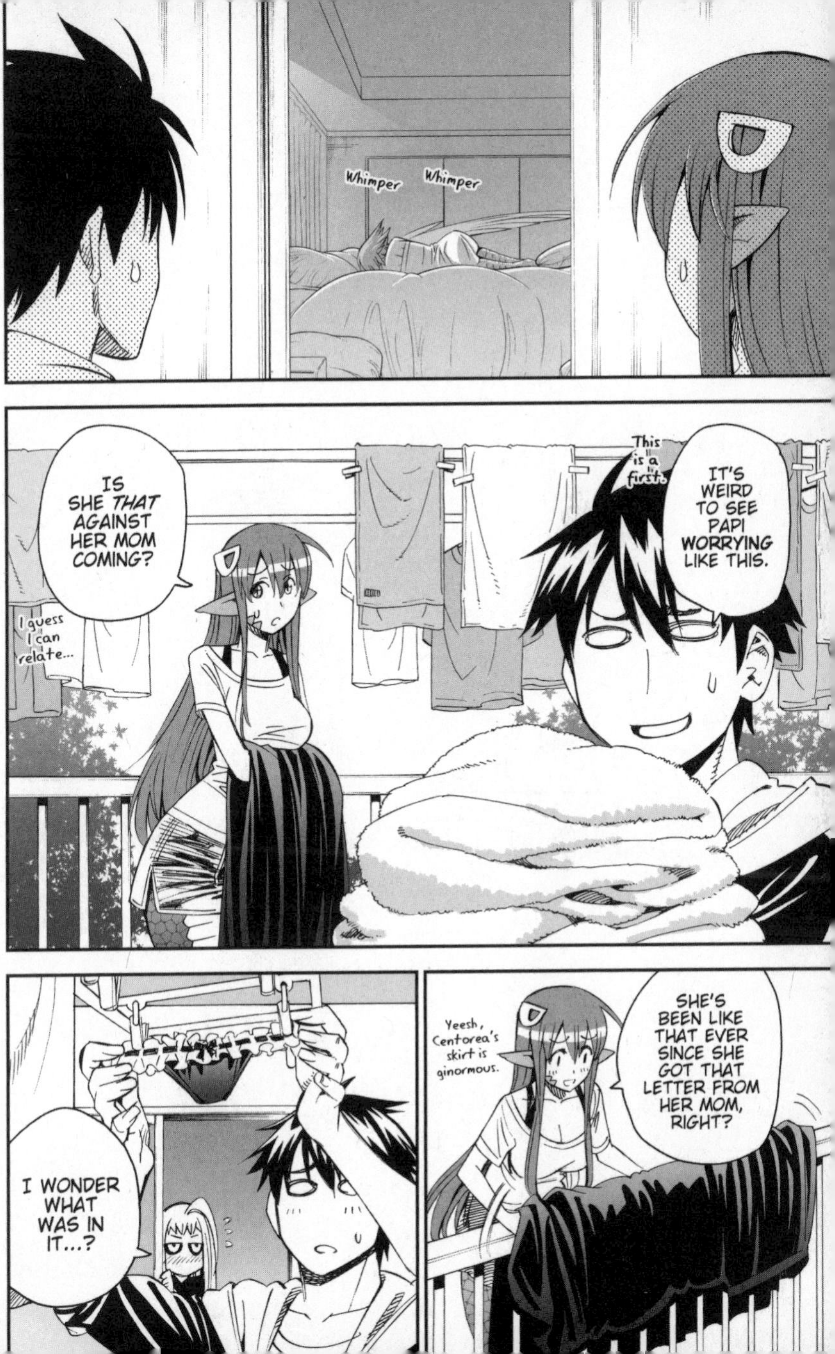
Whimper Whimper
This is a first.
IT'S WEIRD TO SEE PAPI WORRYING LIKE THIS.
IS SHE *THAT* AGAINST HER MOM COMING?
I guess I can relate...
SHE'S BEEN LIKE THAT EVER SINCE SHE GOT THAT LETTER FROM HER MOM, RIGHT?
Yeesh, Centorea's skirt is ginormous.
I WONDER WHAT WAS IN IT...?

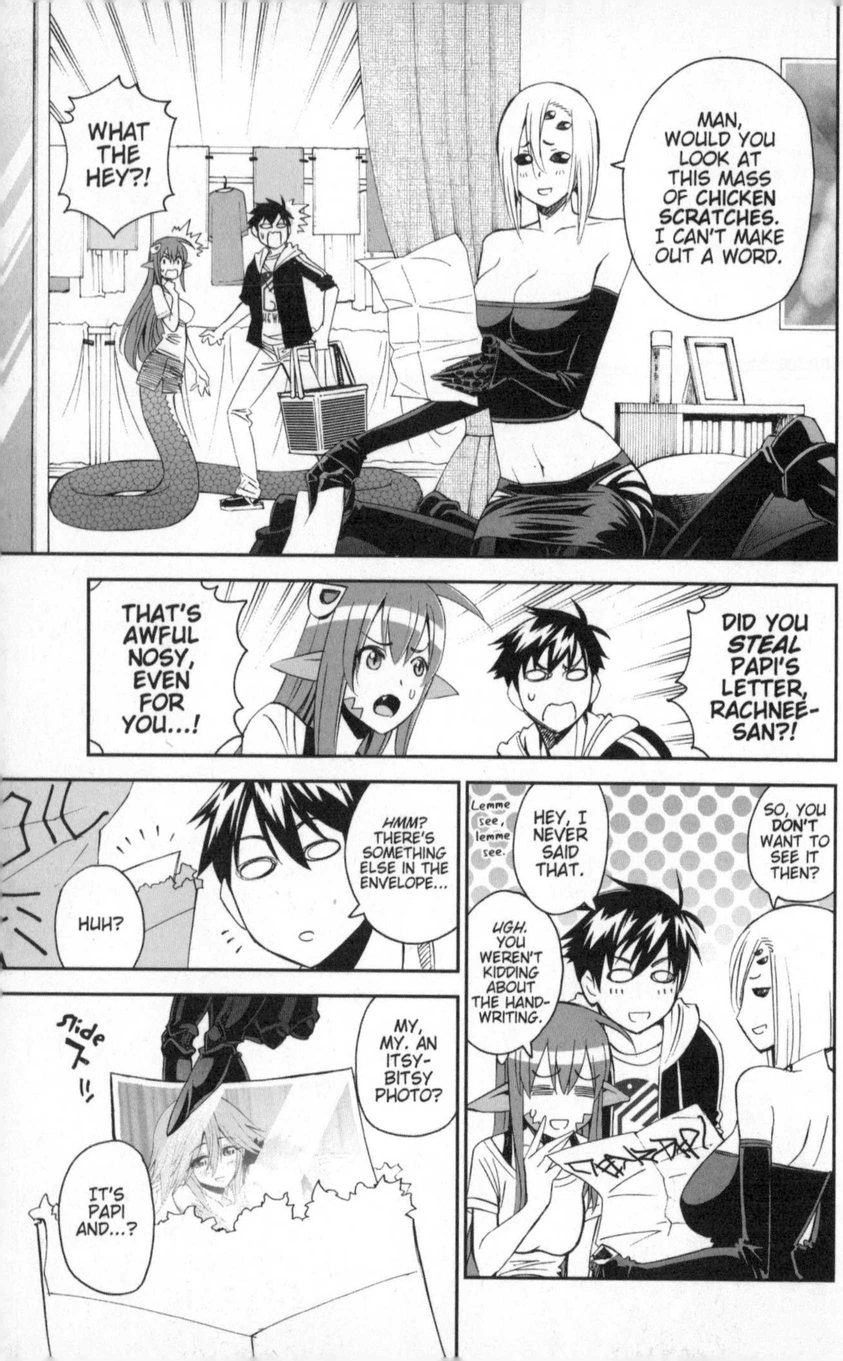

MAN, WOULD YOU LOOK AT THIS MASS OF CHICKEN SCRATCHES. I CAN'T MAKE OUT A WORD.
WHAT THE HEY?!
DID YOU *STEAL* PAPI'S LETTER, RACHNEE-SAN?!
THAT'S AWFUL NOSY, EVEN FOR YOU...!
SO, YOU DON'T WANT TO SEE IT THEN?
HEY, I NEVER SAID THAT.
Lemme see, lemme see.
UGH. YOU WEREN'T KIDDING ABOUT THE HAND-WRITING.
HMM? THERE'S SOMETHING ELSE IN THE ENVELOPE...
HUH?
MY, MY. AN ITSY-BITSY PHOTO?
slide
IT'S PAPI AND...?

Chapter 28

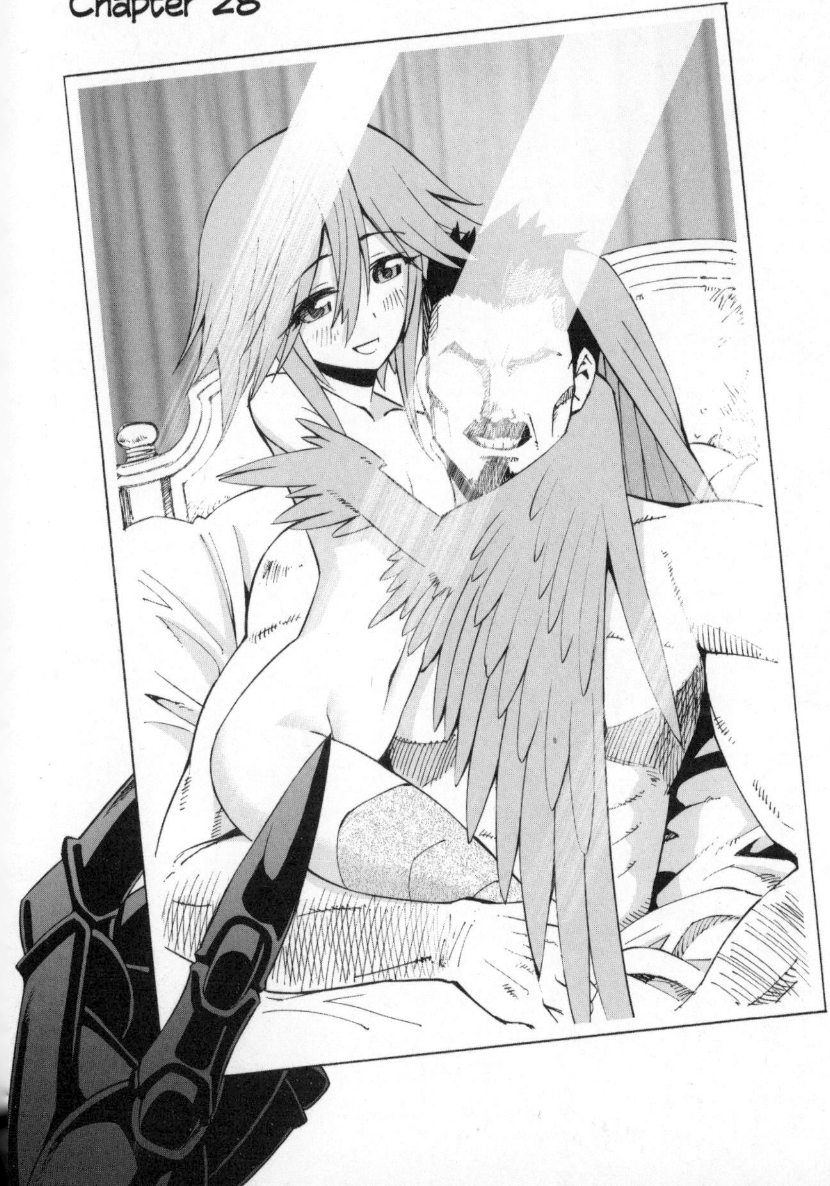

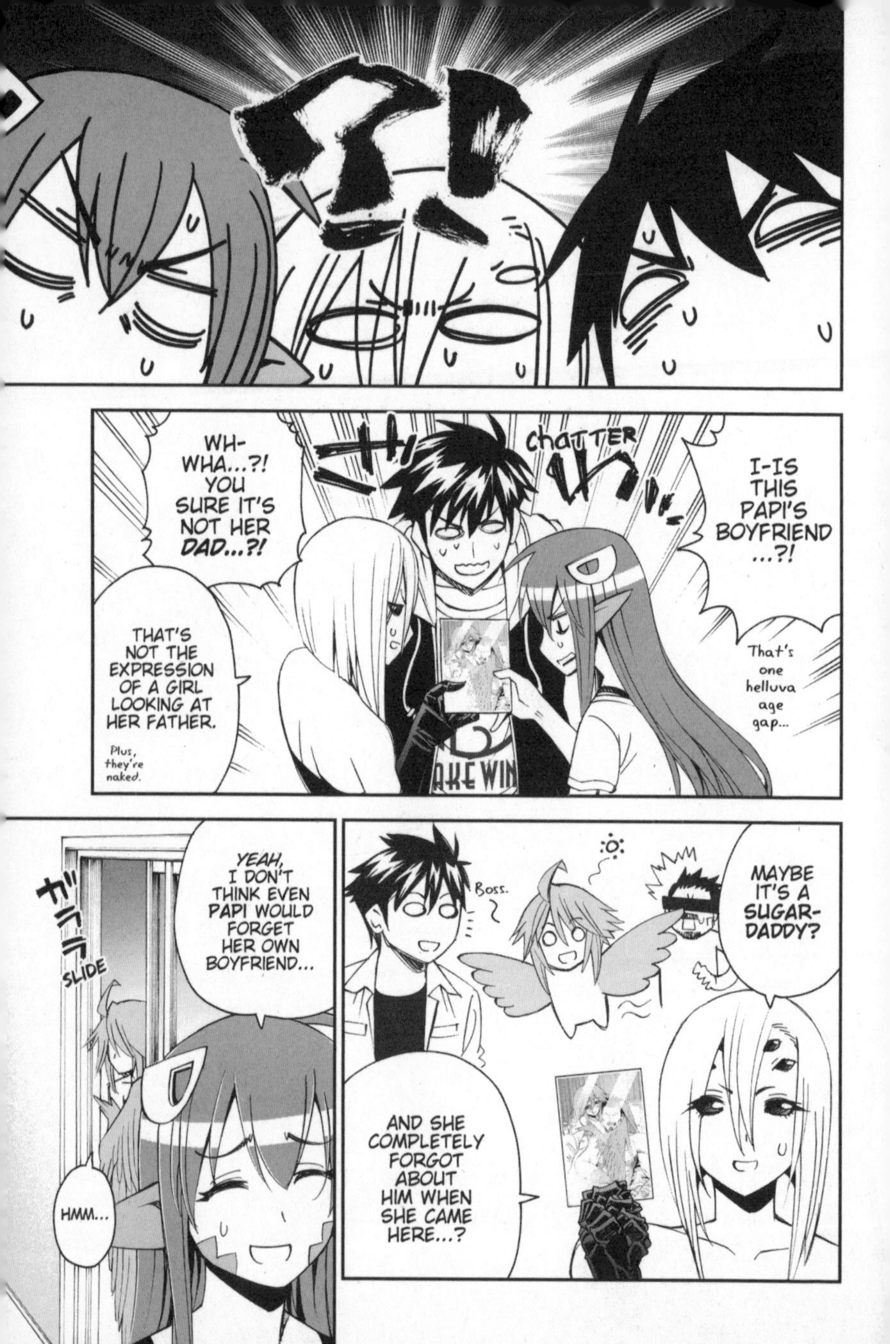
I-IS THIS PAPI'S BOYFRIEND...?!
That's one helluva age gap...
CHATTER
WH-WHA...?! YOU SURE IT'S NOT HER *DAD...?!*
THAT'S NOT THE EXPRESSION OF A GIRL LOOKING AT HER FATHER.
Plus, they're naked.
MAYBE IT'S A SUGAR-DADDY?
Boss.
AND SHE COMPLETELY FORGOT ABOUT HIM WHEN SHE CAME HERE...?
YEAH, I DON'T THINK EVEN PAPI WOULD FORGET HER OWN BOYFRIEND...
SLIDE
HMM...

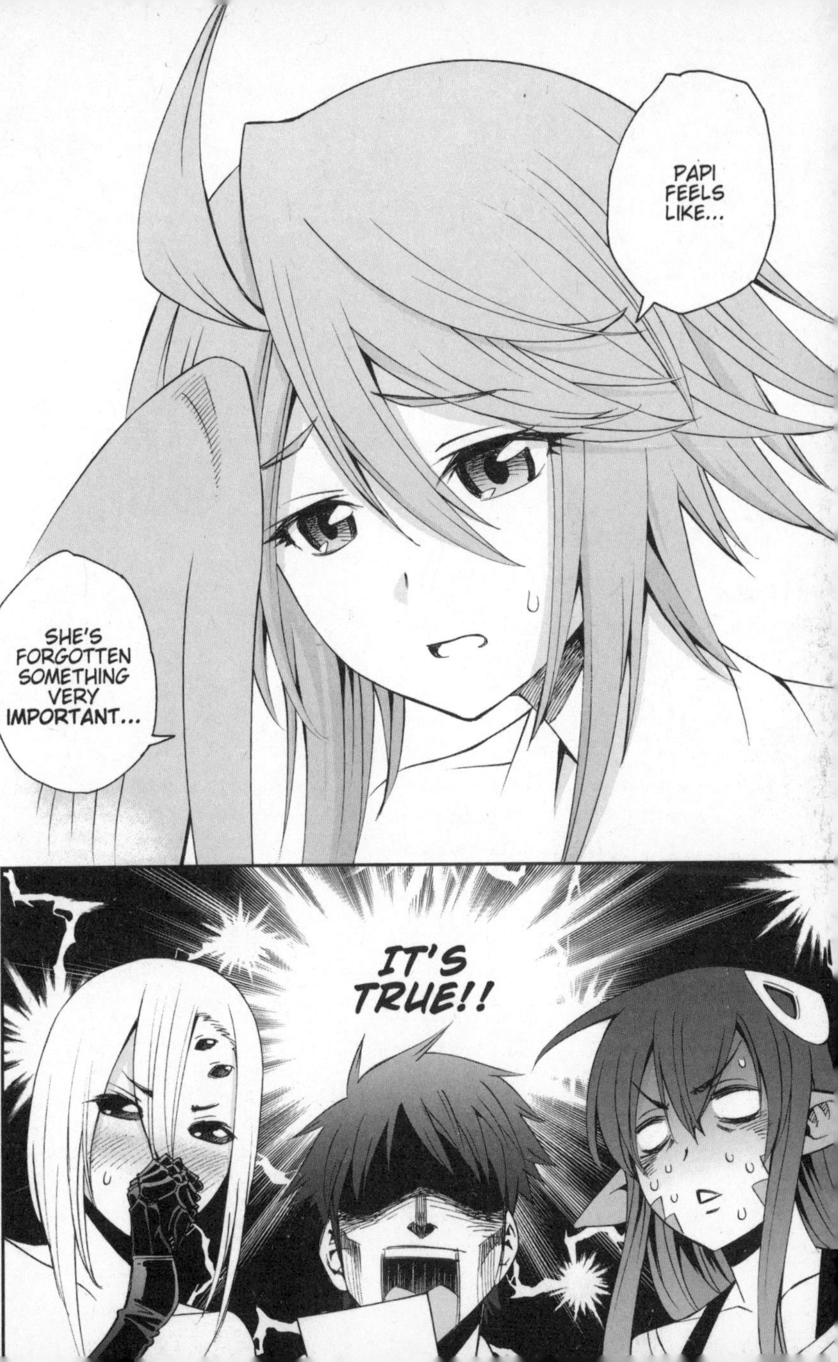
PAPI FEELS LIKE...
SHE'S FORGOTTEN SOMETHING VERY IMPORTANT...
IT'S TRUE!!

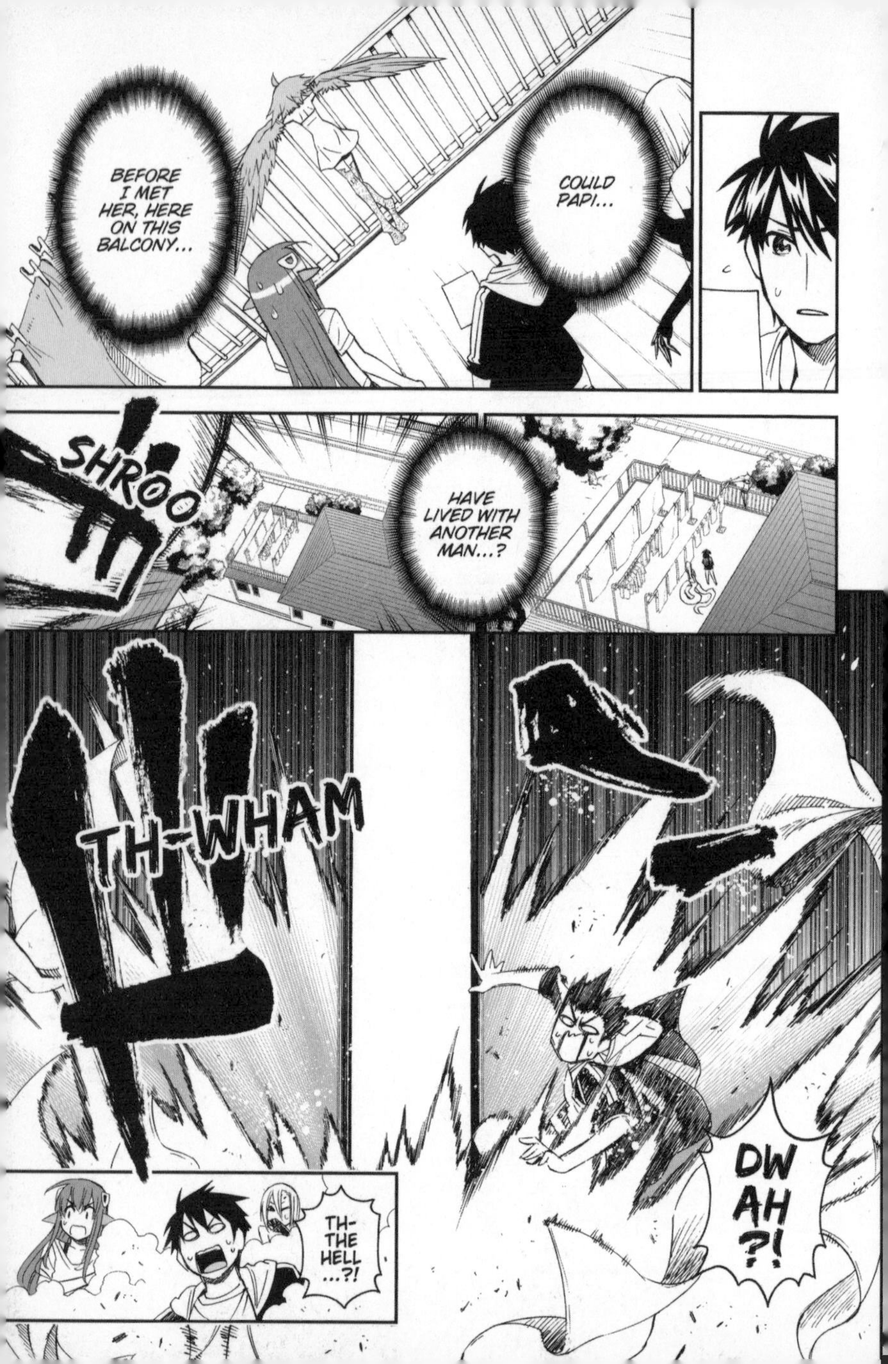

COULD PAPI...
BEFORE I MET HER, HERE ON THIS BALCONY...
HAVE LIVED WITH ANOTHER MAN...?
SHROOO
DW AH ?!
TH-WHAM
TH-THE HELL...?!

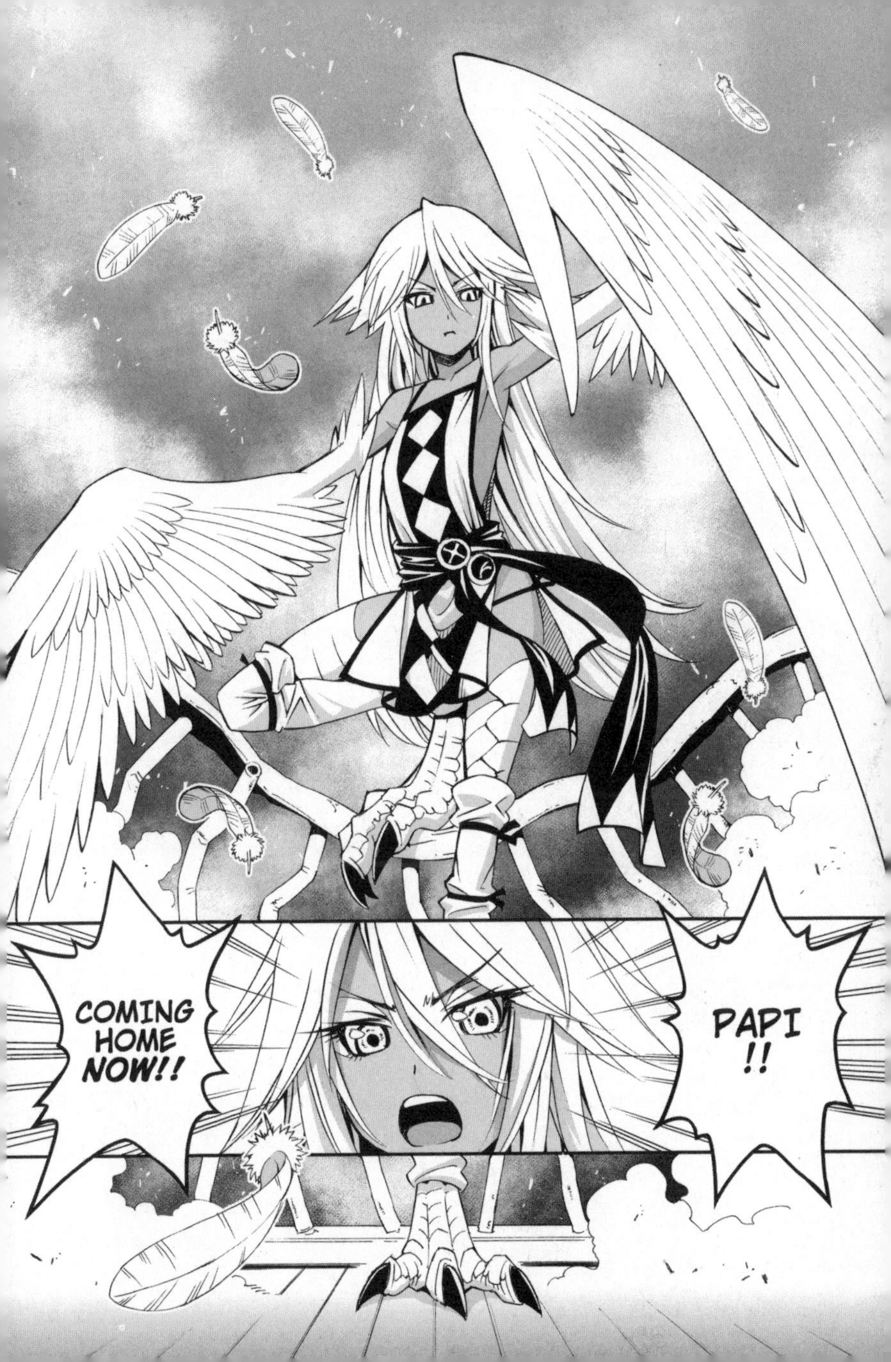
PAPI !!
COMING HOME NOW!!

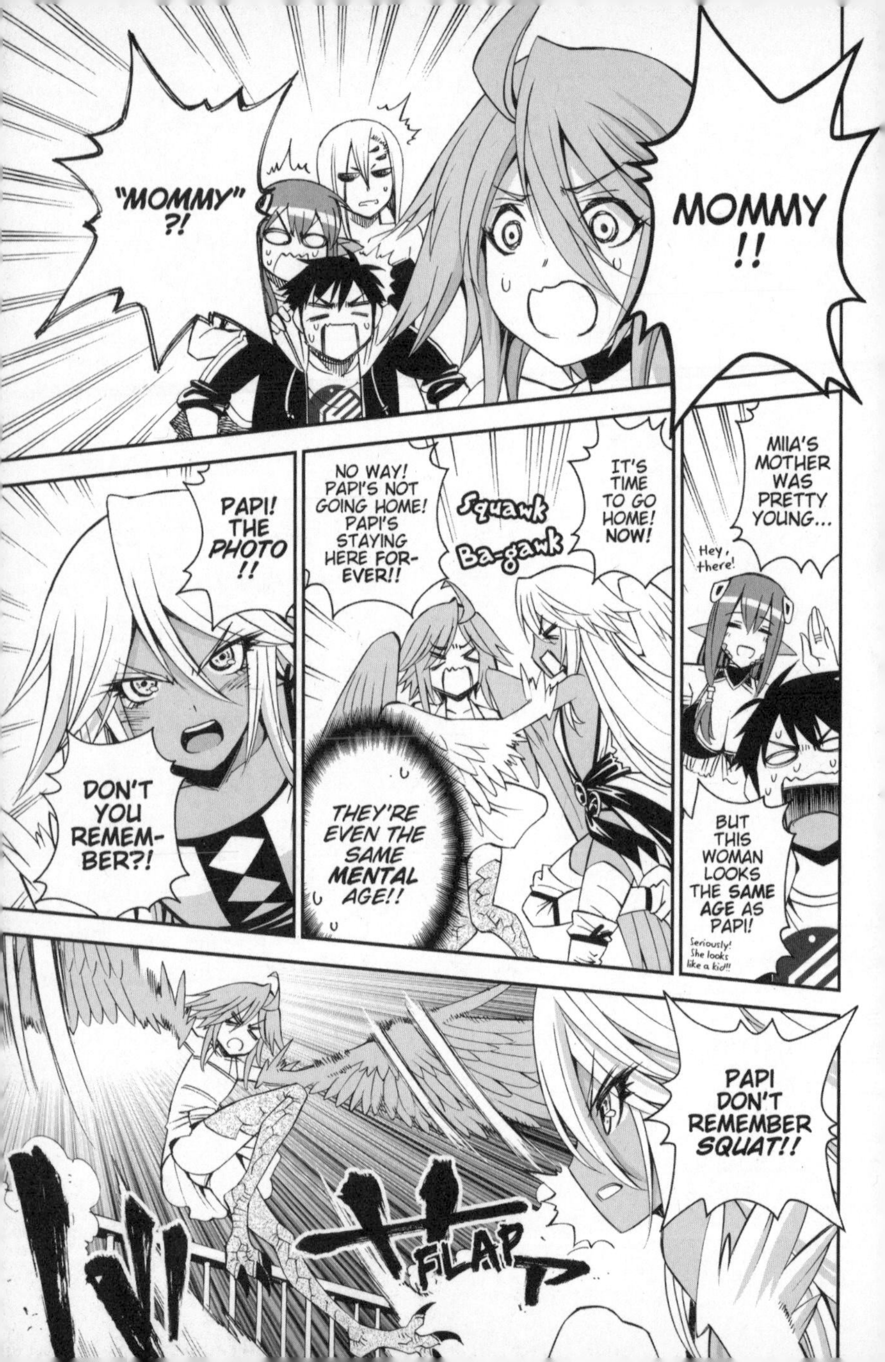
MOMMY !!
"MOMMY" ?!
MIIA'S MOTHER WAS PRETTY YOUNG...
Hey, there!
BUT THIS WOMAN LOOKS THE SAME AGE AS PAPI!
Seriously! She looks like a kid!!
IT'S TIME TO GO HOME! NOW!
Squawk
Ba-gawk
NO WAY! PAPI'S NOT GOING HOME! PAPI'S STAYING HERE FOR-EVER!!
THEY'RE EVEN THE SAME MENTAL AGE!!
PAPI! THE PHOTO !!
DON'T YOU REMEM-BER?!
PAPI DON'T REMEMBER SQUAT!!
FLAP

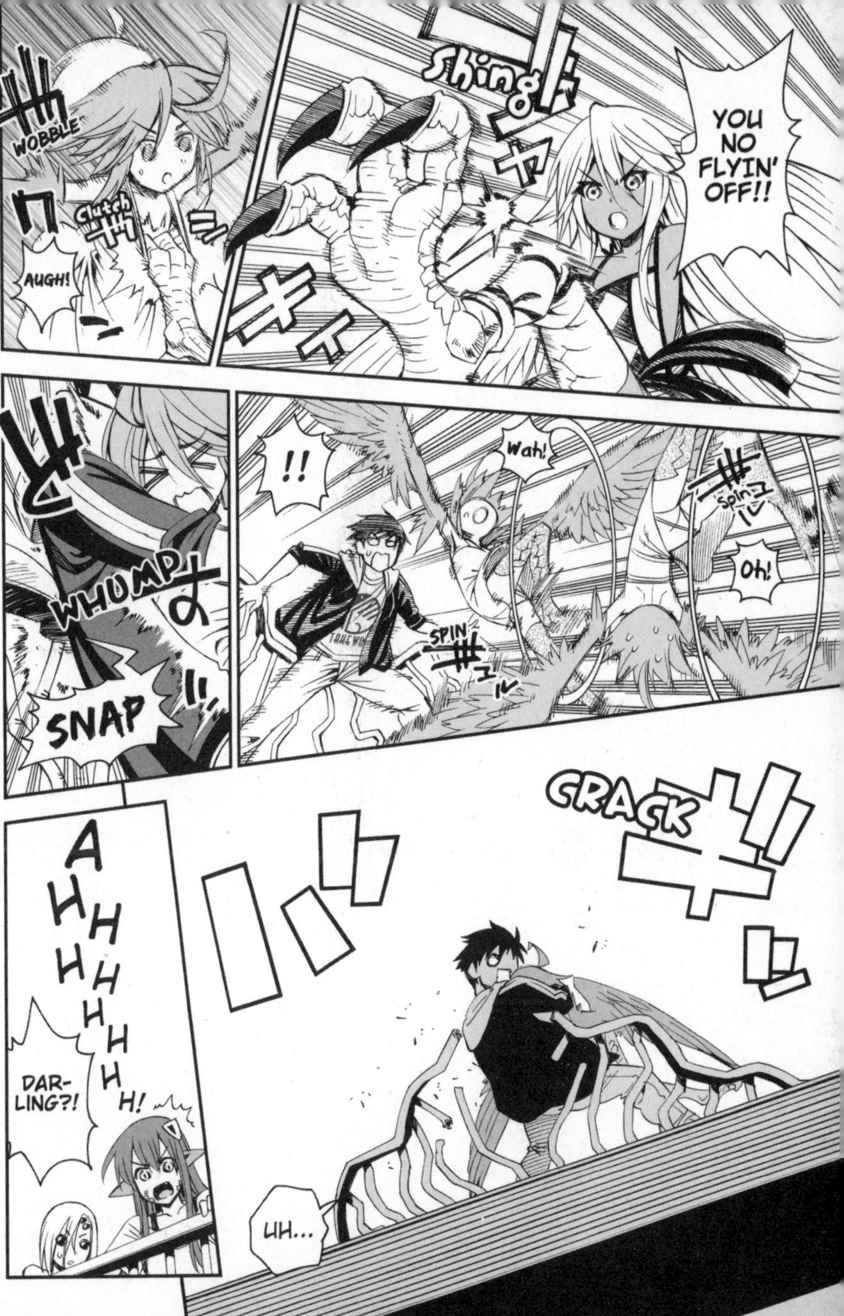
Shing
YOU NO FLYIN' OFF!!
WOBBLE
Clutch
AUGH!
Spin
Wah!
!!
Oh!
SPIN
WHUMP
SNAP
CRACK
UH...
AHHHHHHHHHHHH!
DAR-
LING?!

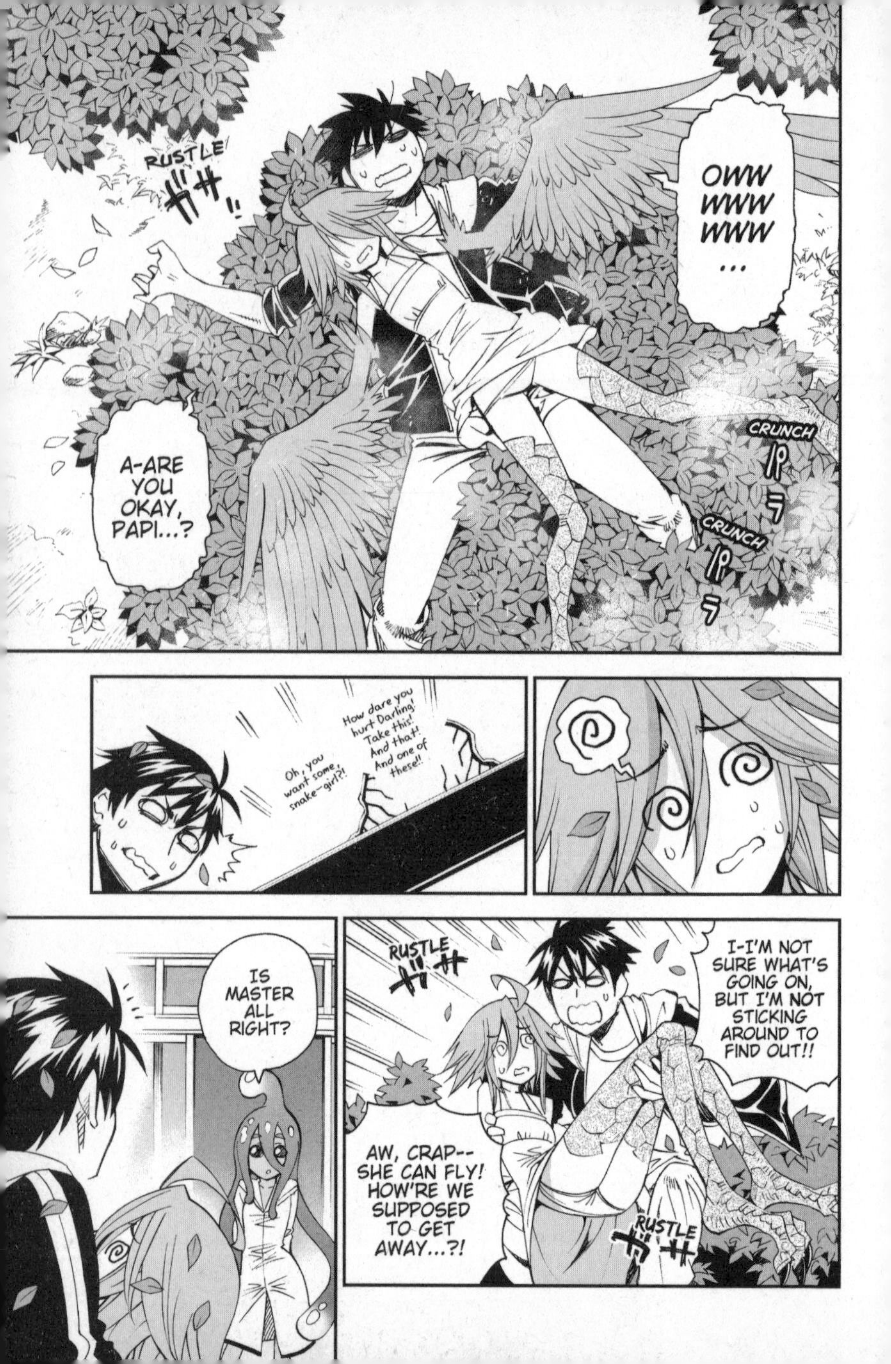
OWW WWW WWW ...
RUSTLE
CRUNCH
CRUNCH
A-ARE YOU OKAY, PAPI...?
How dare you hurt Darling! Take this! And that! And one of these!!
Oh, you want some, snake-girl?!
I-I'M NOT SURE WHAT'S GOING ON, BUT I'M NOT STICKING AROUND TO FIND OUT!!
RUSTLE
AW, CRAP-- SHE CAN FLY! HOW'RE WE SUPPOSED TO GET AWAY...?!
RUSTLE
IS MASTER ALL RIGHT?

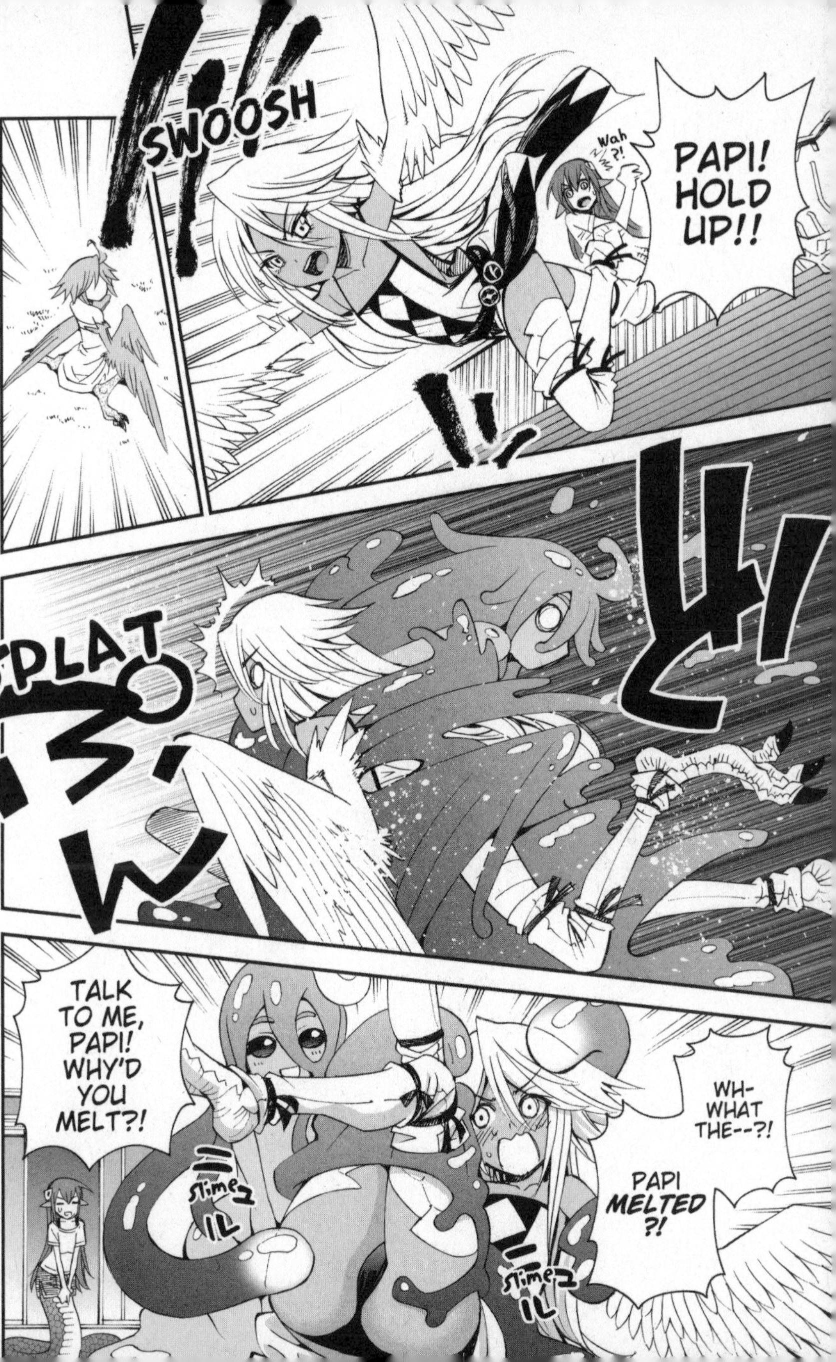
PAPI! HOLD UP!!
Wah ?!
SWOOSH
SPLAT
WH-WHAT THE--?!
PAPI MELTED ?!
TALK TO ME, PAPI! WHY'D YOU MELT?!
slime
slime

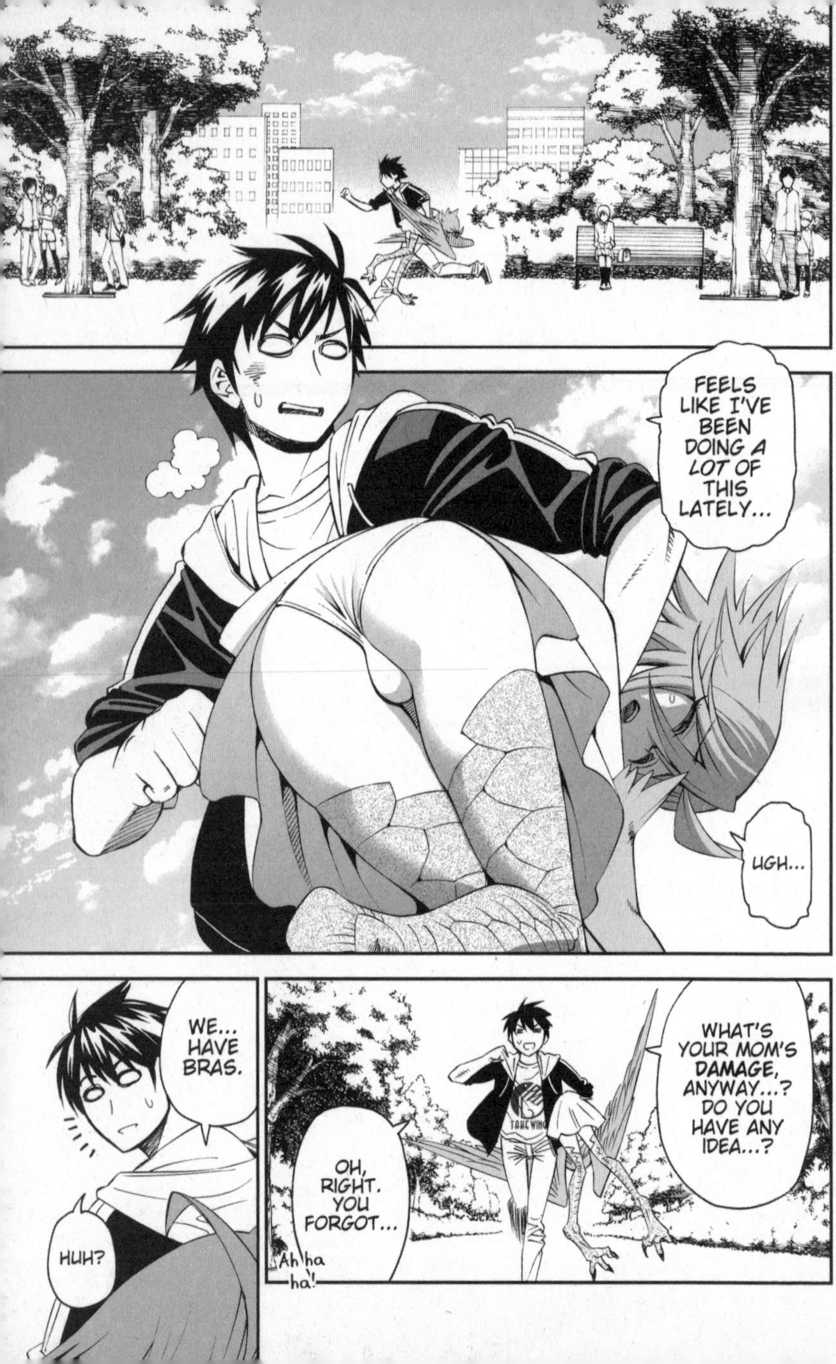
FEELS LIKE I'VE BEEN DOING A LOT OF THIS LATELY...
UGH...
WHAT'S YOUR MOM'S DAMAGE, ANYWAY...? DO YOU HAVE ANY IDEA...?
OH, RIGHT. YOU FORGOT...
Ah ha ha!
WE... HAVE BRAS.
HUH?

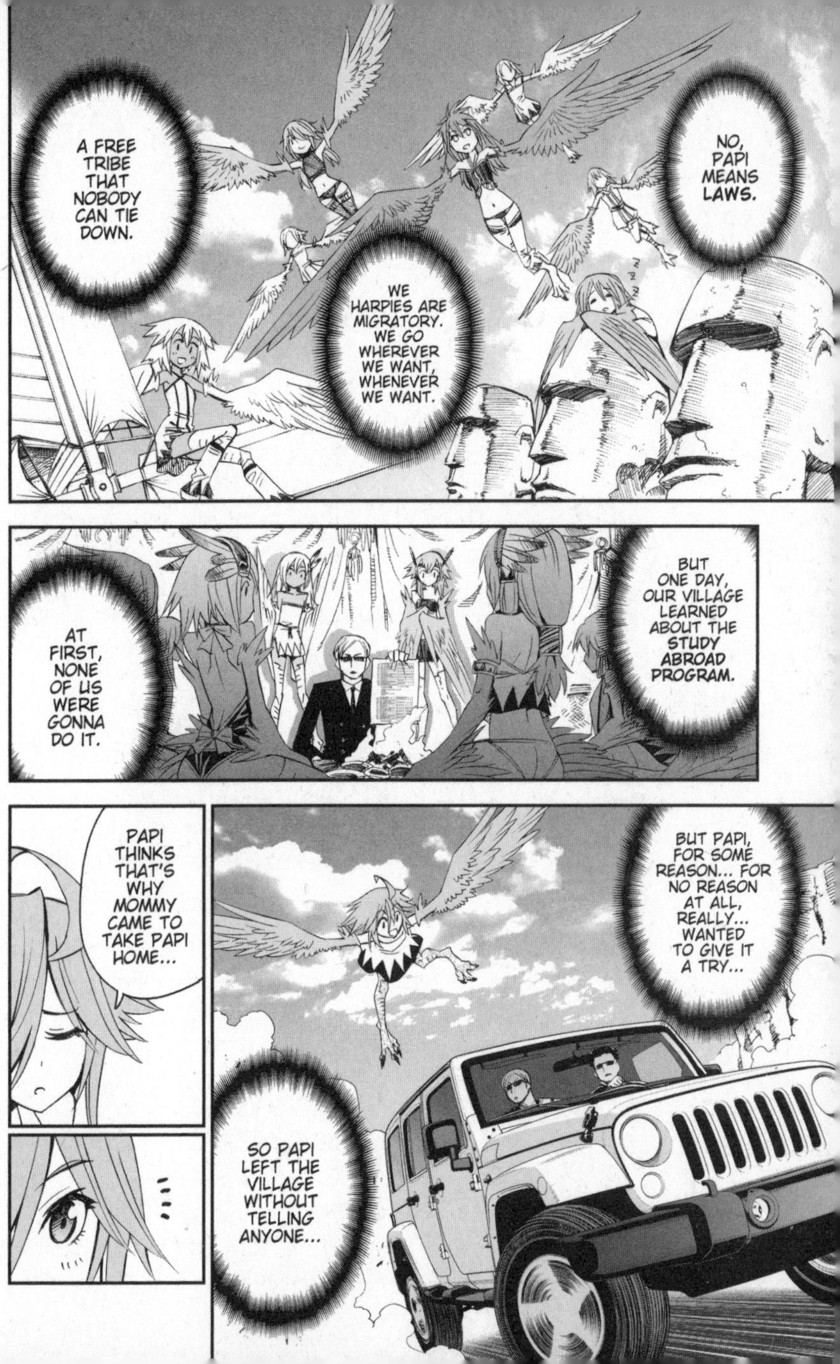
NO, PAPI MEANS LAWS.
WE HARPIES ARE MIGRATORY. WE GO WHEREVER WE WANT, WHENEVER WE WANT.
A FREE TRIBE THAT NOBODY CAN TIE DOWN.
BUT ONE DAY, OUR VILLAGE LEARNED ABOUT THE STUDY ABROAD PROGRAM.
AT FIRST, NONE OF US WERE GONNA DO IT.
BUT PAPI, FOR SOME REASON... FOR NO REASON AT ALL, REALLY... WANTED TO GIVE IT A TRY...
SO PAPI LEFT THE VILLAGE WITHOUT TELLING ANYONE...
PAPI THINKS THAT'S WHY MOMMY CAME TO TAKE PAPI HOME...
...

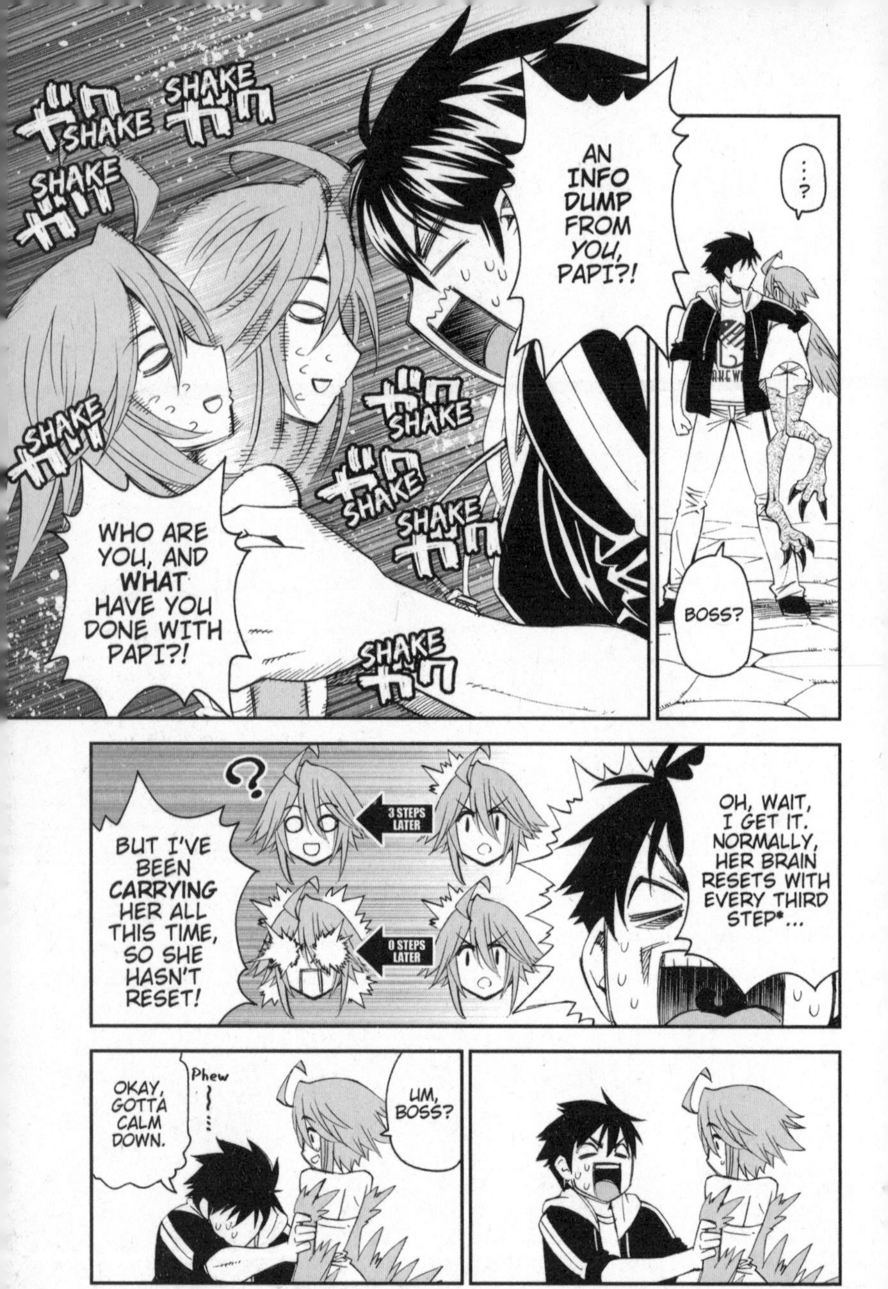

...?
BOSS?
AN INFO DUMP FROM YOU, PAPI?!
SHAKE SHAKE
SHAKE
SHAKE
WHO ARE YOU, AND WHAT HAVE YOU DONE WITH PAPI?!
SHAKE
SHAKE
SHAKE
SHAKE
OH, WAIT, I GET IT. NORMALLY, HER BRAIN RESETS WITH EVERY THIRD STEP*...
3 STEPS LATER
0 STEPS LATER
BUT I'VE BEEN CARRYING HER ALL THIS TIME, SO SHE HASN'T RESET!
UM, BOSS?
Phew ~...
OKAY, GOTTA CALM DOWN.

*According to a well-known Japanese proverb, chickens forget what they were doing after taking three steps.

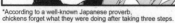

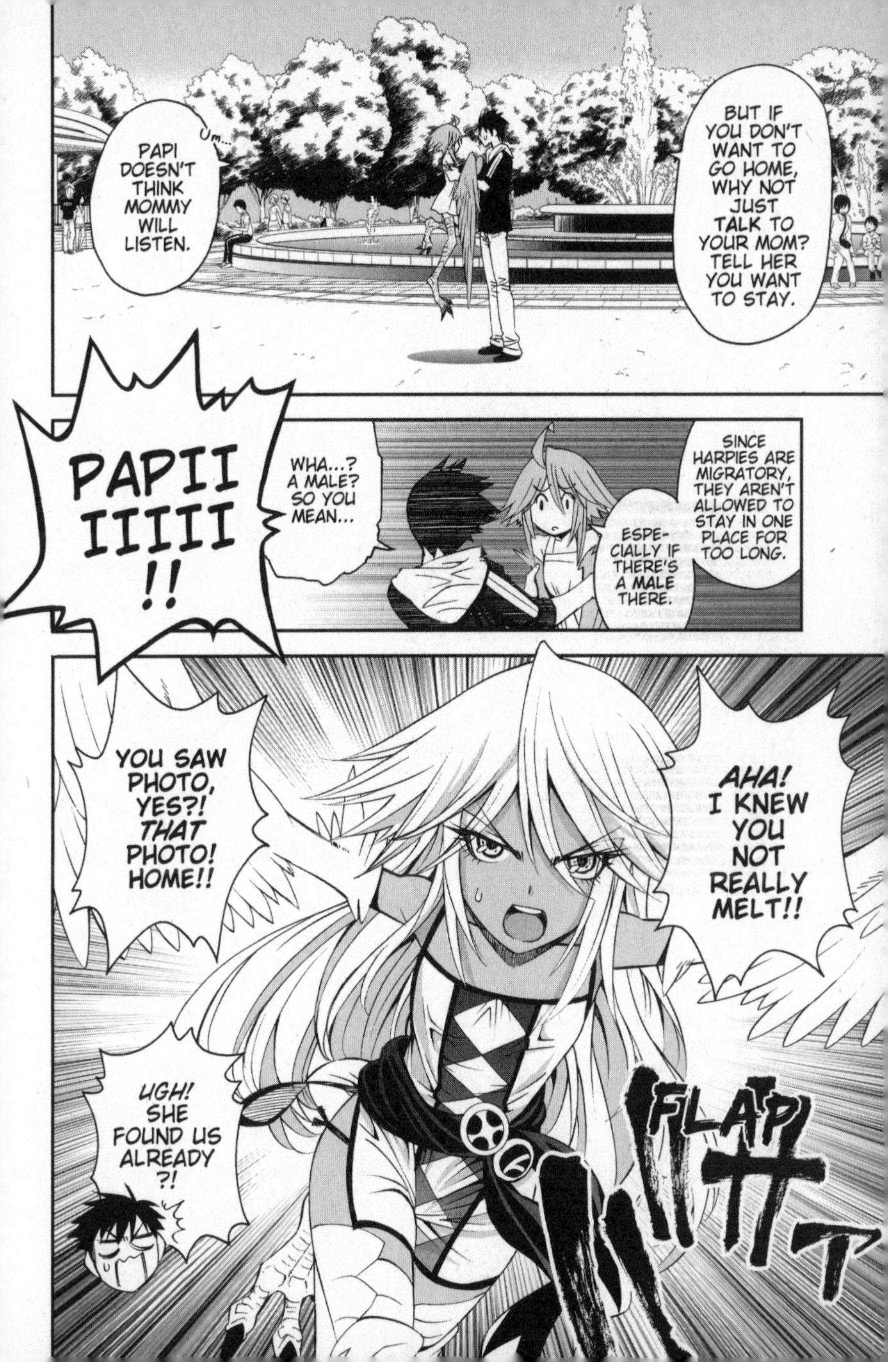

BUT IF YOU DON'T WANT TO GO HOME, WHY NOT JUST TALK TO YOUR MOM? TELL HER YOU WANT TO STAY.
Um...
PAPI DOESN'T THINK MOMMY WILL LISTEN.
SINCE HARPIES ARE MIGRATORY, THEY AREN'T ALLOWED TO STAY IN ONE PLACE FOR TOO LONG.
ESPECIALLY IF THERE'S A MALE THERE.
WHA...? A MALE? SO YOU MEAN...
PAPIIIIIII!!
AHA! I KNEW YOU NOT REALLY MELT!!
YOU SAW PHOTO, YES?! THAT PHOTO! HOME!!
FLAP
UGH! SHE FOUND US ALREADY?!

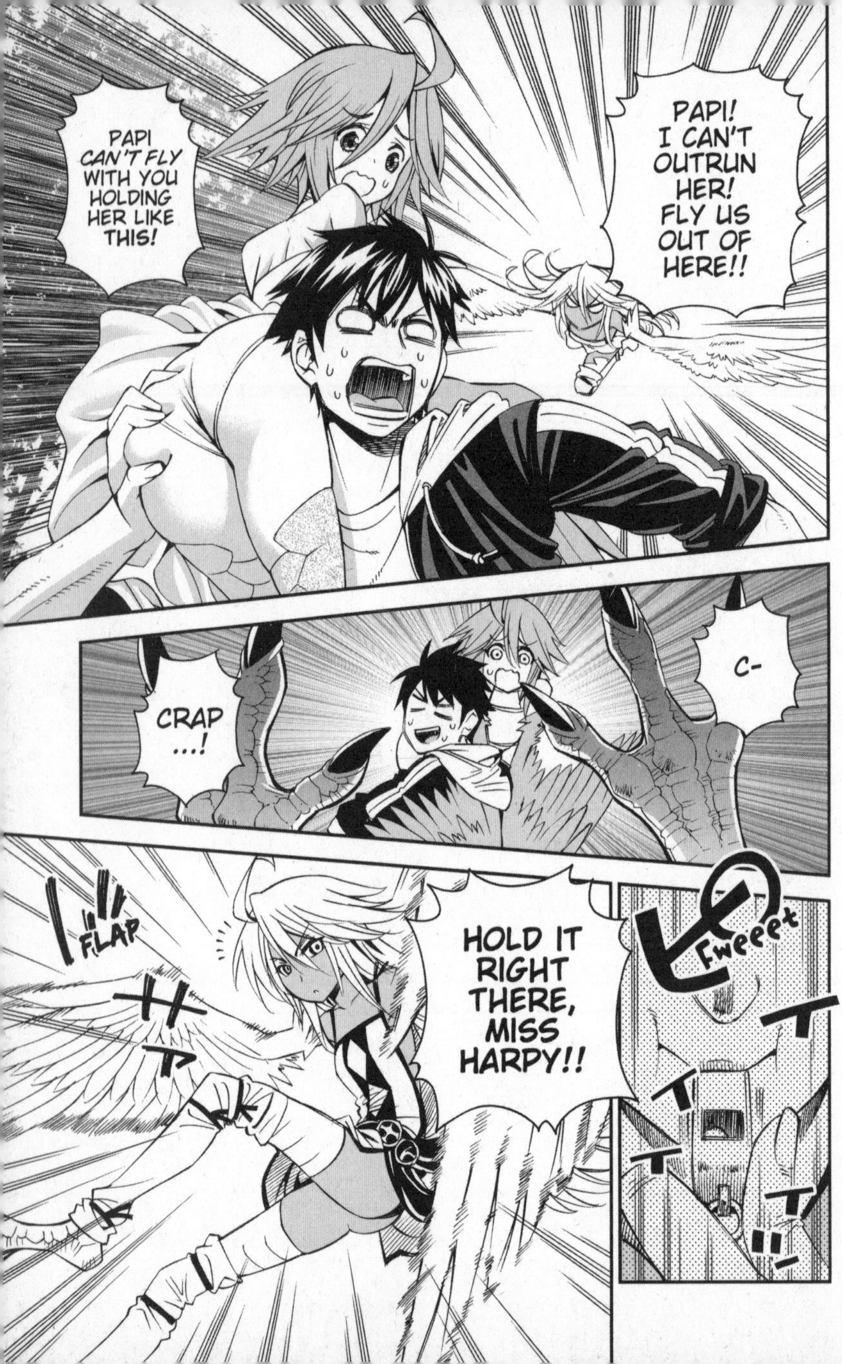
PAPI! I CAN'T OUTRUN HER! FLY US OUT OF HERE!!
PAPI CAN'T FLY WITH YOU HOLDING HER LIKE THIS!
C-
CRAP ...!
Fweeet
HOLD IT RIGHT THERE, MISS HARPY!!
FLAP

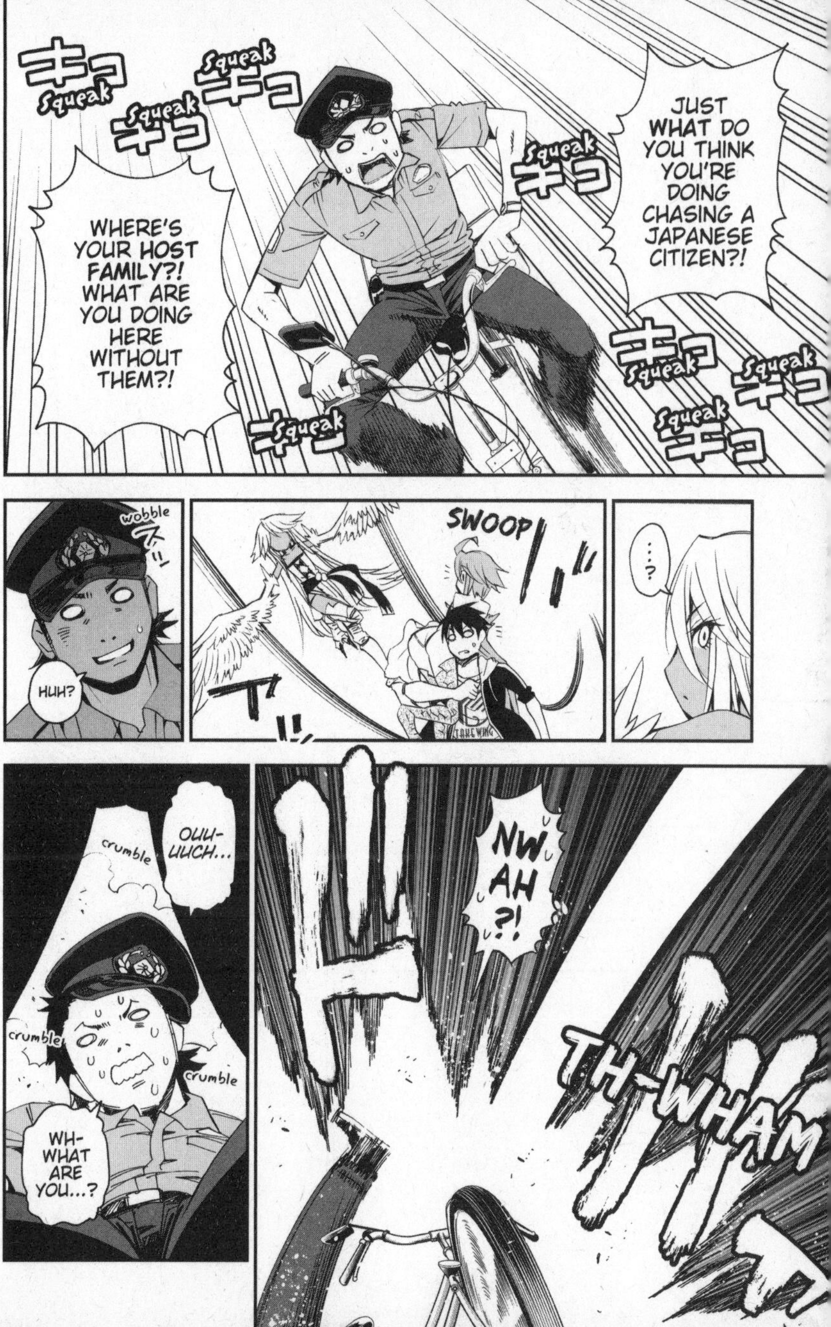
Squeak
Squeak
Squeak
Squeak
JUST WHAT DO YOU THINK YOU'RE DOING CHASING A JAPANESE CITIZEN?!
WHERE'S YOUR HOST FAMILY?! WHAT ARE YOU DOING HERE WITHOUT THEM?!
Squeak
Squeak
Squeak
Squeak
...?
SWOOP
wobble
HUH?
NWAH?!
TH-WHAM
OUUU-UUCH...
crumble
crumble
crumble
WH-WHAT ARE YOU...?

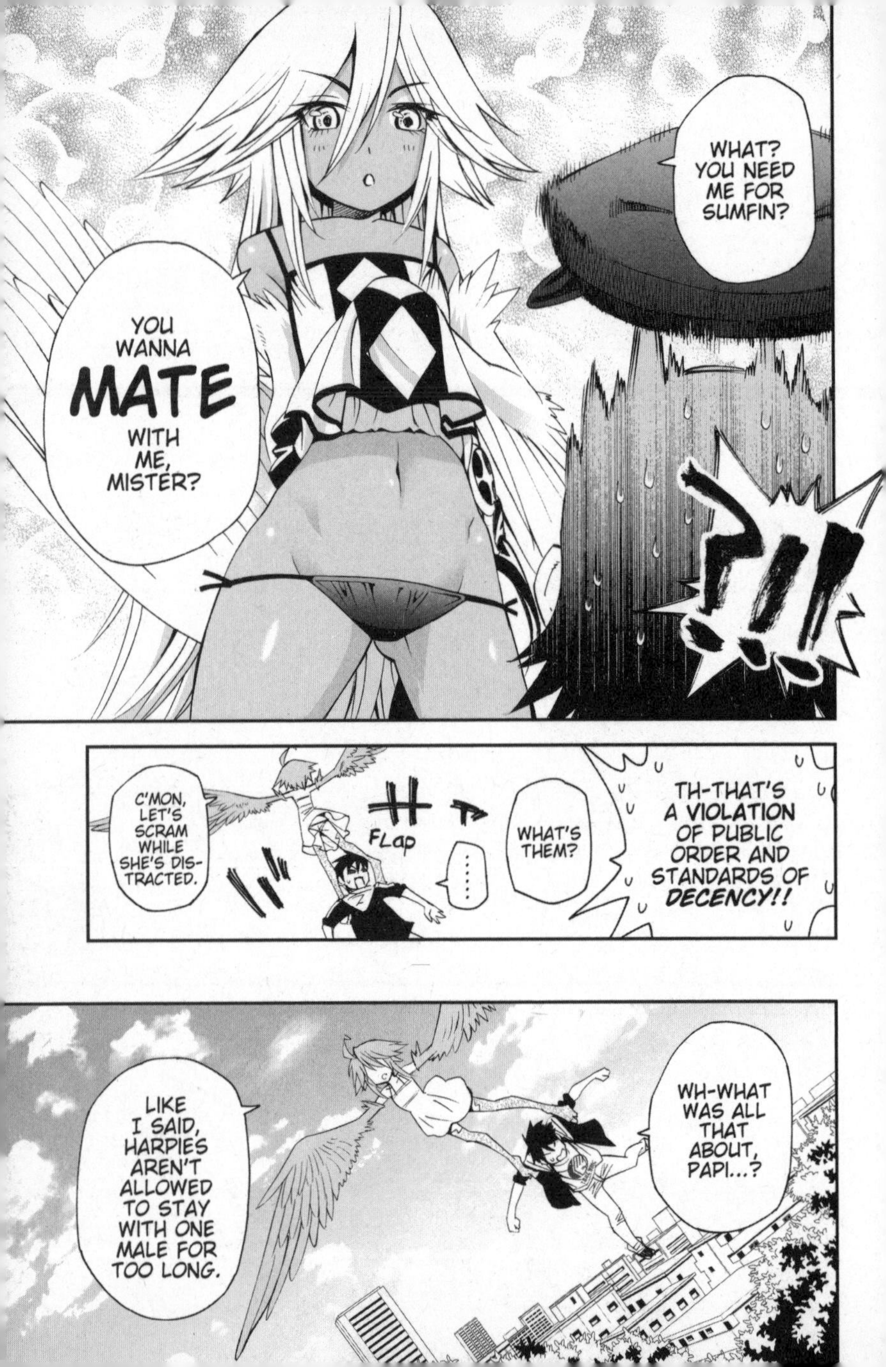
WHAT? YOU NEED ME FOR SUMFIN?
YOU WANNA MATE WITH ME, MISTER?
?!!
TH-THAT'S A VIOLATION OF PUBLIC ORDER AND STANDARDS OF DECENCY!!
WHAT'S THEM?
......
FLap
C'MON, LET'S SCRAM WHILE SHE'S DIS-TRACTED.
WH-WHAT WAS ALL THAT ABOUT, PAPI...?
LIKE I SAID, HARPIES AREN'T ALLOWED TO STAY WITH ONE MALE FOR TOO LONG.

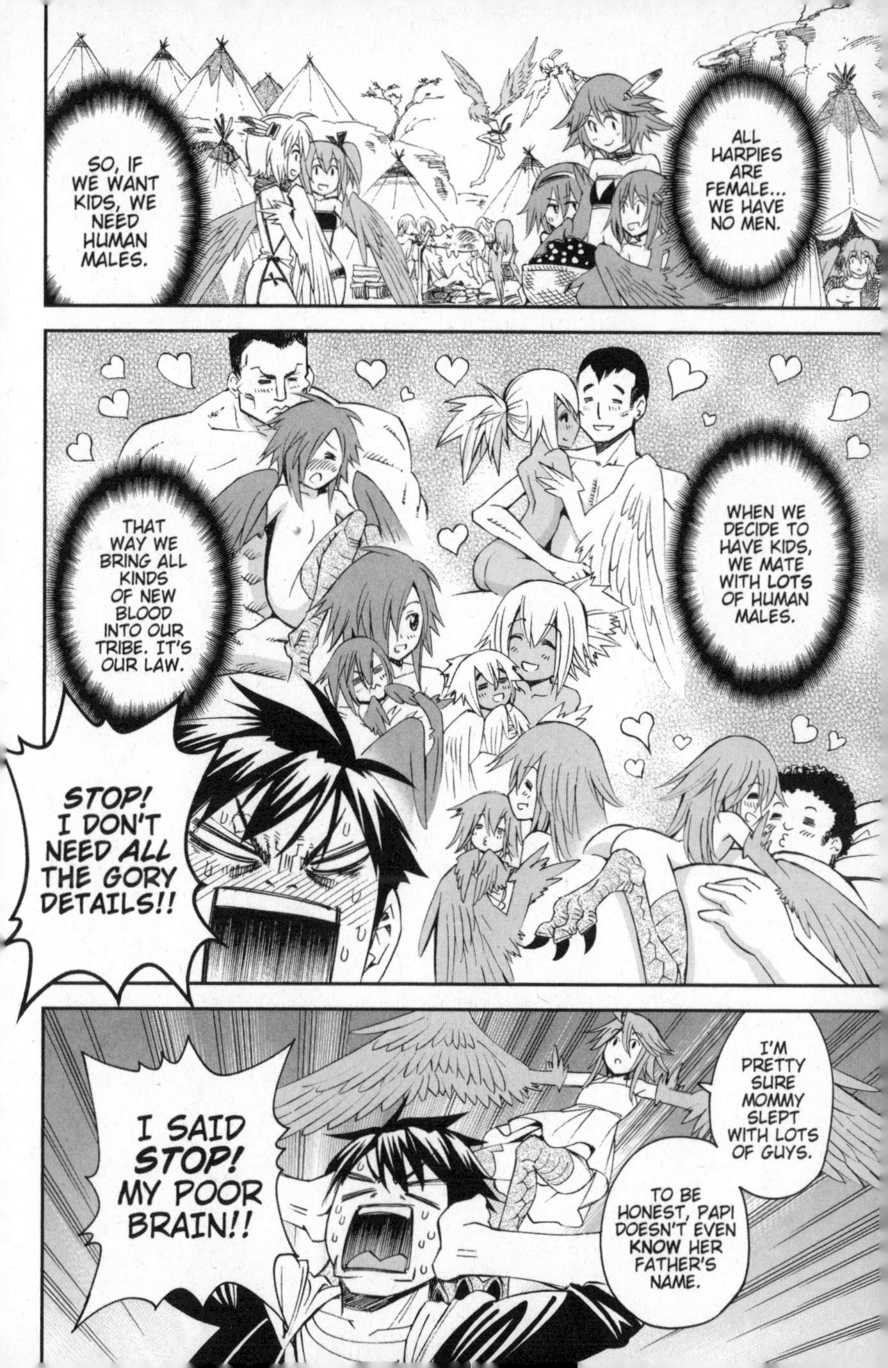
ALL HARPIES ARE FEMALE... WE HAVE NO MEN.
SO, IF WE WANT KIDS, WE NEED HUMAN MALES.
WHEN WE DECIDE TO HAVE KIDS, WE MATE WITH LOTS OF HUMAN MALES.
THAT WAY WE BRING ALL KINDS OF NEW BLOOD INTO OUR TRIBE. IT'S OUR LAW.
STOP! I DON'T NEED ALL THE GORY DETAILS!!
I'M PRETTY SURE MOMMY SLEPT WITH LOTS OF GUYS.
TO BE HONEST, PAPI DOESN'T EVEN KNOW HER FATHER'S NAME.
I SAID STOP! MY POOR BRAIN!!

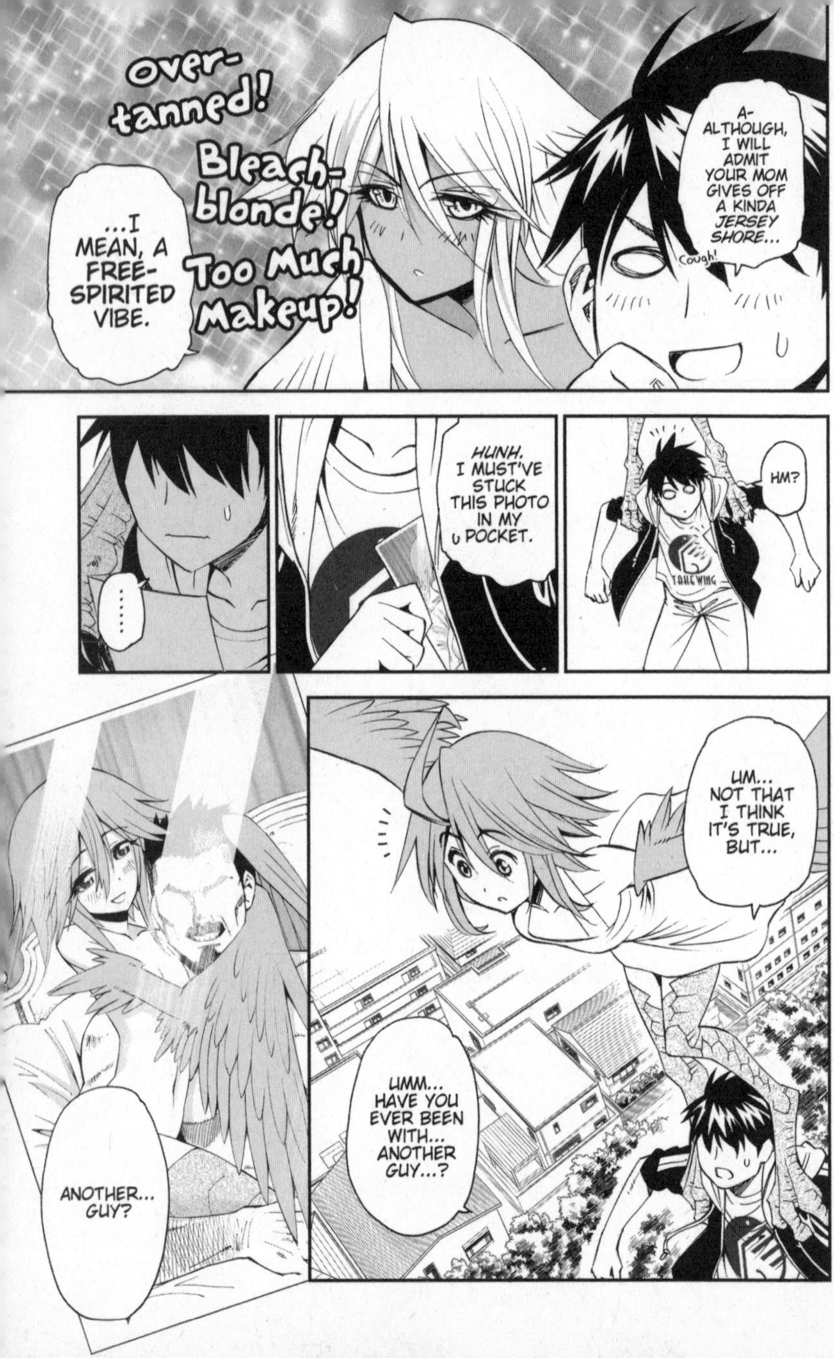
A- ALTHOUGH, I WILL ADMIT YOUR MOM GIVES OFF A KINDA JERSEY SHORE...
Cough!
over-tanned!
Bleach-blonde!
Too Much Makeup!
...I MEAN, A FREE-SPIRITED VIBE.
HM?
HUNH. I MUST'VE STUCK THIS PHOTO IN MY POCKET.
......
UM... NOT THAT I THINK IT'S TRUE, BUT...
UMM... HAVE YOU EVER BEEN WITH... ANOTHER GUY...?
ANOTHER... GUY?

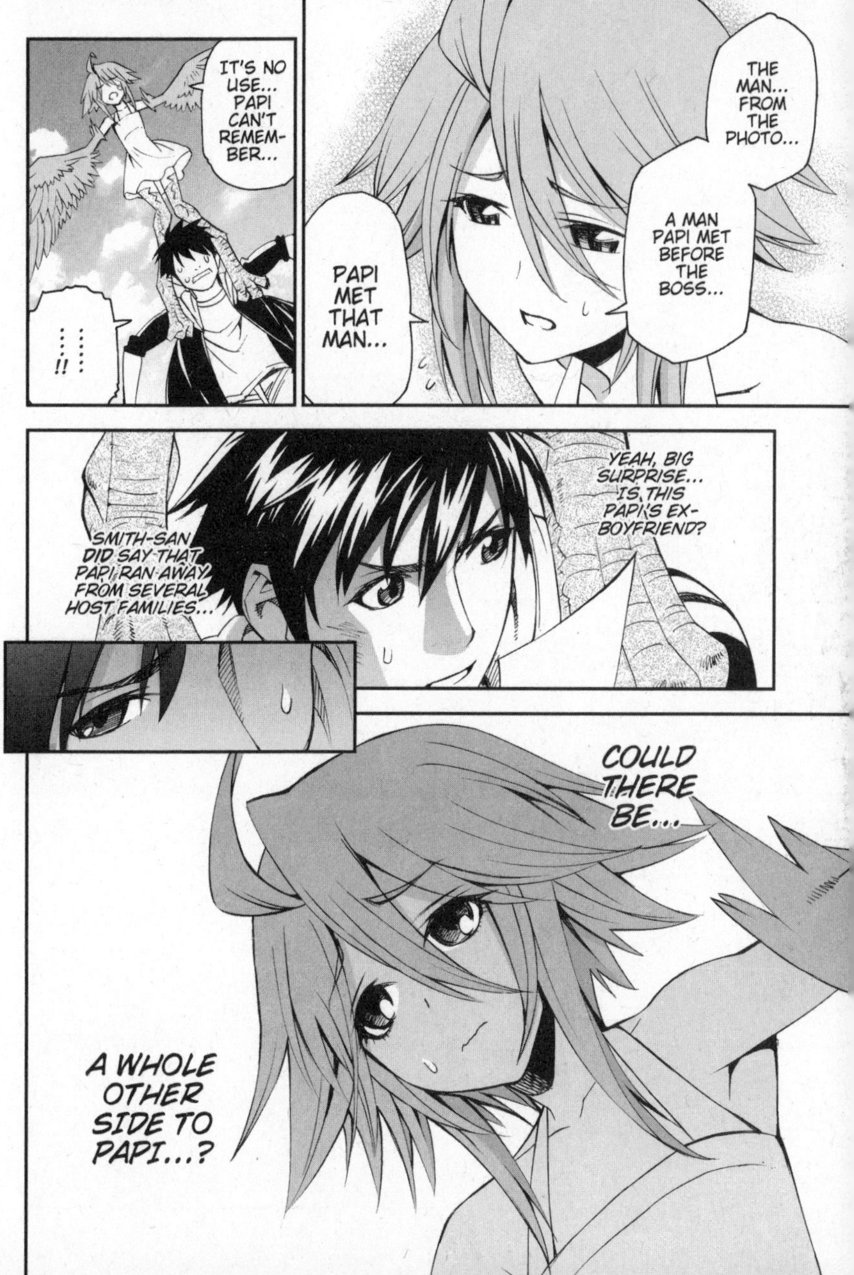
THE MAN... FROM THE PHOTO...
A MAN PAPI MET BEFORE THE BOSS...
PAPI MET THAT MAN...
IT'S NO USE... PAPI CAN'T REMEMBER...
......!!
YEAH, BIG SURPRISE... IS THIS PAPI'S EX-BOYFRIEND?
SMITH-SAN DID SAY THAT PAPI RAN AWAY FROM SEVERAL HOST FAMILIES...
COULD THERE BE...
A WHOLE OTHER SIDE TO PAPI...?

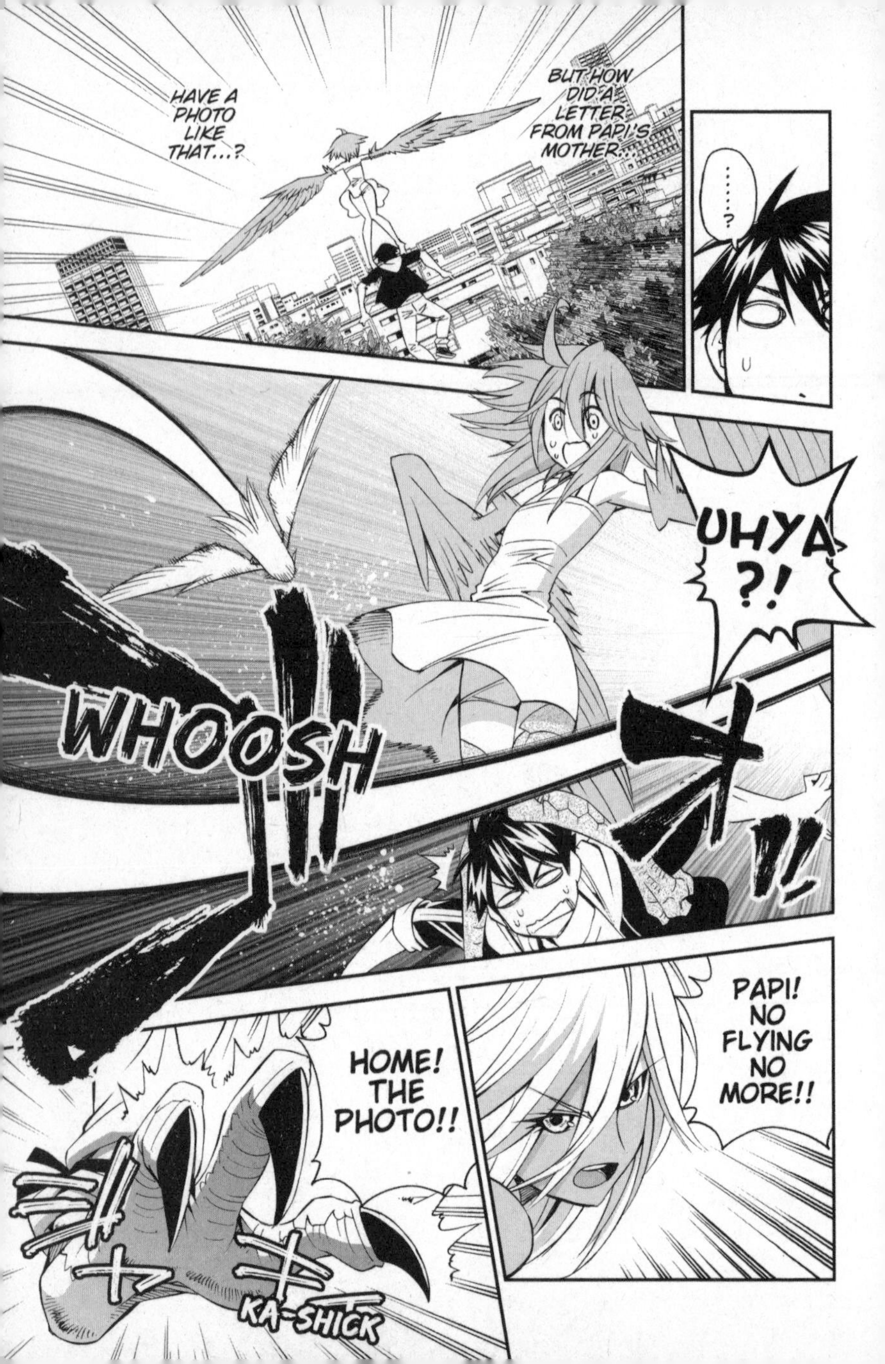
BUT HOW DID A LETTER FROM PAPI'S MOTHER...
HAVE A PHOTO LIKE THAT...?
……?
UHYA ?!
WHOOSH
PAPI! NO FLYING NO MORE!!
HOME! THE PHOTO!!
KA-SHICK

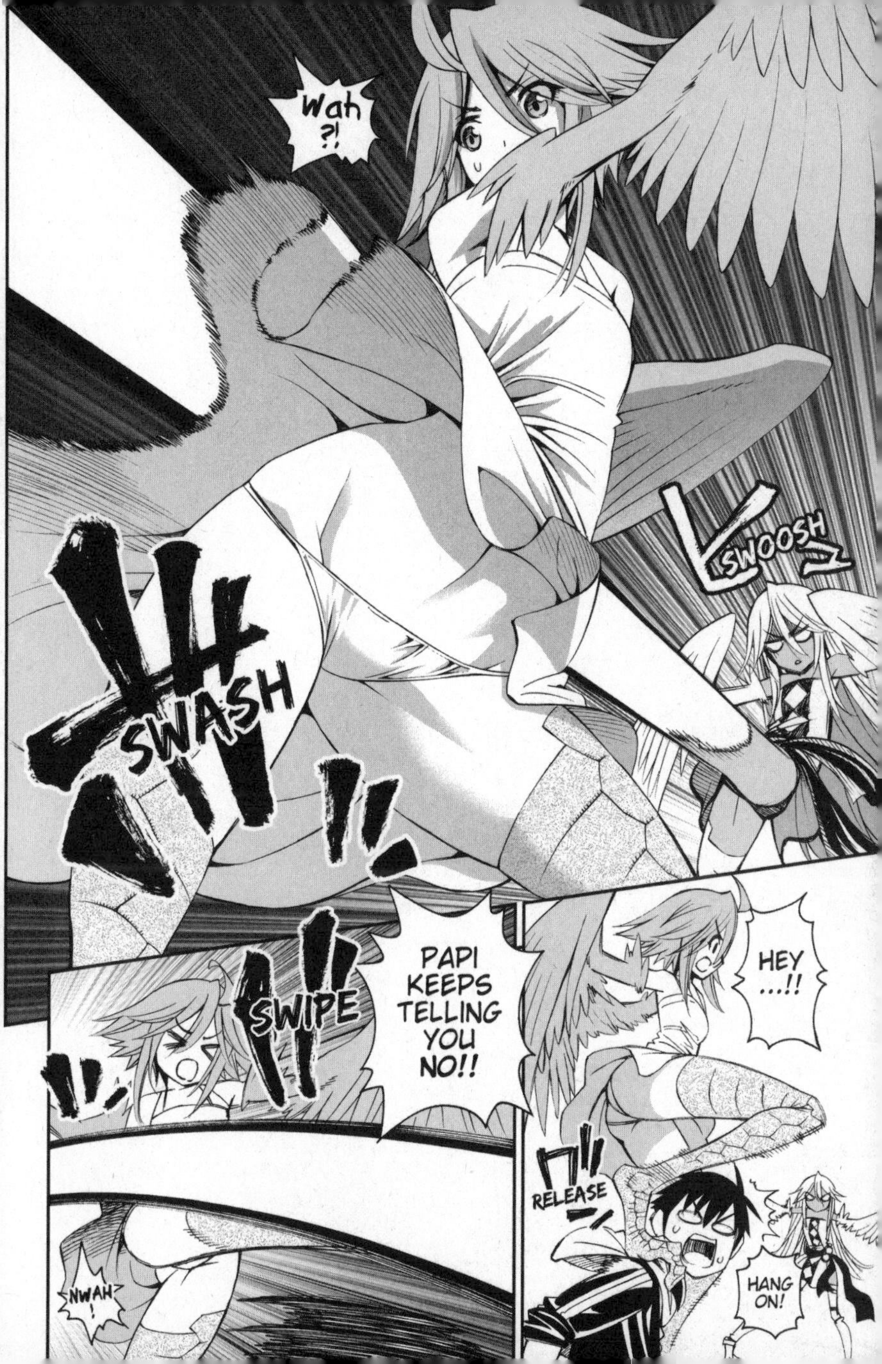
Wah ?!
SWOOSH
SWASH
HEY ...!!
RELEASE
HANG ON!
PAPI KEEPS TELLING YOU NO!!
SWIPE
NWAH !

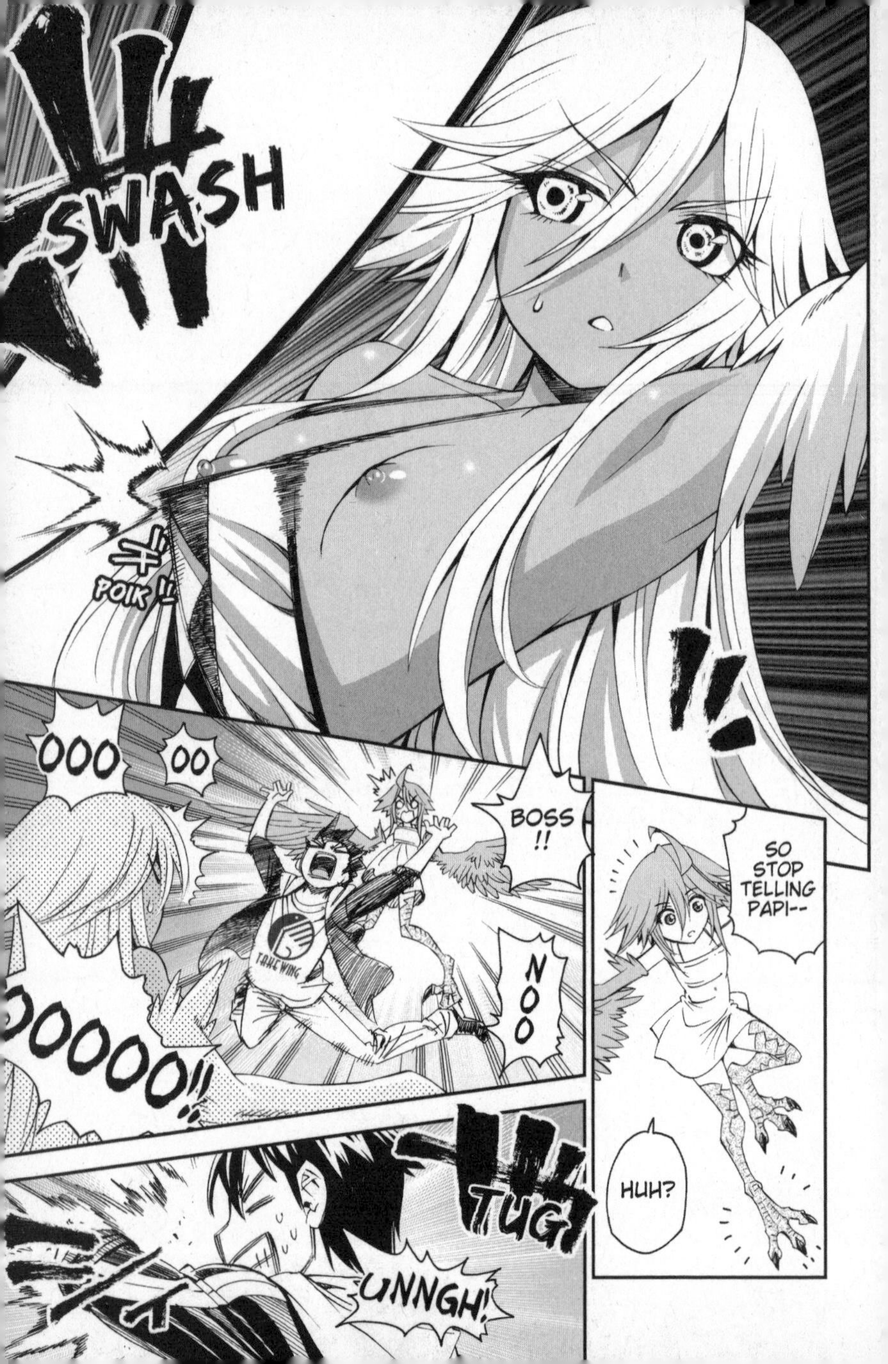
SWASH
POIK!!
SO STOP TELLING PAPI--
HUH?
BOSS!!
NOO
OOO
OO
OOOOOO!!
TUG!
UNNGH!

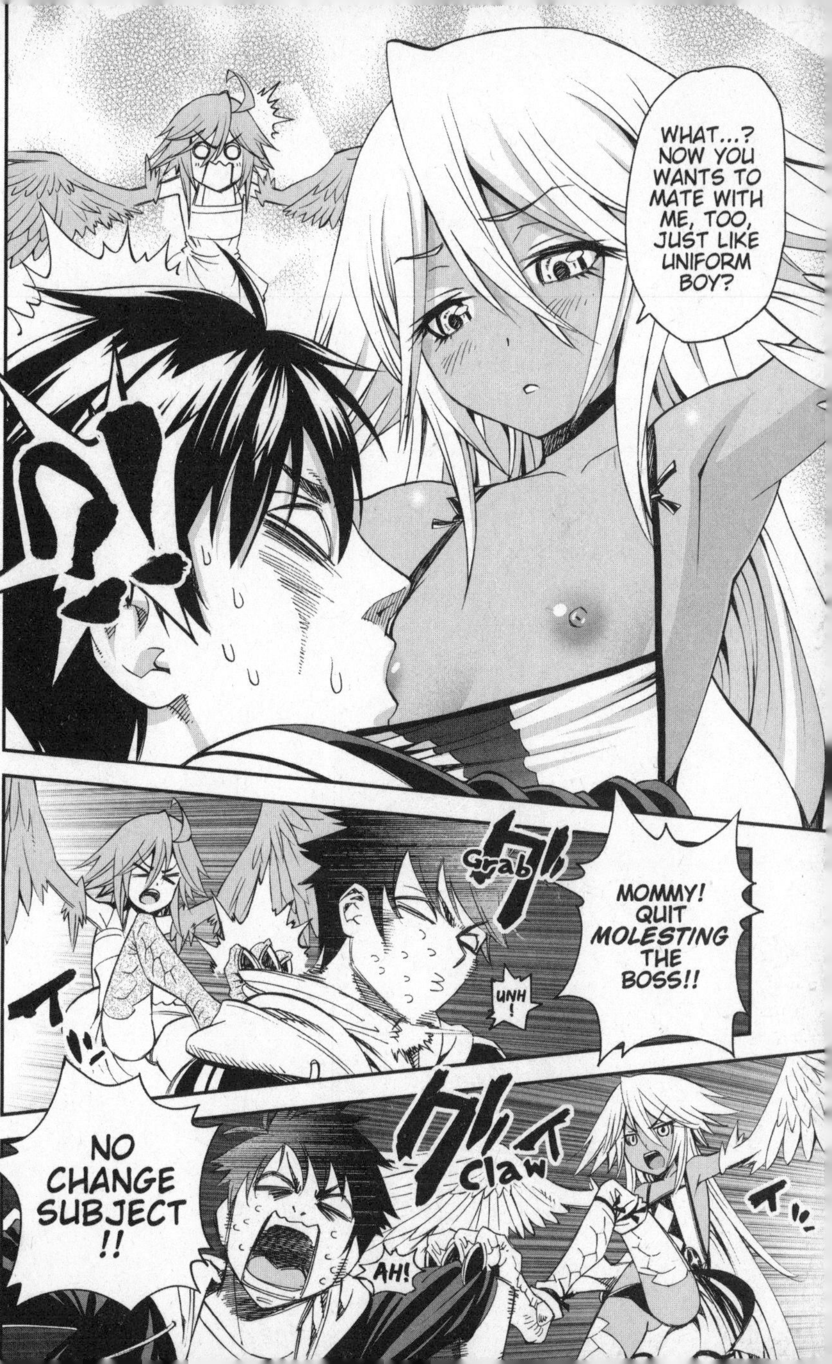
WHAT...? NOW YOU WANTS TO MATE WITH ME, TOO, JUST LIKE UNIFORM BOY?
MOMMY! QUIT MOLESTING THE BOSS!!
Grab
UNH!
Claw
NO CHANGE SUBJECT!!
AH!

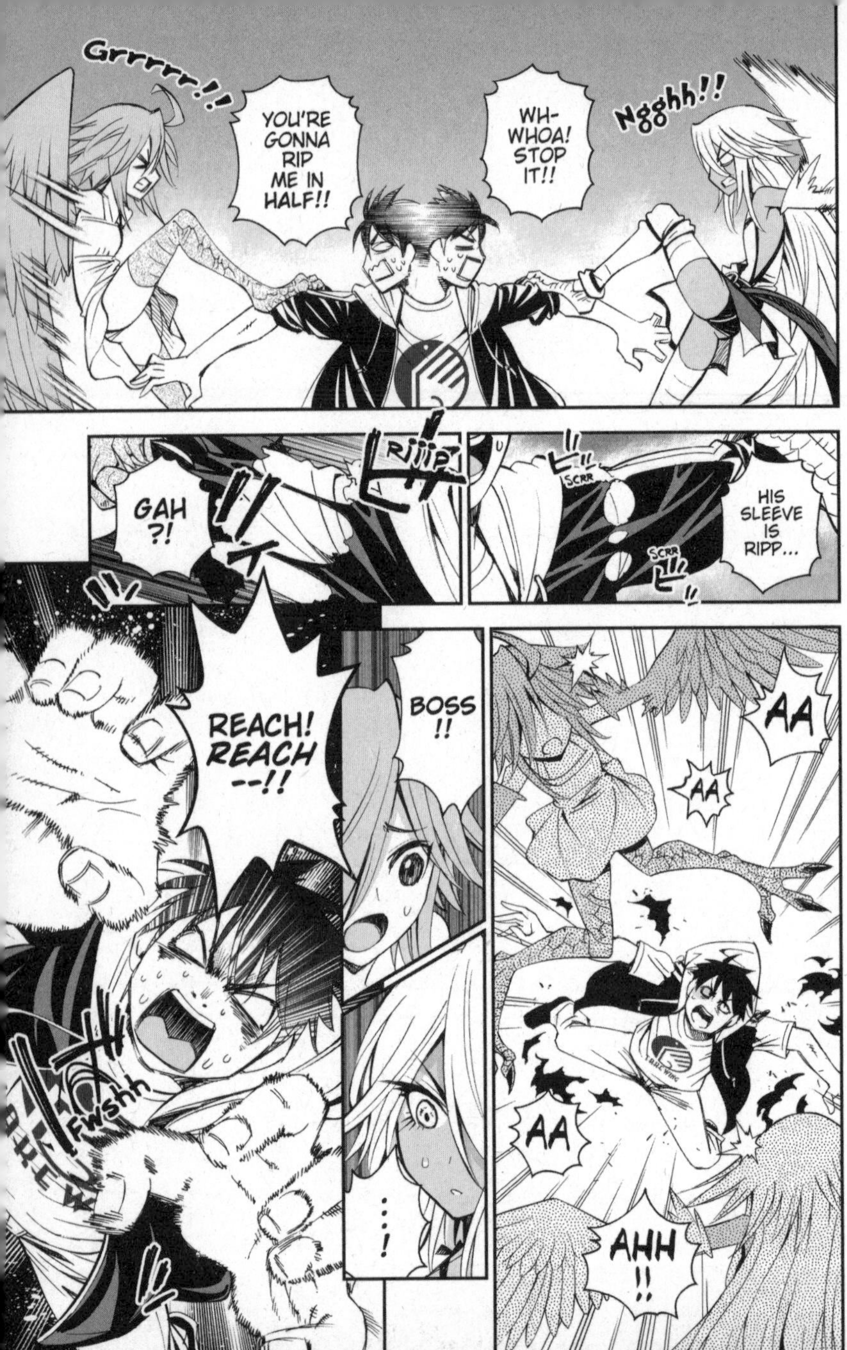
Ngghh!!
WH-WHOA! STOP IT!!
YOU'RE GONNA RIP ME IN HALF!!
Grrrrr!!
SCRR
HIS SLEEVE IS RIPP...
SCRR
RIIIP
GAH?!
AA
AA
AA
AHH!!
BOSS!!
...!
REACH! REACH--!!
Fwshh

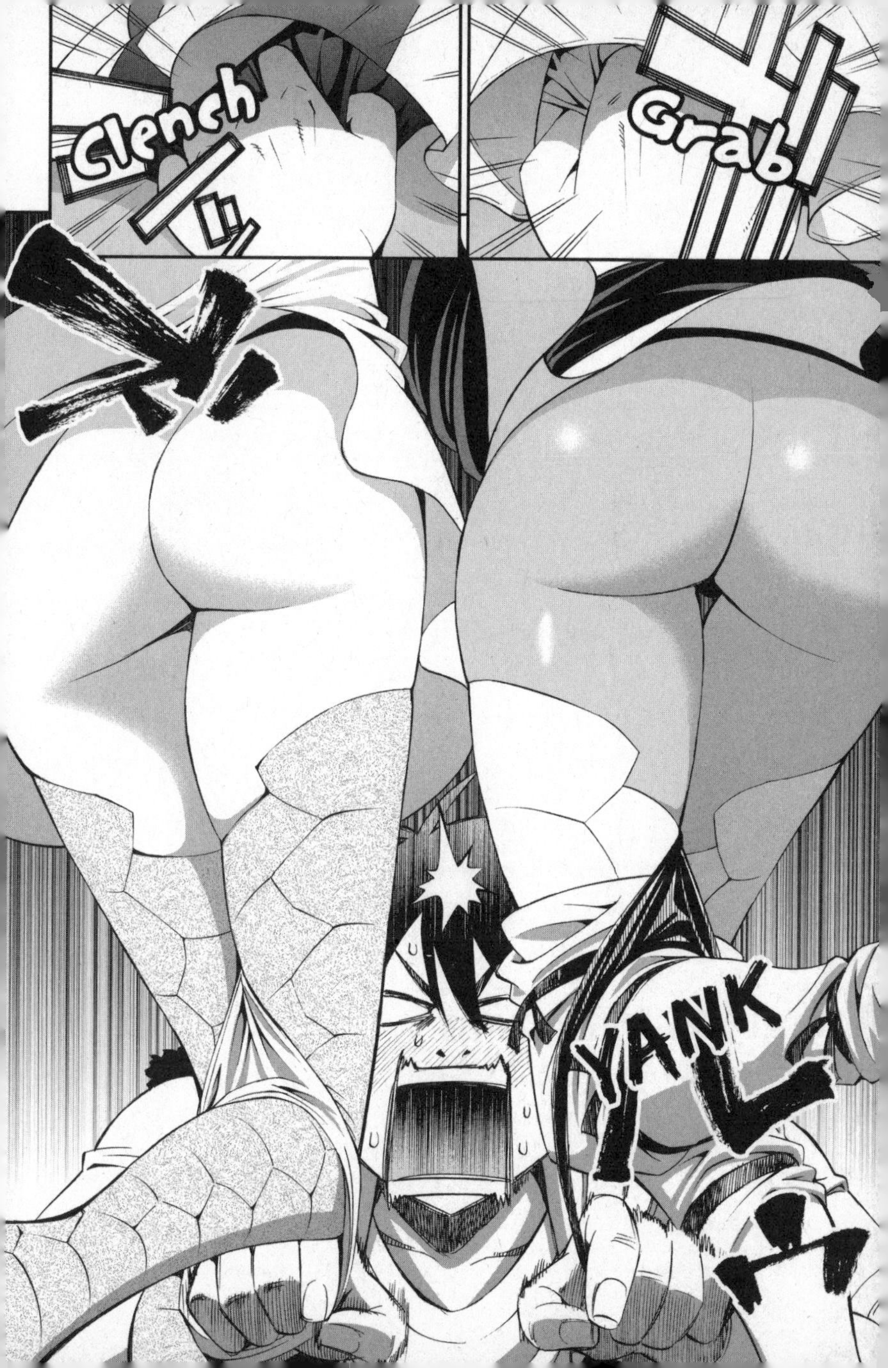
Grab
Clench
YANK

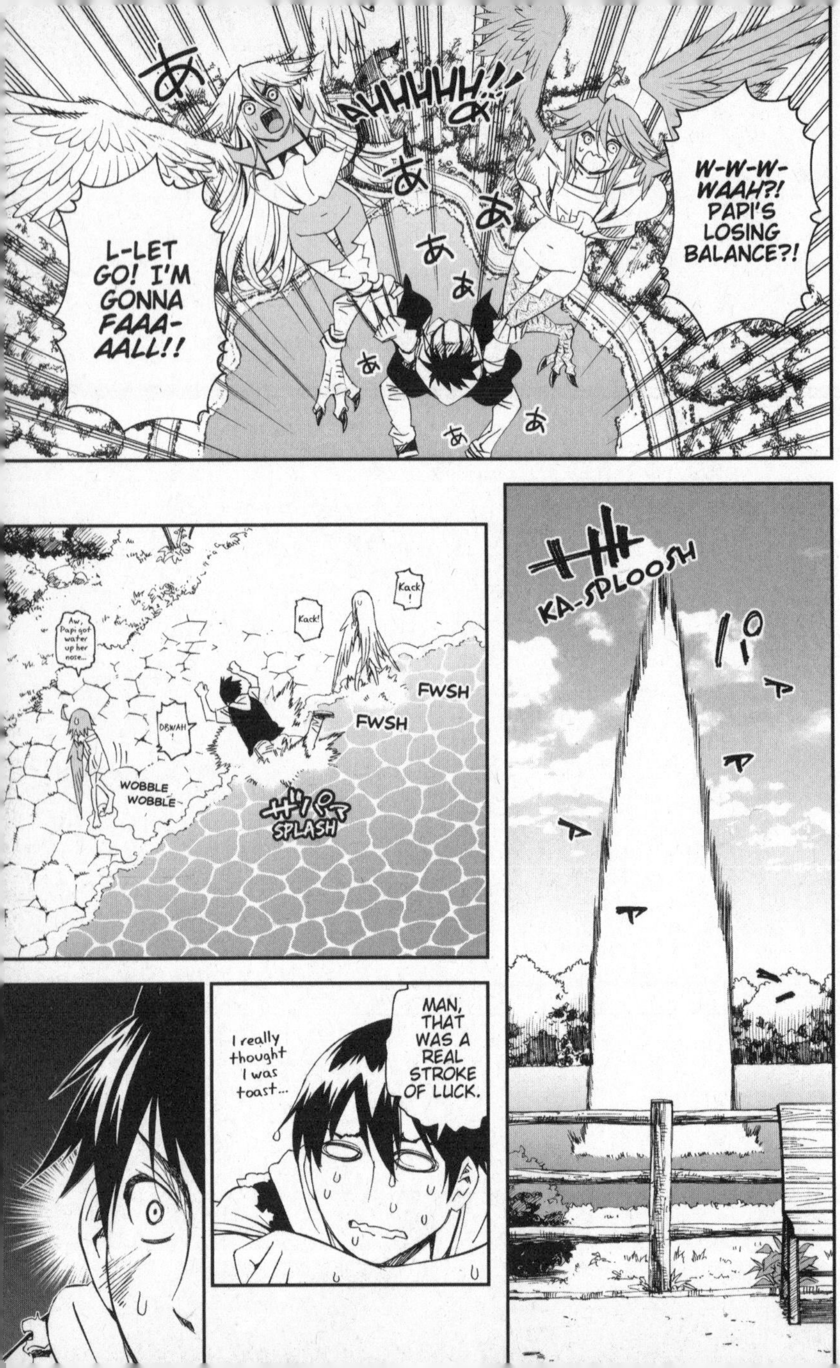

AHHHHH!!
W-W-W-WAAH?! PAPI'S LOSING BALANCE?!
L-LET GO! I'M GONNA FAAAA-AALL!!
KA-SPLOOSH
Kack!
Kack!
FWSH
FWSH
Aw, Papi got water up her nose...
OBWAH!
WOBBLE WOBBLE
SPLASH
MAN, THAT WAS A REAL STROKE OF LUCK.
I really thought I was toast...

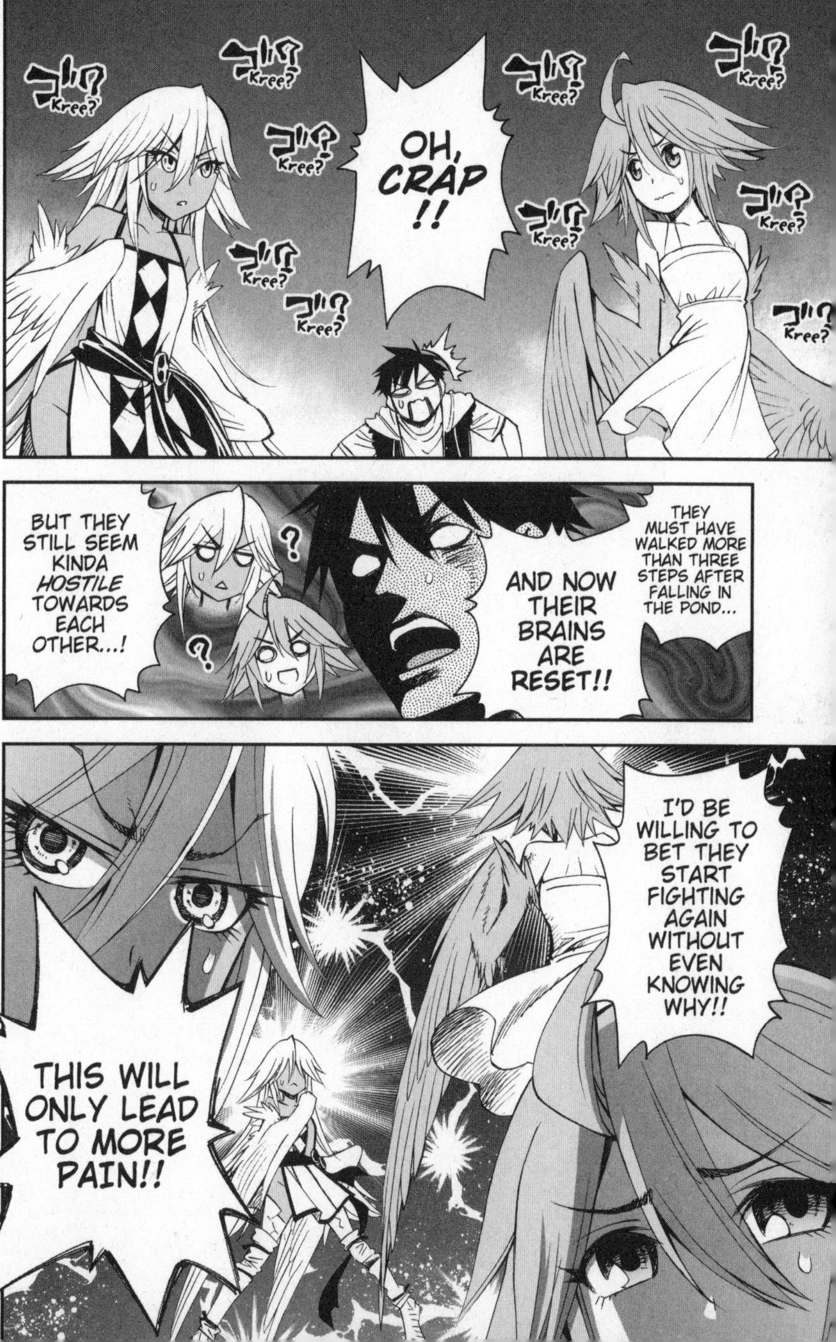
Kree?
Kree?
Kree?
Kree?
Kree?
OH, CRAP!!
Kree?
Kree?
Kree?
Kree?
Kree?
THEY MUST HAVE WALKED MORE THAN THREE STEPS AFTER FALLING IN THE POND...
AND NOW THEIR BRAINS ARE RESET!!
BUT THEY STILL SEEM KINDA *HOSTILE* TOWARDS EACH OTHER...!
I'D BE WILLING TO BET THEY START FIGHTING AGAIN WITHOUT EVEN KNOWING WHY!!
THIS WILL ONLY LEAD TO MORE PAIN!!

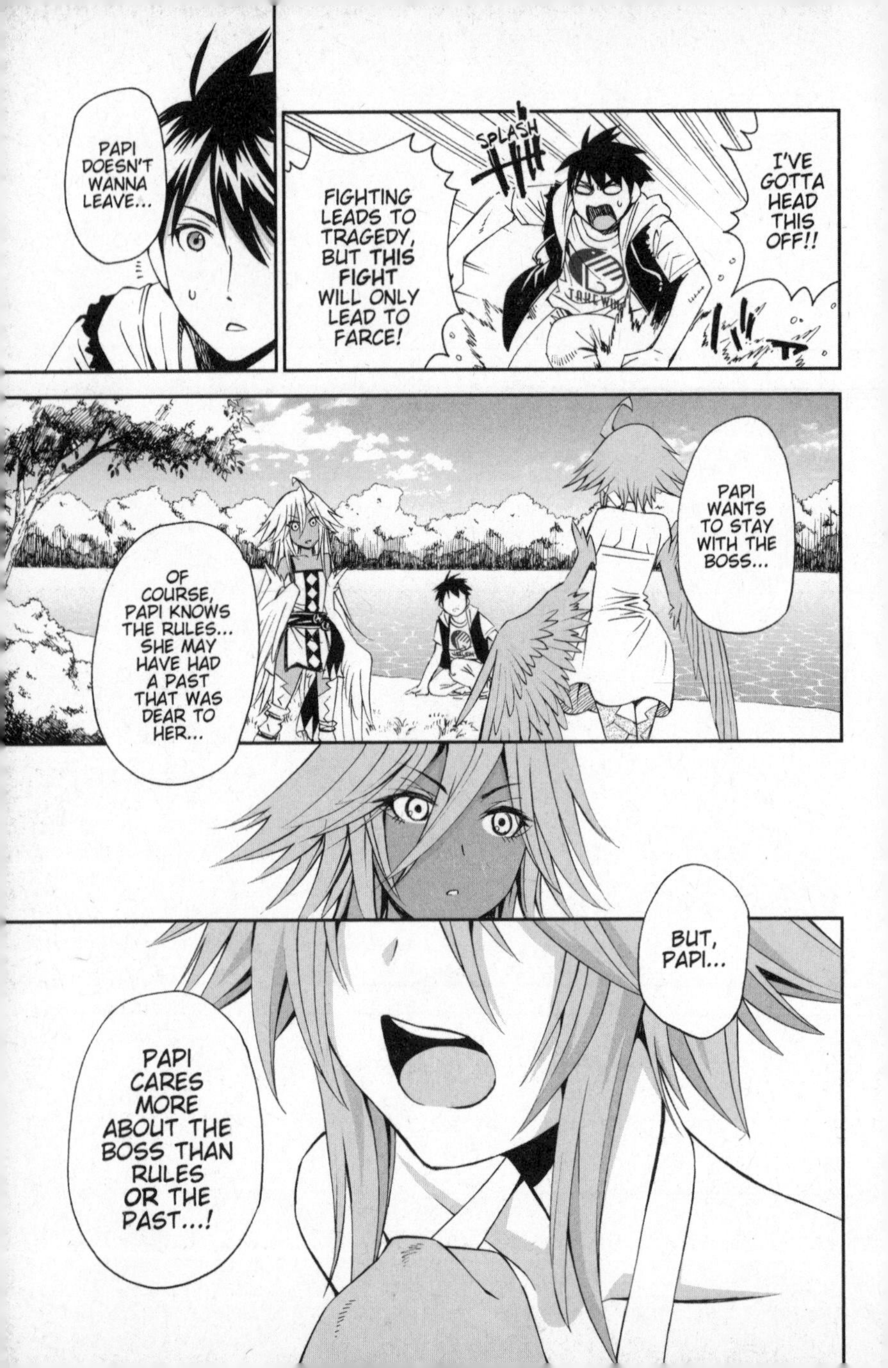
I'VE GOTTA HEAD THIS OFF!!
SPLASH
FIGHTING LEADS TO TRAGEDY, BUT THIS FIGHT WILL ONLY LEAD TO FARCE!
PAPI DOESN'T WANNA LEAVE...
PAPI WANTS TO STAY WITH THE BOSS...
OF COURSE, PAPI KNOWS THE RULES... SHE MAY HAVE HAD A PAST THAT WAS DEAR TO HER...
BUT, PAPI...
PAPI CARES MORE ABOUT THE BOSS THAN RULES OR THE PAST...!

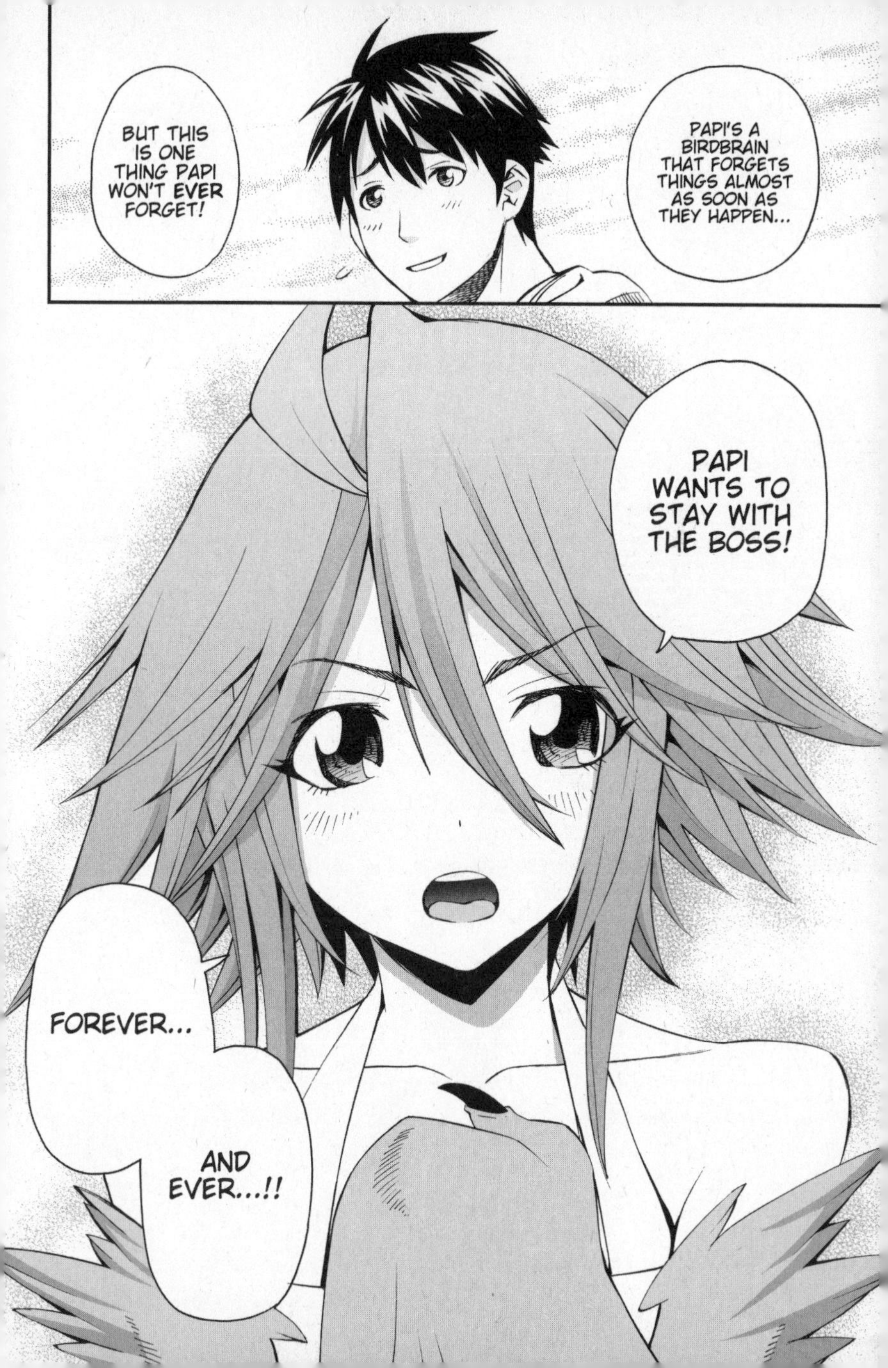
PAPI'S A BIRDBRAIN THAT FORGETS THINGS ALMOST AS SOON AS THEY HAPPEN...
BUT THIS IS ONE THING PAPI WON'T EVER FORGET!
PAPI WANTS TO STAY WITH THE BOSS!
FOREVER... AND EVER...!!

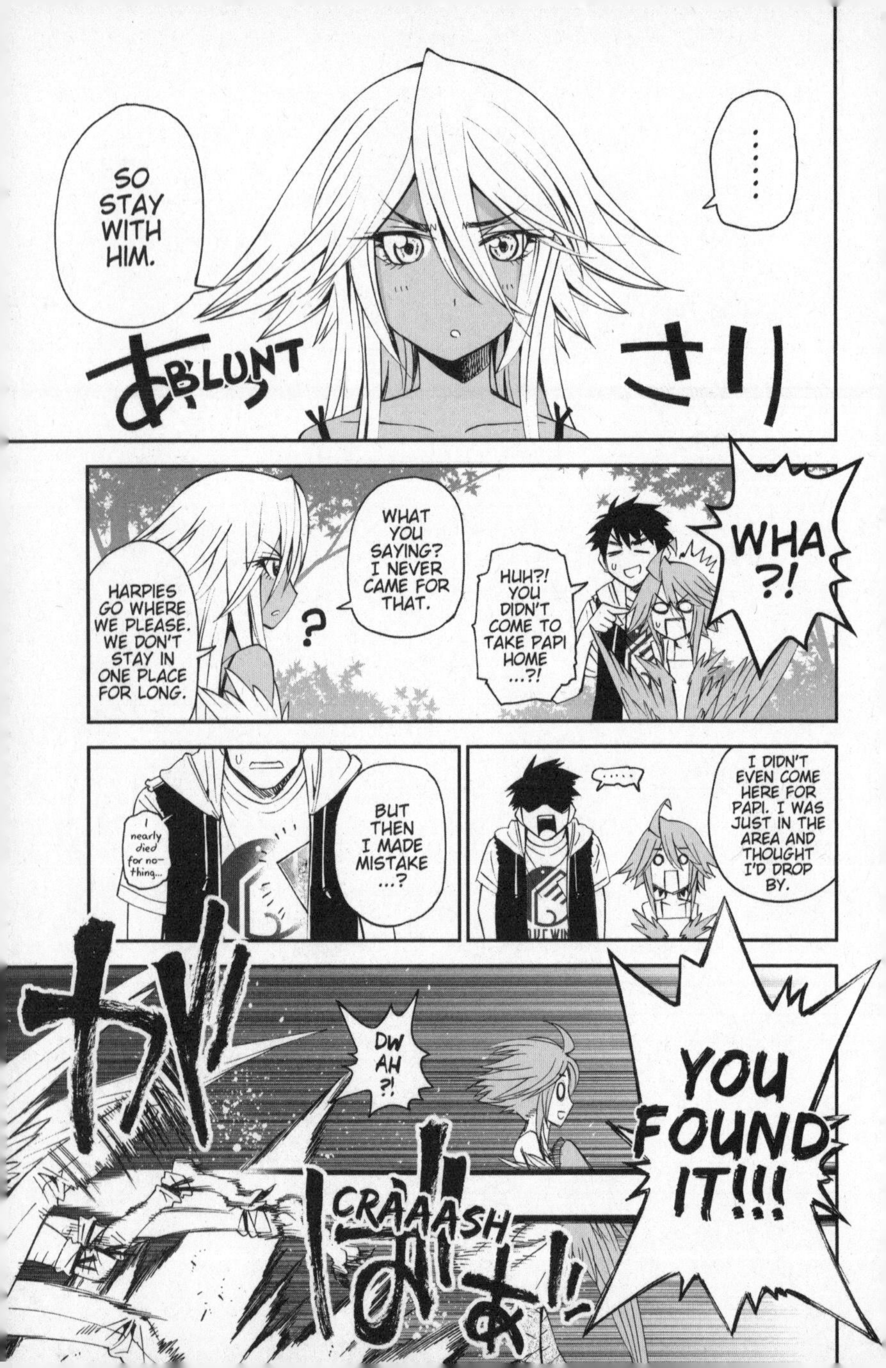
......
さり
SO STAY WITH HIM.
BLUNT
WHA?!
HUH?! YOU DIDN'T COME TO TAKE PAPI HOME ...?!
WHAT YOU SAYING? I NEVER CAME FOR THAT.
?
HARPIES GO WHERE WE PLEASE. WE DON'T STAY IN ONE PLACE FOR LONG.
I DIDN'T EVEN COME HERE FOR PAPI. I WAS JUST IN THE AREA AND THOUGHT I'D DROP BY.
.....
BUT THEN I MADE MISTAKE ...?
I nearly died for no-thing...
YOU FOUND IT!!!
DW AH ?!
CRAAASH

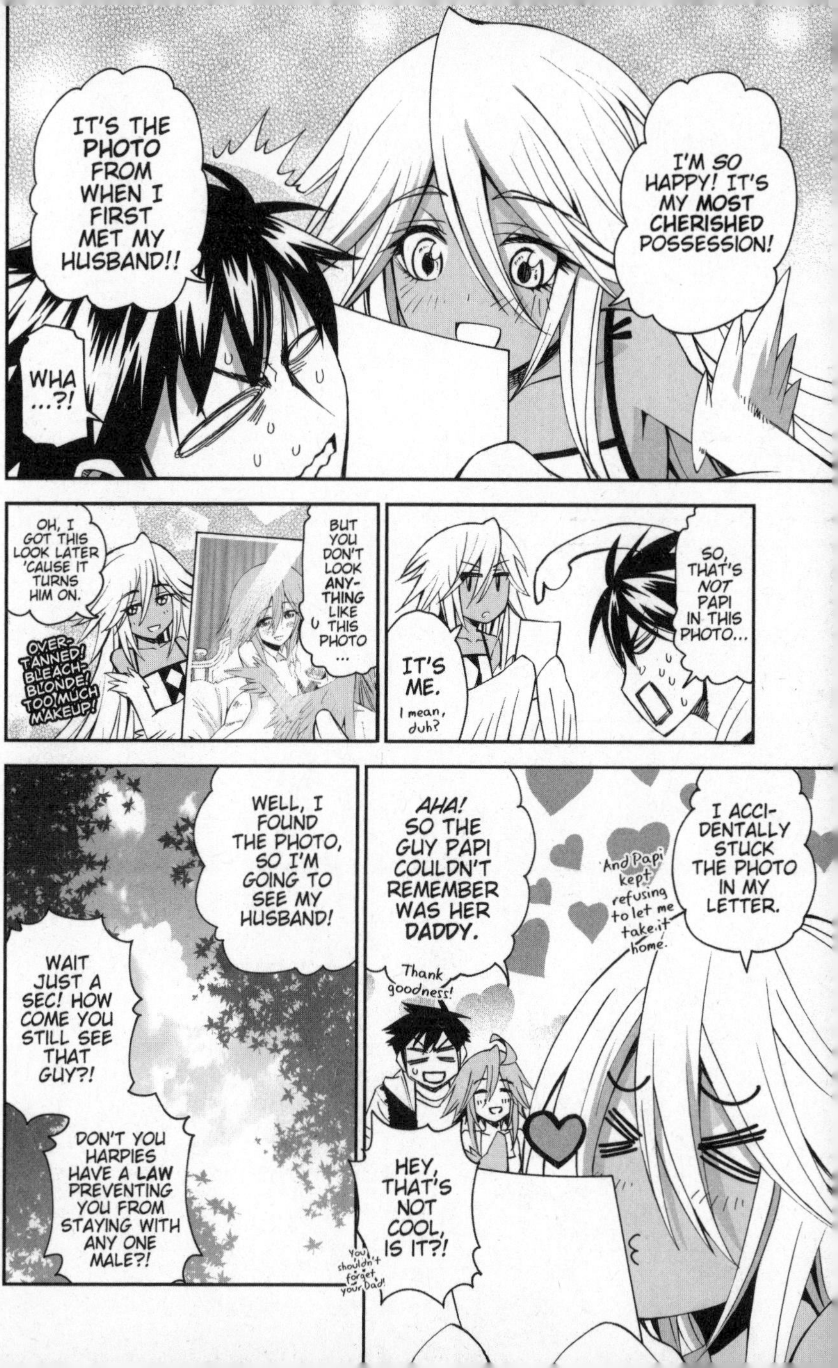
I'M SO HAPPY! IT'S MY MOST CHERISHED POSSESSION!
IT'S THE PHOTO FROM WHEN I FIRST MET MY HUSBAND!!
WHA...?!
SO, THAT'S NOT PAPI IN THIS PHOTO...
IT'S ME.
I mean, duh?
BUT YOU DON'T LOOK ANYTHING LIKE THIS PHOTO...
OH, I GOT THIS LOOK LATER 'CAUSE IT TURNS HIM ON.
OVER-TANNED! BLEACH-BLONDE! TOO MUCH MAKEUP!
I ACCIDENTALLY STUCK THE PHOTO IN MY LETTER.
And Papi kept refusing to let me take it home.
AHA! SO THE GUY PAPI COULDN'T REMEMBER WAS HER DADDY.
Thank goodness!
HEY, THAT'S NOT COOL, IS IT?!
You shouldn't forget your Dad!
WELL, I FOUND THE PHOTO, SO I'M GOING TO SEE MY HUSBAND!
WAIT JUST A SEC! HOW COME YOU STILL SEE THAT GUY?!
DON'T YOU HARPIES HAVE A LAW PREVENTING YOU FROM STAYING WITH ANY ONE MALE?!

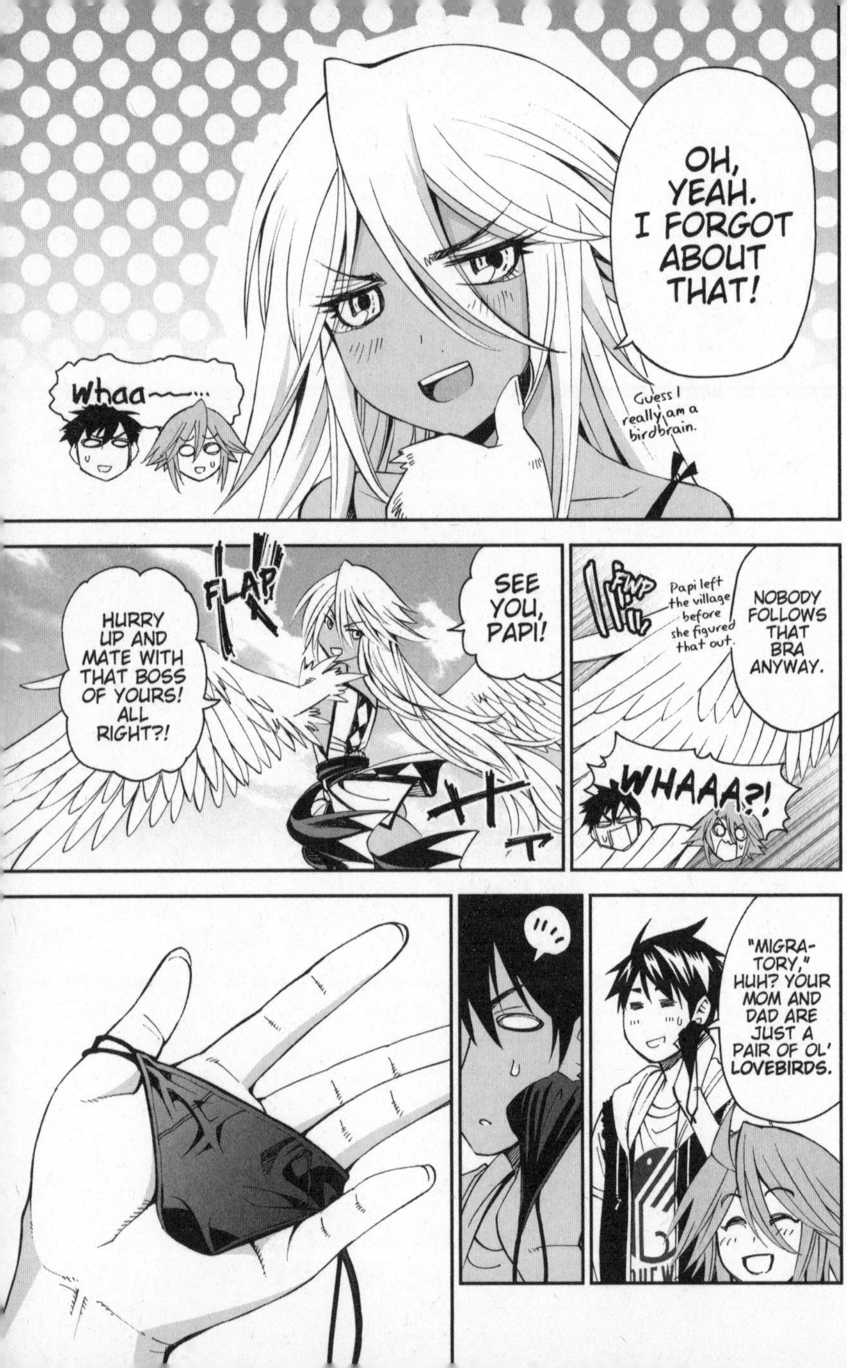
OH, YEAH. I FORGOT ABOUT THAT!
Guess I really am a birdbrain.
Whaa~...
NOBODY FOLLOWS THAT BRA ANYWAY.
Papi left the village before she figured that out.
FWP
WHAAA?!
SEE YOU, PAPI!
FLAP
HURRY UP AND MATE WITH THAT BOSS OF YOURS! ALL RIGHT?!
"MIGRATORY," HUH? YOUR MOM AND DAD ARE JUST A PAIR OF OL' LOVEBIRDS.

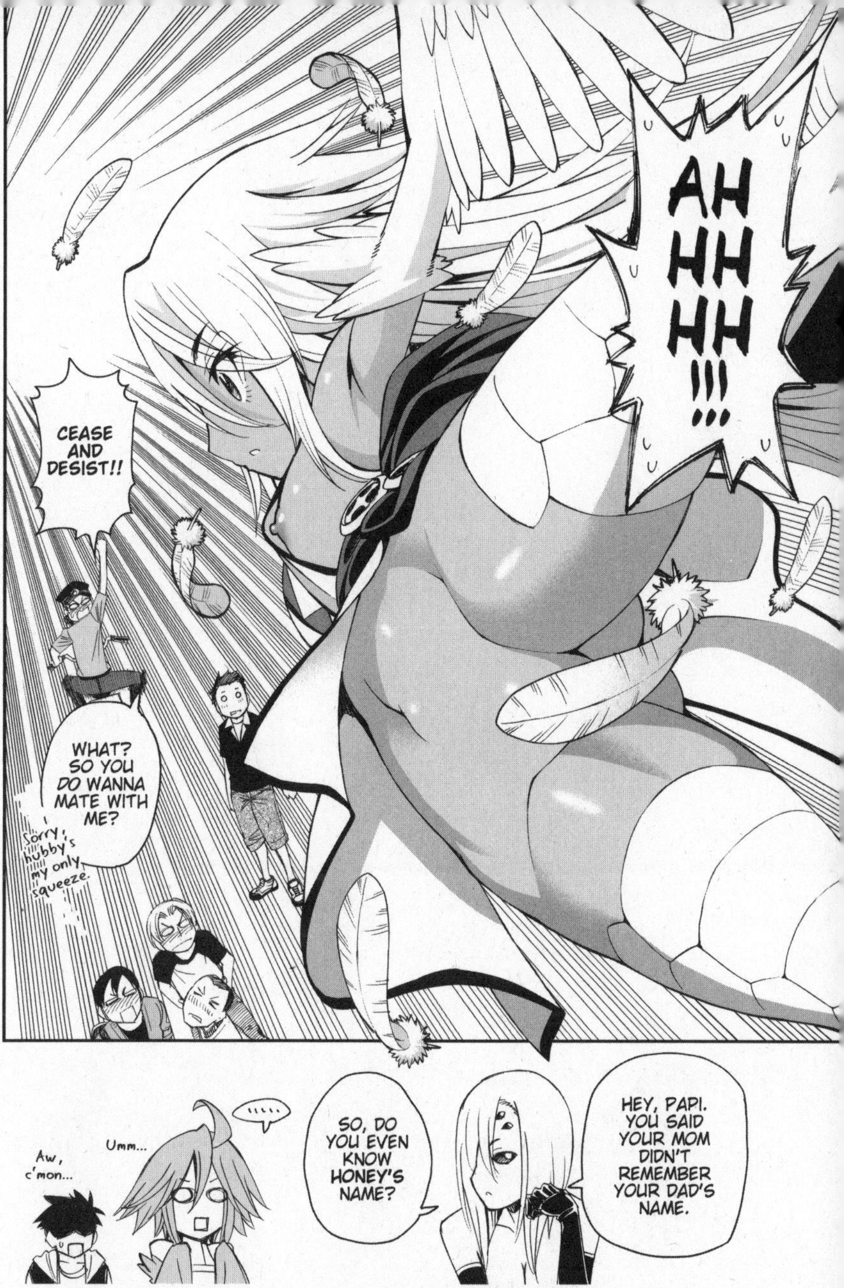
AHHHHHH!!!
CEASE AND DESIST!!
WHAT? SO YOU DO WANNA MATE WITH ME?
Sorry, hubby's my only squeeze.
HEY, PAPI. YOU SAID YOUR MOM DIDN'T REMEMBER YOUR DAD'S NAME.
SO, DO YOU EVEN KNOW HONEY'S NAME?
......
Umm...
Aw, c'mon...

Monster Musume

Everyday Life with Monster Girls

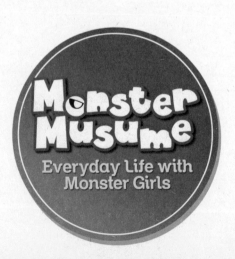

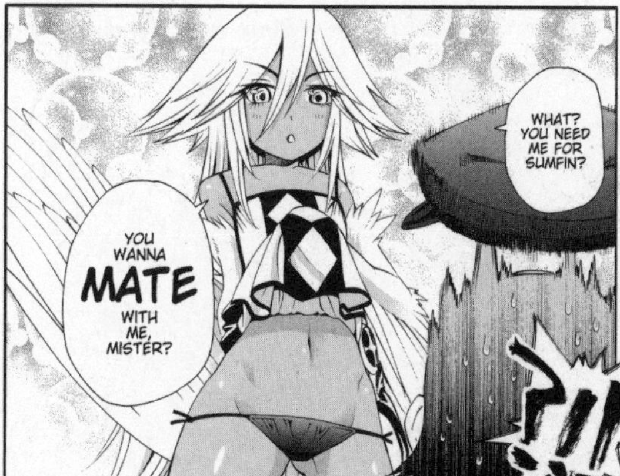
WHAT? YOU NEED ME FOR SUMFIN?
YOU WANNA MATE WITH ME, MISTER?
?!!

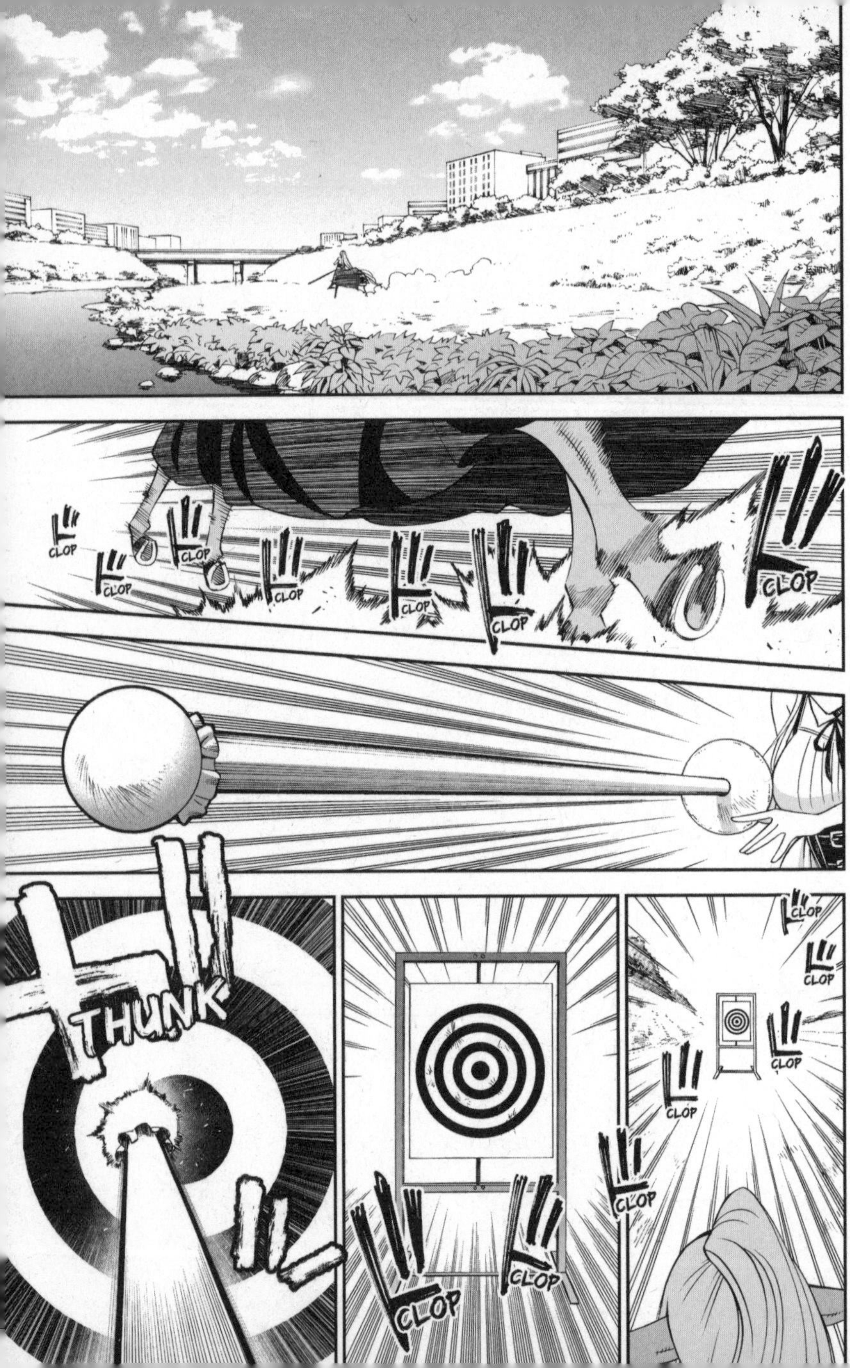
CLOP
CLOP
CLOP
CLOP
CLOP
CLOP
CLOP
CLOP
CLOP
CLOP
CLOP
CLOP
CLOP
CLOP
THUNK

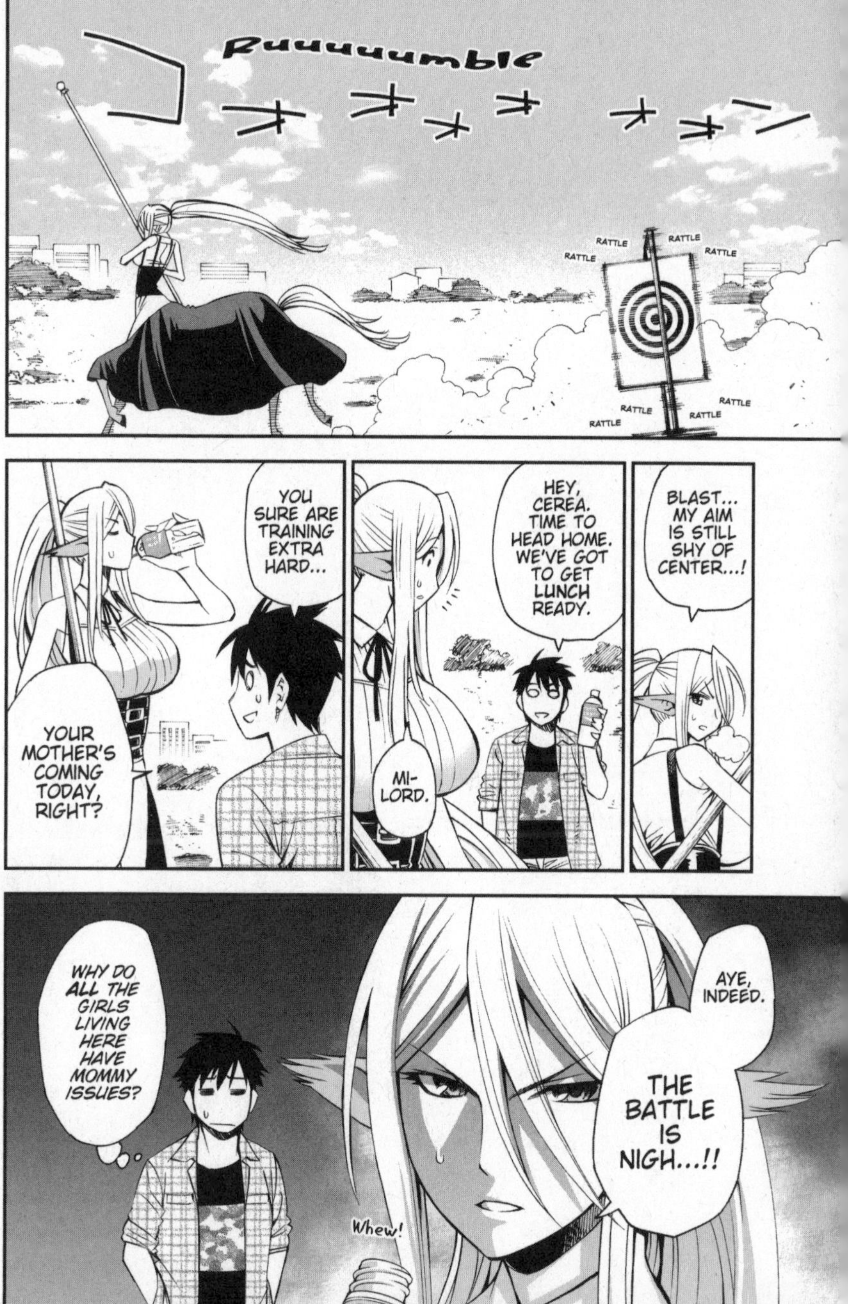
Ruuuuumble
コオオオオーン
RATTLE
RATTLE
RATTLE
RATTLE
RATTLE
RATTLE
RATTLE
RATTLE
BLAST... MY AIM IS STILL SHY OF CENTER...!
HEY, CEREA. TIME TO HEAD HOME. WE'VE GOT TO GET LUNCH READY.
MI-LORD.
YOU SURE ARE TRAINING EXTRA HARD...
YOUR MOTHER'S COMING TODAY, RIGHT?
AYE, INDEED.
THE BATTLE IS NIGH...!!
Whew!
WHY DO ALL THE GIRLS LIVING HERE HAVE MOMMY ISSUES?

Chapter 29

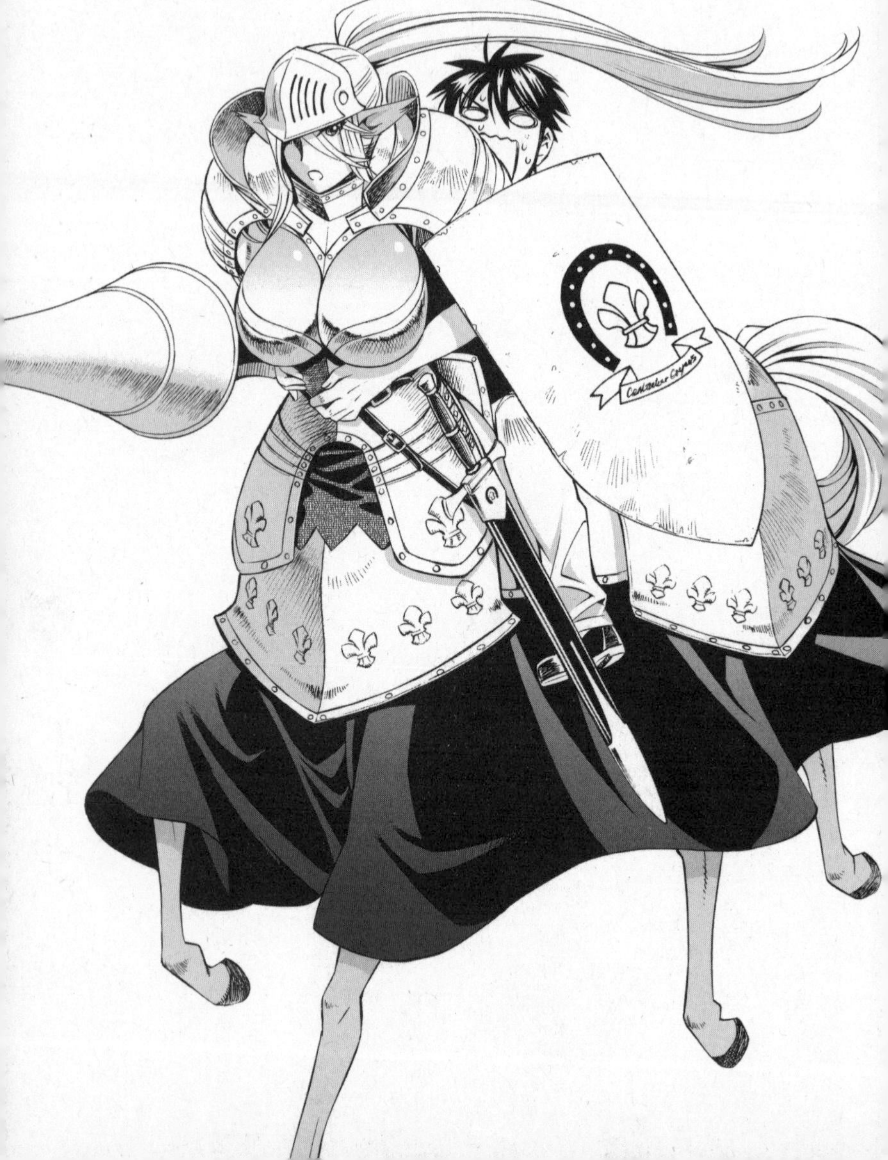

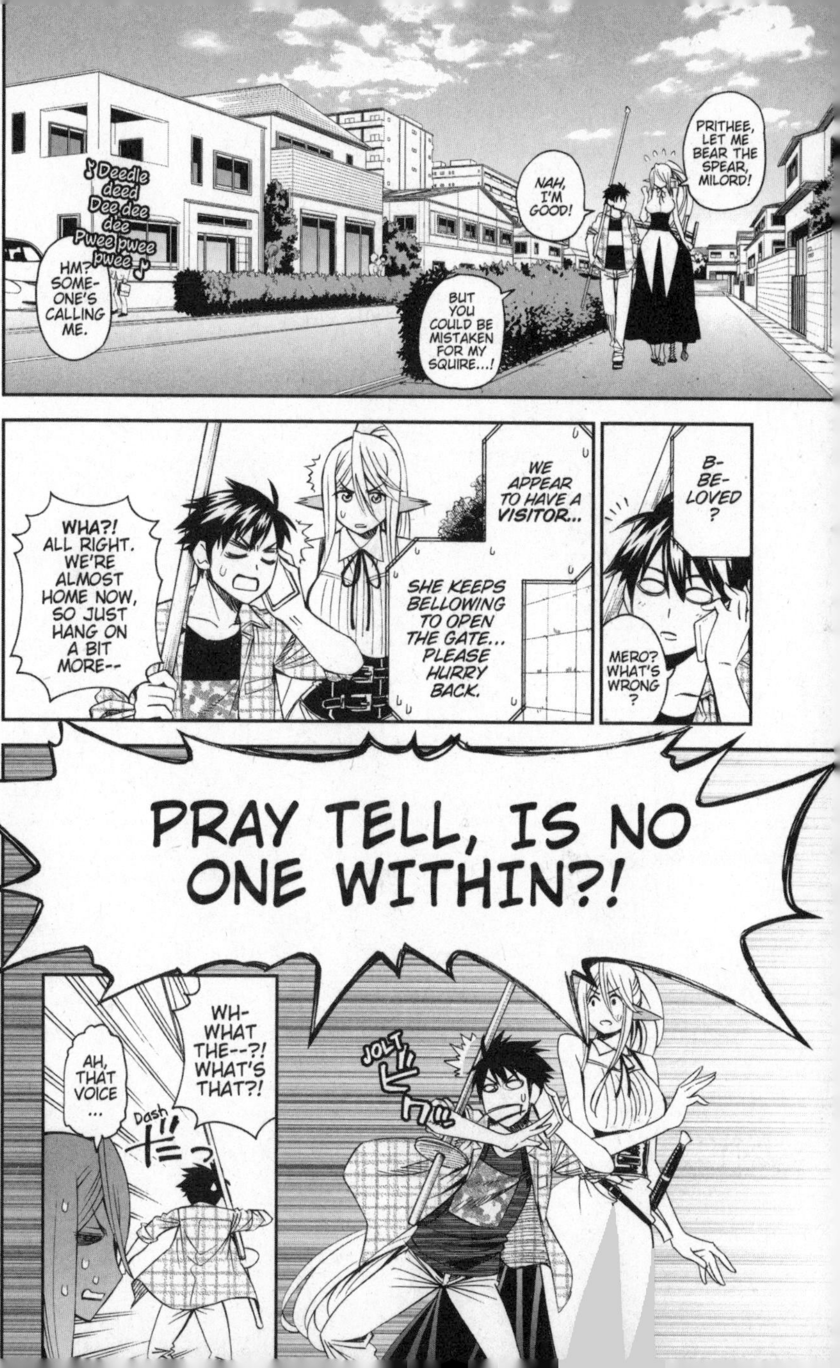
PRITHEE, LET ME BEAR THE SPEAR, MILORD!
NAH, I'M GOOD!
BUT YOU COULD BE MISTAKEN FOR MY SQUIRE...!
Deedle deed Dee dee dee Pwee pwee pwee
HM? SOMEONE'S CALLING ME.
B-BELOVED?
MERO? WHAT'S WRONG?
WE APPEAR TO HAVE A VISITOR...
SHE KEEPS BELLOWING TO OPEN THE GATE... PLEASE HURRY BACK.
WHA?! ALL RIGHT. WE'RE ALMOST HOME NOW, SO JUST HANG ON A BIT MORE--
PRAY TELL, IS NO ONE WITHIN?!
JOLT
WH-WHAT THE--?! WHAT'S THAT?!
AH, THAT VOICE...
Dash

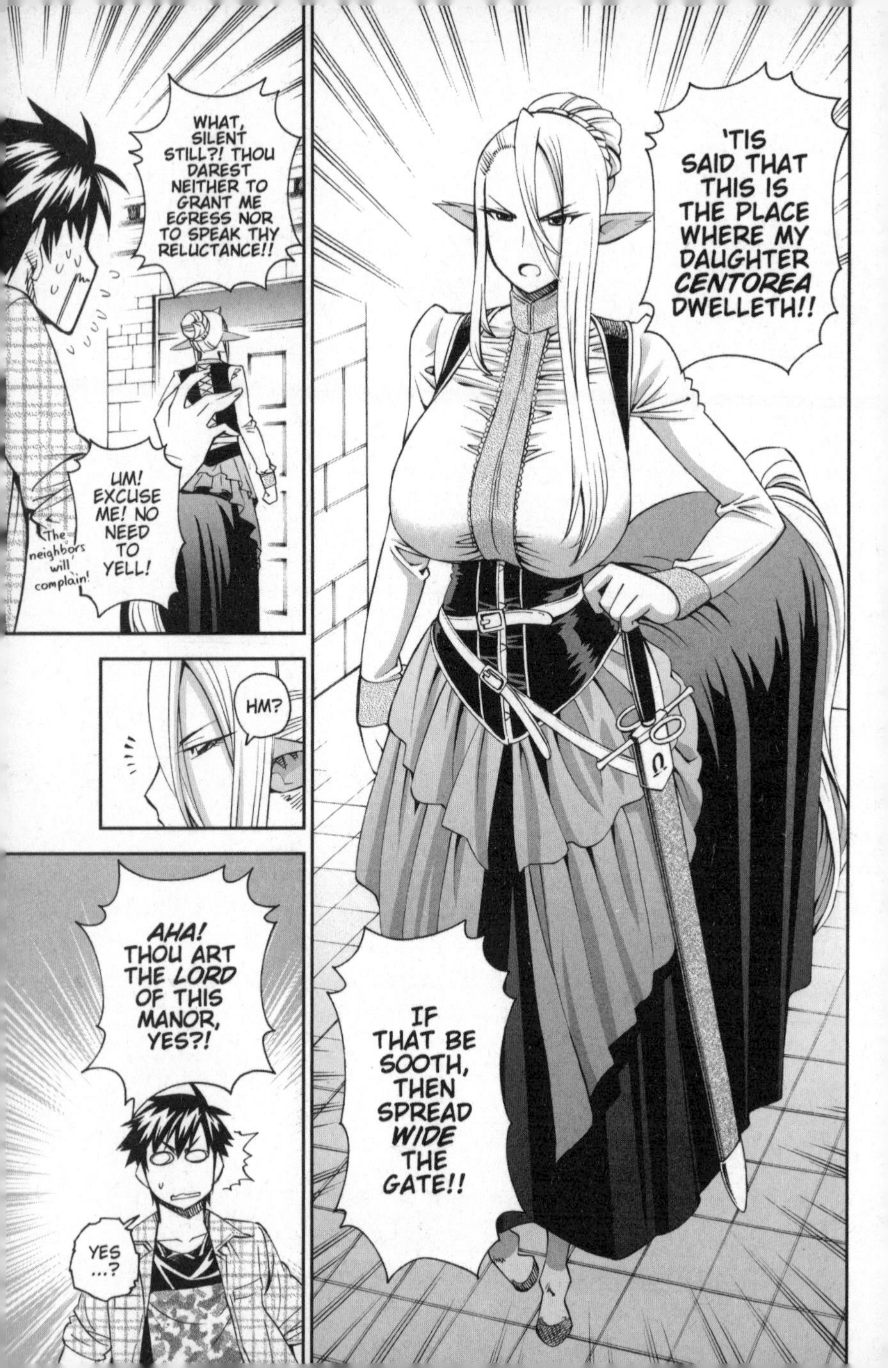
'TIS SAID THAT THIS IS THE PLACE WHERE MY DAUGHTER *CENTOREA* DWELLETH!!
IF THAT BE SOOTH, THEN SPREAD *WIDE* THE GATE!!
WHAT, SILENT STILL?! THOU DAREST NEITHER TO GRANT ME EGRESS NOR TO SPEAK THY RELUCTANCE!!
UM! EXCUSE ME! NO NEED TO YELL!
The neighbors will complain!
HM?
AHA! THOU ART THE *LORD* OF THIS MANOR, YES?!
YES ...?

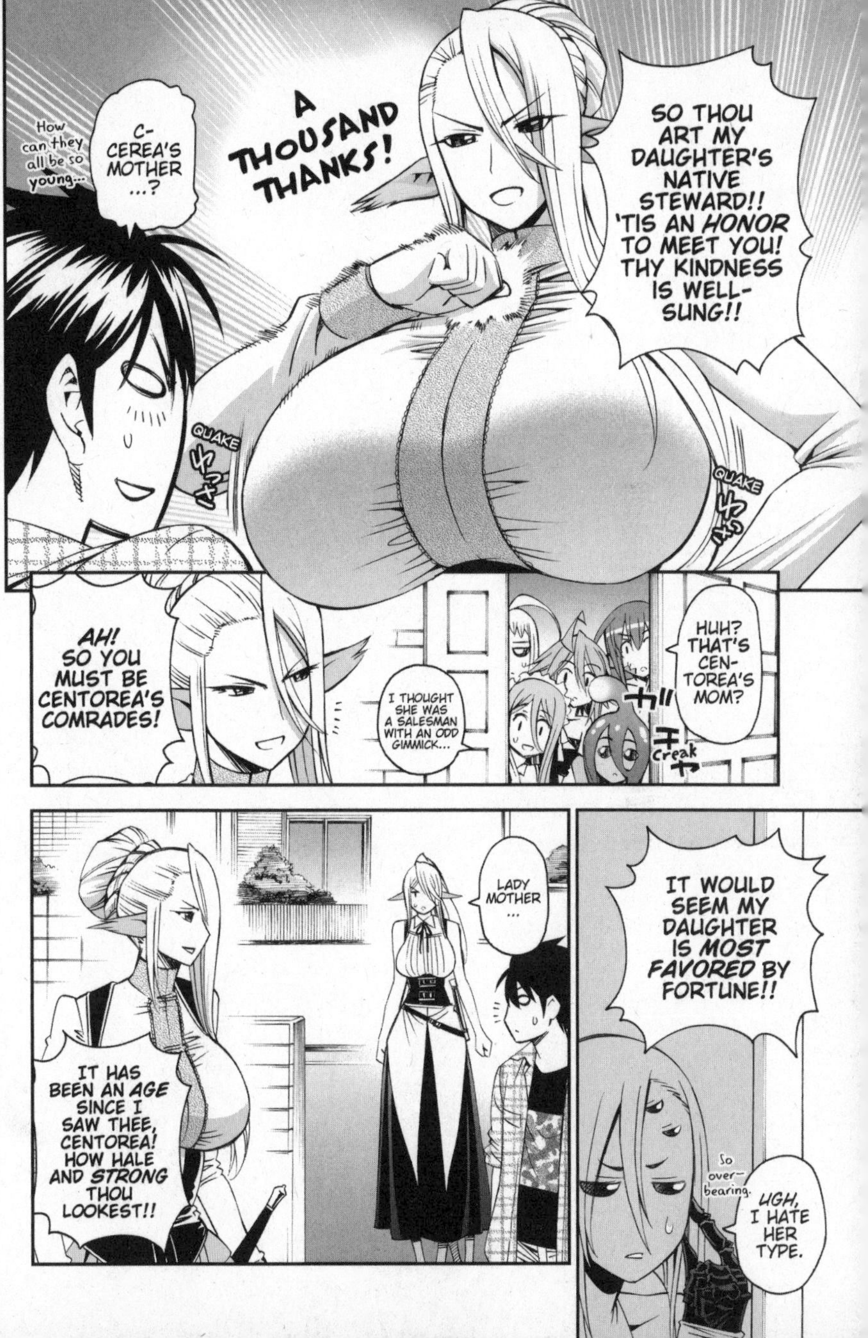
SO THOU ART MY DAUGHTER'S NATIVE STEWARD!! 'TIS AN *HONOR* TO MEET YOU! THY KINDNESS IS WELL-SUNG!!
A THOUSAND THANKS!
C-CEREA'S MOTHER ...?
How can they all be so young...
QUAKE
QUAKE
HUH? THAT'S CENTOREA'S MOM?
Creak
I THOUGHT SHE WAS A SALESMAN WITH AN ODD GIMMICK...
AH! SO YOU MUST BE CENTOREA'S COMRADES!
IT WOULD SEEM MY DAUGHTER IS *MOST FAVORED* BY FORTUNE!!
UGH, I HATE HER TYPE.
So over-bearing.
LADY MOTHER ...
IT HAS BEEN AN *AGE* SINCE I SAW THEE, CENTOREA! HOW HALE AND *STRONG* THOU LOOKEST!!

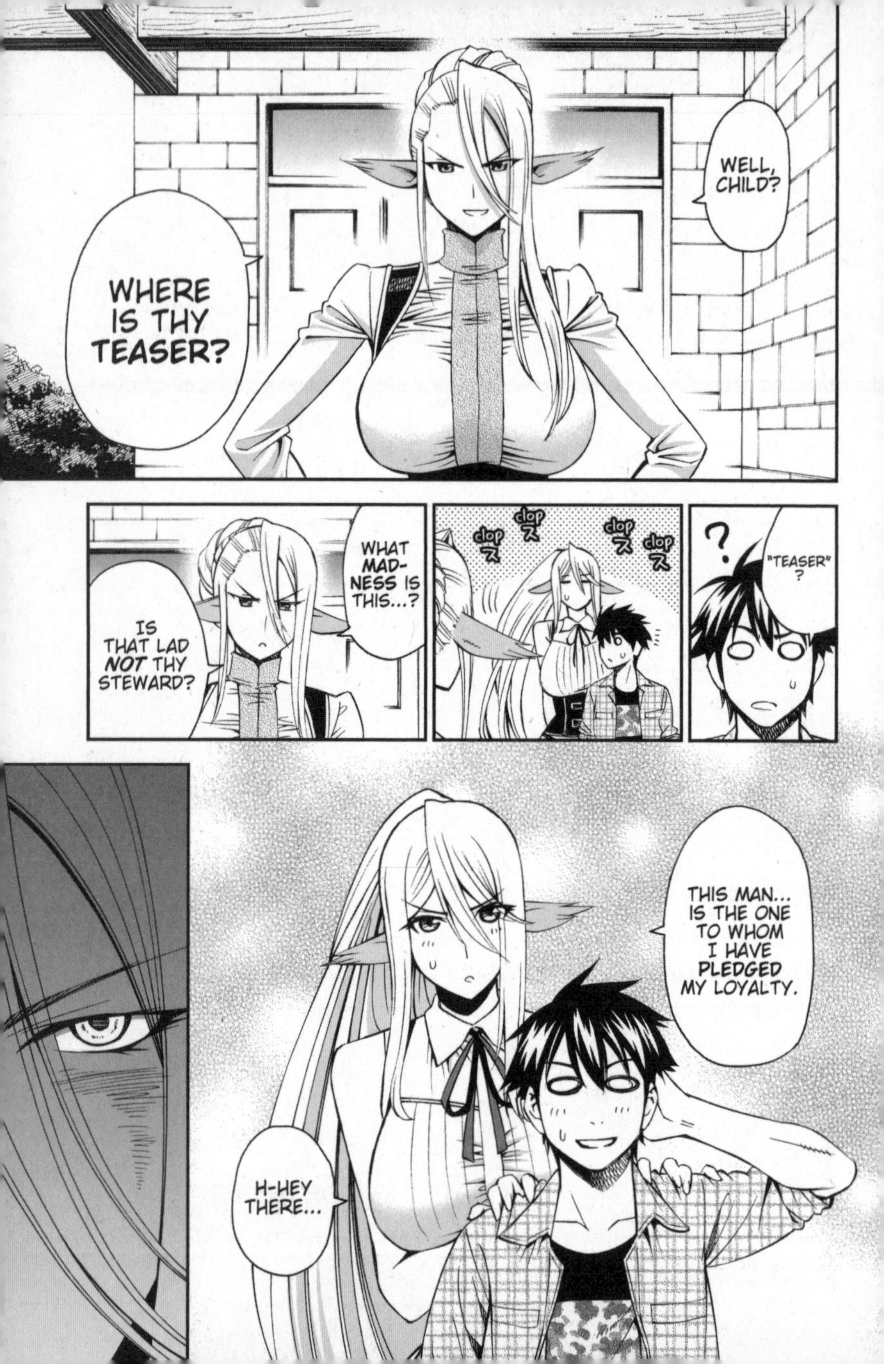
WELL, CHILD?
WHERE IS THY TEASER?
?
"TEASER"?
clop ス
clop ス
clop ス
clop ス
WHAT MADNESS IS THIS...?
IS THAT LAD *NOT* THY STEWARD?
THIS MAN... IS THE ONE TO WHOM I HAVE PLEDGED MY LOYALTY.
H-HEY THERE...

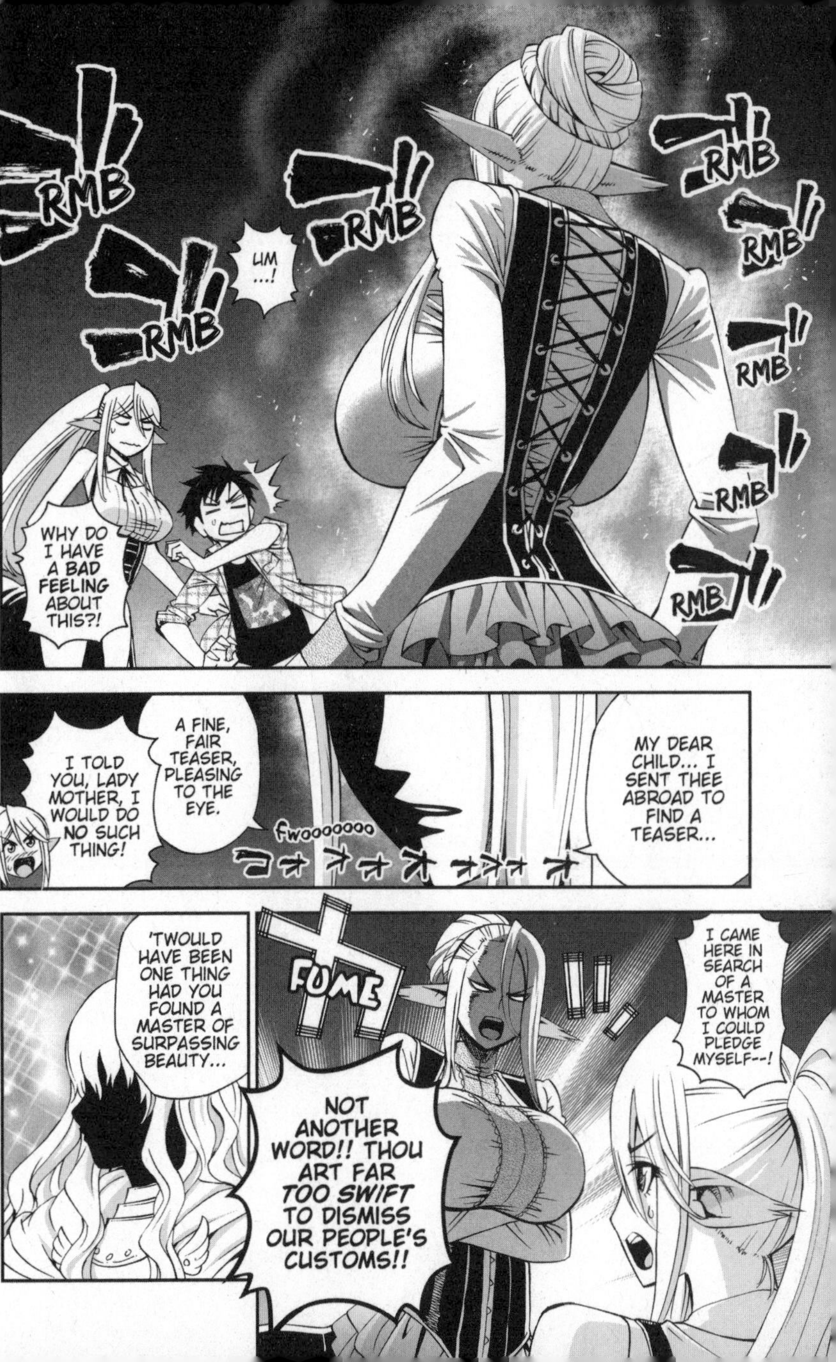
RMB
RMB
RMB
RMB
RMB
RMB
UM ...!
RMB
RMB
WHY DO I HAVE A BAD FEELING ABOUT THIS?!
MY DEAR CHILD... I SENT THEE ABROAD TO FIND A TEASER...
fwoooooo
A FINE, FAIR TEASER, PLEASING TO THE EYE.
I TOLD YOU, LADY MOTHER, I WOULD DO NO SUCH THING!
I CAME HERE IN SEARCH OF A MASTER TO WHOM I COULD PLEDGE MYSELF--!
FUME
'TWOULD HAVE BEEN ONE THING HAD YOU FOUND A MASTER OF SURPASSING BEAUTY...
NOT ANOTHER WORD!! THOU ART FAR TOO SWIFT TO DISMISS OUR PEOPLE'S CUSTOMS!!

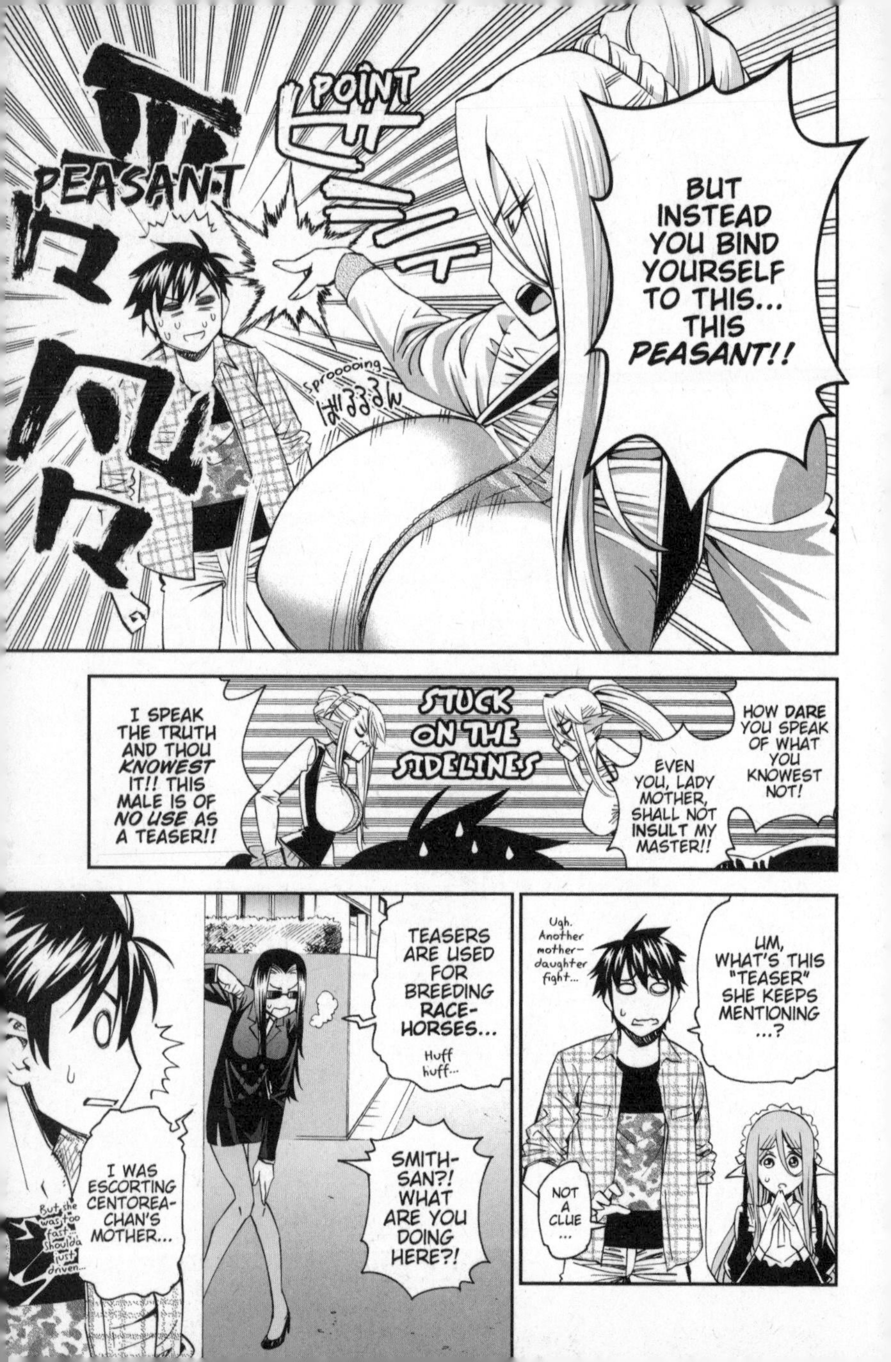
BUT INSTEAD YOU BIND YOURSELF TO THIS... THIS PEASANT!!
POINT
sproooing
PEASANT
HOW DARE YOU SPEAK OF WHAT YOU KNOWEST NOT!
EVEN YOU, LADY MOTHER, SHALL NOT INSULT MY MASTER!!
STUCK ON THE SIDELINES
I SPEAK THE TRUTH AND THOU KNOWEST IT!! THIS MALE IS OF NO USE AS A TEASER!!
UM, WHAT'S THIS "TEASER" SHE KEEPS MENTIONING ...?
Ugh. Another mother-daughter fight...
NOT A CLUE ...
TEASERS ARE USED FOR BREEDING RACE-HORSES...
Huff huff...
SMITH-SAN?! WHAT ARE YOU DOING HERE?!
I WAS ESCORTING CENTOREA-CHAN'S MOTHER...
But she was too fast... Should'a just driven...

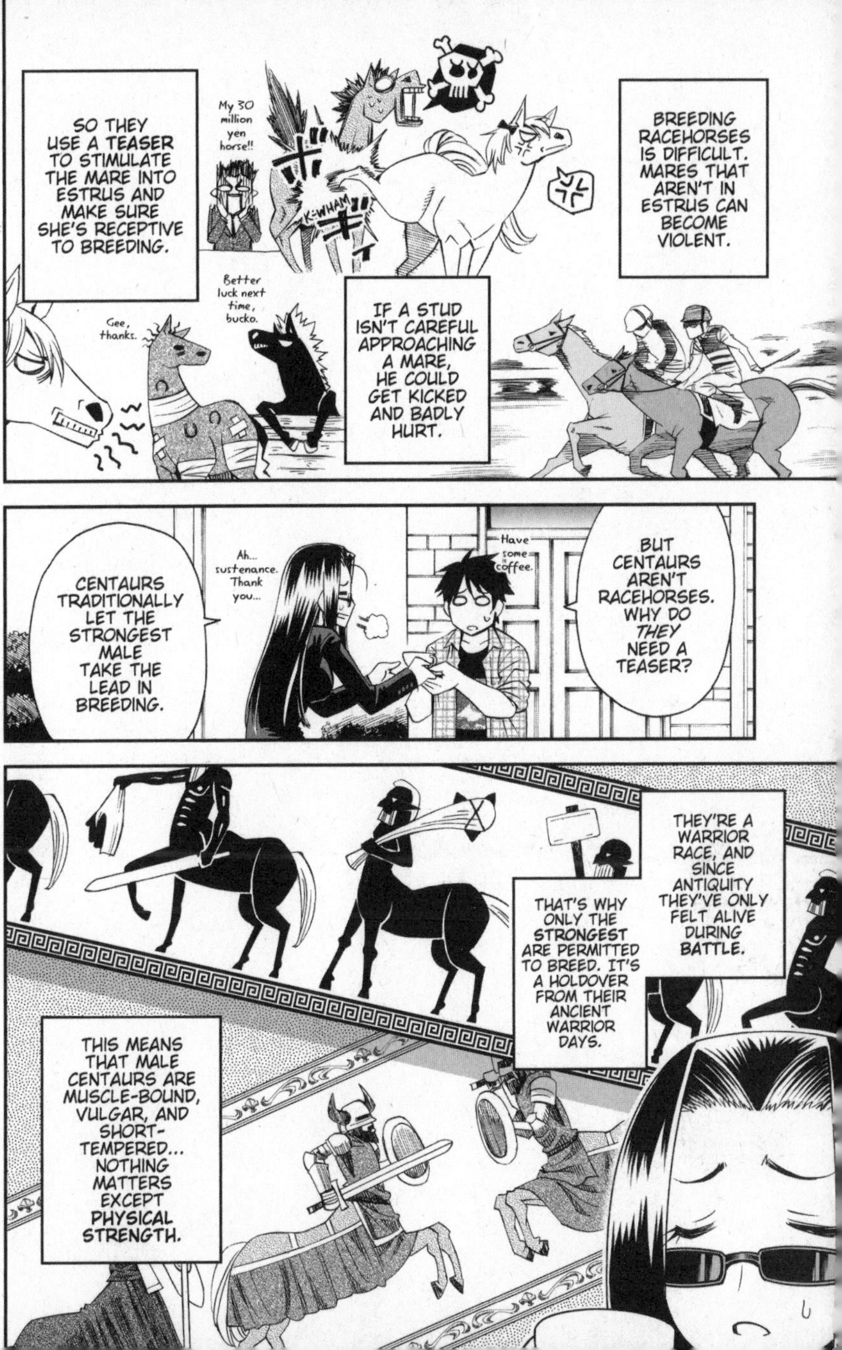
BREEDING RACEHORSES IS DIFFICULT. MARES THAT AREN'T IN ESTRUS CAN BECOME VIOLENT.
IF A STUD ISN'T CAREFUL APPROACHING A MARE, HE COULD GET KICKED AND BADLY HURT.
My 30 million yen horse!!
K-WHAM
SO THEY USE A TEASER TO STIMULATE THE MARE INTO ESTRUS AND MAKE SURE SHE'S RECEPTIVE TO BREEDING.
Better luck next time, bucko.
Gee, thanks.
BUT CENTAURS AREN'T RACEHORSES. WHY DO *THEY* NEED A TEASER?
Have some coffee.
Ah... sustenance. Thank you...
CENTAURS TRADITIONALLY LET THE STRONGEST MALE TAKE THE LEAD IN BREEDING.
THEY'RE A WARRIOR RACE, AND SINCE ANTIQUITY THEY'VE ONLY FELT ALIVE DURING BATTLE.
THAT'S WHY ONLY THE STRONGEST ARE PERMITTED TO BREED. IT'S A HOLDOVER FROM THEIR ANCIENT WARRIOR DAYS.
THIS MEANS THAT MALE CENTAURS ARE MUSCLE-BOUND, VULGAR, AND SHORT-TEMPERED... NOTHING MATTERS EXCEPT PHYSICAL STRENGTH.

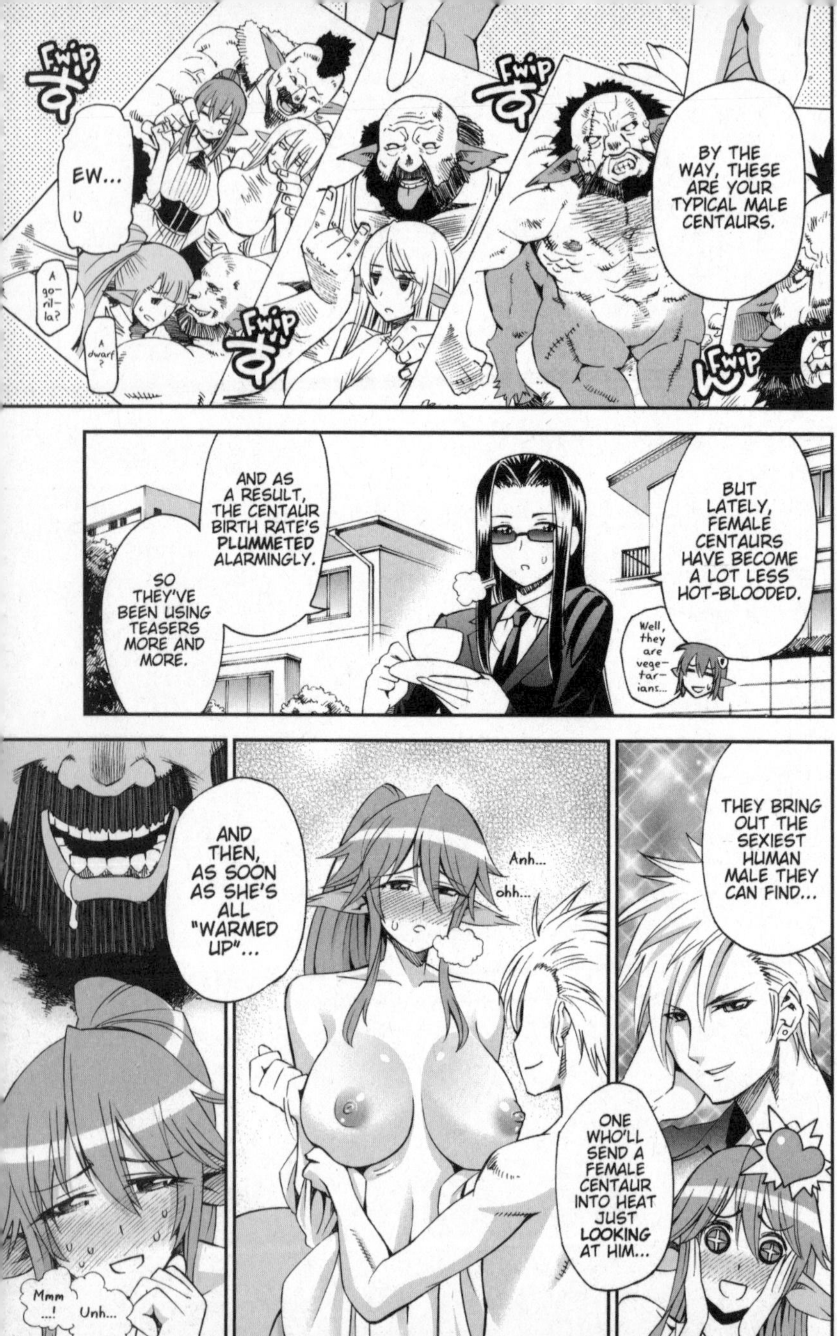
Fwip
BY THE WAY, THESE ARE YOUR TYPICAL MALE CENTAURS.
Fwip
Fwip
Fwip
EW...
A go-ril-la?
A dwarf?
BUT LATELY, FEMALE CENTAURS HAVE BECOME A LOT LESS HOT-BLOODED.
Well, they are vege-tar-ians...
AND AS A RESULT, THE CENTAUR BIRTH RATE'S PLUMMETED ALARMINGLY.
SO THEY'VE BEEN USING TEASERS MORE AND MORE.
THEY BRING OUT THE SEXIEST HUMAN MALE THEY CAN FIND...
ONE WHO'LL SEND A FEMALE CENTAUR INTO HEAT JUST LOOKING AT HIM...
Anh...
ohh...
AND THEN, AS SOON AS SHE'S ALL "WARMED UP"...
Mmm...!
Unh...

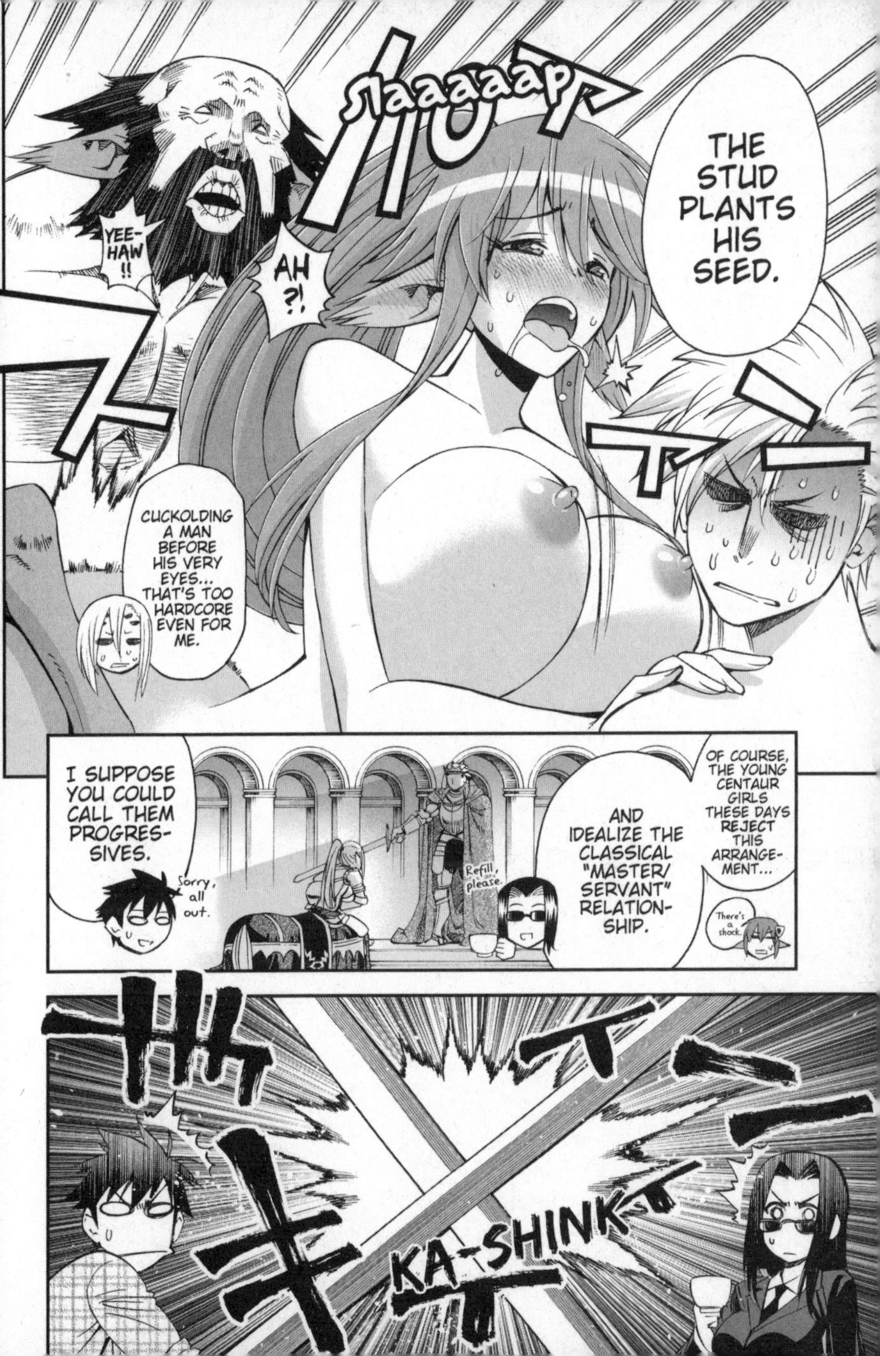
slaaaaap
THE STUD PLANTS HIS SEED.
AH ?!
YEE-HAW !!
CUCKOLDING A MAN BEFORE HIS VERY EYES... THAT'S TOO HARDCORE EVEN FOR ME.
OF COURSE, THE YOUNG CENTAUR GIRLS THESE DAYS REJECT THIS ARRANGE-MENT...
There's a shock.
AND IDEALIZE THE CLASSICAL "MASTER/SERVANT" RELATION-SHIP.
Refill, please.
Sorry, all out.
I SUPPOSE YOU COULD CALL THEM PROGRES-SIVES.
KA-SHINK

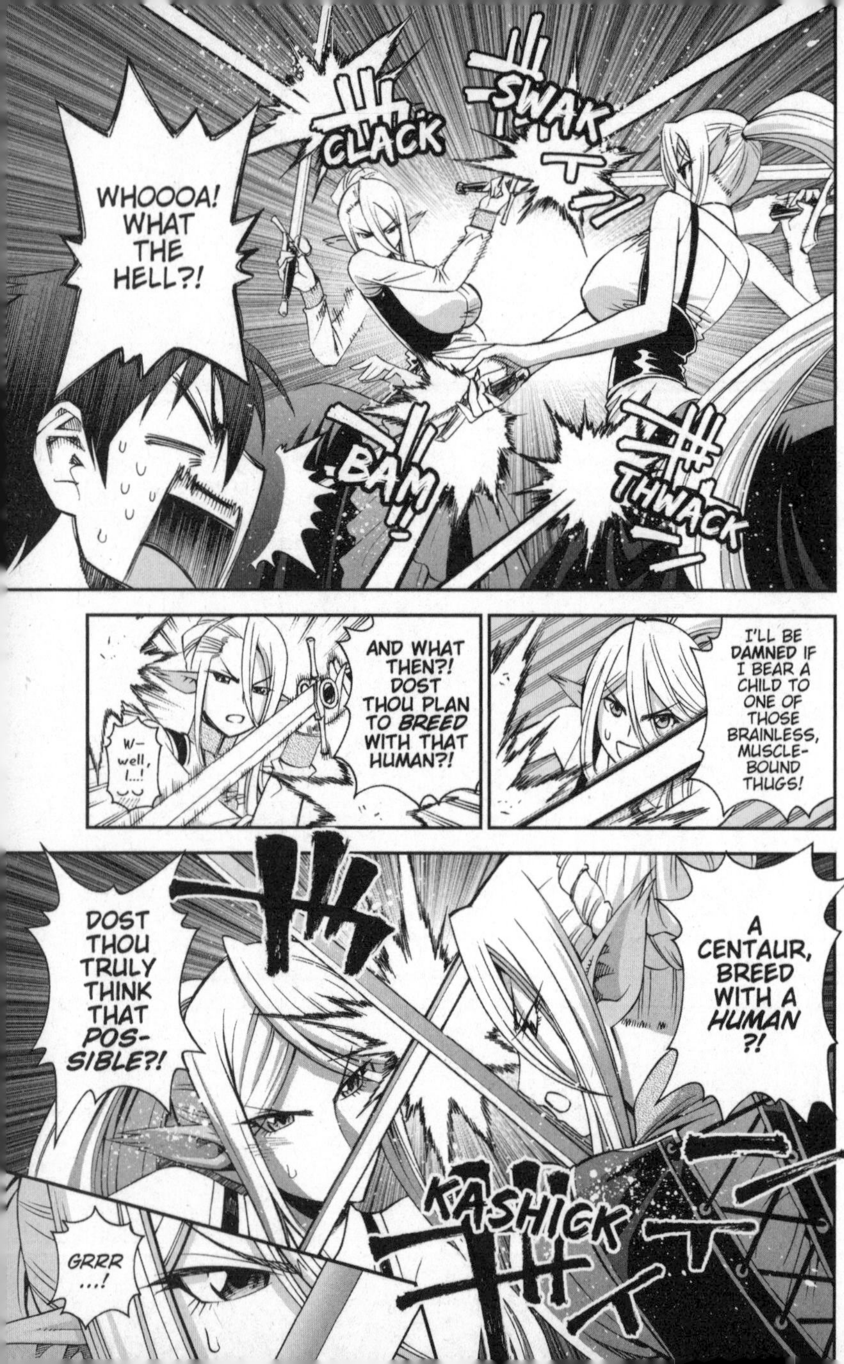
SWAK
CLACK
WHOOOA! WHAT THE HELL?!
THWACK
BAM
I'LL BE DAMNED IF I BEAR A CHILD TO ONE OF THOSE BRAINLESS, MUSCLE-BOUND THUGS!
AND WHAT THEN?! DOST THOU PLAN TO *BREED* WITH THAT HUMAN?!
W-well, I...!
A CENTAUR, BREED WITH A *HUMAN*?!
DOST THOU TRULY THINK THAT *POSSIBLE*?!
KASHICK
GRRR ...!

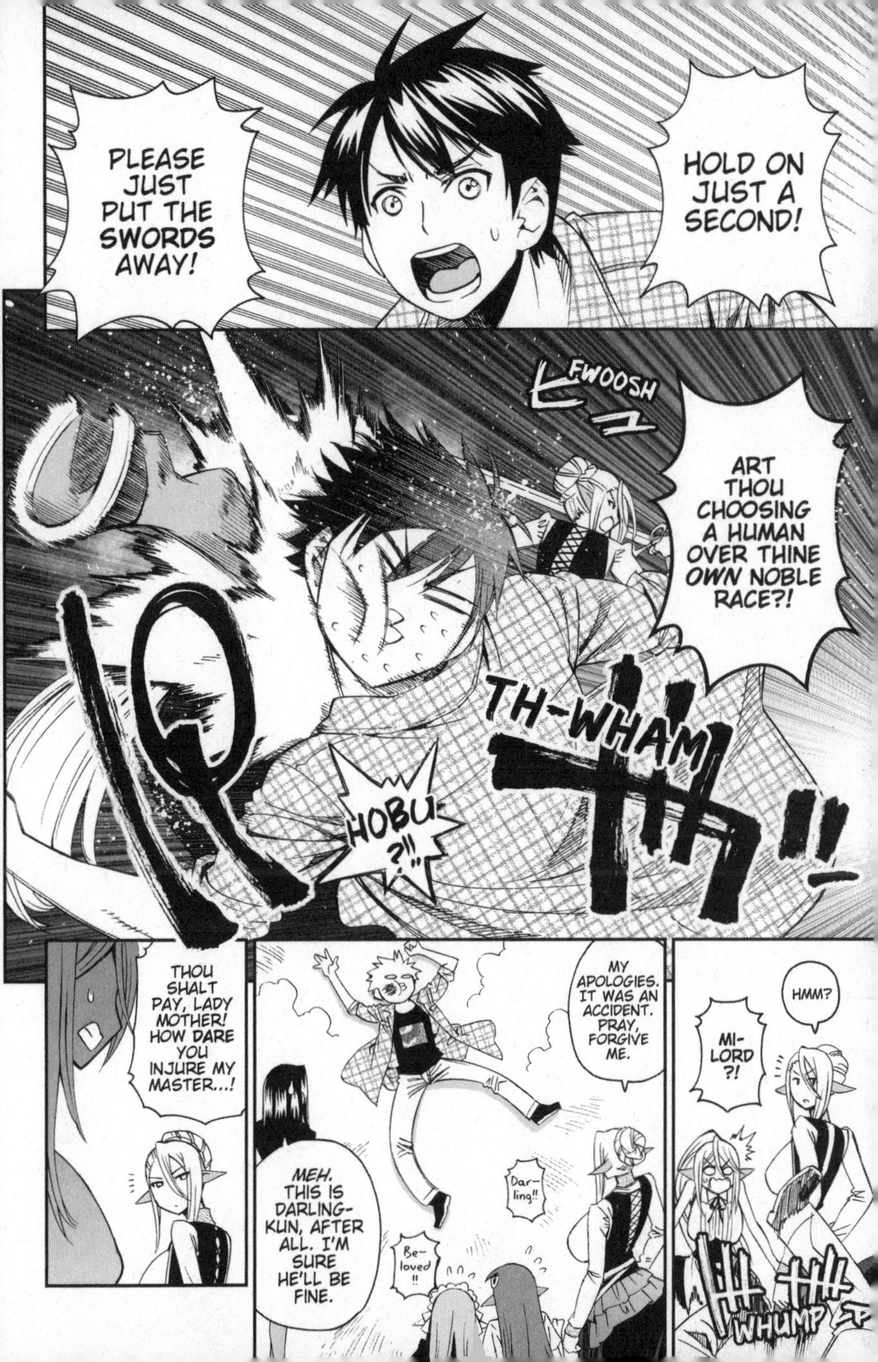
HOLD ON JUST A SECOND!
PLEASE JUST PUT THE SWORDS AWAY!
FWOOSH
ART THOU CHOOSING A HUMAN OVER THINE OWN NOBLE RACE?!
TH-WHAM
HOBU ?!!
HMM?
MI-LORD ?!
WHUMP
MY APOLOGIES. IT WAS AN ACCIDENT. PRAY, FORGIVE ME.
Darling!!
MEH. THIS IS DARLING-KUN, AFTER ALL. I'M SURE HE'LL BE FINE.
Be-loved !!
THOU SHALT PAY, LADY MOTHER! HOW DARE YOU INJURE MY MASTER...!

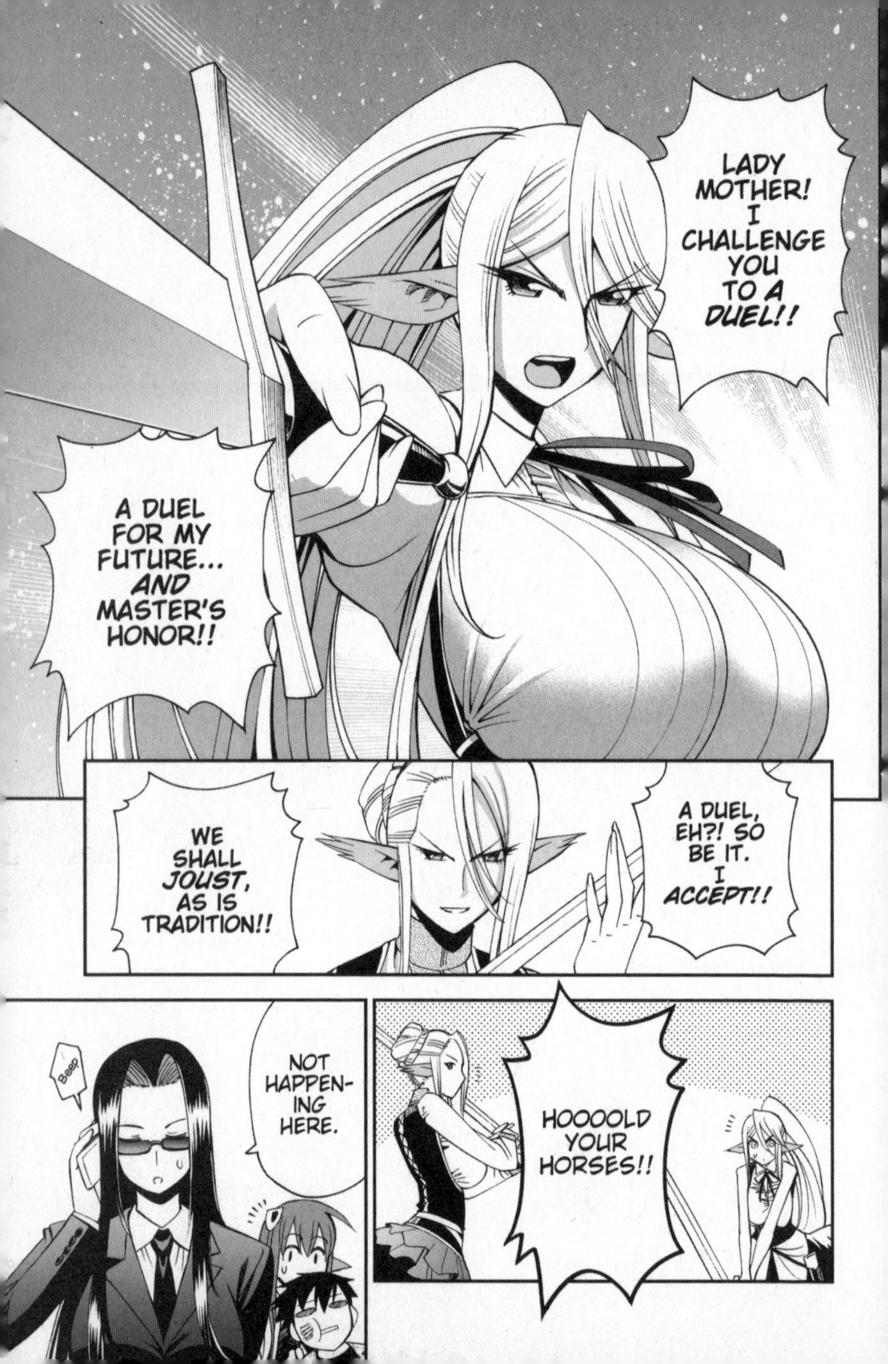
LADY MOTHER! I CHALLENGE YOU TO A DUEL!!
A DUEL FOR MY FUTURE... AND MASTER'S HONOR!!
A DUEL, EH?! SO BE IT. I ACCEPT!!
WE SHALL JOUST, AS IS TRADITION!!
HOOOOLD YOUR HORSES!!
NOT HAPPENING HERE.
Beep

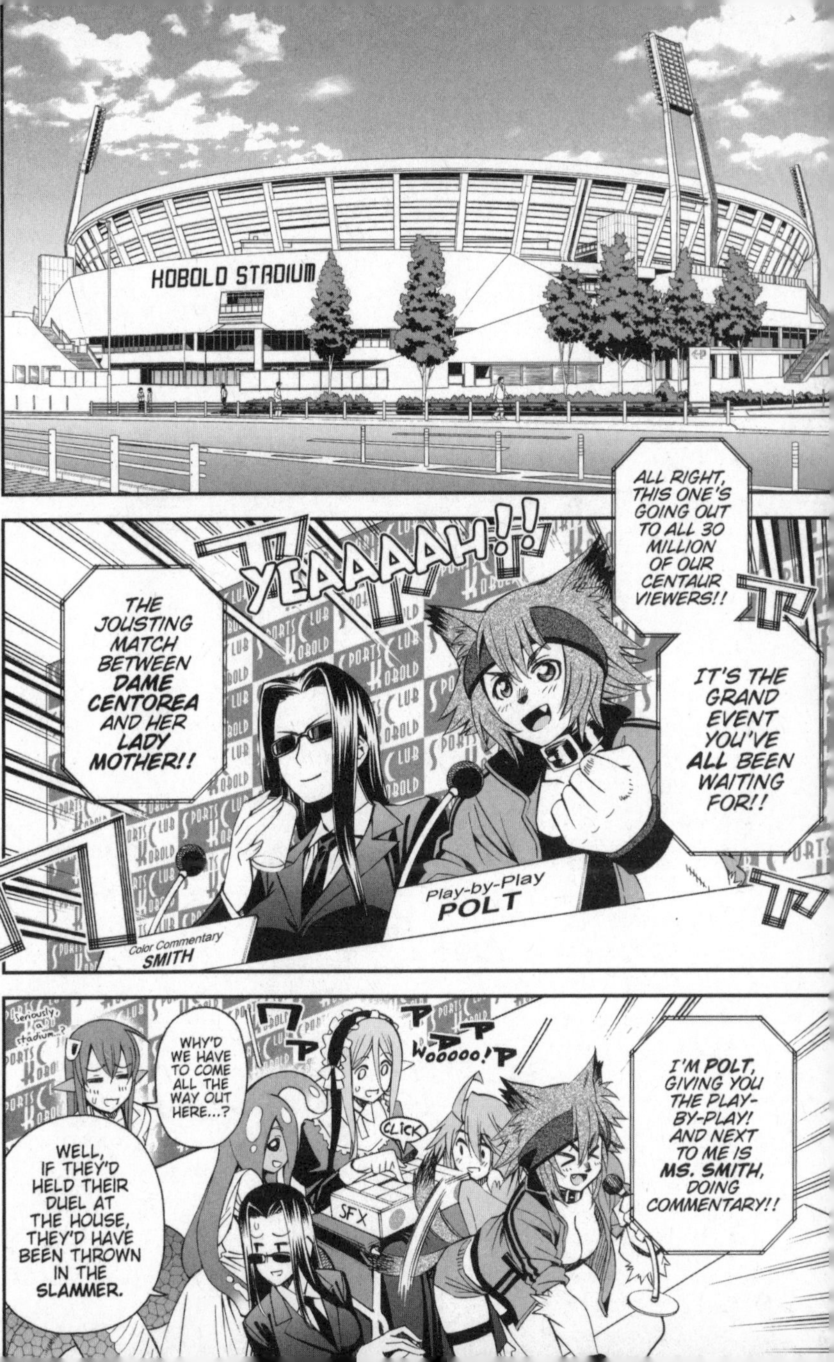
KOBOLD STADIUM
ALL RIGHT, THIS ONE'S GOING OUT TO ALL 30 MILLION OF OUR CENTAUR VIEWERS!!
IT'S THE GRAND EVENT YOU'VE ALL BEEN WAITING FOR!!
YEAAAAH!!
THE JOUSTING MATCH BETWEEN DAME CENTOREA AND HER LADY MOTHER!!
Play-by-Play POLT
Color Commentary SMITH
I'M POLT, GIVING YOU THE PLAY-BY-PLAY! AND NEXT TO ME IS MS. SMITH, DOING COMMENTARY!!
WOOOOO!
CLICK
SFX
WHY'D WE HAVE TO COME ALL THE WAY OUT HERE...?
Seriously, a stadium...?
WELL, IF THEY'D HELD THEIR DUEL AT THE HOUSE, THEY'D HAVE BEEN THROWN IN THE SLAMMER.

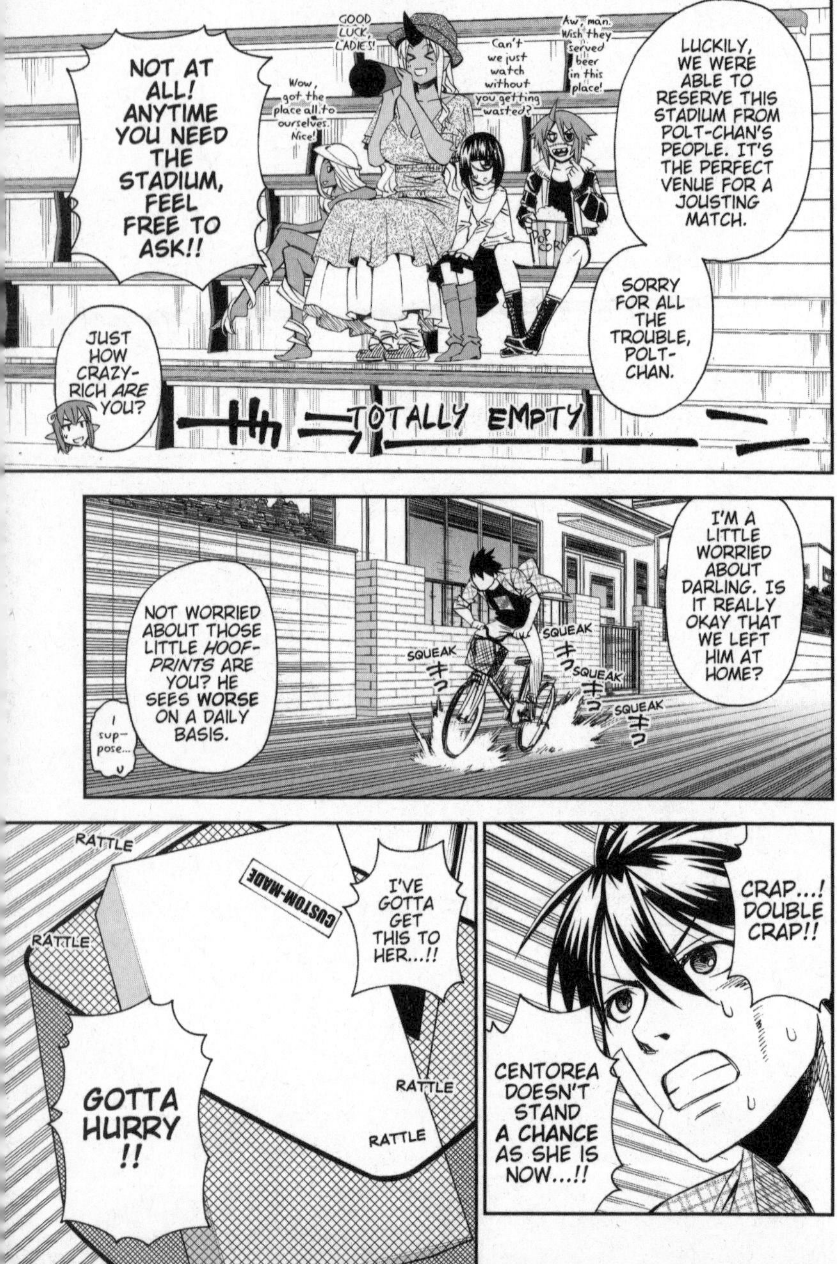

LUCKILY, WE WERE ABLE TO RESERVE THIS STADIUM FROM POLT-CHAN'S PEOPLE. IT'S THE PERFECT VENUE FOR A JOUSTING MATCH.
SORRY FOR ALL THE TROUBLE, POLT-CHAN.
Aw, man. Wish they served beer in this place!
Can't we just watch without you getting wasted?
GOOD LUCK, LADIES!
Wow, got the place all to ourselves. Nice!
NOT AT ALL! ANYTIME YOU NEED THE STADIUM, FEEL FREE TO ASK!!
TOTALLY EMPTY
JUST HOW CRAZY-RICH ARE YOU?
I'M A LITTLE WORRIED ABOUT DARLING. IS IT REALLY OKAY THAT WE LEFT HIM AT HOME?
SQUEAK
SQUEAK
SQUEAK
SQUEAK
NOT WORRIED ABOUT THOSE LITTLE HOOF-PRINTS ARE YOU? HE SEES WORSE ON A DAILY BASIS.
I sup-pose...
CRAP...! DOUBLE CRAP!!
CENTOREA DOESN'T STAND A CHANCE AS SHE IS NOW...!!
RATTLE
RATTLE
CUSTOM-MADE
I'VE GOTTA GET THIS TO HER...!!
RATTLE
RATTLE
GOTTA HURRY!!

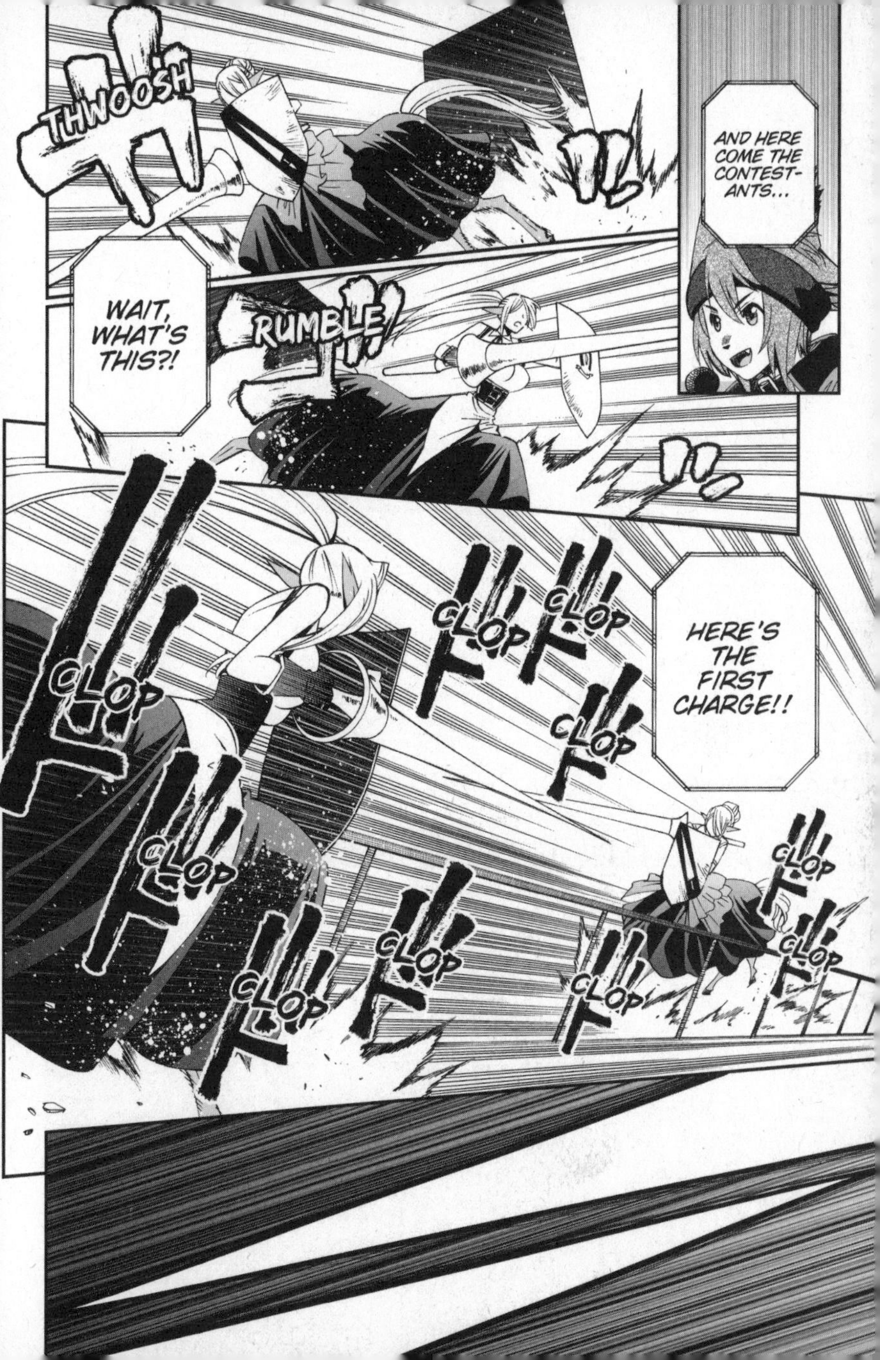
AND HERE COME THE CONTESTANTS...
THWOOSH
WAIT, WHAT'S THIS?!
RUMBLE
HERE'S THE FIRST CHARGE!!
CLOP
CLOP
CLOP
CLOP
CLOP
CLOP
CLOP
CLOP
CLOP
CLOP
CLOP

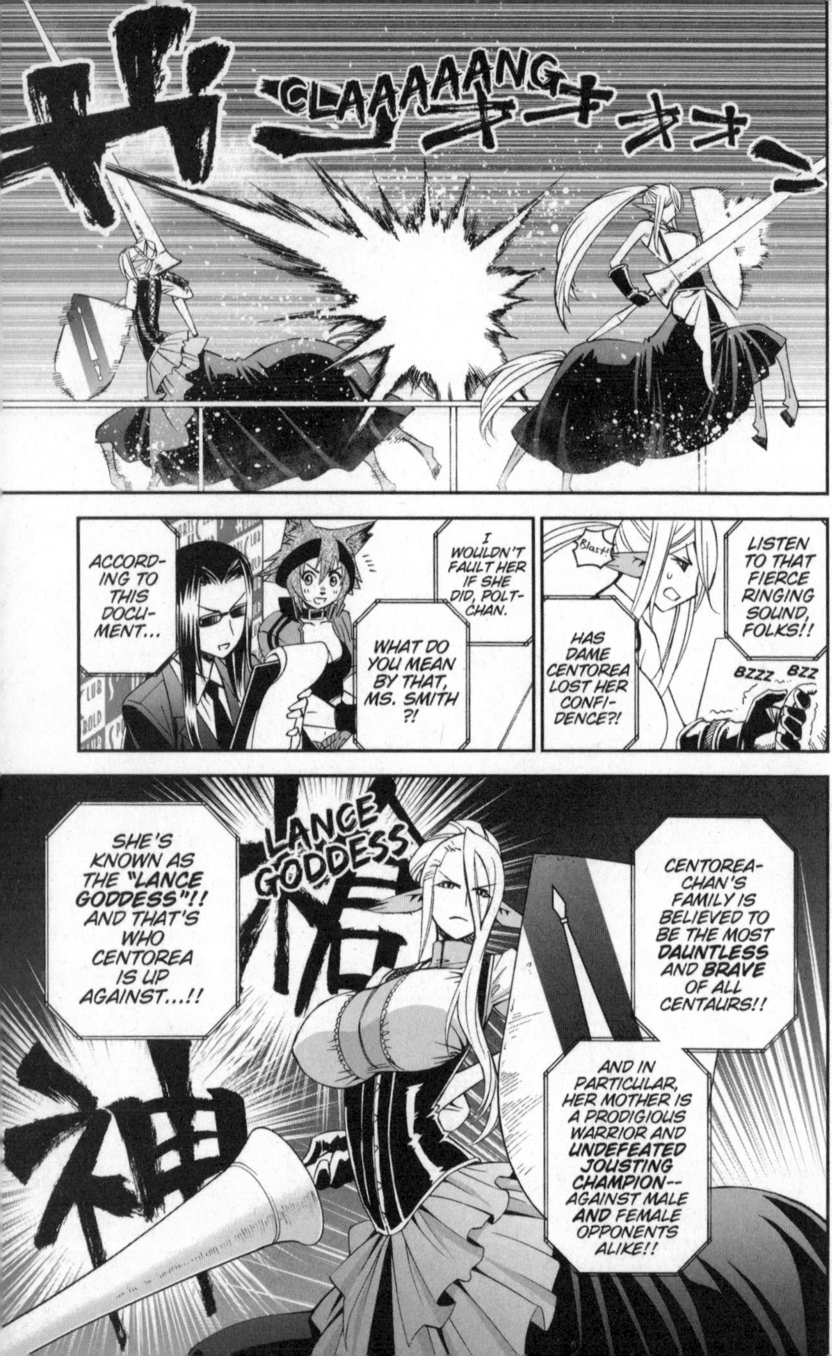
CLAAAAANG
LISTEN TO THAT FIERCE RINGING SOUND, FOLKS!!
Blast!!
HAS DAME CENTOREA LOST HER CONFIDENCE?!
BZZZ~ BZZ
I WOULDN'T FAULT HER IF SHE DID, POLT-CHAN.
WHAT DO YOU MEAN BY THAT, MS. SMITH?!
ACCORDING TO THIS DOCUMENT...
CENTOREA-CHAN'S FAMILY IS BELIEVED TO BE THE MOST DAUNTLESS AND BRAVE OF ALL CENTAURS!!
AND IN PARTICULAR, HER MOTHER IS A PRODIGIOUS WARRIOR AND UNDEFEATED JOUSTING CHAMPION-- AGAINST MALE AND FEMALE OPPONENTS ALIKE!!
LANCE GODDESS
SHE'S KNOWN AS THE "LANCE GODDESS"!! AND THAT'S WHO CENTOREA IS UP AGAINST...!!

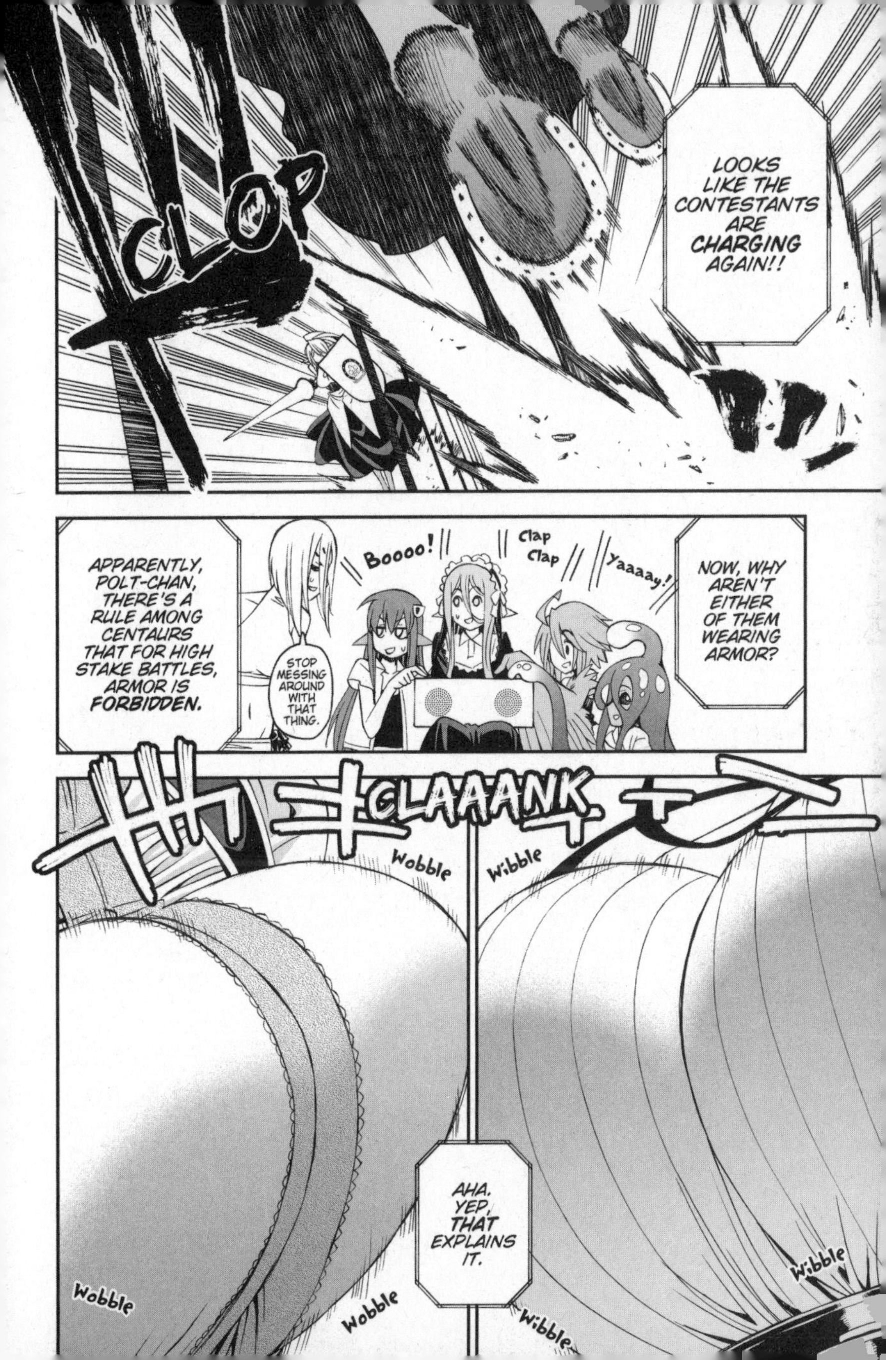
LOOKS LIKE THE CONTESTANTS ARE CHARGING AGAIN!!
CLOP
NOW, WHY AREN'T EITHER OF THEM WEARING ARMOR?
Yaaaay!
Clap Clap
Boooo!
STOP MESSING AROUND WITH THAT THING.
APPARENTLY, POLT-CHAN, THERE'S A RULE AMONG CENTAURS THAT FOR HIGH STAKE BATTLES, ARMOR IS FORBIDDEN.
CLAAANK
wibble
Wobble
AHA. YEP, THAT EXPLAINS IT.
wibble
wibble
wobble
wobble

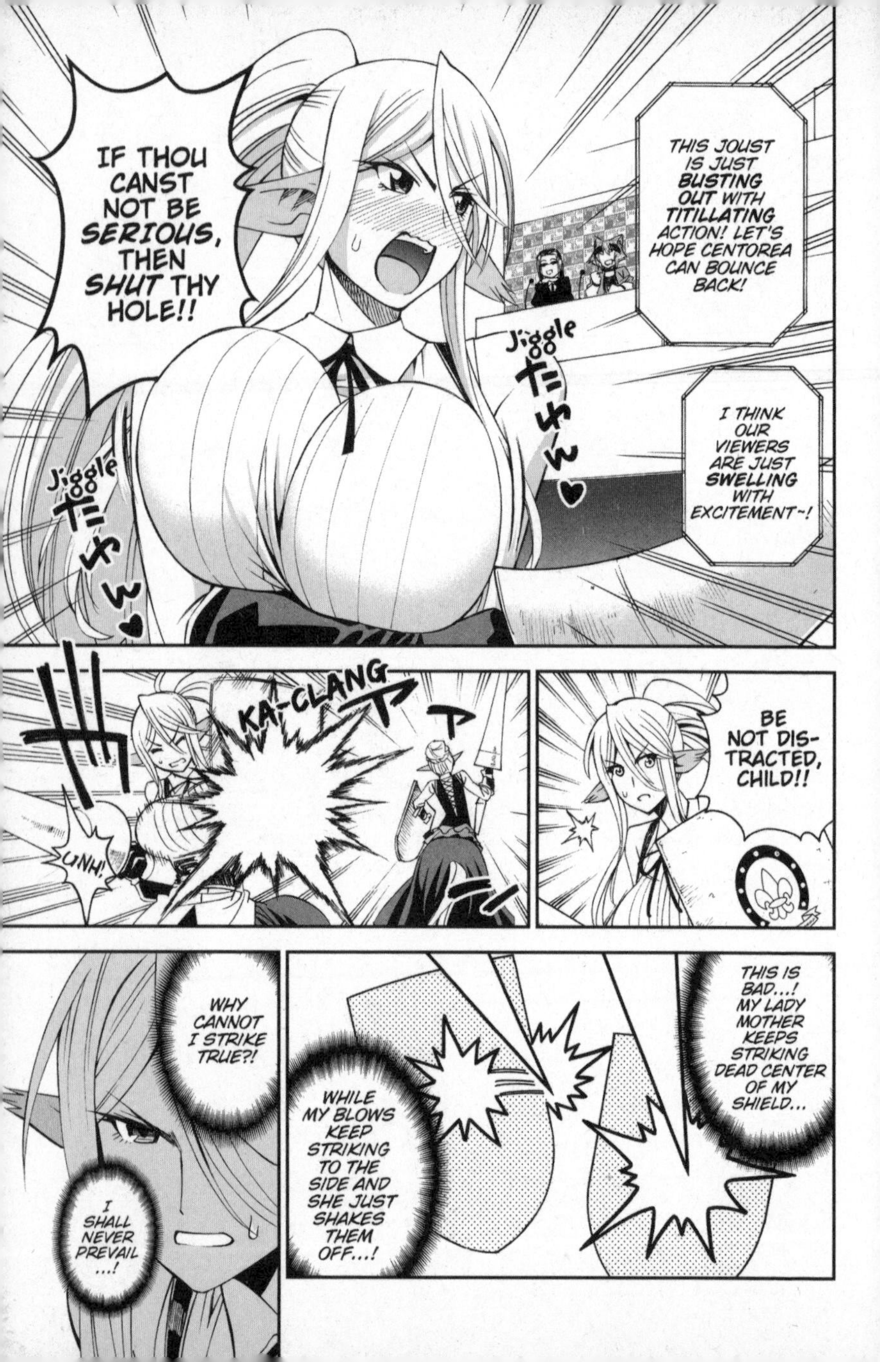
THIS JOUST IS JUST BUSTING OUT WITH TITILLATING ACTION! LET'S HOPE CENTOREA CAN BOUNCE BACK!
I THINK OUR VIEWERS ARE JUST SWELLING WITH EXCITEMENT~!
IF THOU CANST NOT BE SERIOUS, THEN SHUT THY HOLE!!
Jiggle
たゆん
Jiggle
たゆん
BE NOT DIS-TRACTED, CHILD!!
KA-CLANG
UNH!
THIS IS BAD...! MY LADY MOTHER KEEPS STRIKING DEAD CENTER OF MY SHIELD...
WHILE MY BLOWS KEEP STRIKING TO THE SIDE AND SHE JUST SHAKES THEM OFF...!
WHY CANNOT I STRIKE TRUE?!
I SHALL NEVER PREVAIL...!

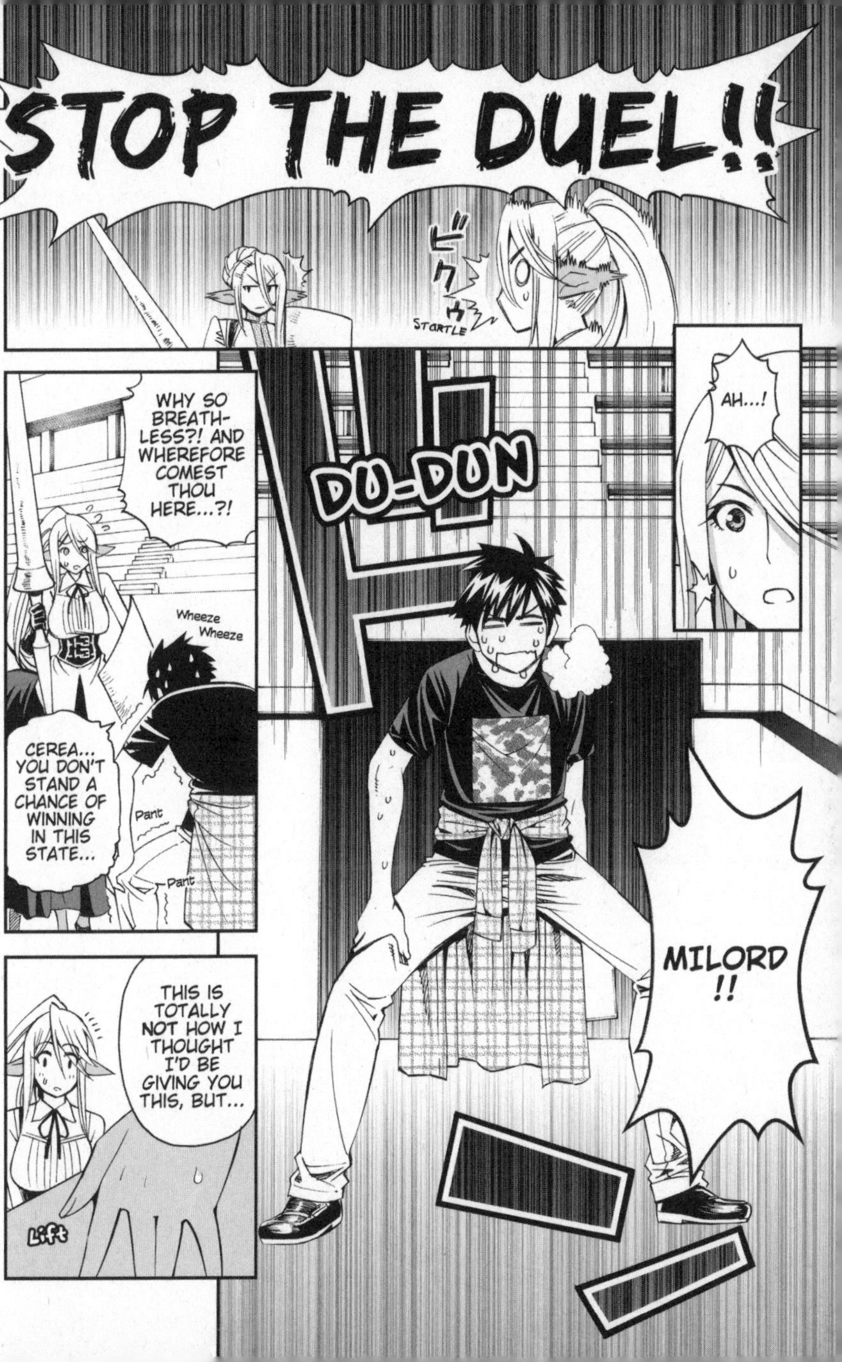
STOP THE DUEL!!
ビクゥ
STARTLE
AH...!
DU-DUN
MILORD !!
WHY SO BREATH-LESS?! AND WHEREFORE COMEST THOU HERE...?!
Wheeze Wheeze
CEREA... YOU DON'T STAND A CHANCE OF WINNING IN THIS STATE...
Pant
Pant
THIS IS TOTALLY NOT HOW I THOUGHT I'D BE GIVING YOU THIS, BUT...
Lift

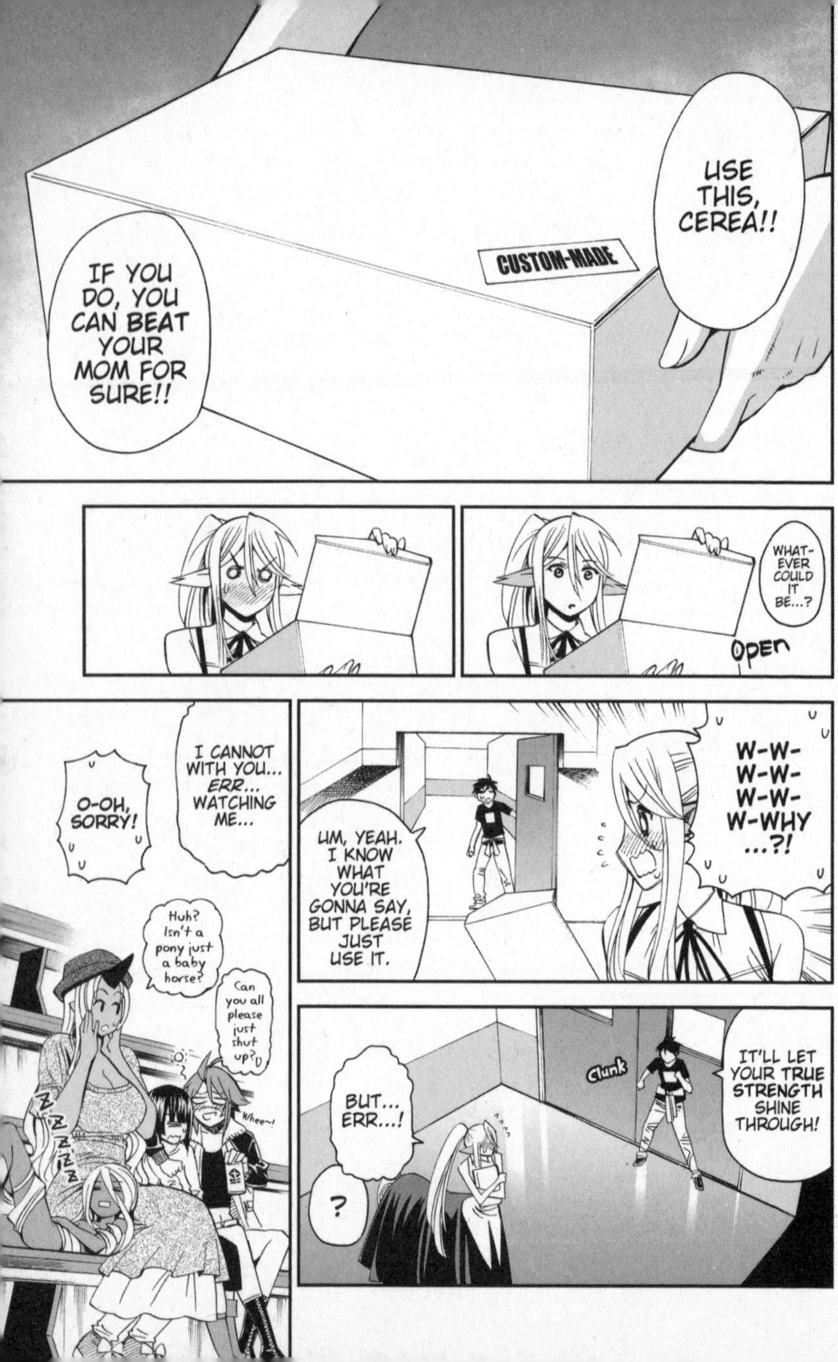
USE THIS, CEREA!!
CUSTOM-MADE
IF YOU DO, YOU CAN BEAT YOUR MOM FOR SURE!!
WHAT-EVER COULD IT BE...?
Open
W-W-W-W-W-W-W-WHY...?!
UM, YEAH. I KNOW WHAT YOU'RE GONNA SAY, BUT PLEASE JUST USE IT.
IT'LL LET YOUR TRUE STRENGTH SHINE THROUGH!
Clunk
BUT... ERR...!
?
I CANNOT WITH YOU... ERR... WATCHING ME...
O-OH, SORRY!
Huh? Isn't a pony just a baby horse?
Can you all please just shut up?
Whee~!
ZZZZZ

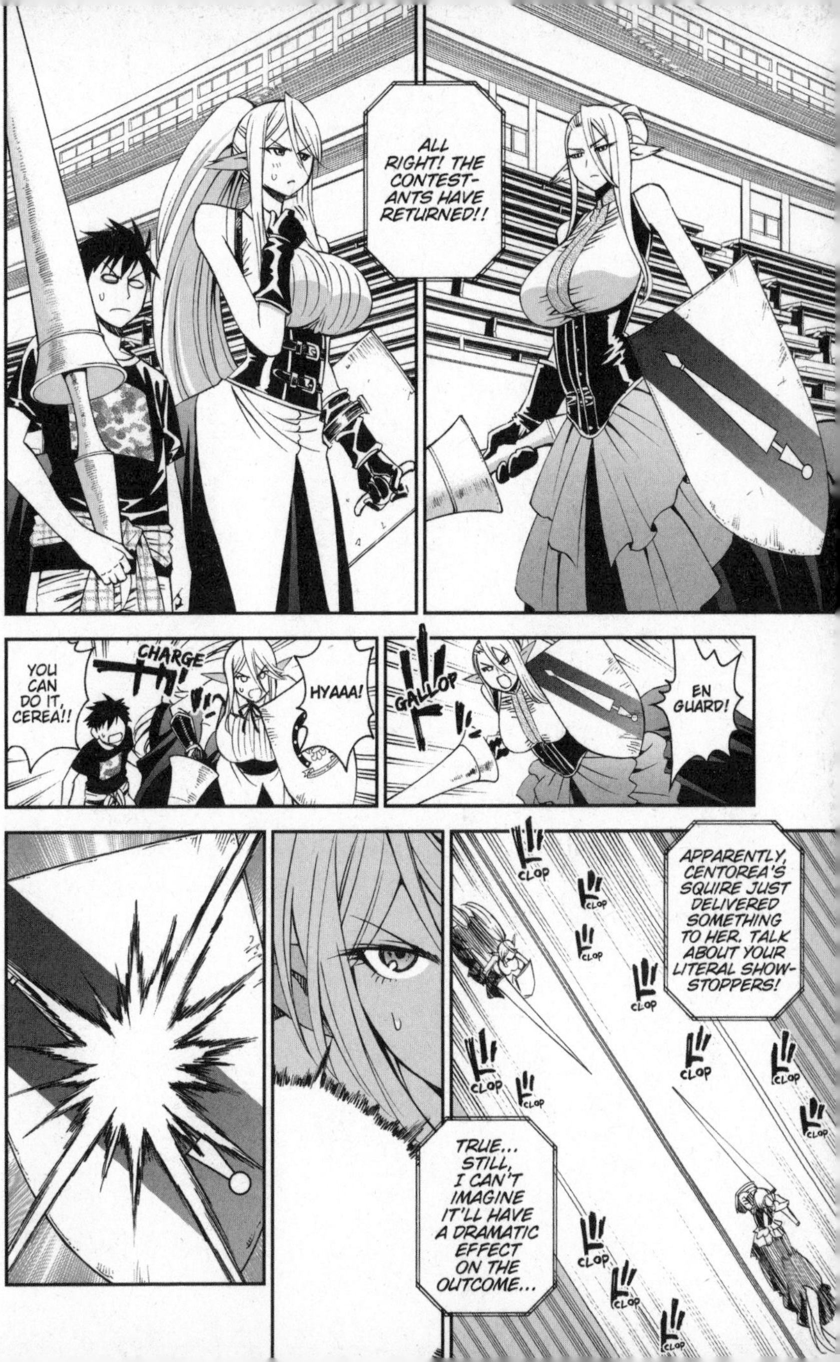

ALL RIGHT! THE CONTEST-ANTS HAVE RETURNED!!
GALLOP
EN GUARD!
CHARGE
HYAAA!
YOU CAN DO IT, CEREA!!
APPARENTLY, CENTOREA'S SQUIRE JUST DELIVERED SOMETHING TO HER. TALK ABOUT YOUR LITERAL SHOW-STOPPERS!
CLOP
TRUE... STILL, I CAN'T IMAGINE IT'LL HAVE A DRAMATIC EFFECT ON THE OUTCOME...

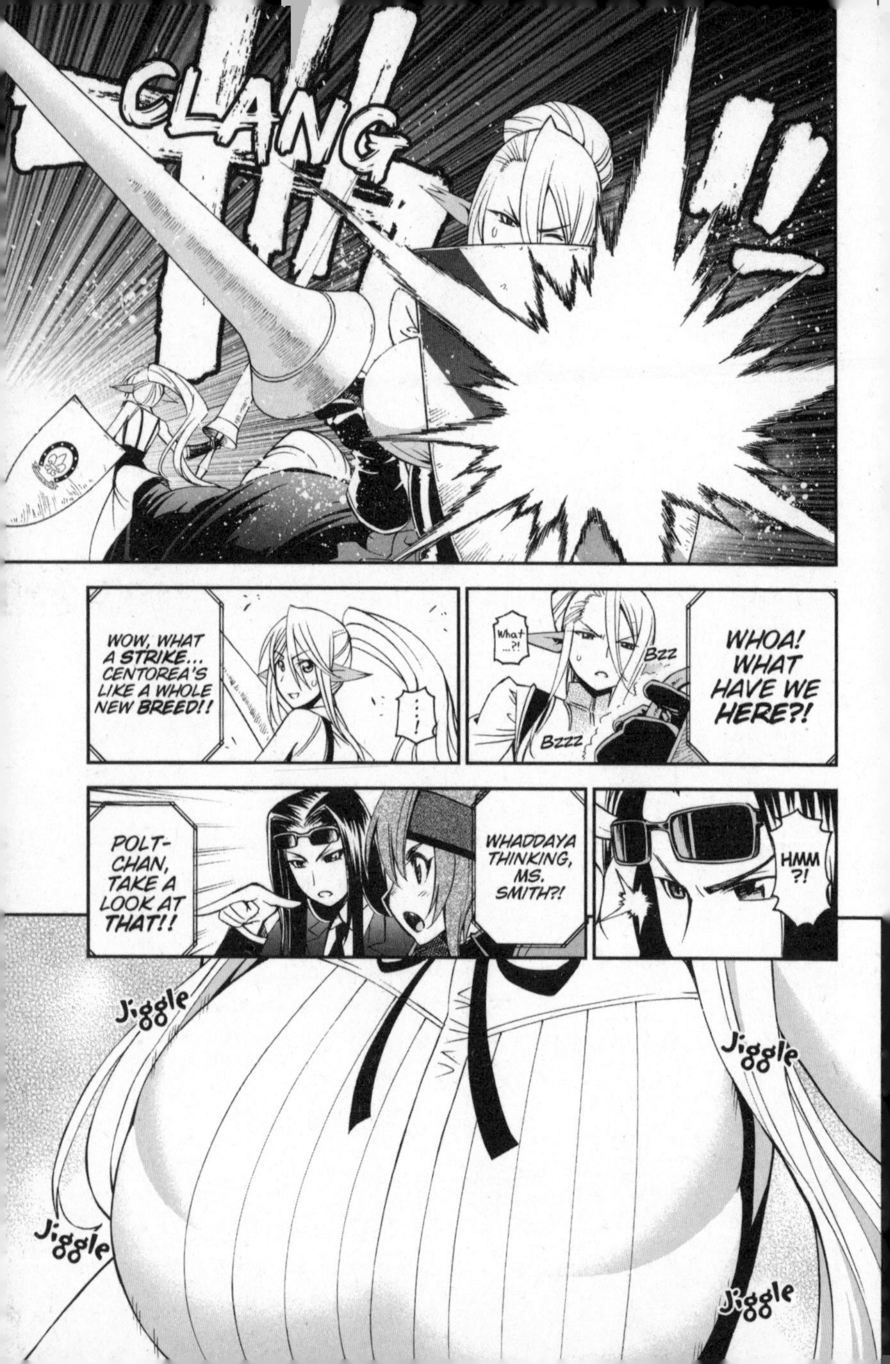
CLANG
WHOA! WHAT HAVE WE HERE?!
Bzz
What ...?!
Bzzz
WOW, WHAT A STRIKE... CENTOREA'S LIKE A WHOLE NEW BREED!!
...!
HMM ?!
WHADDAYA THINKING, MS. SMITH?!
POLT-CHAN, TAKE A LOOK AT THAT!!
Jiggle
Jiggle
Jiggle
Jiggle

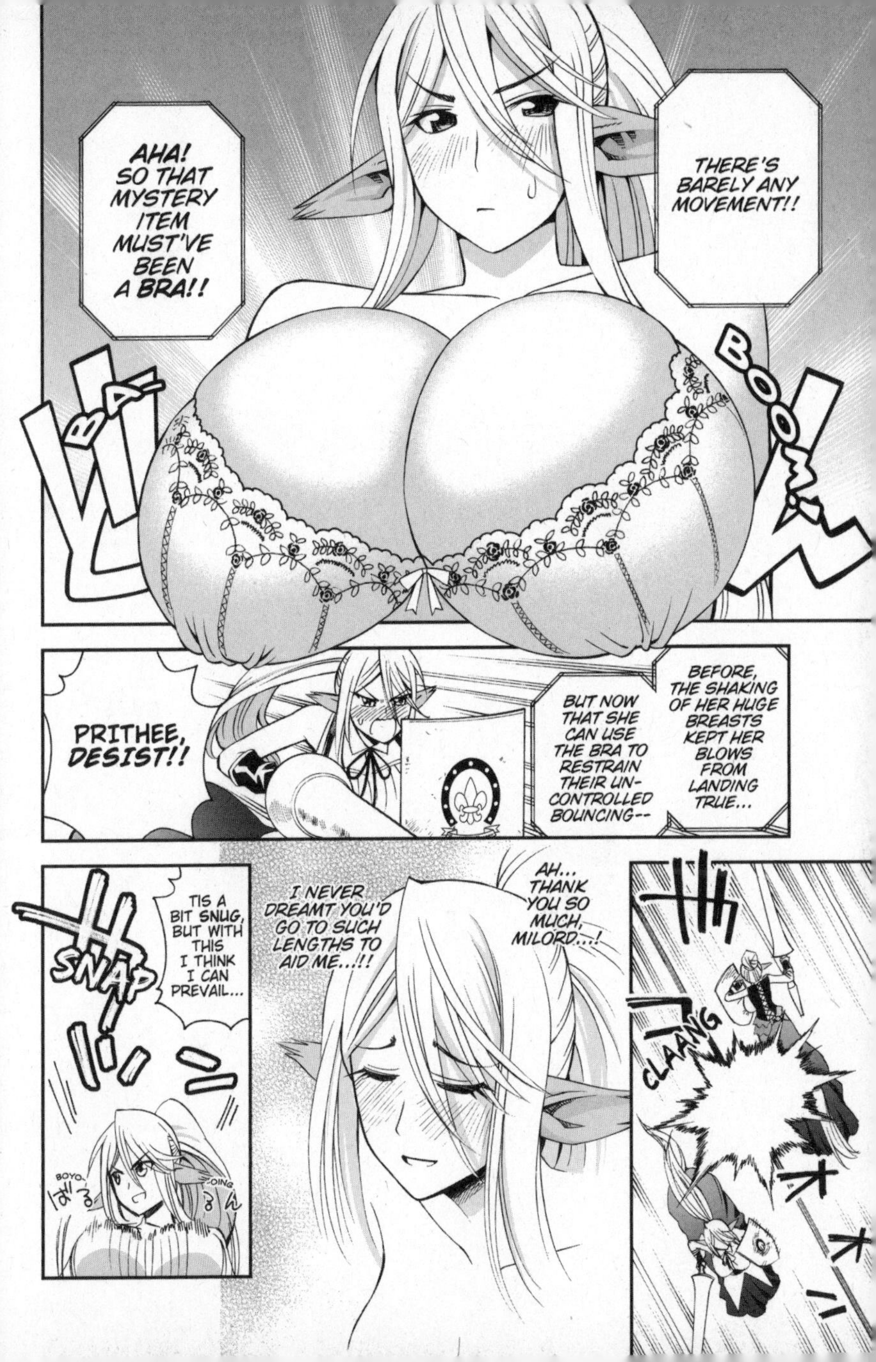
THERE'S BARELY ANY MOVEMENT!!
AHA! SO THAT MYSTERY ITEM MUST'VE BEEN A BRA!!
BOOM!
BA-
BEFORE, THE SHAKING OF HER HUGE BREASTS KEPT HER BLOWS FROM LANDING TRUE...
BUT NOW THAT SHE CAN USE THE BRA TO RESTRAIN THEIR UN-CONTROLLED BOUNCING--
PRITHEE, DESIST!!
CLAANG
AH... THANK YOU SO MUCH, MILORD...!
I NEVER DREAMT YOU'D GO TO SUCH LENGTHS TO AID ME...!!
TIS A BIT SNUG, BUT WITH THIS I THINK I CAN PREVAIL...
SNAP
BOING
BOYO

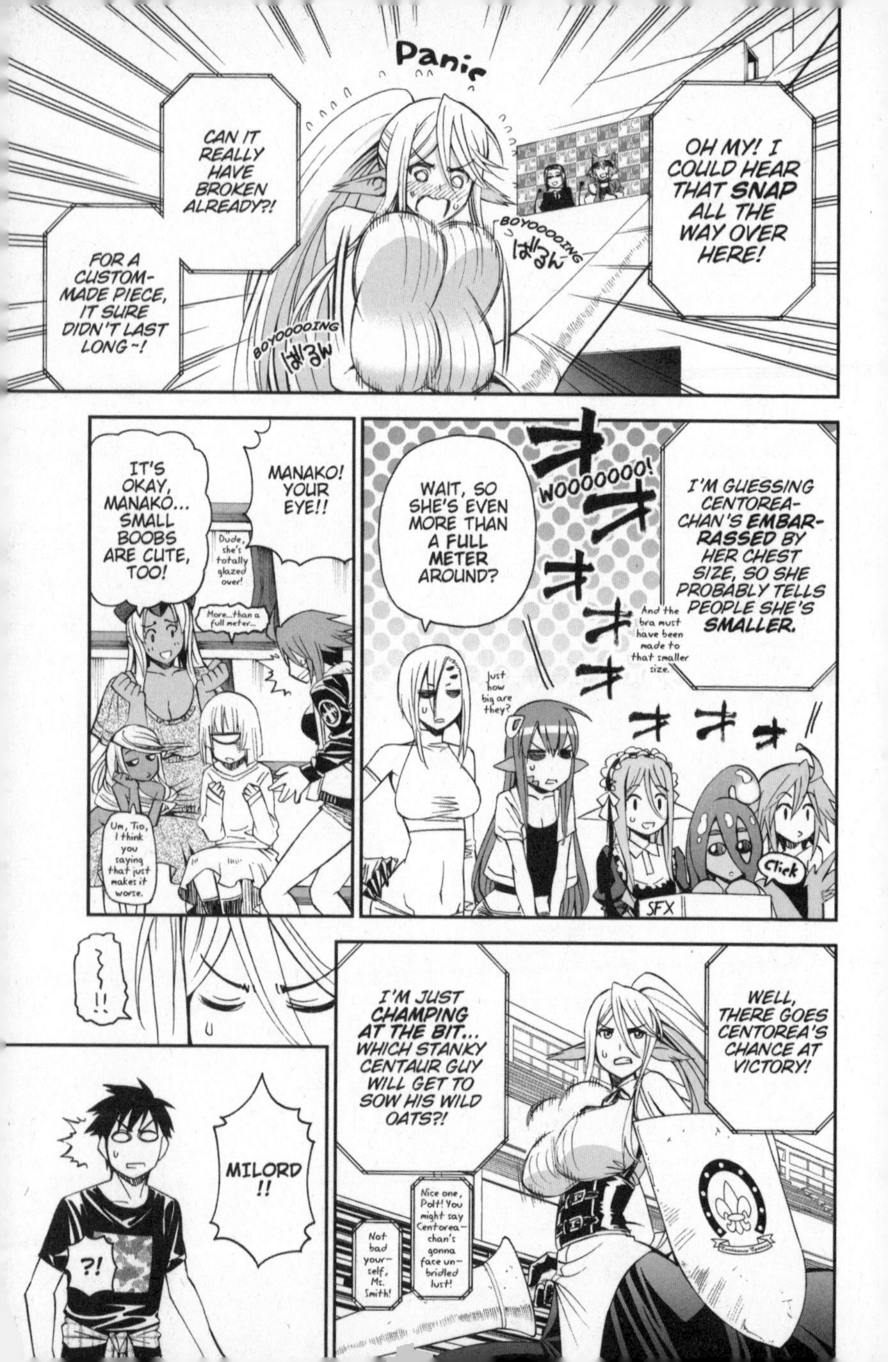
Panic
OH MY! I COULD HEAR THAT SNAP ALL THE WAY OVER HERE!
BOYOOOOING
ばるん
CAN IT REALLY HAVE BROKEN ALREADY?!
BOYOOOOING
ばるん
FOR A CUSTOM-MADE PIECE, IT SURE DIDN'T LAST LONG~!
I'M GUESSING CENTOREA-CHAN'S EMBARRASSED BY HER CHEST SIZE, SO SHE PROBABLY TELLS PEOPLE SHE'S SMALLER.
And the bra must have been made to that smaller size.
WOOOOOOO!
WAIT, SO SHE'S EVEN MORE THAN A FULL METER AROUND?
Just how big are they?
Click
SFX
MANAKO! YOUR EYE!!
IT'S OKAY, MANAKO... SMALL BOOBS ARE CUTE, TOO!
Dude, she's totally glazed over!
More...than a full meter...
Um, Tio, I think you saying that just makes it worse.
WELL, THERE GOES CENTOREA'S CHANCE AT VICTORY!
I'M JUST CHAMPING AT THE BIT... WHICH STANKY CENTAUR GUY WILL GET TO SOW HIS WILD OATS?!
Nice one, Polt! You might say Centorea-chan's gonna face unbridled lust!
Not bad yourself, Ms. Smith!
~~!!
MILORD!!
?!

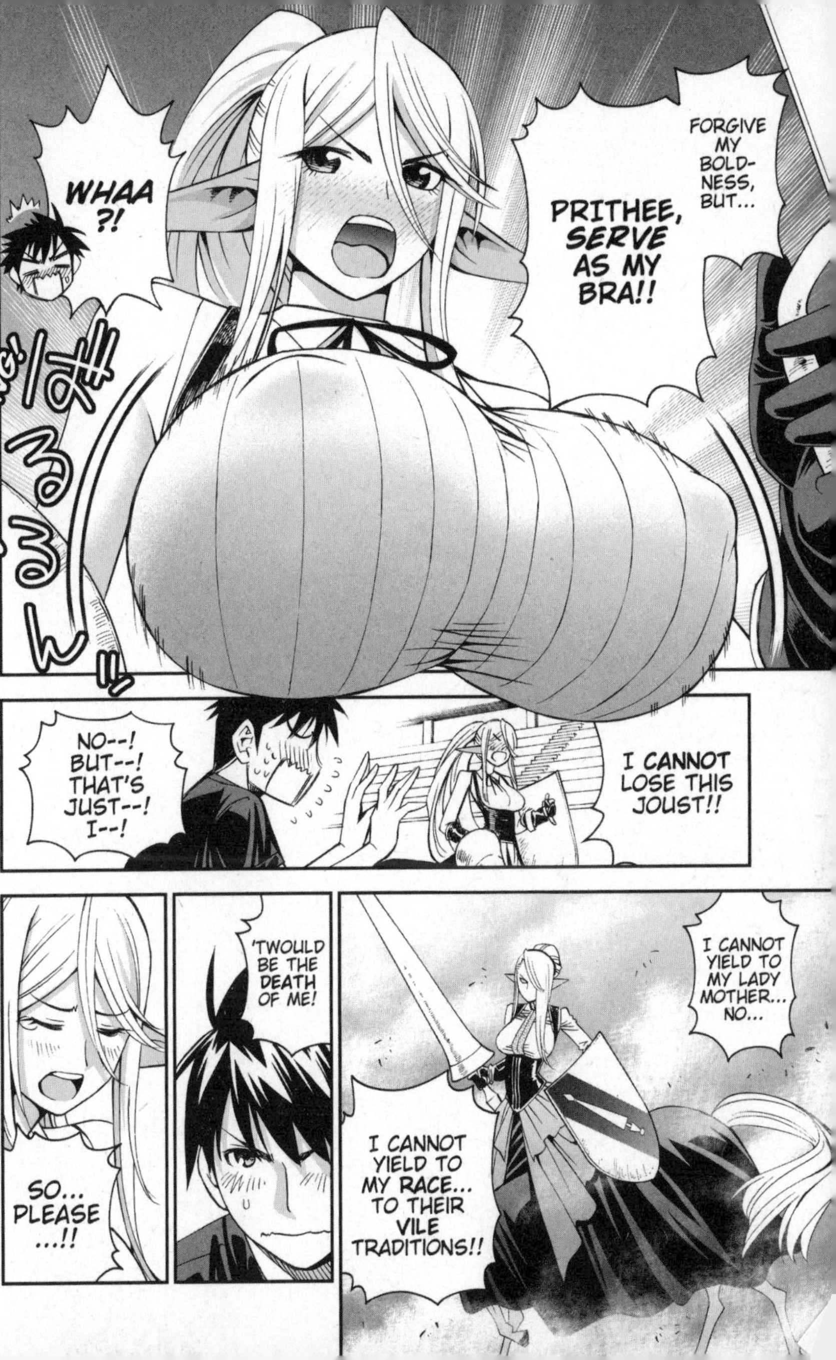

FORGIVE MY BOLDNESS, BUT...
PRITHEE, SERVE AS MY BRA!!
WHAA ?!
BOYOOOING!
I CANNOT LOSE THIS JOUST!!
NO--! BUT--! THAT'S JUST--! I--!
I CANNOT YIELD TO MY LADY MOTHER... NO...
I CANNOT YIELD TO MY RACE... TO THEIR VILE TRADITIONS!!
'TWOULD BE THE DEATH OF ME!
SO... PLEASE ...!!

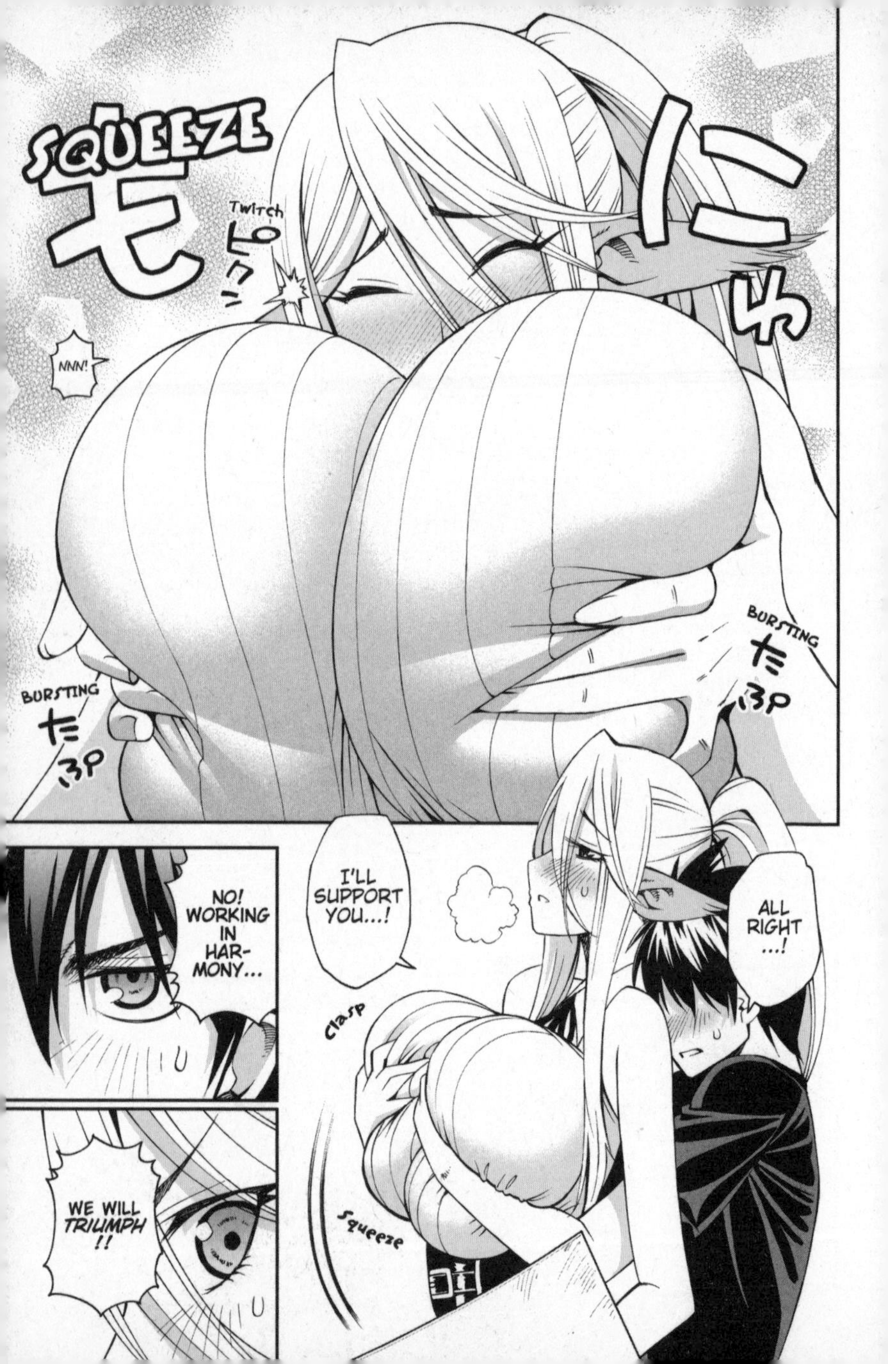
SQUEEZE
TWITCH
NNN!
BURSTING
BURSTING
ALL RIGHT ...!
I'LL SUPPORT YOU...!
CLASP
SQUEEZE
NO! WORKING IN HAR-MONY...
WE WILL TRIUMPH !!

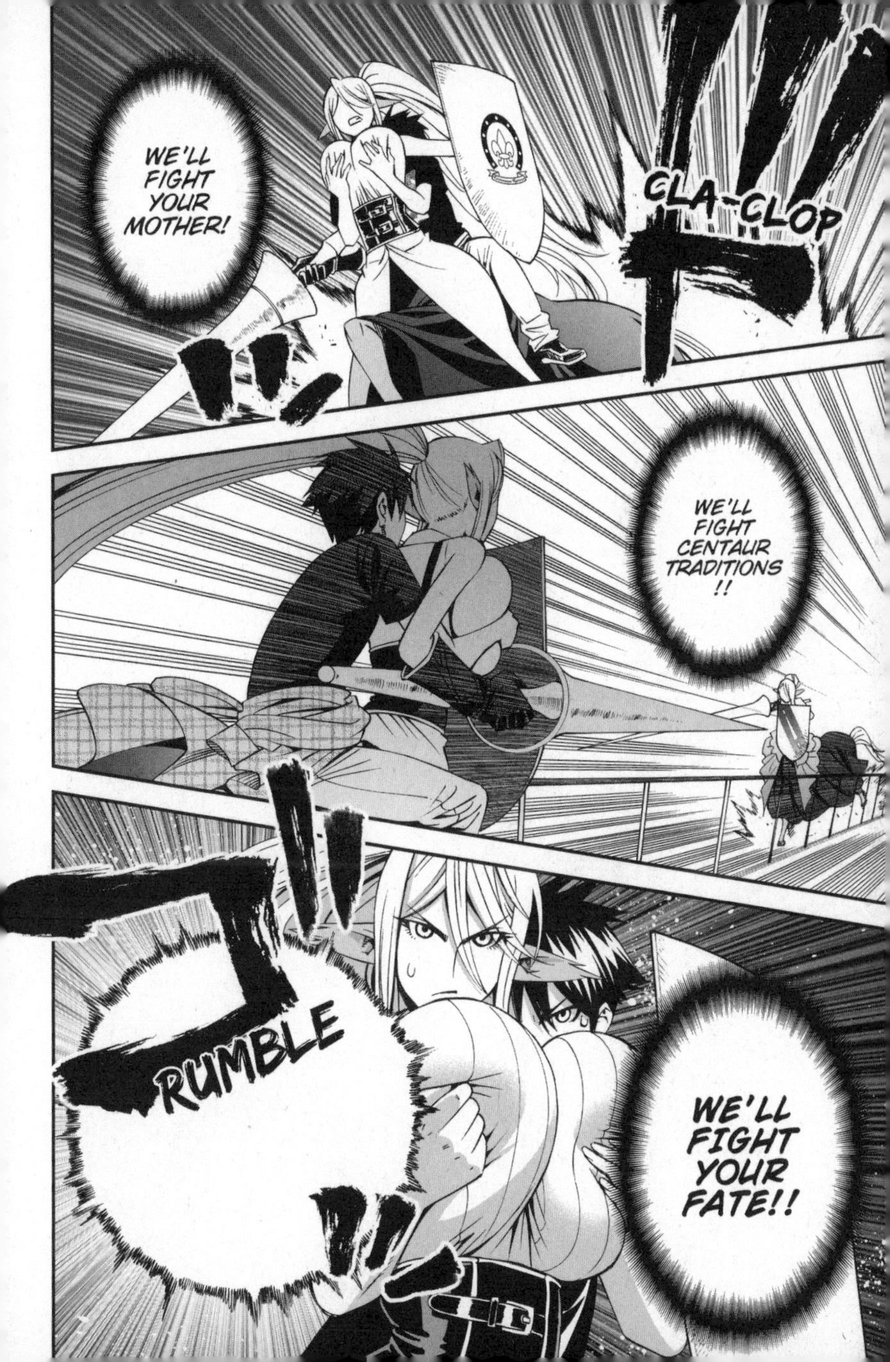
CLA-CLOP
WE'LL FIGHT YOUR MOTHER!
WE'LL FIGHT CENTAUR TRADITIONS!!
WE'LL FIGHT YOUR FATE!!
RUMBLE

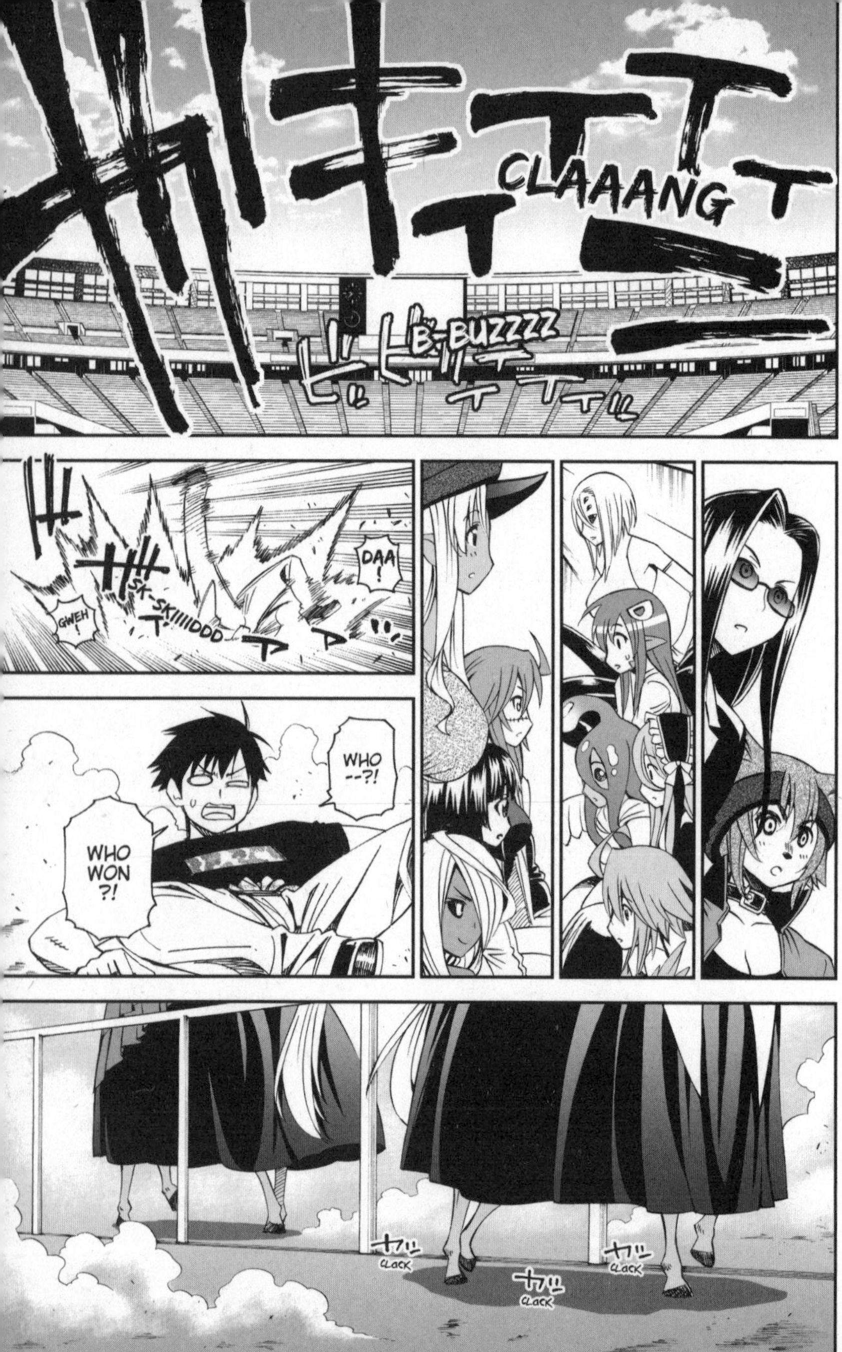
CLAAANG
B-BUZZZZ
DAA!
SK-SKIIIIDDD
GWEH!
WHO--?!
WHO WON?!
CLACK
CLACK
CLACK

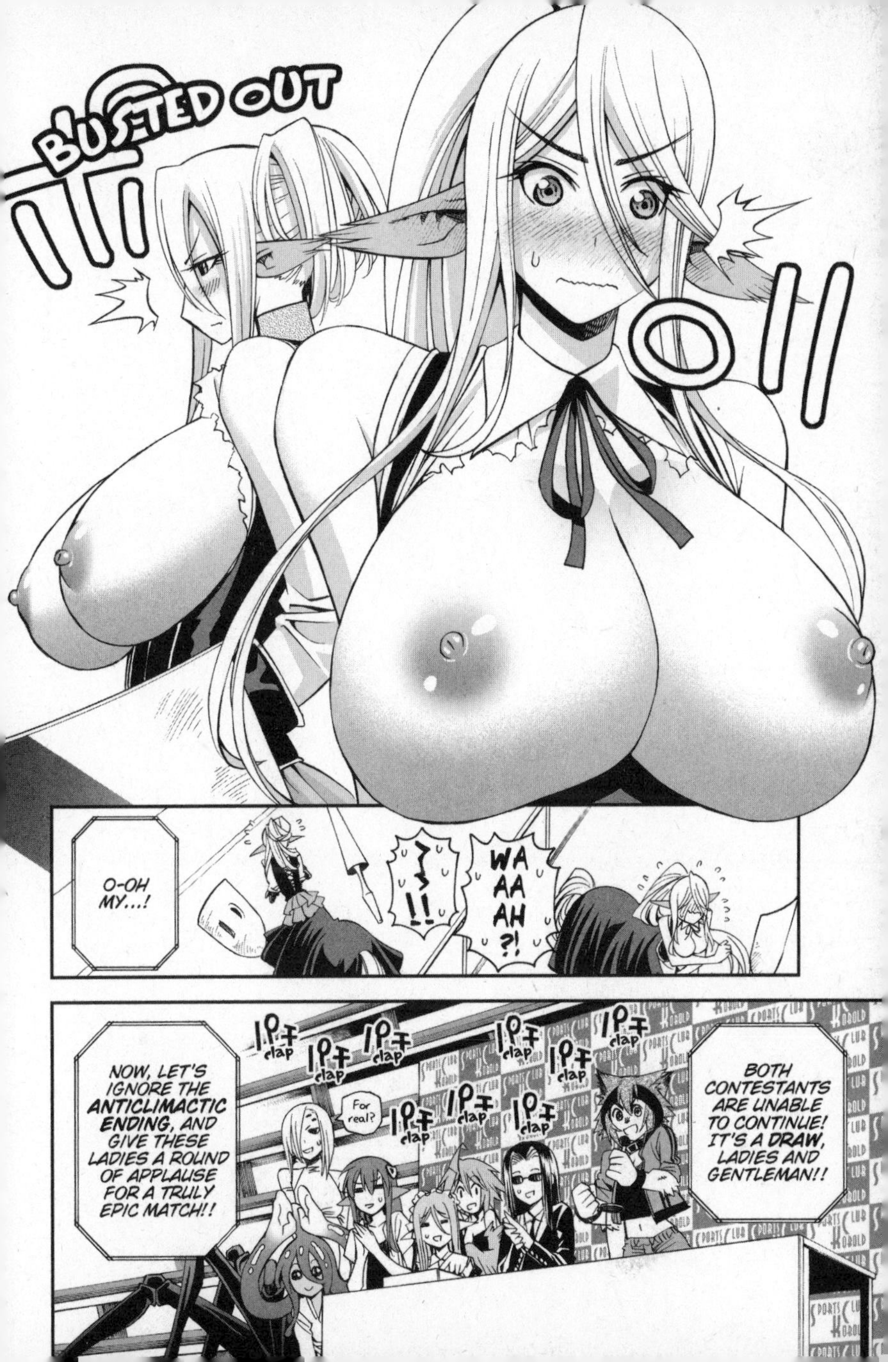
BUSTED OUT
WAAAAH?!
O-OH MY...!
BOTH CONTESTANTS ARE UNABLE TO CONTINUE! IT'S A DRAW, LADIES AND GENTLEMAN!!
For real?
NOW, LET'S IGNORE THE ANTICLIMACTIC ENDING, AND GIVE THESE LADIES A ROUND OF APPLAUSE FOR A TRULY EPIC MATCH!!

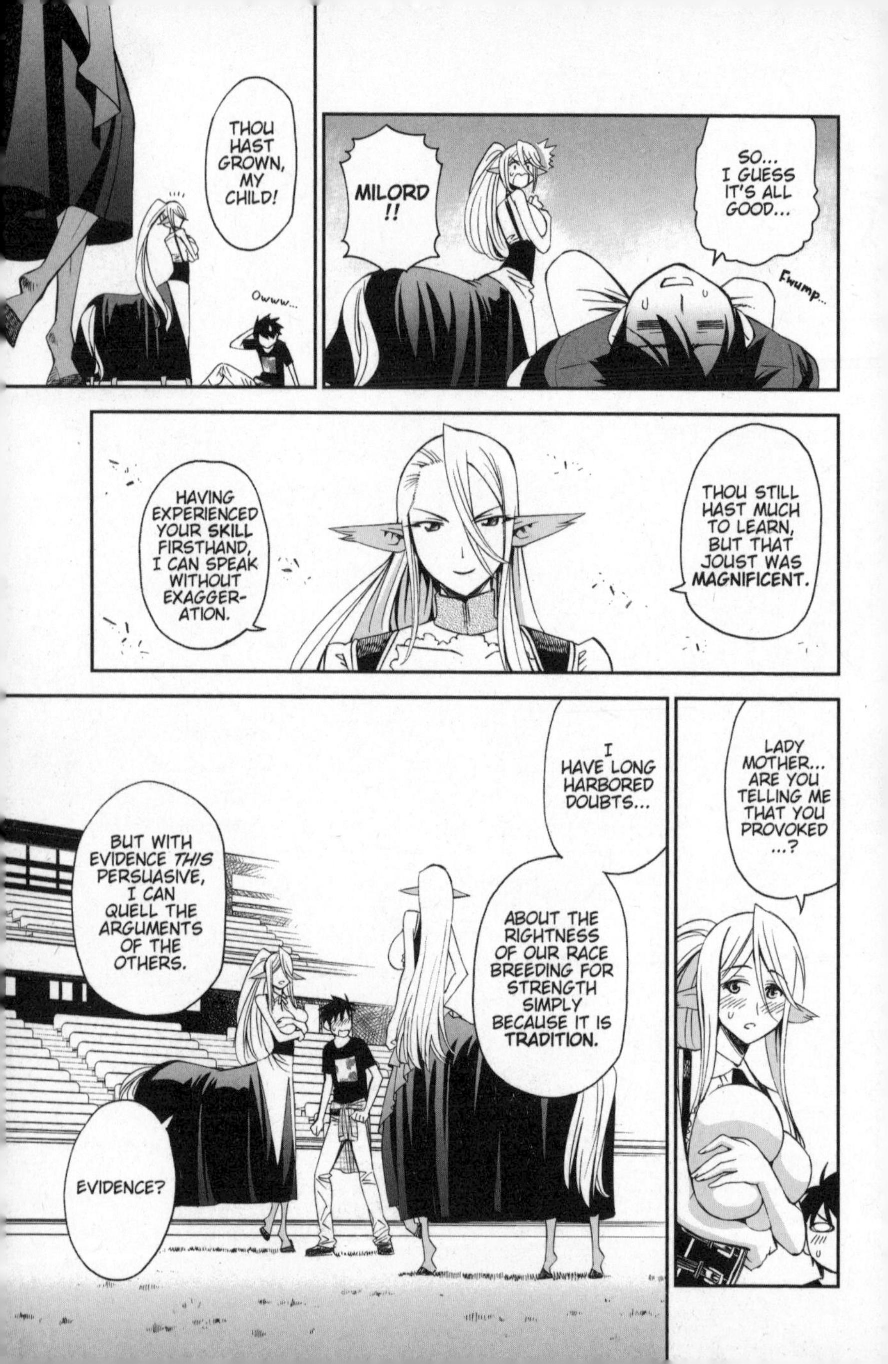
SO... I GUESS IT'S ALL GOOD...
Fwump...
MILORD !!
THOU HAST GROWN, MY CHILD!
Owww...
THOU STILL HAST MUCH TO LEARN, BUT THAT JOUST WAS MAGNIFICENT.
HAVING EXPERIENCED YOUR SKILL FIRSTHAND, I CAN SPEAK WITHOUT EXAGGER-ATION.
LADY MOTHER... ARE YOU TELLING ME THAT YOU PROVOKED ...?
I HAVE LONG HARBORED DOUBTS...
ABOUT THE RIGHTNESS OF OUR RACE BREEDING FOR STRENGTH SIMPLY BECAUSE IT IS TRADITION.
BUT WITH EVIDENCE *THIS* PERSUASIVE, I CAN QUELL THE ARGUMENTS OF THE OTHERS.
EVIDENCE?

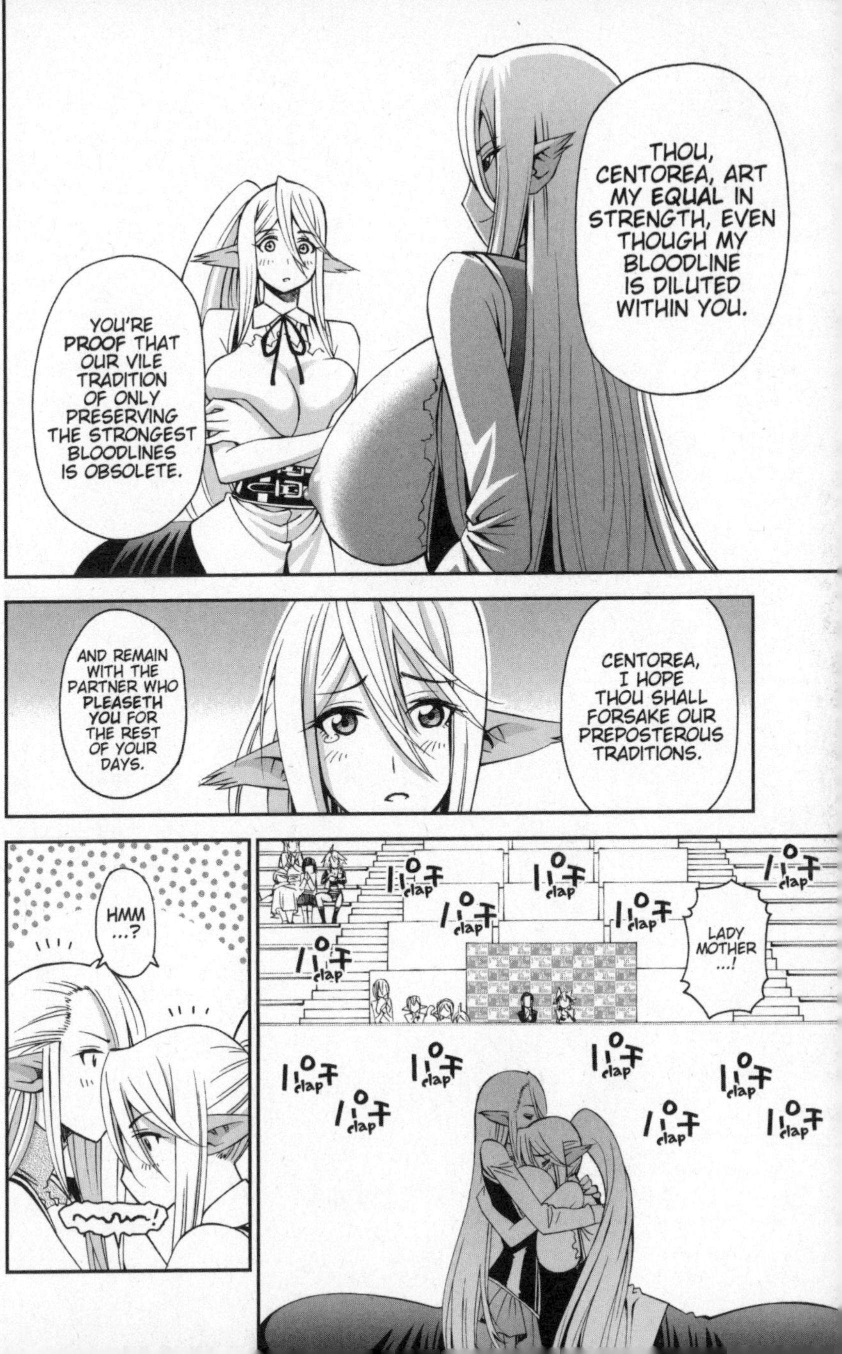
THOU, CENTOREA, ART MY EQUAL IN STRENGTH, EVEN THOUGH MY BLOODLINE IS DILUTED WITHIN YOU.
YOU'RE PROOF THAT OUR VILE TRADITION OF ONLY PRESERVING THE STRONGEST BLOODLINES IS OBSOLETE.
CENTOREA, I HOPE THOU SHALL FORSAKE OUR PREPOSTEROUS TRADITIONS.
AND REMAIN WITH THE PARTNER WHO PLEASETH YOU FOR THE REST OF YOUR DAYS.
パチ clap
パチ clap
パチ clap
パチ clap
パチ clap
パチ clap
LADY MOTHER ...!
パチ clap
パチ clap
パチ clap
パチ clap
パチ clap
パチ clap
パチ clap
HMM ...?

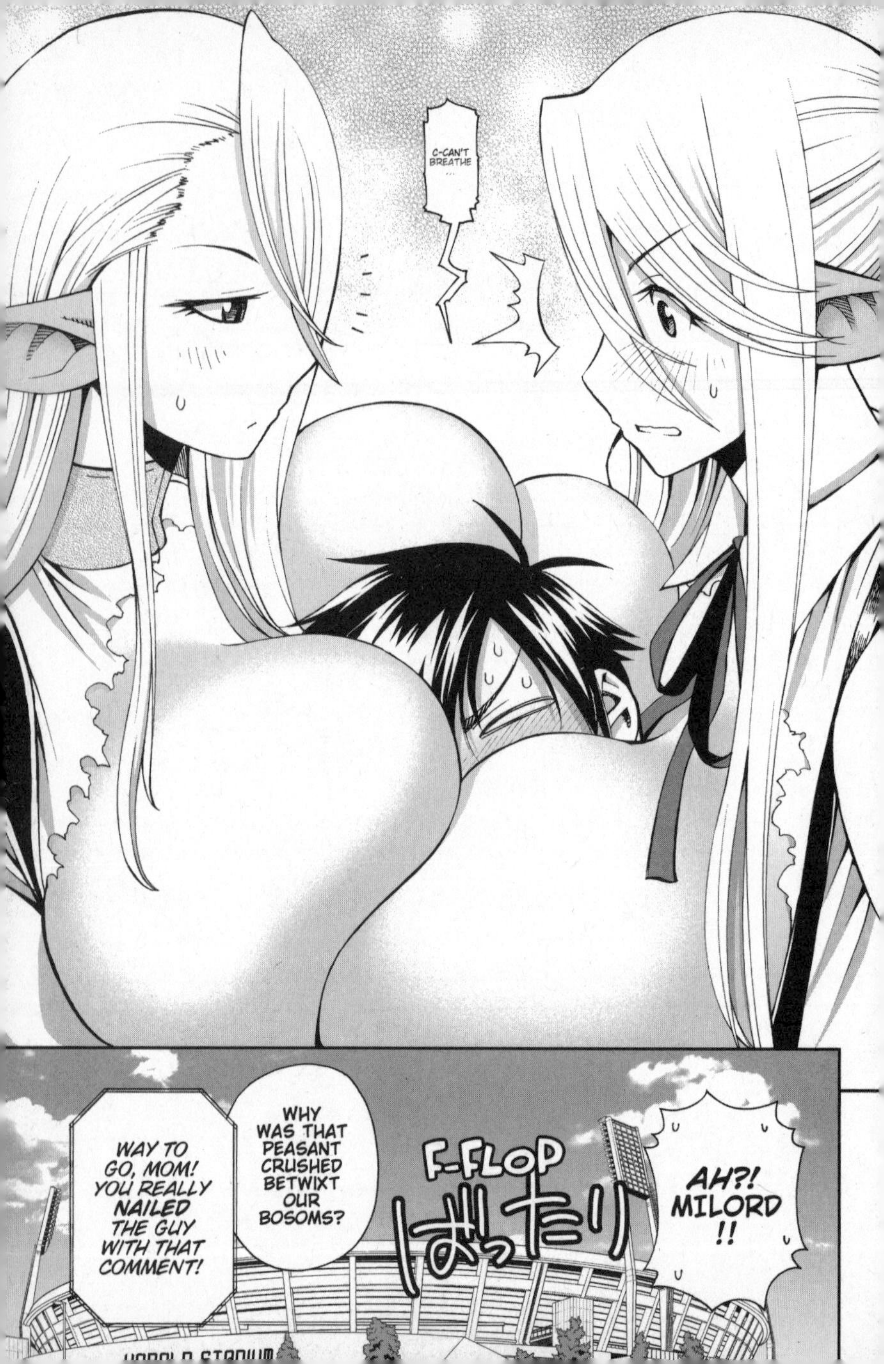
C-CAN'T BREATHE ...
AH?! MILORD !!
F-FLOP
ぱったり
WHY WAS THAT PEASANT CRUSHED BETWIXT OUR BOSOMS?
WAY TO GO, MOM! YOU REALLY NAILED THE GUY WITH THAT COMMENT!

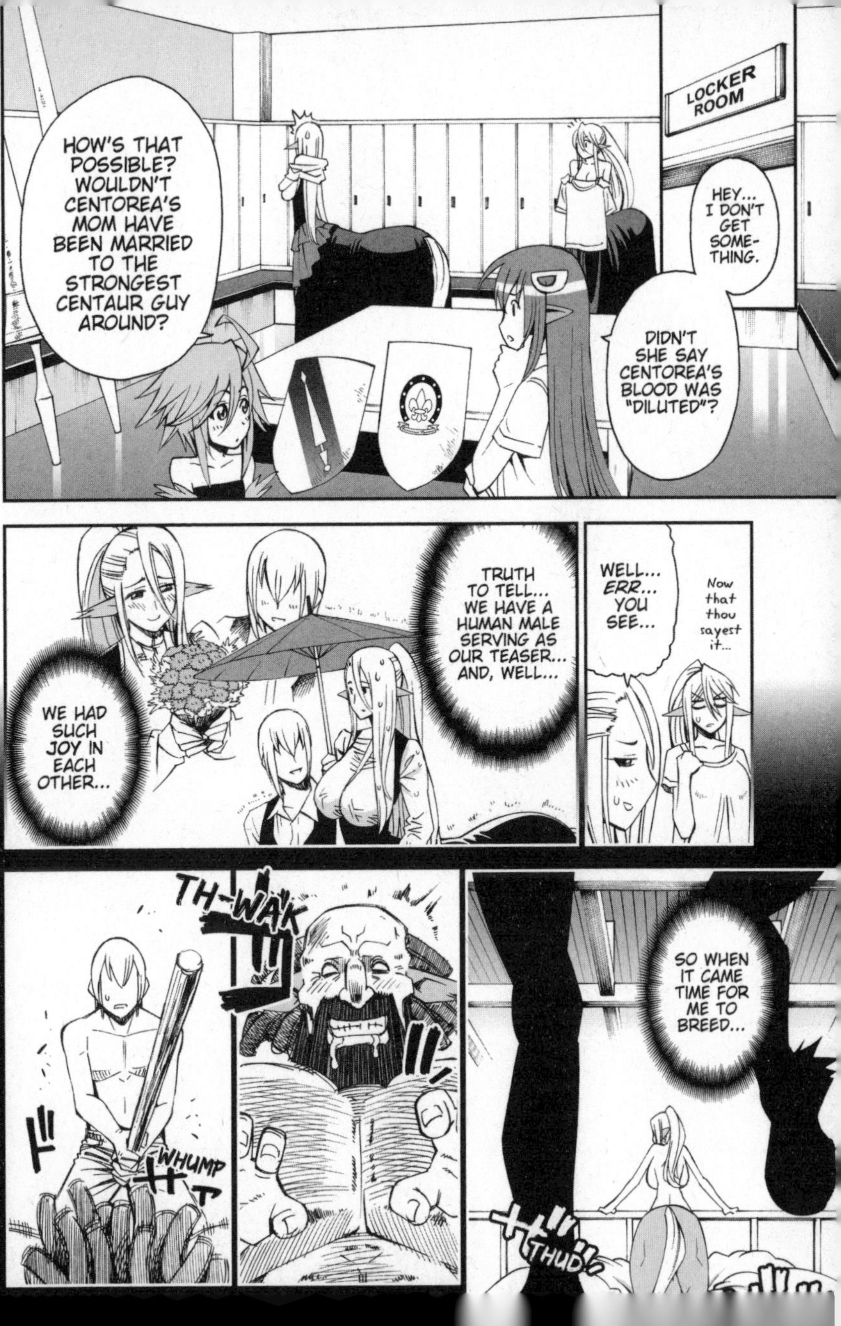
LOCKER ROOM
HEY... I DON'T GET SOMETHING.
DIDN'T SHE SAY CENTOREA'S BLOOD WAS "DILUTED"?
HOW'S THAT POSSIBLE? WOULDN'T CENTOREA'S MOM HAVE BEEN MARRIED TO THE STRONGEST CENTAUR GUY AROUND?
Now that thou sayest it...
WELL... ERR... YOU SEE...
TRUTH TO TELL... WE HAVE A HUMAN MALE SERVING AS OUR TEASER... AND, WELL...
WE HAD SUCH JOY IN EACH OTHER...
SO WHEN IT CAME TIME FOR ME TO BREED...
THUD
TH-WAK
WHUMP

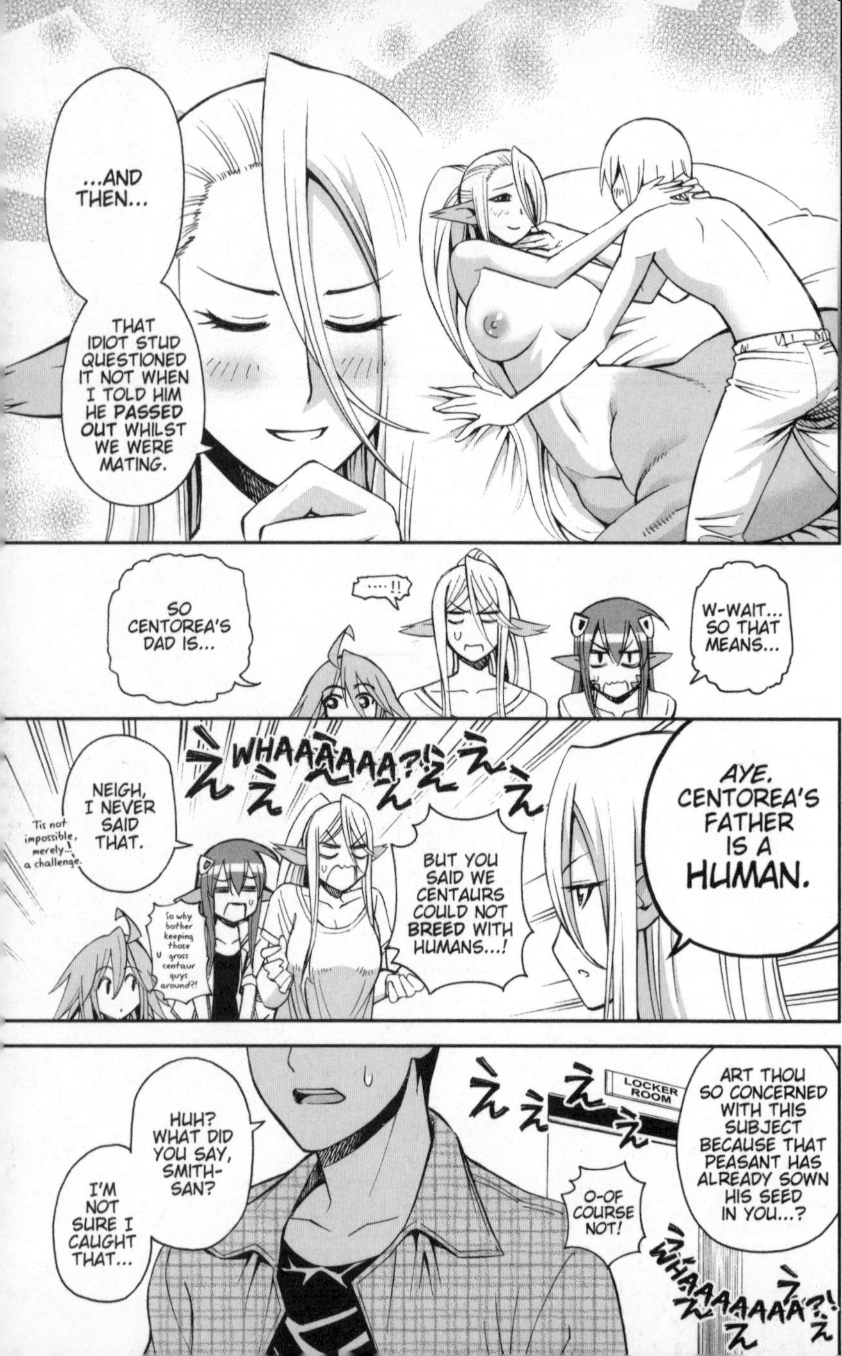

...AND THEN...
THAT IDIOT STUD QUESTIONED IT NOT WHEN I TOLD HIM HE PASSED OUT WHILST WE WERE MATING.
W-WAIT... SO THAT MEANS...
....!!
SO CENTOREA'S DAD IS...
AYE. CENTOREA'S FATHER IS A HUMAN.
WHAAAAAAA?!
BUT YOU SAID WE CENTAURS COULD NOT BREED WITH HUMANS...!
So why bother keeping those gross centaur guys around?!
NEIGH, I NEVER SAID THAT.
Tis not impossible, merely... a challenge.
ART THOU SO CONCERNED WITH THIS SUBJECT BECAUSE THAT PEASANT HAS ALREADY SOWN HIS SEED IN YOU...?
WHAAAAAAAA?!
LOCKER ROOM
O-OF COURSE NOT!
HUH? WHAT DID YOU SAY, SMITH-SAN?
I'M NOT SURE I CAUGHT THAT...

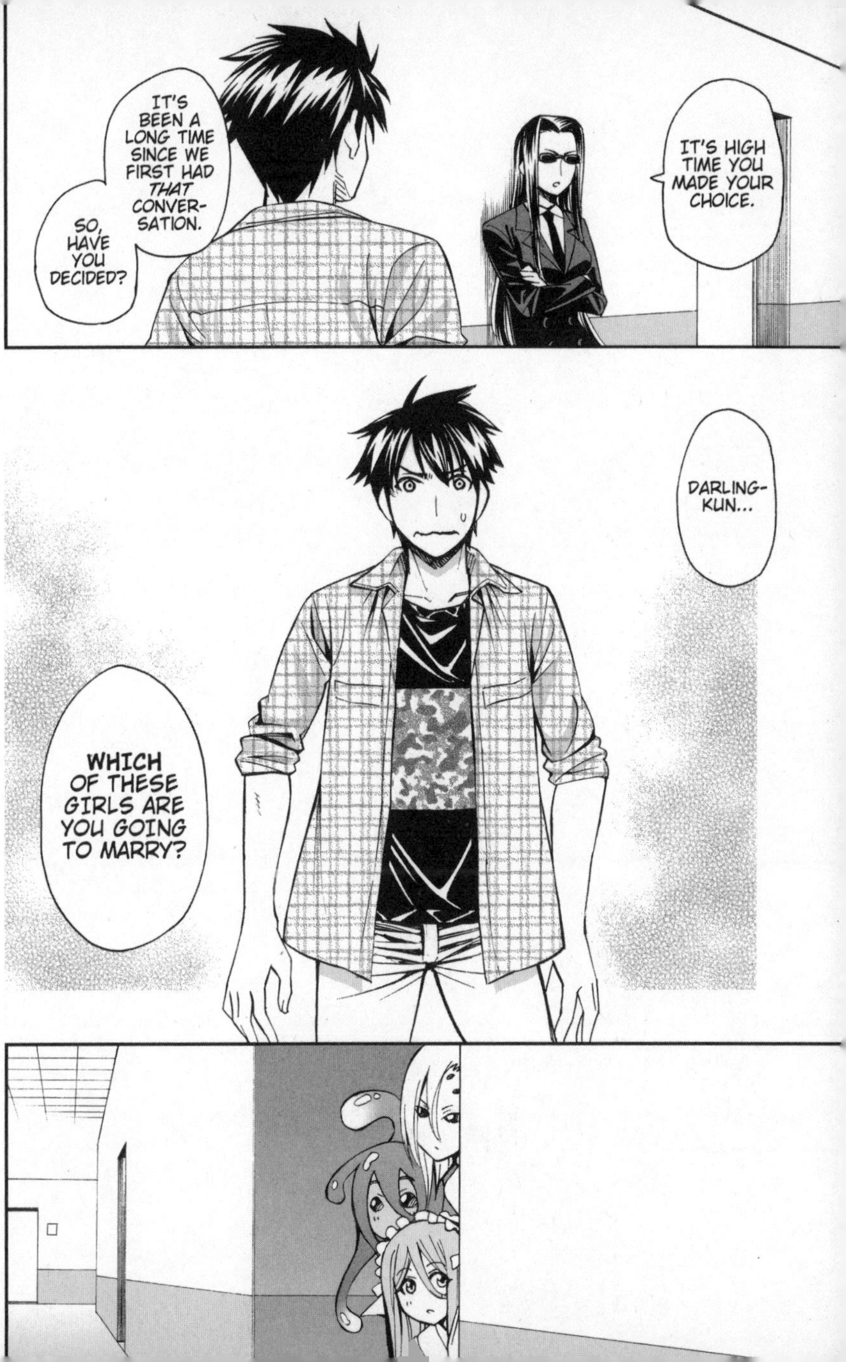
IT'S HIGH TIME YOU MADE YOUR CHOICE.
IT'S BEEN A LONG TIME SINCE WE FIRST HAD *THAT* CONVERSATION.
SO, HAVE YOU DECIDED?
DARLING-KUN...
WHICH OF THESE GIRLS ARE YOU GOING TO MARRY?

Monster Musume

Everyday Life with Monster Girls

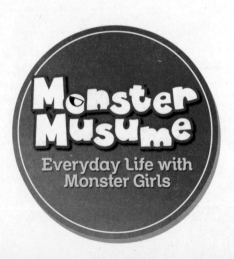

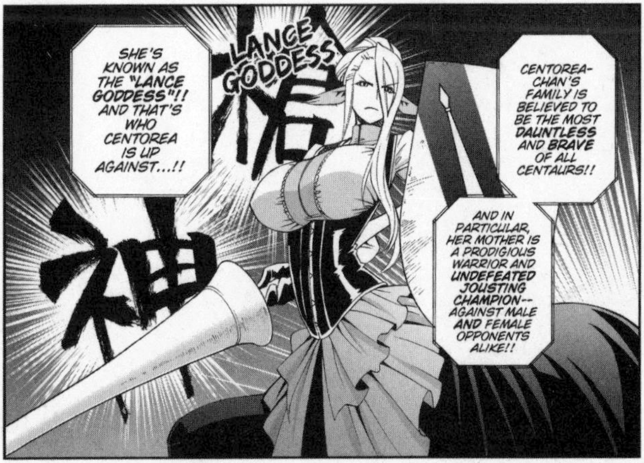
CENTOREA-CHAN'S FAMILY IS BELIEVED TO BE THE MOST DAUNTLESS AND BRAVE OF ALL CENTAURS!!
AND IN PARTICULAR, HER MOTHER IS A PRODIGIOUS WARRIOR AND UNDEFEATED JOUSTING CHAMPION--AGAINST MALE AND FEMALE OPPONENTS ALIKE!!
LANCE GODDESS
SHE'S KNOWN AS THE "LANCE GODDESS"!! AND THAT'S WHO CENTOREA IS UP AGAINST...!!

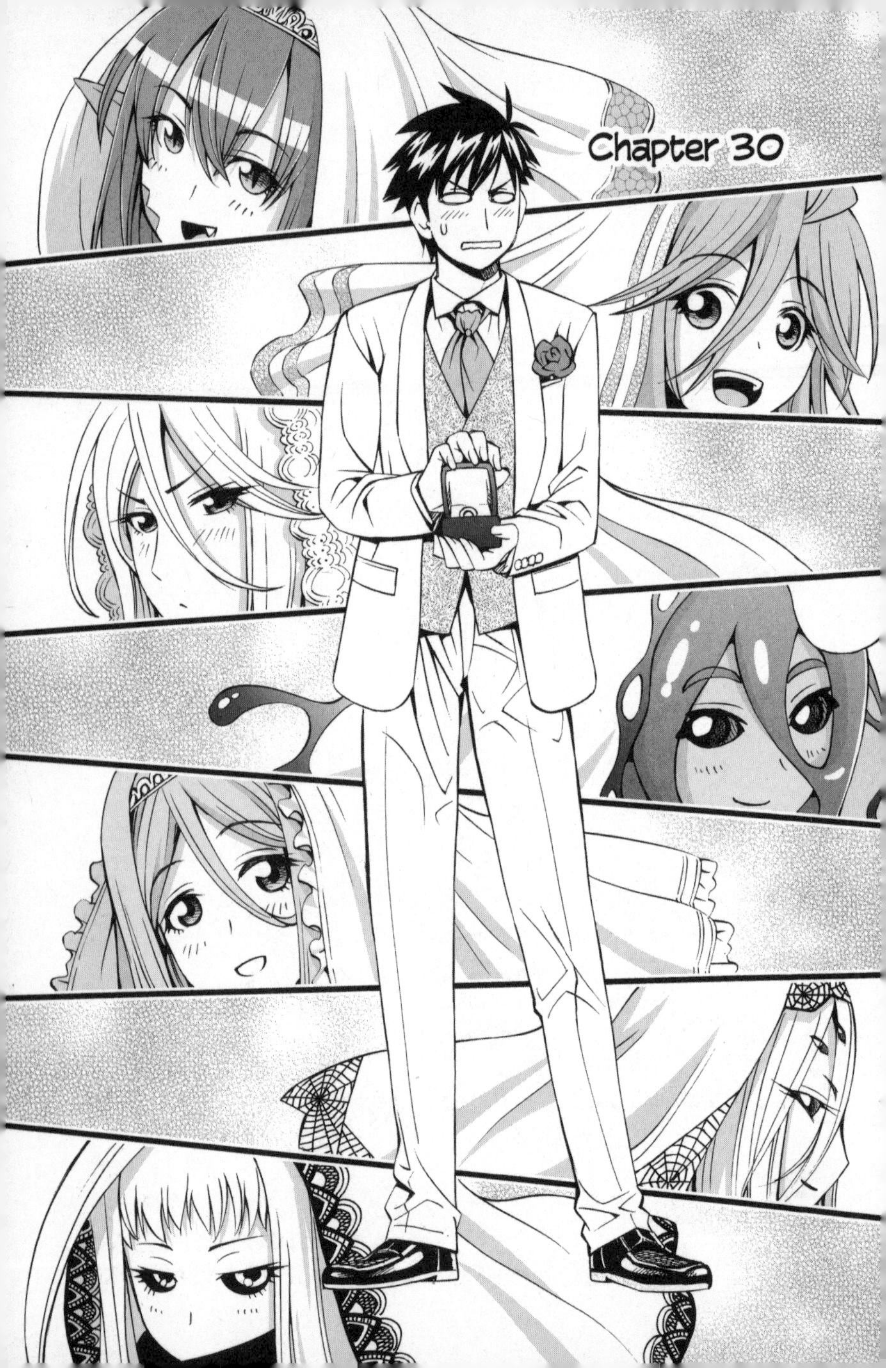
Chapter 30

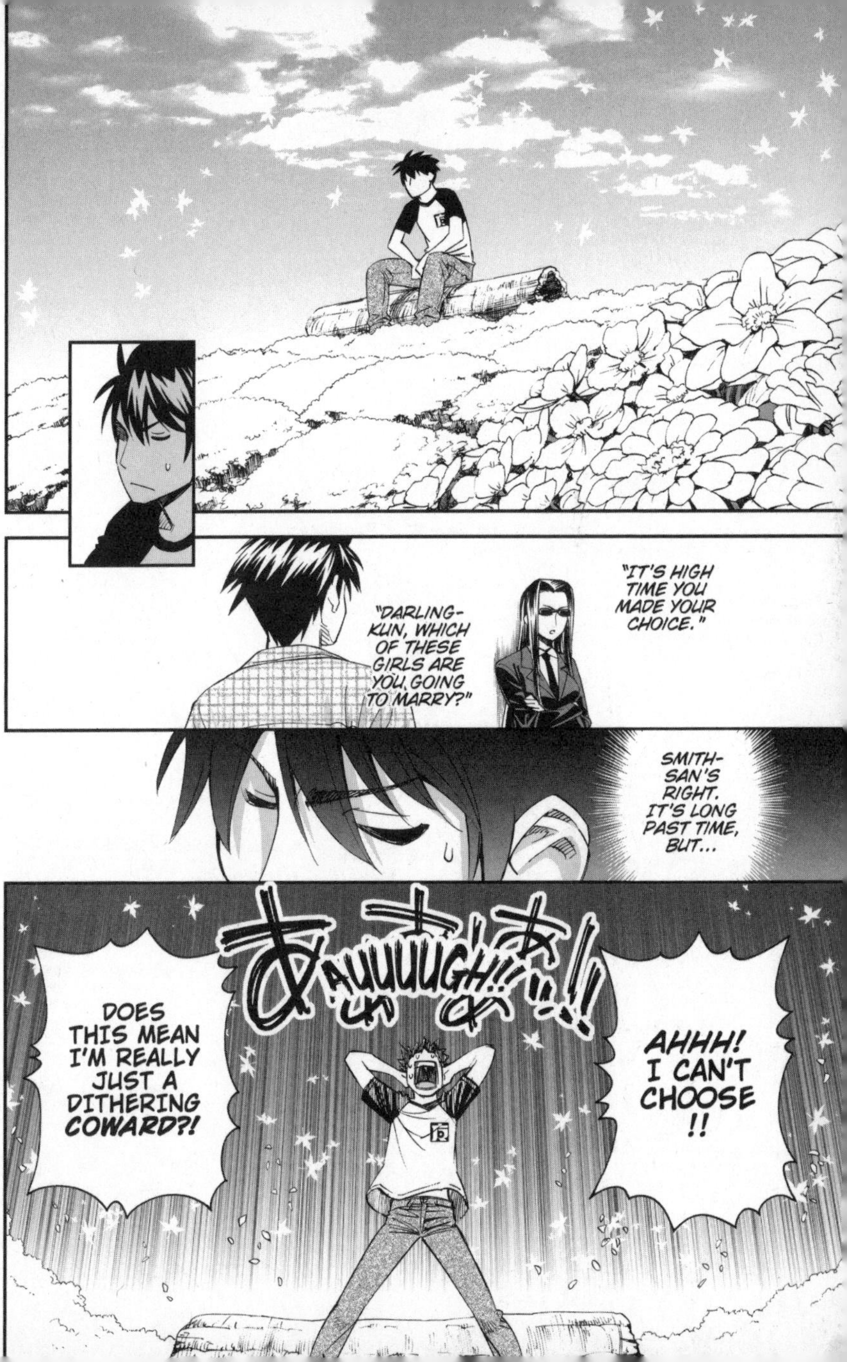
"IT'S HIGH TIME YOU MADE YOUR CHOICE."
"DARLING-KUN, WHICH OF THESE GIRLS ARE YOU GOING TO MARRY?"
SMITH-SAN'S RIGHT. IT'S LONG PAST TIME, BUT...
AUUUUGH!!
AHHH! I CAN'T CHOOSE !!
DOES THIS MEAN I'M REALLY JUST A DITHERING COWARD?!

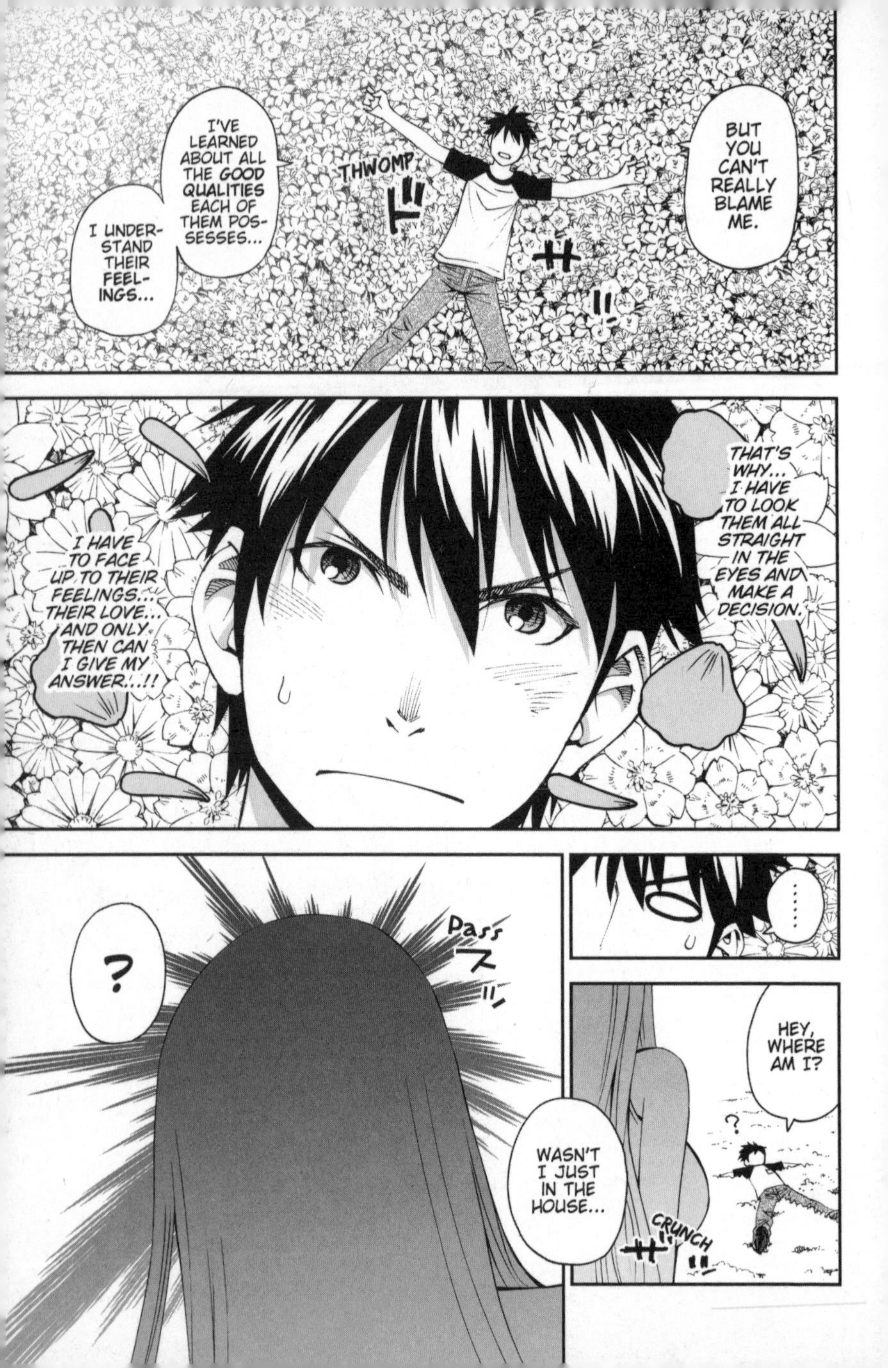
BUT YOU CAN'T REALLY BLAME ME.
THWOMP
I'VE LEARNED ABOUT ALL THE GOOD QUALITIES EACH OF THEM POSSESSES...
I UNDER-STAND THEIR FEEL-INGS...
THAT'S WHY... I HAVE TO LOOK THEM ALL STRAIGHT IN THE EYES AND MAKE A DECISION.
I HAVE TO FACE UP TO THEIR FEELINGS... THEIR LOVE... AND ONLY THEN CAN I GIVE MY ANSWER...!!
......
HEY, WHERE AM I?
?
WASN'T I JUST IN THE HOUSE...
CRUNCH
Pass
?

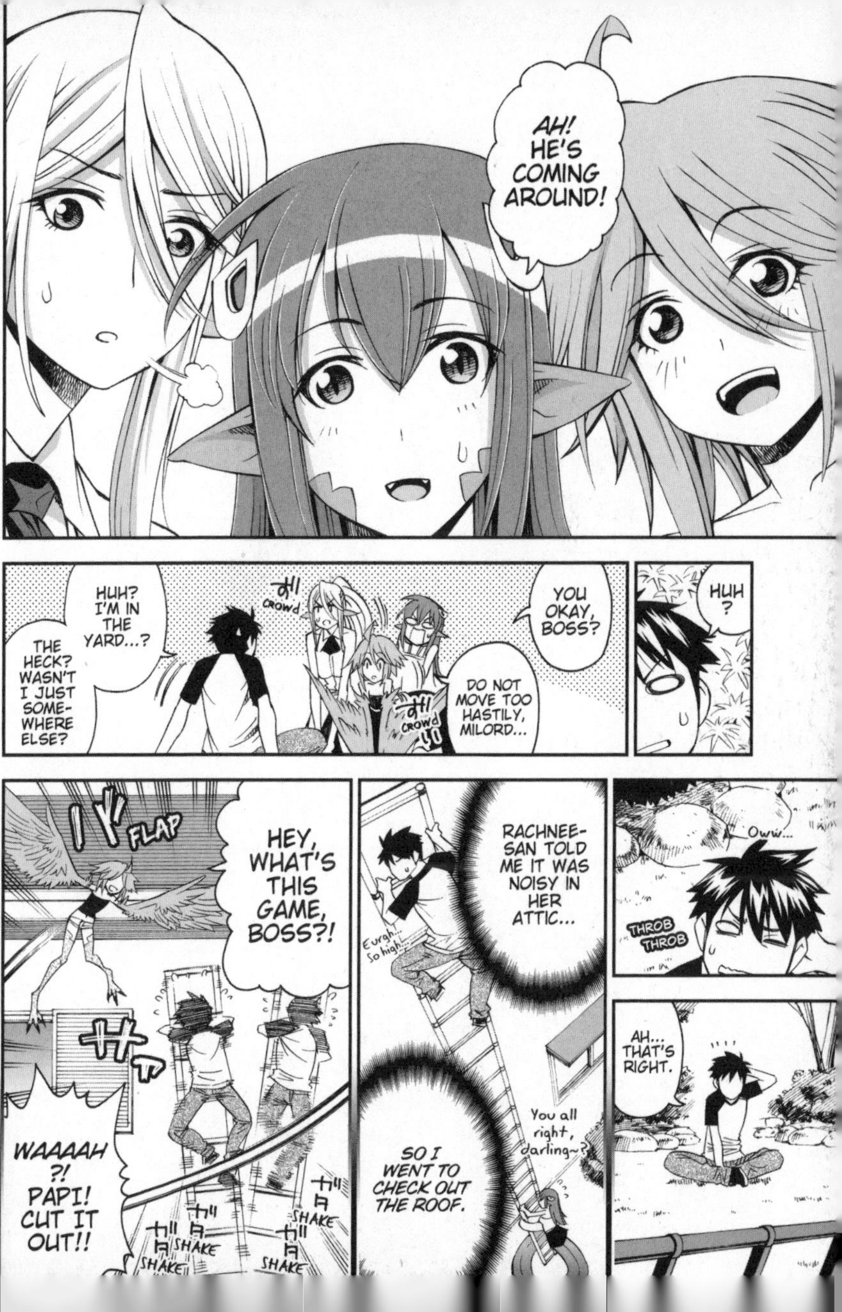
AH! HE'S COMING AROUND!
HUH?
YOU OKAY, BOSS?
CROWD
DO NOT MOVE TOO HASTILY, MILORD...
CROWD
HUH? I'M IN THE YARD...?
THE HECK? WASN'T I JUST SOME-WHERE ELSE?
Oww...
THROB THROB
AH... THAT'S RIGHT.
RACHNEE-SAN TOLD ME IT WAS NOISY IN HER ATTIC...
Eurgh... So high...
You all right, darling~?
SO I WENT TO CHECK OUT THE ROOF.
HEY, WHAT'S THIS GAME, BOSS?!
FLAP
WAAAAH?! PAPI! CUT IT OUT!!
SHAKE
SHAKE
SHAKE
SHAKE

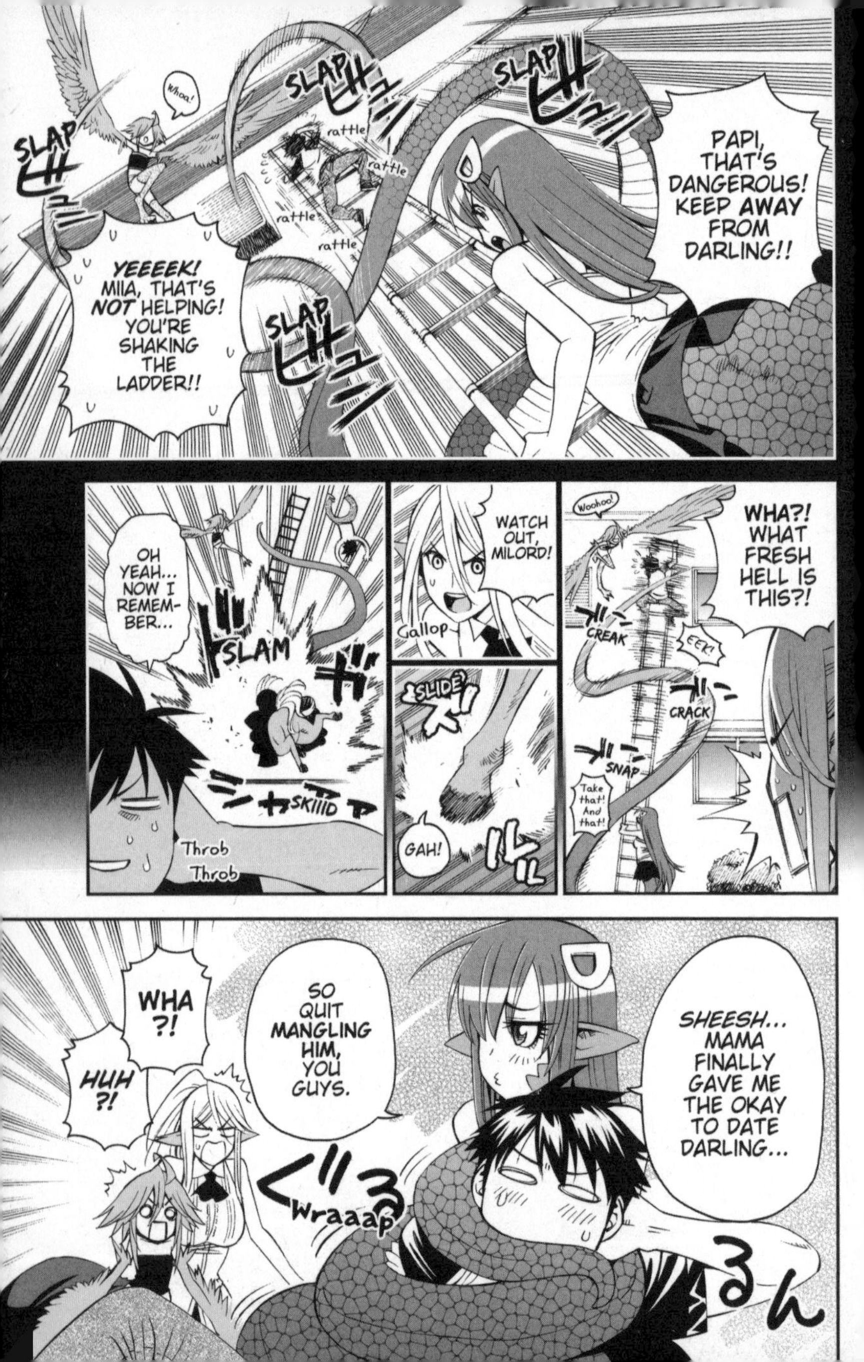
PAPI, THAT'S DANGEROUS! KEEP AWAY FROM DARLING!!
SLAP
SLAP
rattle
rattle
rattle
rattle
Whoa!
SLAP
SLAP
YEEEEK! MIIA, THAT'S NOT HELPING! YOU'RE SHAKING THE LADDER!!
WHA?! WHAT FRESH HELL IS THIS?!
Woohoo!
CREAK
EEK!
CRACK
SNAP
Take that! And that!
WATCH OUT, MILORD!
Gallop
SLIDE
GAH!
OH YEAH... NOW I REMEMBER...
SLAM
SKIIID
Throb Throb
SHEESH... MAMA FINALLY GAVE ME THE OKAY TO DATE DARLING...
SO QUIT MANGLING HIM, YOU GUYS.
WHA ?!
HUH ?!
Wraaap

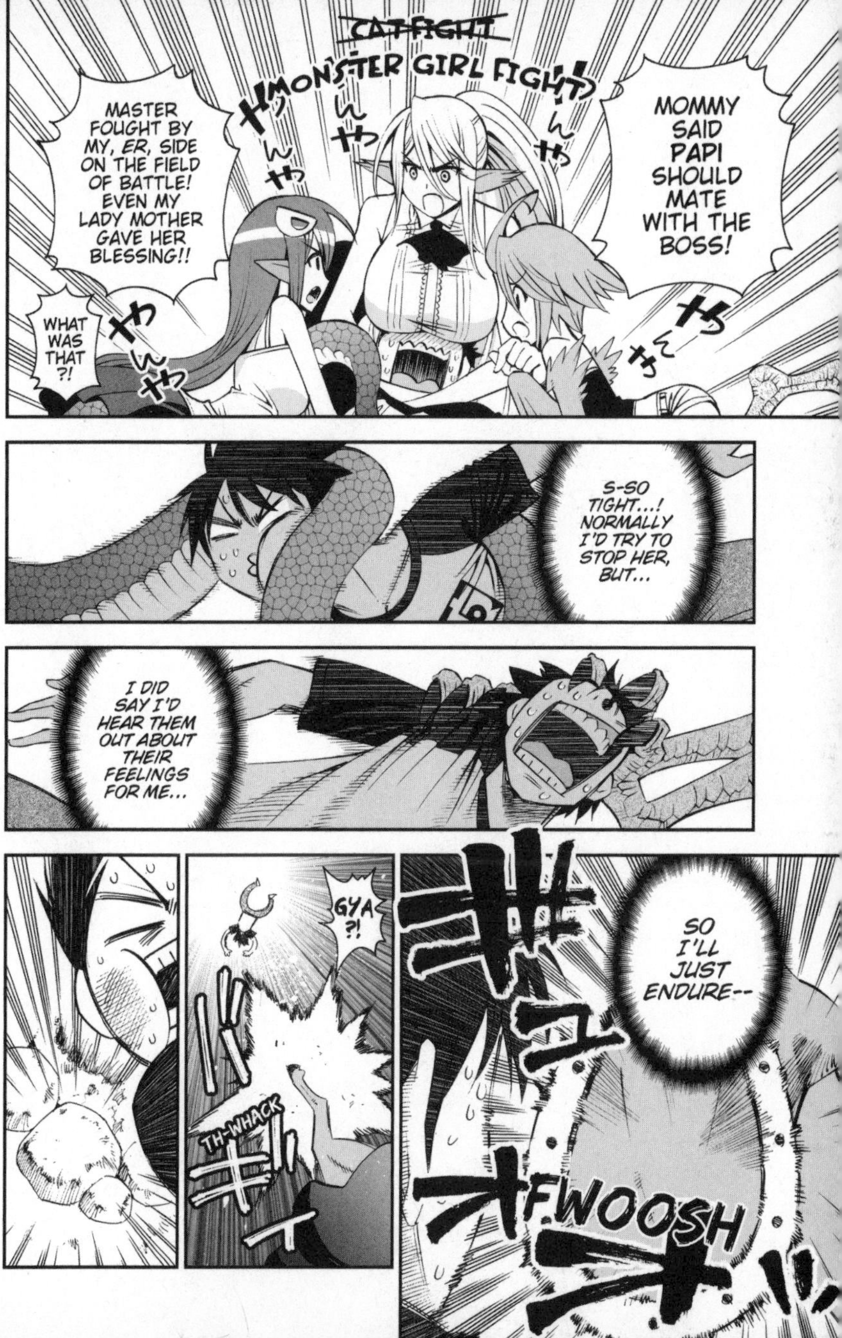
~~CAT FIGHT~~
MONSTER GIRL FIGHT!!
MOMMY SAID PAPI SHOULD MATE WITH THE BOSS!
MASTER FOUGHT BY MY, *ER*, SIDE ON THE FIELD OF BATTLE! EVEN MY LADY MOTHER GAVE HER BLESSING!!
WHAT WAS THAT?!
S-SO TIGHT...! NORMALLY I'D TRY TO STOP HER, BUT...
I DID SAY I'D HEAR THEM OUT ABOUT THEIR FEELINGS FOR ME...
SO I'LL JUST ENDURE--
FWOOSH
GYA?!
TH-WHACK

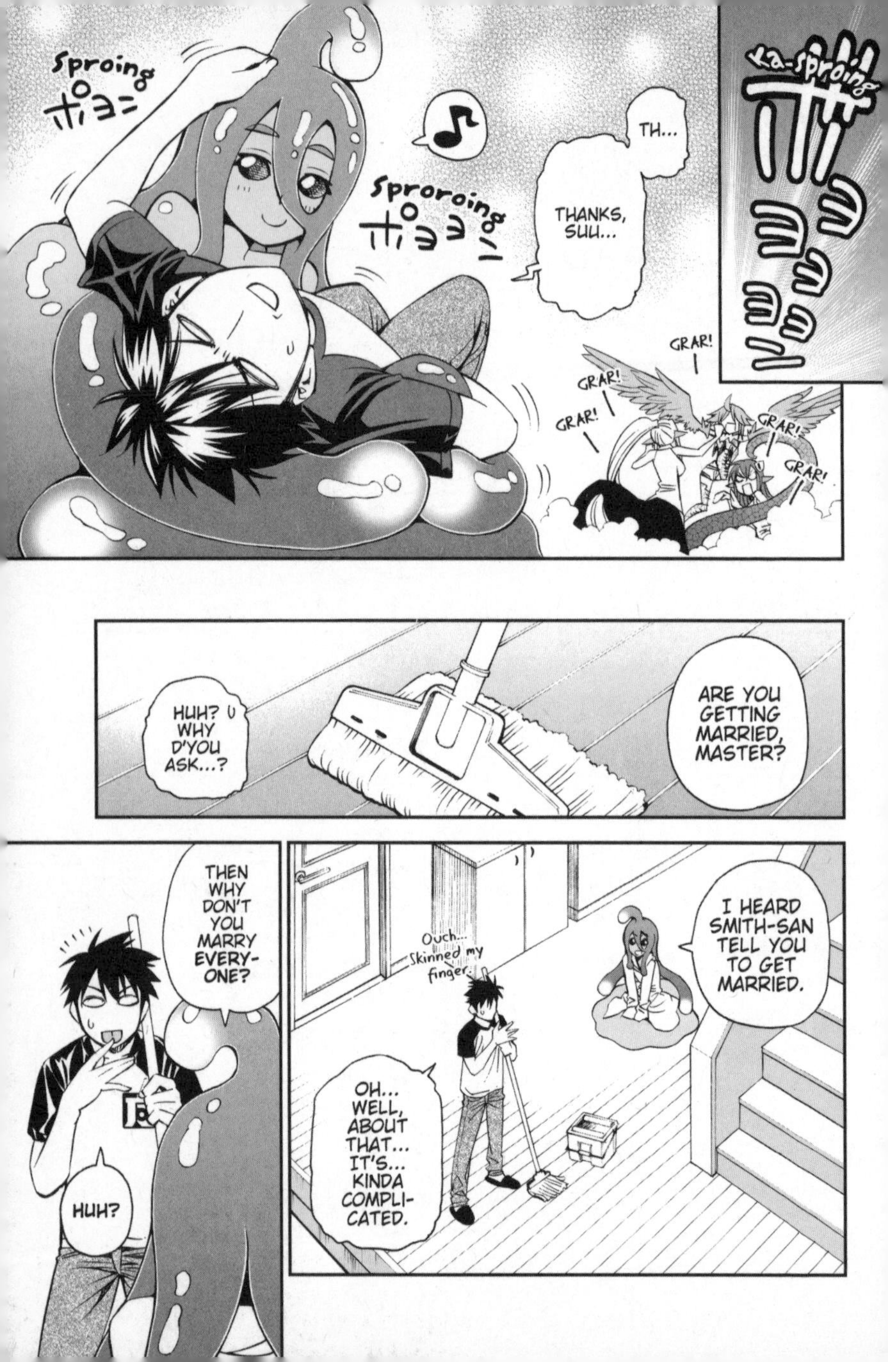

Ka-sproing
TH...
THANKS, SUU...
GRAR!
GRAR!
GRAR!
GRAR!
GRAR!
Sproroing
ポヨヨン
♪
Sproing
ポヨン
ARE YOU GETTING MARRIED, MASTER?
HUH? WHY D'YOU ASK...?
I HEARD SMITH-SAN TELL YOU TO GET MARRIED.
Ouch... Skinned my finger.
OH... WELL, ABOUT THAT... IT'S... KINDA COMPLICATED.
THEN WHY DON'T YOU MARRY EVERYONE?
HUH?

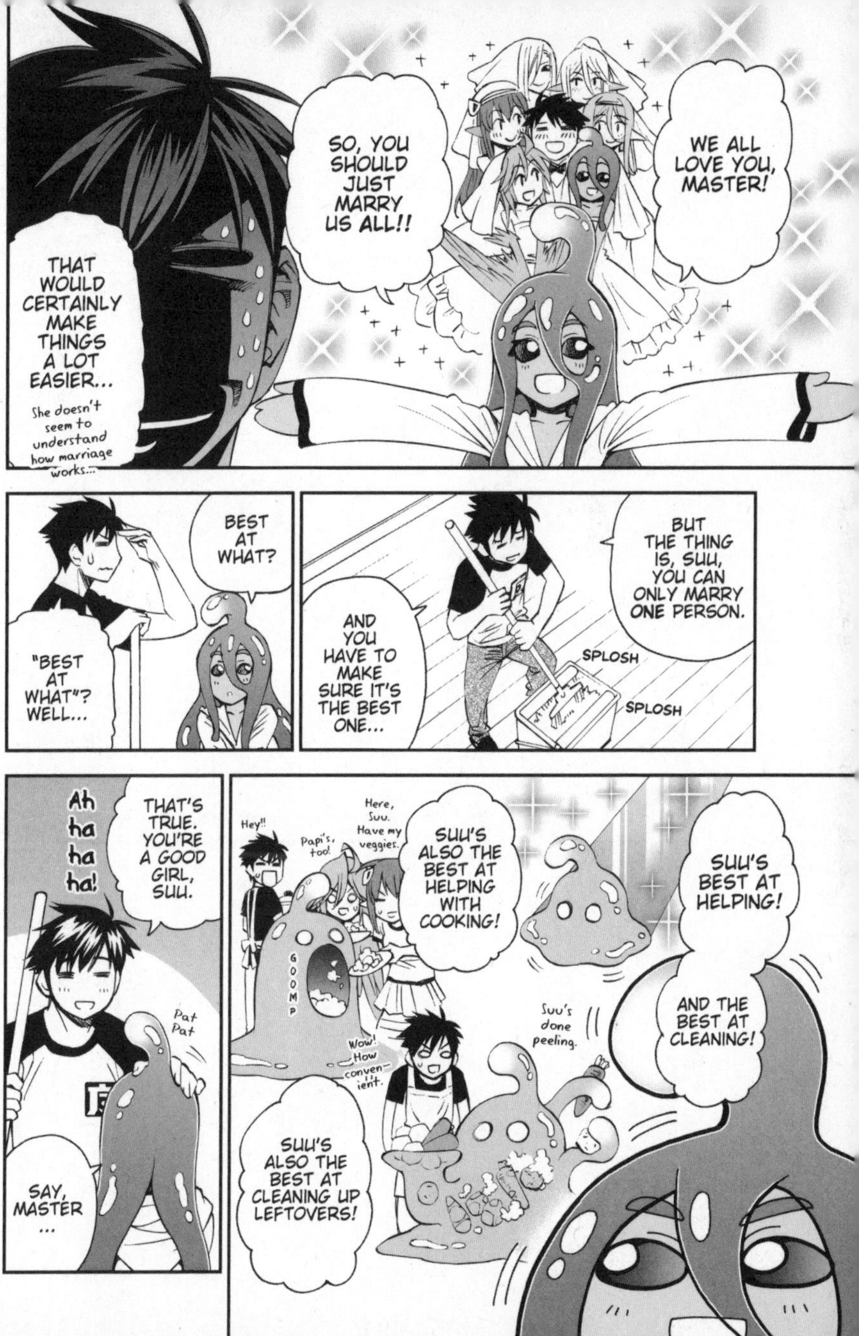
WE ALL LOVE YOU, MASTER!
SO, YOU SHOULD JUST MARRY US ALL!!
THAT WOULD CERTAINLY MAKE THINGS A LOT EASIER...
She doesn't seem to understand how marriage works...
BUT THE THING IS, SUU, YOU CAN ONLY MARRY ONE PERSON.
AND YOU HAVE TO MAKE SURE IT'S THE BEST ONE...
SPLOSH
SPLOSH
BEST AT WHAT?
"BEST AT WHAT"? WELL...
SUU'S BEST AT HELPING!
SUU'S ALSO THE BEST AT HELPING WITH COOKING!
Here, Suu. Have my veggies.
Papi's, too!
Hey!!
GOOOMP
AND THE BEST AT CLEANING!
Suu's done peeling.
Wow! How conven-ient.
SUU'S ALSO THE BEST AT CLEANING UP LEFTOVERS!
THAT'S TRUE. YOU'RE A GOOD GIRL, SUU.
Ah ha ha ha!
Pat Pat
SAY, MASTER ...

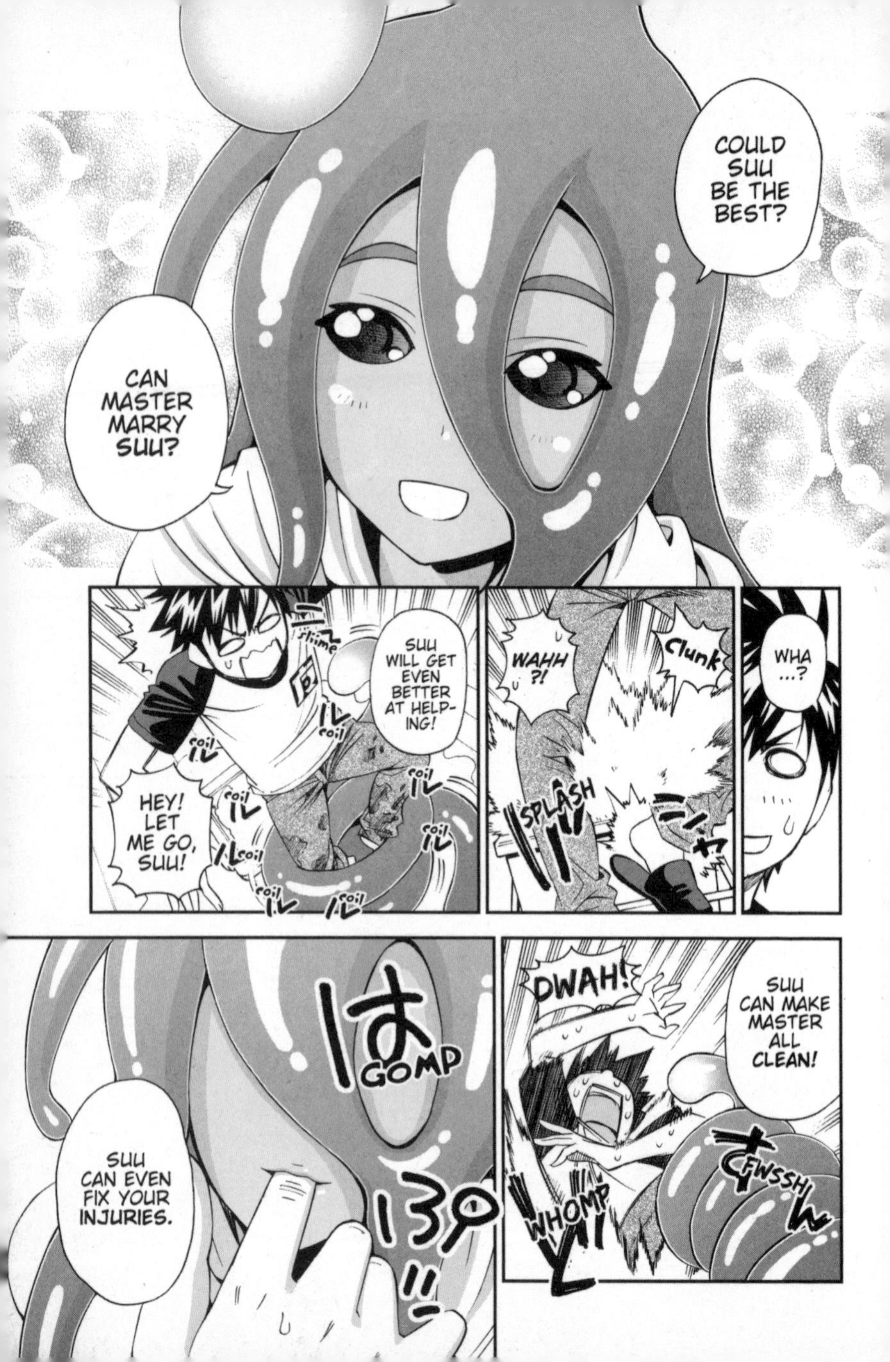
COULD SUU BE THE BEST?
CAN MASTER MARRY SUU?
WHA ...?
Clunk
WAHH ?!
SPLASH
sliime
SUU WILL GET EVEN BETTER AT HELP-ING!
HEY! LET ME GO, SUU!
coil
DWAH!
SUU CAN MAKE MASTER ALL CLEAN!
FWSSH
WHOMP
GOMP
SUU CAN EVEN FIX YOUR INJURIES.

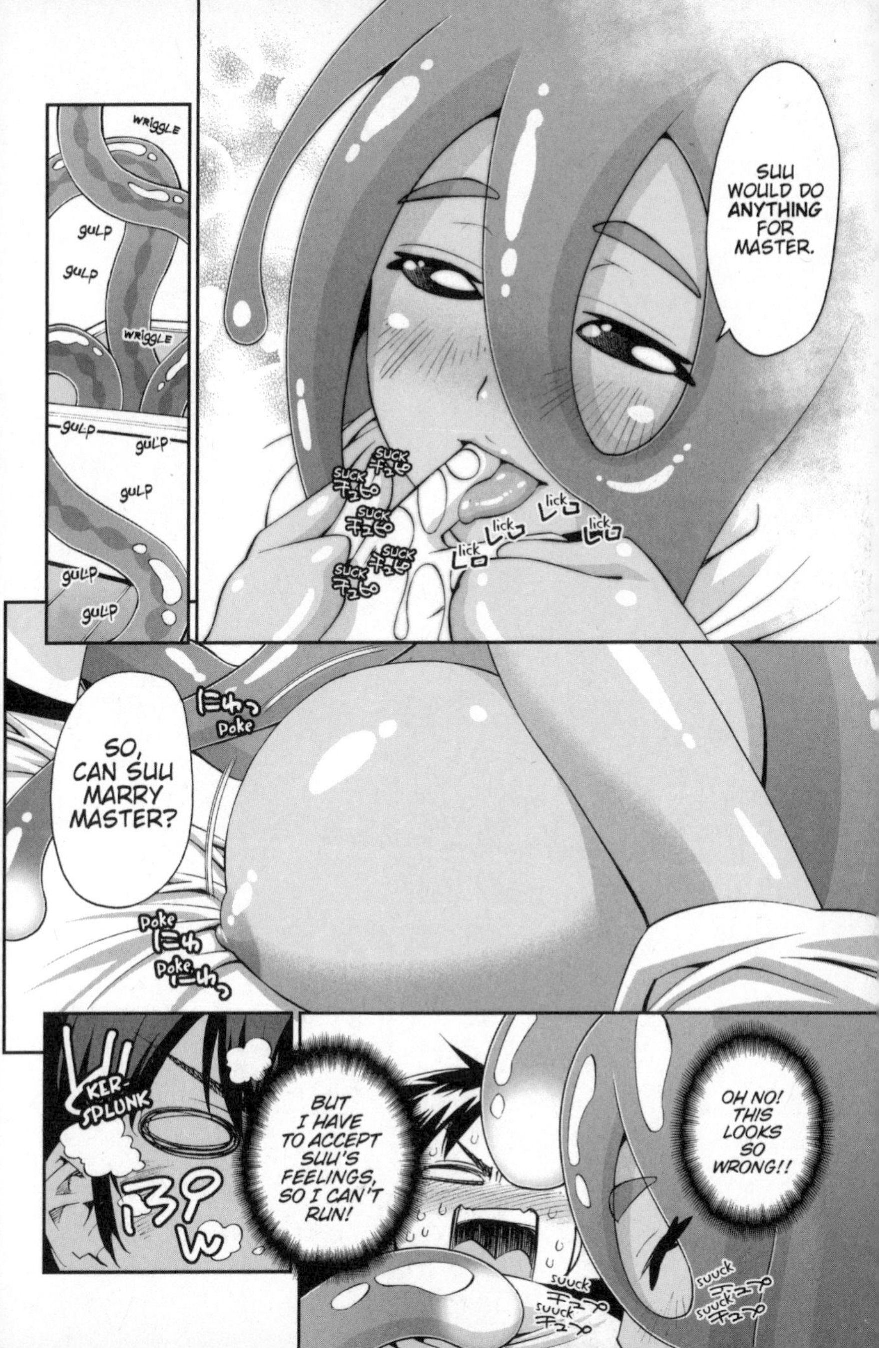
SUU WOULD DO ANYTHING FOR MASTER.
suck
suck
suck
suck
suck
lick
lick
lick
lick
wriggle
gulp
gulp
wriggle
gulp
gulp
gulp
gulp
gulp
SO, CAN SUU MARRY MASTER?
poke
poke
poke
OH NO! THIS LOOKS SO WRONG!!
BUT I HAVE TO ACCEPT SUU'S FEELINGS, SO I CAN'T RUN!
suuck
suuck
suuck
suuck
KER-SPLUNK

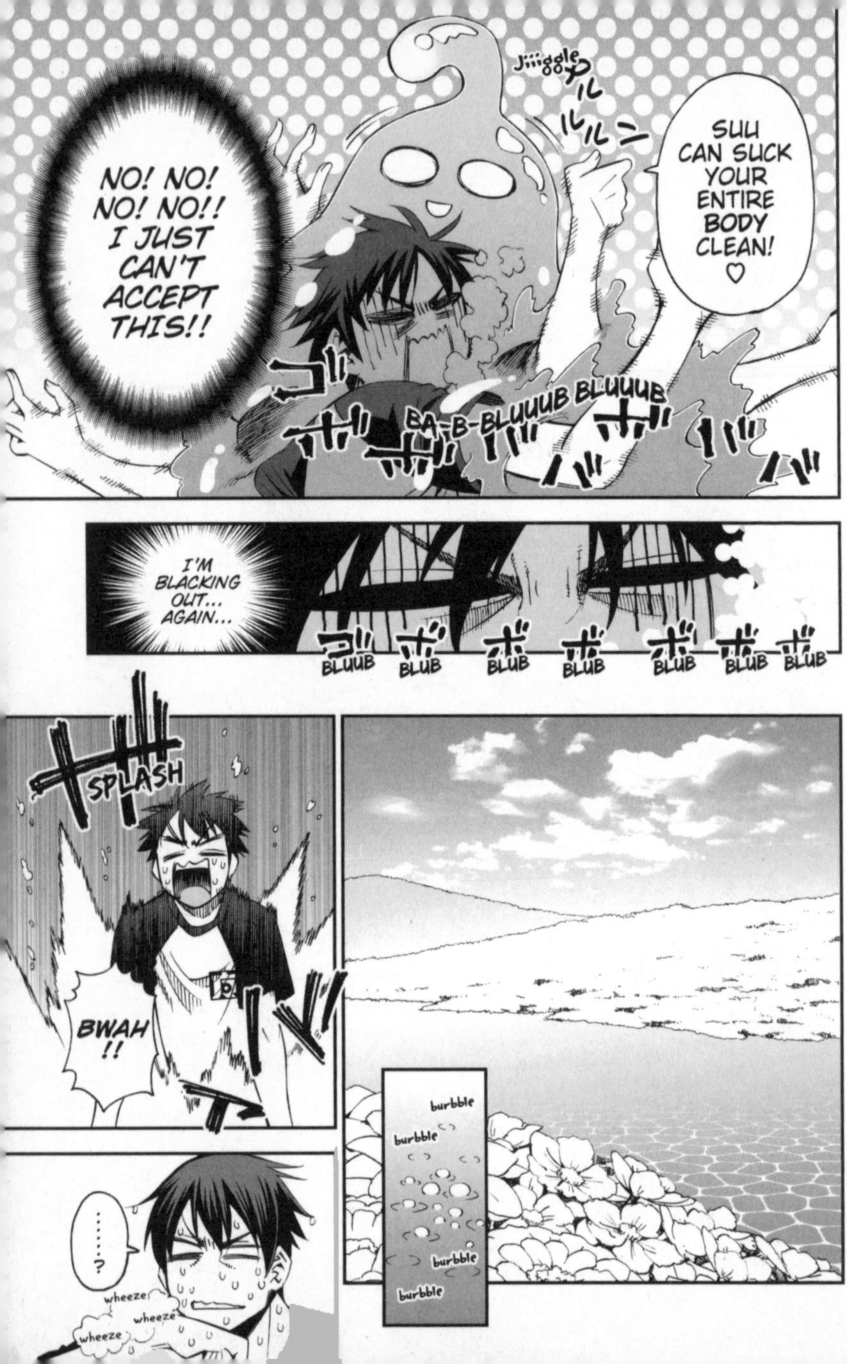
Jiiiggle
SUU CAN SUCK YOUR ENTIRE BODY CLEAN! ♡
NO! NO! NO! NO!! I JUST CAN'T ACCEPT THIS!!
BA-B-BLUUUB BLUUUB
I'M BLACKING OUT... AGAIN...
BLUUB BLUB BLUB BLUB BLUB BLUB BLUB
burbble
burbble
burbble
burbble
SPLASH
BWAH !!
......?
wheeze
wheeze
wheeze

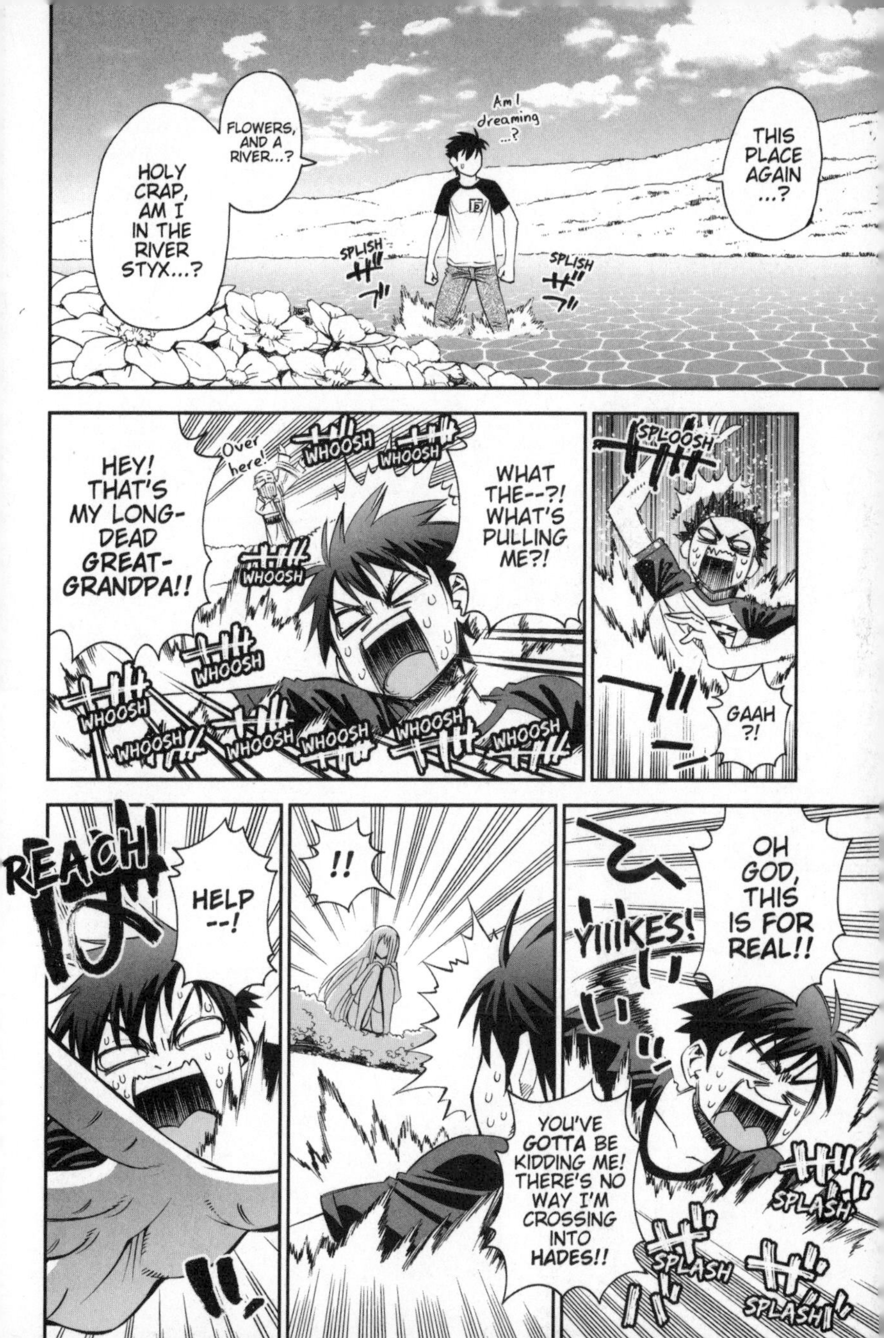
THIS PLACE AGAIN ...?
Am I dreaming ...?
FLOWERS, AND A RIVER...?
HOLY CRAP, AM I IN THE RIVER STYX...?
SPLISH
SPLISH
SPLOOSH
GAAH ?!
WHAT THE--?! WHAT'S PULLING ME?!
WHOOSH
WHOOSH
Over here!
HEY! THAT'S MY LONG-DEAD GREAT-GRANDPA!!
WHOOSH
WHOOSH
WHOOSH
WHOOSH
WHOOSH
WHOOSH
WHOOSH
WHOOSH
OH GOD, THIS IS FOR REAL!!
YIIIKES!
YOU'VE GOTTA BE KIDDING ME! THERE'S NO WAY I'M CROSSING INTO HADES!!
SPLASH
SPLASH
SPLASH
!!
REACH
HELP --!

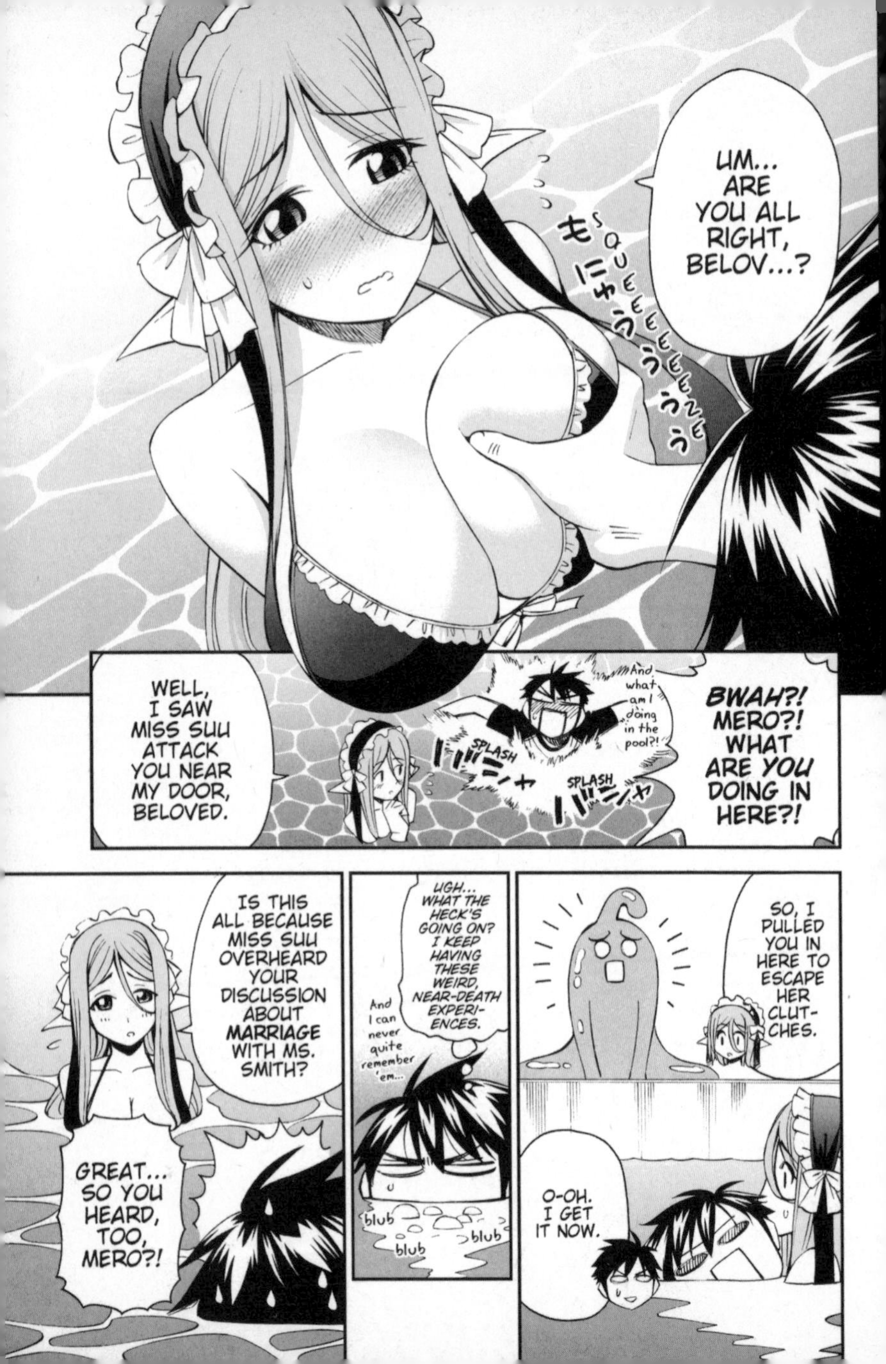
UM... ARE YOU ALL RIGHT, BELOV...?
SQUEEEEEEZE
もにゅうぅぅう
BWAH?! MERO?! WHAT ARE YOU DOING IN HERE?!
And what am I doing in the pool?!
SPLASH
SPLASH
WELL, I SAW MISS SUU ATTACK YOU NEAR MY DOOR, BELOVED.
SO, I PULLED YOU IN HERE TO ESCAPE HER CLUTCHES.
O-OH. I GET IT NOW.
UGH... WHAT THE HECK'S GOING ON? I KEEP HAVING THESE WEIRD, NEAR-DEATH EXPERI-ENCES.
And I can never quite remember 'em...
blub
blub
blub
IS THIS ALL BECAUSE MISS SUU OVERHEARD YOUR DISCUSSION ABOUT MARRIAGE WITH MS. SMITH?
GREAT... SO YOU HEARD, TOO, MERO?!

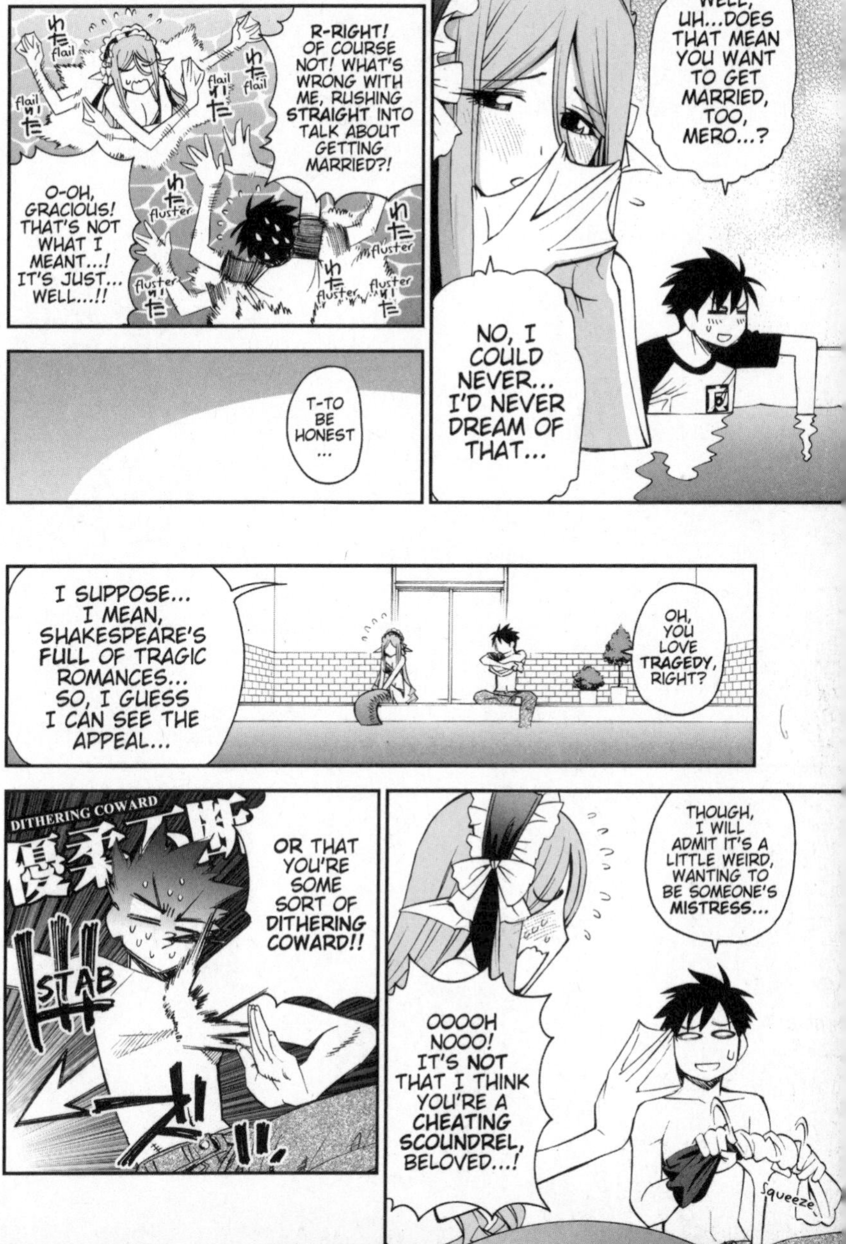
WELL, UH...DOES THAT MEAN YOU WANT TO GET MARRIED, TOO, MERO...?
NO, I COULD NEVER... I'D NEVER DREAM OF THAT...
R-RIGHT! OF COURSE NOT! WHAT'S WRONG WITH ME, RUSHING STRAIGHT INTO TALK ABOUT GETTING MARRIED?!
O-OH, GRACIOUS! THAT'S NOT WHAT I MEANT...! IT'S JUST... WELL...!!
flail
fluster
T-TO BE HONEST...
OH, YOU LOVE TRAGEDY, RIGHT?
I SUPPOSE... I MEAN, SHAKESPEARE'S FULL OF TRAGIC ROMANCES... SO, I GUESS I CAN SEE THE APPEAL...
THOUGH, I WILL ADMIT IT'S A LITTLE WEIRD, WANTING TO BE SOMEONE'S MISTRESS...
OOOOH NOOO! IT'S NOT THAT I THINK YOU'RE A CHEATING SCOUNDREL, BELOVED...!
Squeeze
DITHERING COWARD
優柔不断
OR THAT YOU'RE SOME SORT OF DITHERING COWARD!!
STAB

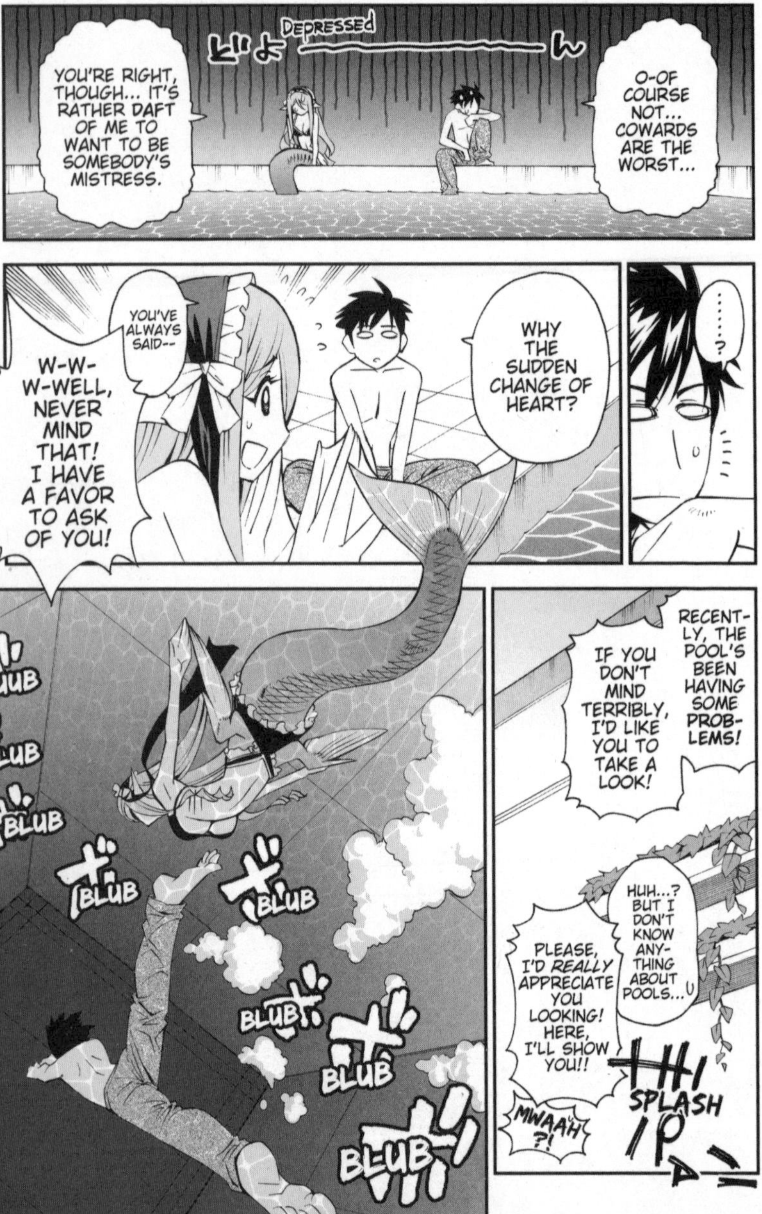
どよ DEPRESSED ん
O-OF COURSE NOT... COWARDS ARE THE WORST...
YOU'RE RIGHT, THOUGH... IT'S RATHER DAFT OF ME TO WANT TO BE SOMEBODY'S MISTRESS.
......?
WHY THE SUDDEN CHANGE OF HEART?
YOU'VE ALWAYS SAID--
W-W-W-WELL, NEVER MIND THAT! I HAVE A FAVOR TO ASK OF YOU!
RECENTLY, THE POOL'S BEEN HAVING SOME PROBLEMS!
IF YOU DON'T MIND TERRIBLY, I'D LIKE YOU TO TAKE A LOOK!
HUH...? BUT I DON'T KNOW ANYTHING ABOUT POOLS...
PLEASE, I'D *REALLY* APPRECIATE YOU LOOKING! HERE, I'LL SHOW YOU!!
SPLASH
MWAAH?!
BLUUB
BLUB
BLUB
BLUB
BLUB
BLUB
BLUB
BLUB

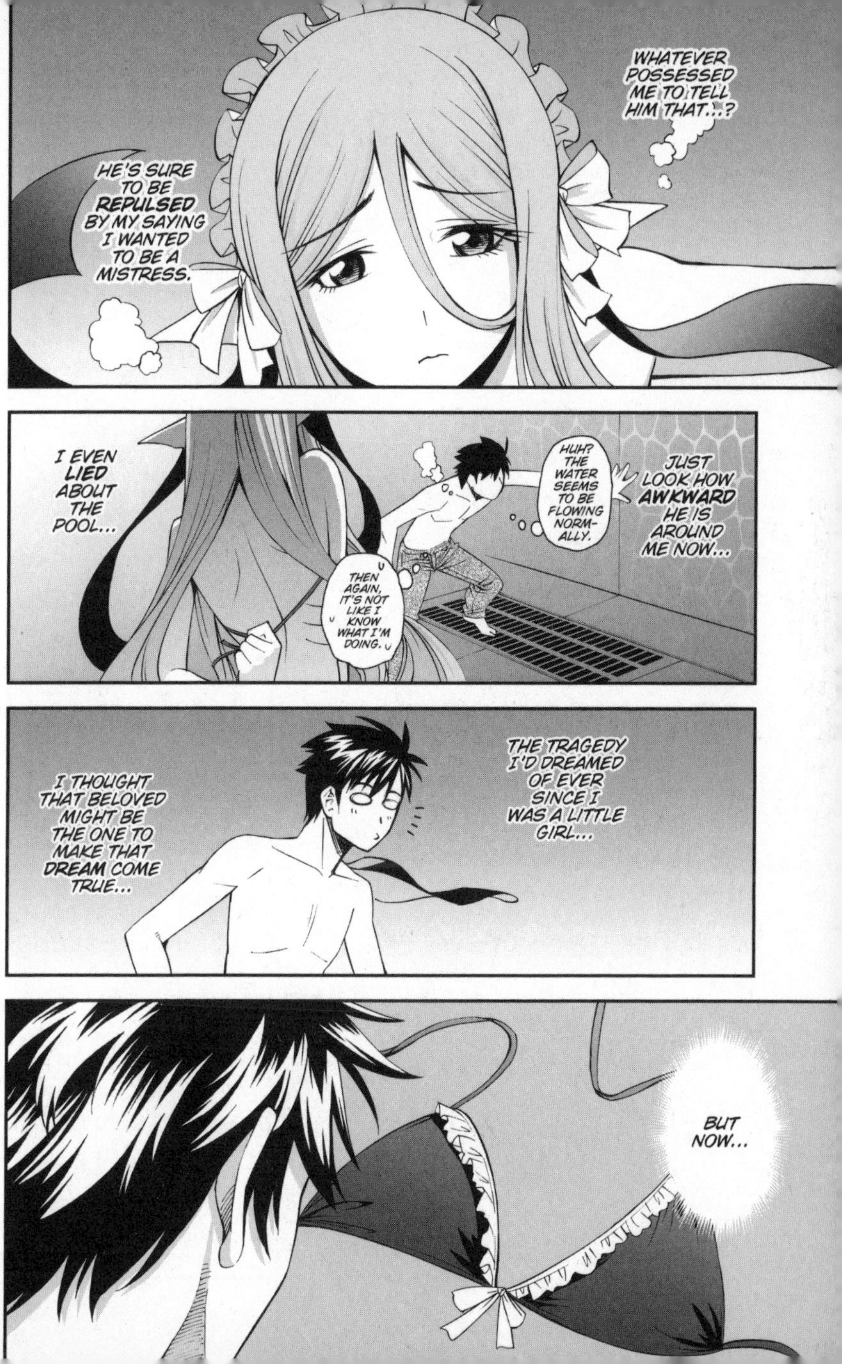
WHATEVER POSSESSED ME TO TELL HIM THAT...?
HE'S SURE TO BE REPULSED BY MY SAYING I WANTED TO BE A MISTRESS.
JUST LOOK HOW AWKWARD HE IS AROUND ME NOW...
HUH? THE WATER SEEMS TO BE FLOWING NORM-ALLY.
I EVEN LIED ABOUT THE POOL...
THEN AGAIN, IT'S NOT LIKE I KNOW WHAT I'M DOING.
THE TRAGEDY I'D DREAMED OF EVER SINCE I WAS A LITTLE GIRL...
I THOUGHT THAT BELOVED MIGHT BE THE ONE TO MAKE THAT DREAM COME TRUE...
BUT NOW...

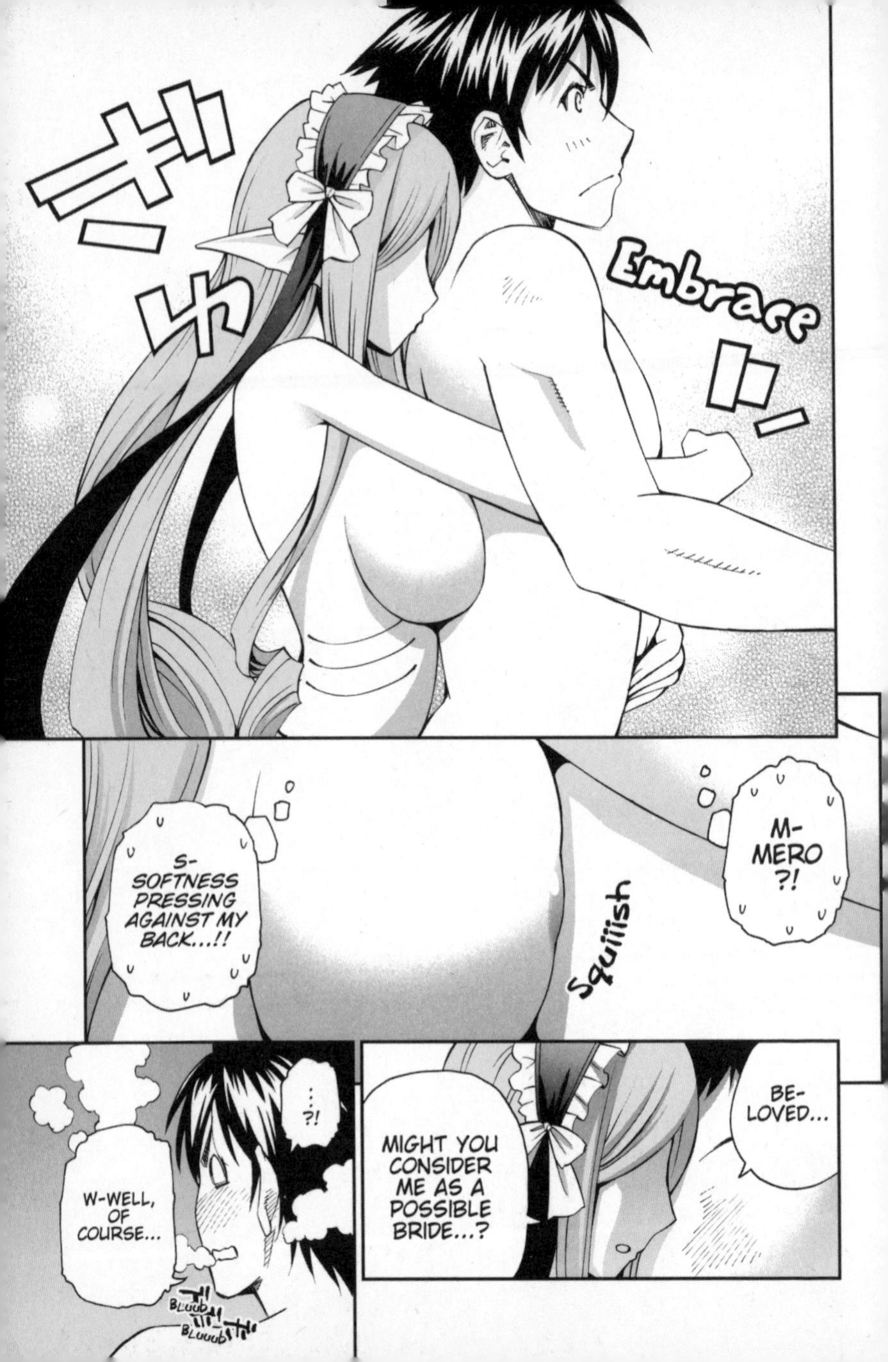

Embrace
M-MERO?!
S-SOFTNESS PRESSING AGAINST MY BACK...!!
Squiiish
BE-LOVED...
MIGHT YOU CONSIDER ME AS A POSSIBLE BRIDE...?
...?!
W-WELL, OF COURSE...
Bluuub
Bluuub

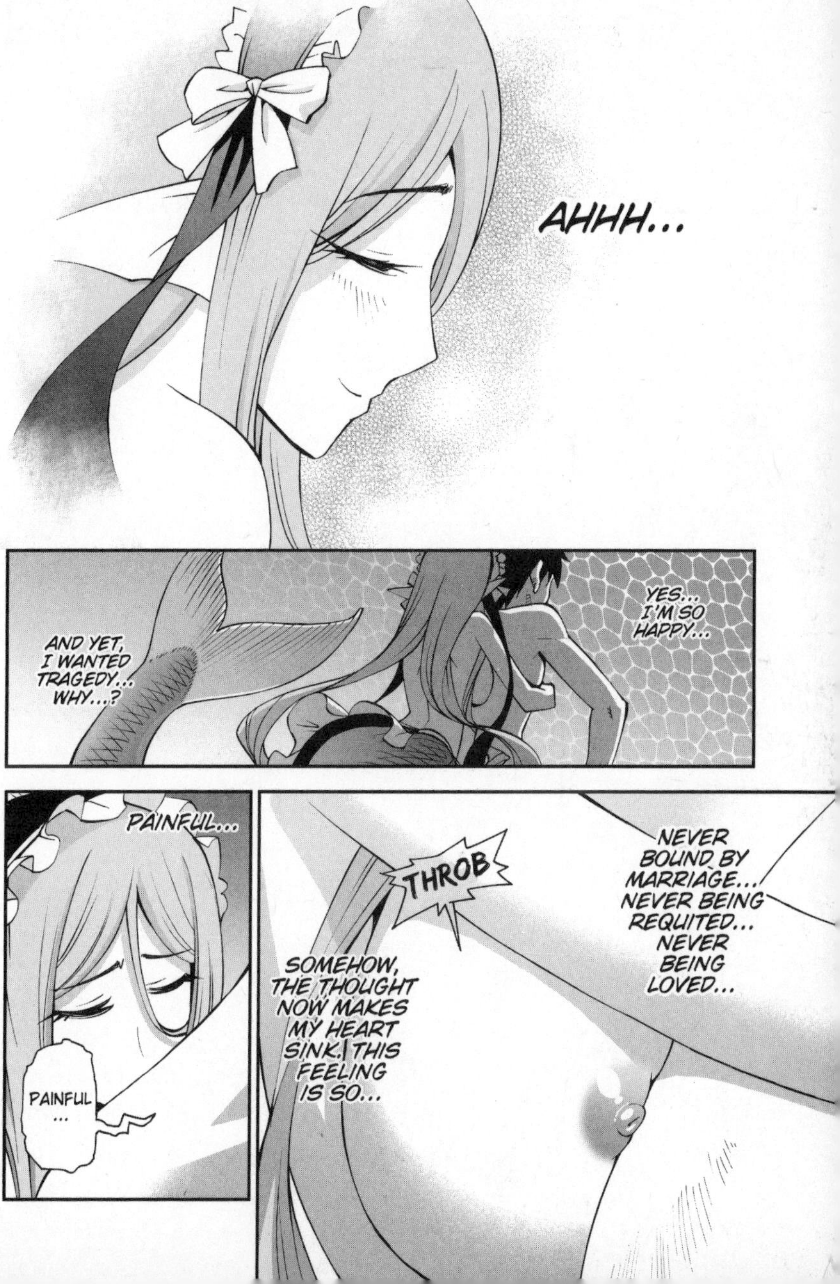
AHHH...
YES... I'M SO HAPPY...
AND YET, I WANTED TRAGEDY... WHY...?
NEVER BOUND BY MARRIAGE... NEVER BEING REQUITED... NEVER BEING LOVED...
THROB
SOMEHOW, THE THOUGHT NOW MAKES MY HEART SINK. THIS FEELING IS SO...
PAINFUL...
PAINFUL ...

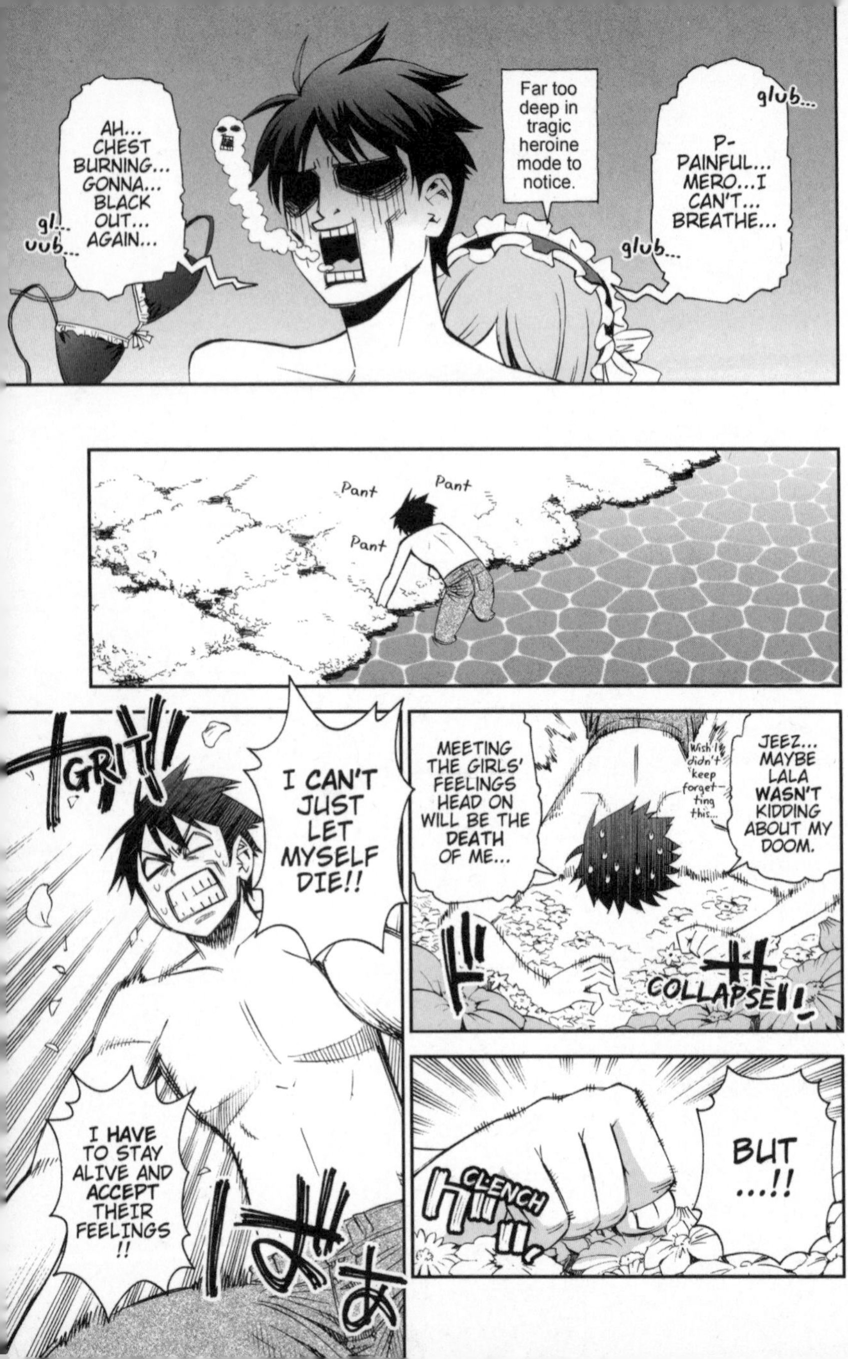
glub...
P-PAINFUL... MERO...I CAN'T... BREATHE...
glub...
Far too deep in tragic heroine mode to notice.
AH... CHEST BURNING... GONNA... BLACK OUT... AGAIN...
gl... uub...
Pant
Pant
Pant
JEEZ... MAYBE LALA WASN'T KIDDING ABOUT MY DOOM.
Wish I didn't keep forget-ting this...
MEETING THE GIRLS' FEELINGS HEAD ON WILL BE THE DEATH OF ME...
COLLAPSE!!
BUT ...!!
CLENCH
GRIT!!
I CAN'T JUST LET MYSELF DIE!!
I HAVE TO STAY ALIVE AND ACCEPT THEIR FEELINGS !!

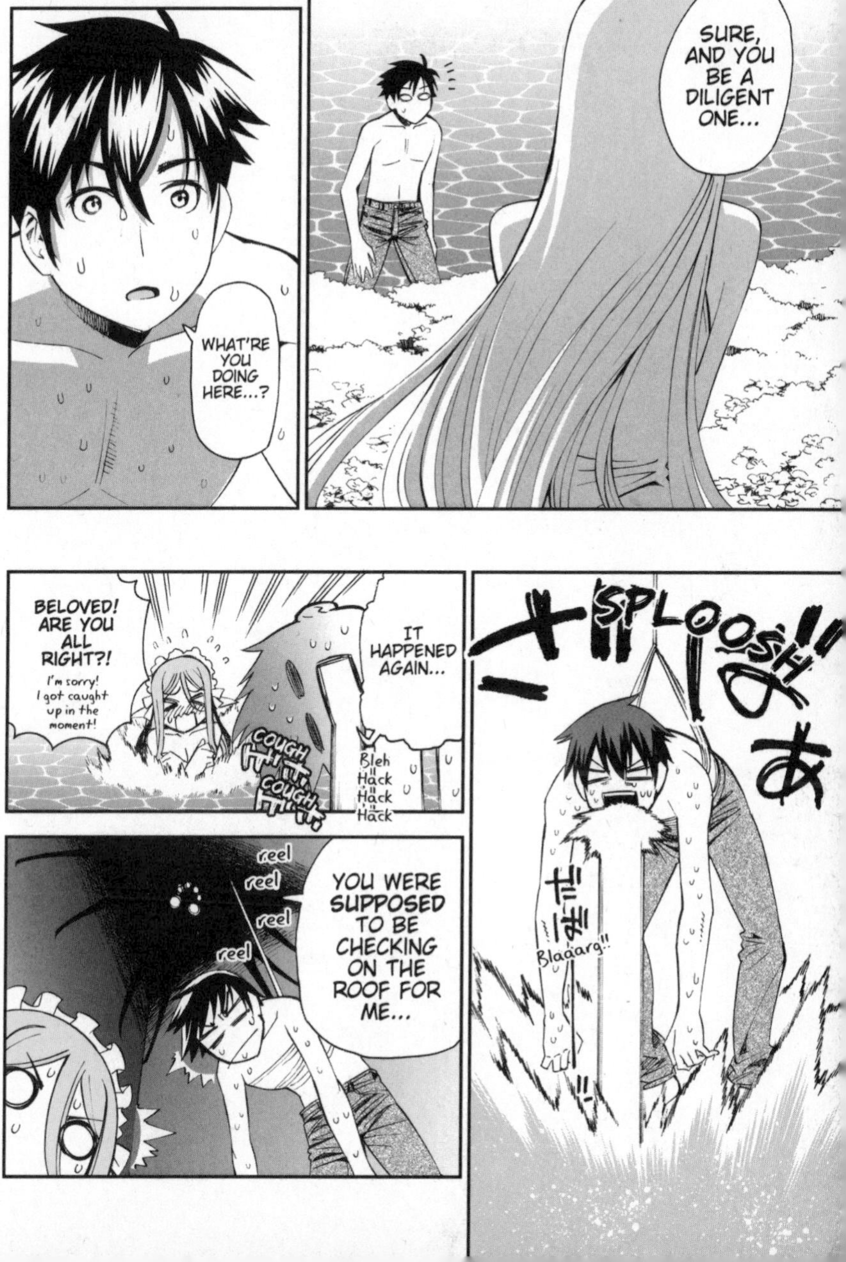
SURE, AND YOU BE A DILIGENT ONE...
WHAT'RE YOU DOING HERE...?
SPLOOSH!!
Blaaarg!!
IT HAPPENED AGAIN...
Bleh Hack Hack Hack
BELOVED! ARE YOU ALL RIGHT?!
I'm sorry! I got caught up in the moment!
COUGH COUGH
reel reel reel reel
YOU WERE SUPPOSED TO BE CHECKING ON THE ROOF FOR ME...

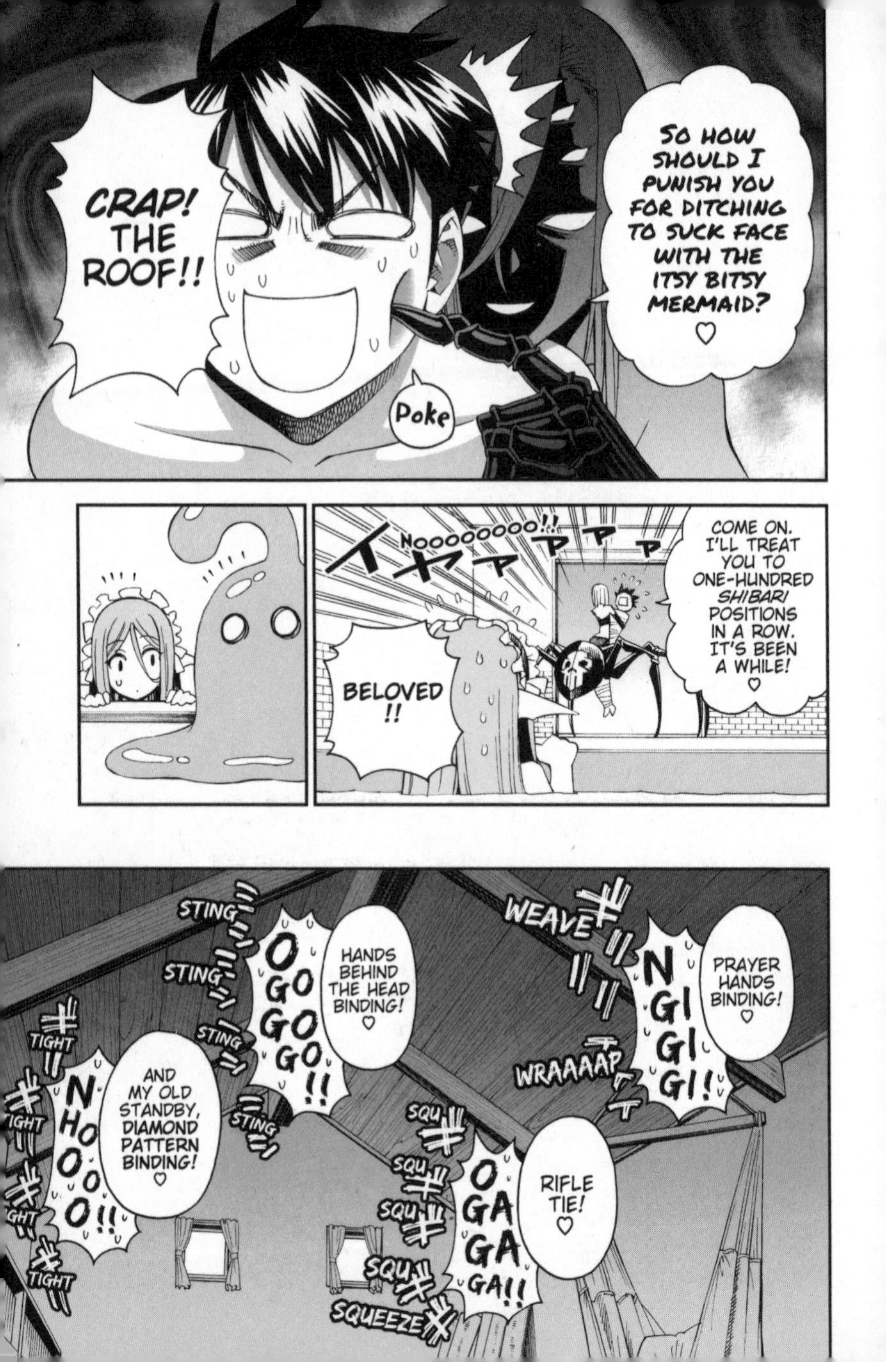
SO HOW SHOULD I PUNISH YOU FOR DITCHING TO SUCK FACE WITH THE ITSY BITSY MERMAID? ♡
CRAP! THE ROOF!!
Poke
COME ON. I'LL TREAT YOU TO ONE-HUNDRED *SHIBARI* POSITIONS IN A ROW. IT'S BEEN A WHILE! ♡
NOOOOOOOO!!
BELOVED !!
PRAYER HANDS BINDING! ♡
NGIGIGI!
WEAVE
WRAAAAP
HANDS BEHIND THE HEAD BINDING! ♡
OGOGOGO!!
STING
STING
STING
STING
RIFLE TIE! ♡
OGAGAGA!!
SQU
SQU
SQU
SQU
SQUEEZE
AND MY OLD STANDBY, DIAMOND PATTERN BINDING! ♡
NHOOOO!!
TIGHT
TIGHT

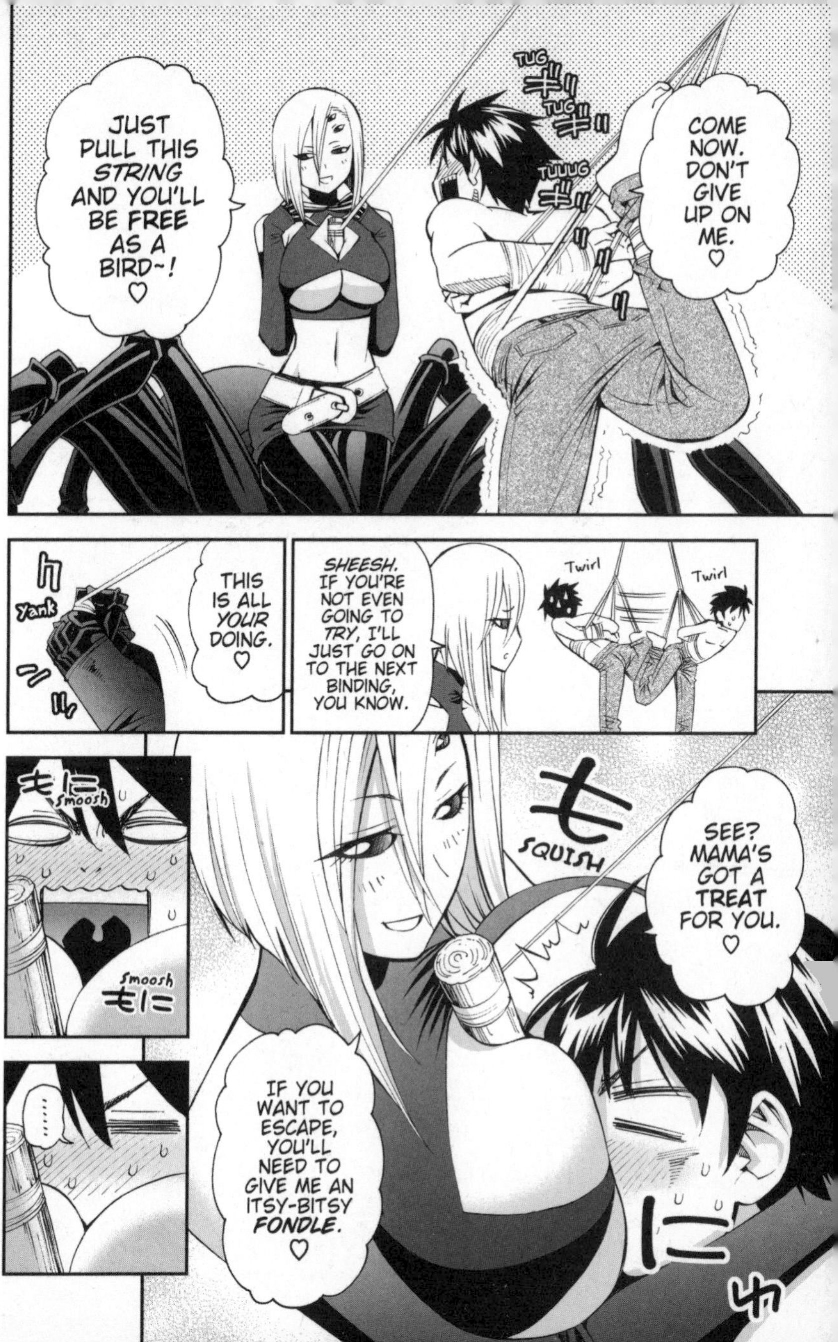
TUG
TUG
TUUUG
COME NOW. DON'T GIVE UP ON ME. ♡
JUST PULL THIS *STRING* AND YOU'LL BE FREE AS A BIRD~! ♡
Twirl
Twirl
SHEESH. IF YOU'RE NOT EVEN GOING TO *TRY*, I'LL JUST GO ON TO THE NEXT BINDING, YOU KNOW.
THIS IS ALL *YOUR* DOING. ♡
Yank
SEE? MAMA'S GOT A TREAT FOR YOU. ♡
SQUISH
IF YOU WANT TO ESCAPE, YOU'LL NEED TO GIVE ME AN ITSY-BITSY *FONDLE*. ♡
Smoosh
Smoosh
......

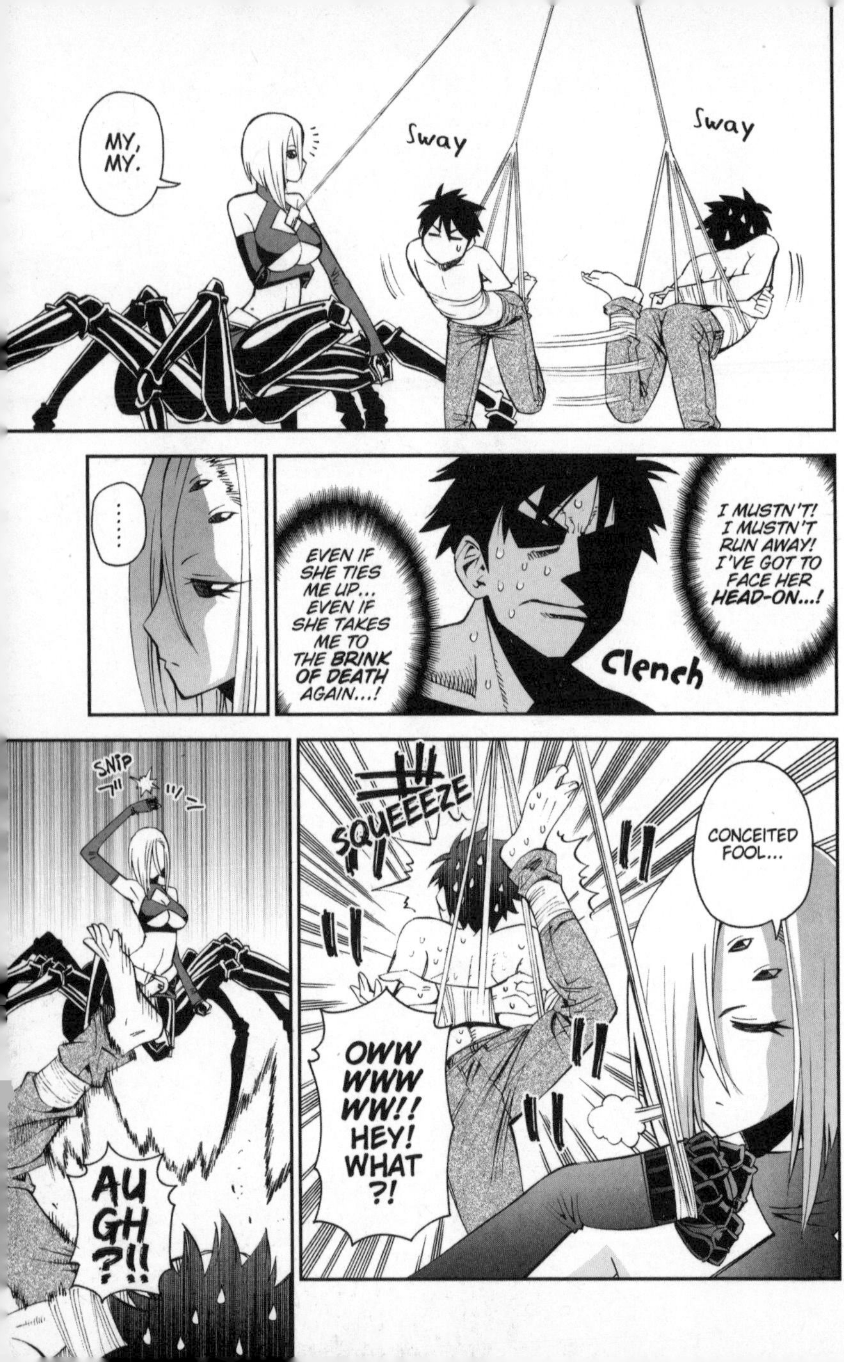
Sway
Sway
MY, MY.
I MUSTN'T! I MUSTN'T RUN AWAY! I'VE GOT TO FACE HER HEAD-ON...!
EVEN IF SHE TIES ME UP... EVEN IF SHE TAKES ME TO THE BRINK OF DEATH AGAIN...!
Clench
......
CONCEITED FOOL...
SQUEEEZE
OWW WWW WW!! HEY! WHAT ?!
SNIP
AUGH ?!!

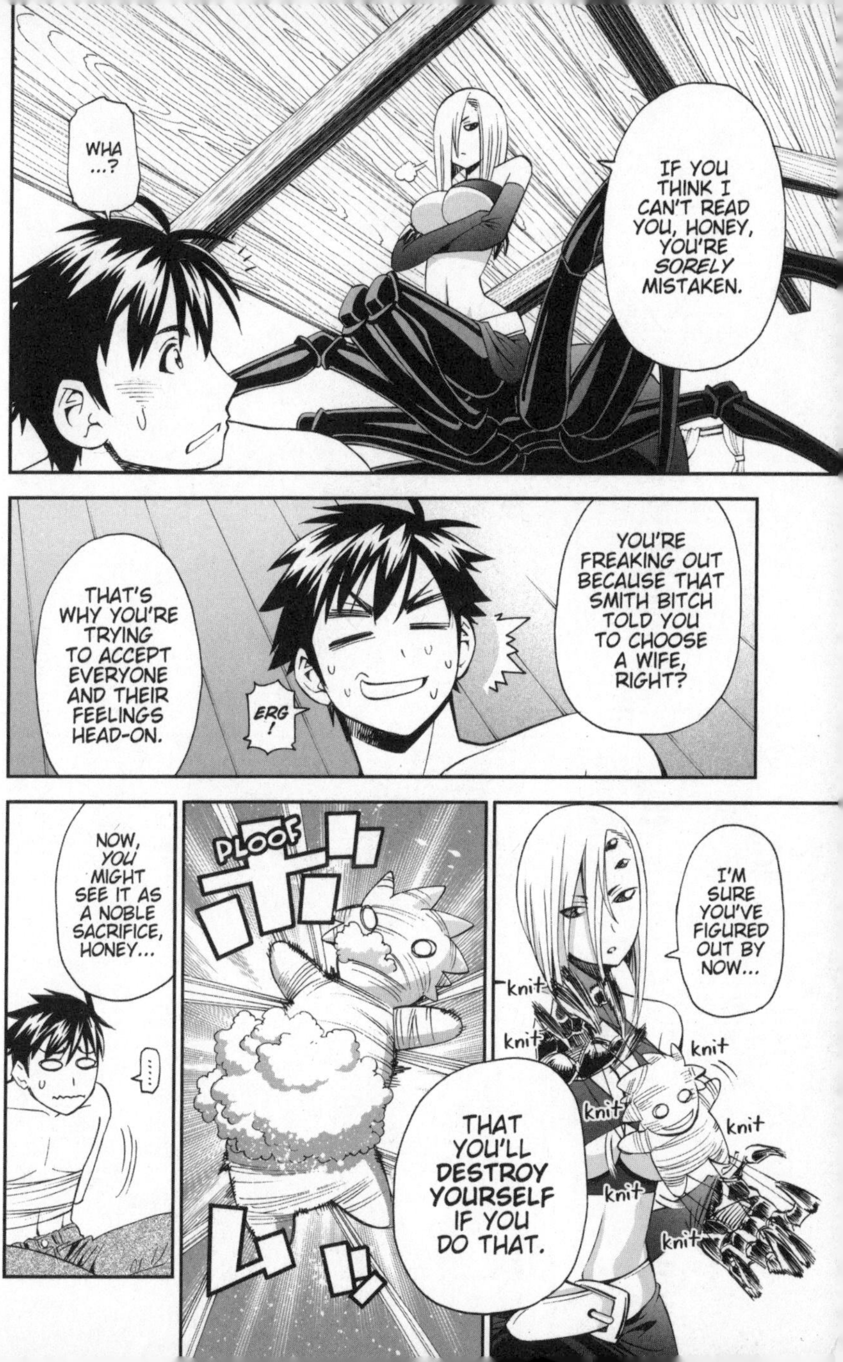
IF YOU THINK I CAN'T READ YOU, HONEY, YOU'RE SORELY MISTAKEN.
WHA ...?
YOU'RE FREAKING OUT BECAUSE THAT SMITH BITCH TOLD YOU TO CHOOSE A WIFE, RIGHT?
ERG!
THAT'S WHY YOU'RE TRYING TO ACCEPT EVERYONE AND THEIR FEELINGS HEAD-ON.
I'M SURE YOU'VE FIGURED OUT BY NOW...
knit
knit
knit
knit
knit
knit
knit
THAT YOU'LL DESTROY YOURSELF IF YOU DO THAT.
PLOOF
NOW, YOU MIGHT SEE IT AS A NOBLE SACRIFICE, HONEY...
......

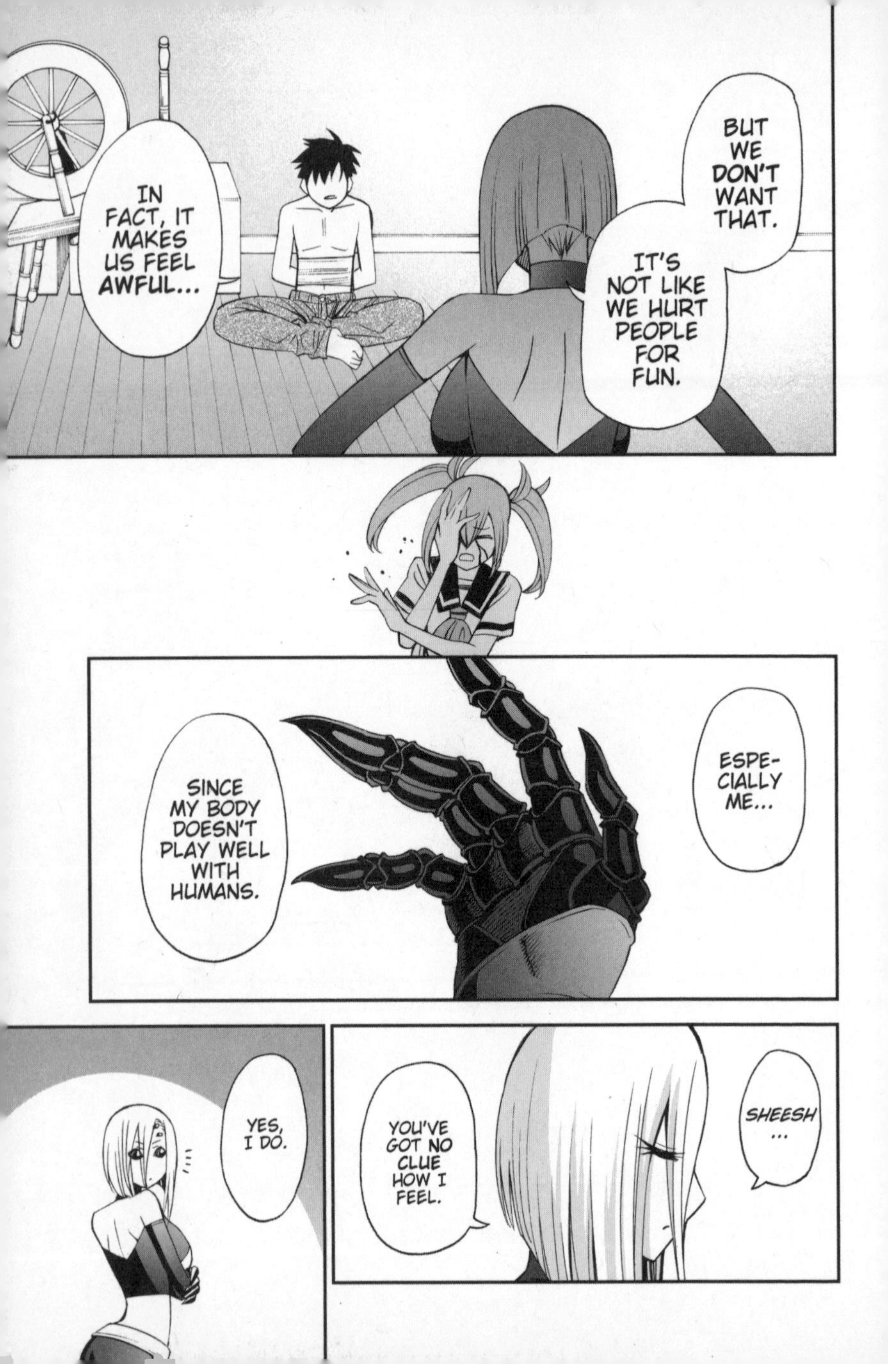
BUT WE DON'T WANT THAT.
IT'S NOT LIKE WE HURT PEOPLE FOR FUN.
IN FACT, IT MAKES US FEEL AWFUL...
ESPE-CIALLY ME...
SINCE MY BODY DOESN'T PLAY WELL WITH HUMANS.
SHEESH...
YOU'VE GOT NO CLUE HOW I FEEL.
YES, I DO.

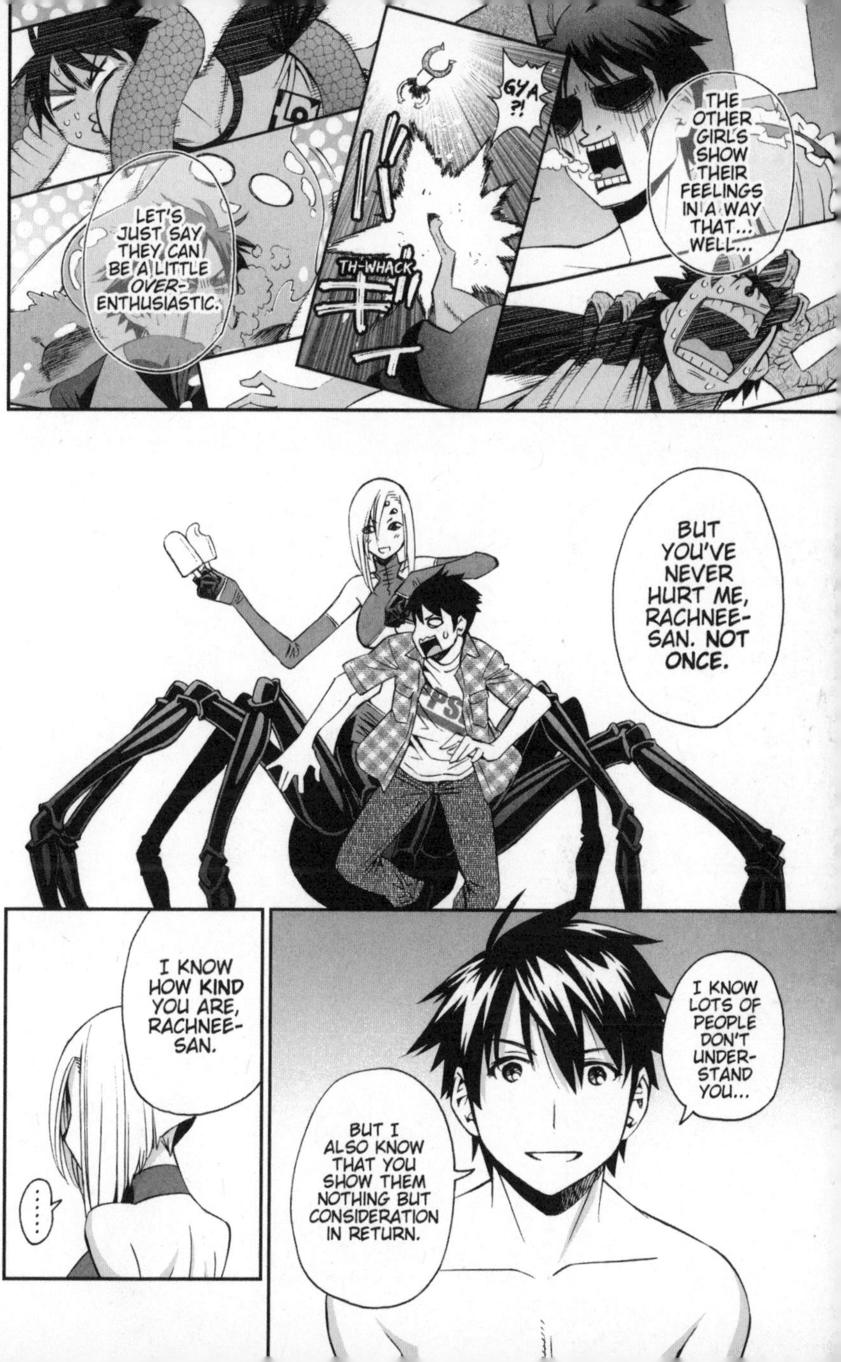
THE OTHER GIRLS SHOW THEIR FEELINGS IN A WAY THAT... WELL...
GYA?!
TH-WHACK
LET'S JUST SAY THEY CAN BE A LITTLE OVER-ENTHUSIASTIC.
BUT YOU'VE NEVER HURT ME, RACHNEE-SAN. NOT ONCE.
I KNOW LOTS OF PEOPLE DON'T UNDERSTAND YOU...
BUT I ALSO KNOW THAT YOU SHOW THEM NOTHING BUT CONSIDERATION IN RETURN.
I KNOW HOW KIND YOU ARE, RACHNEE-SAN.
......

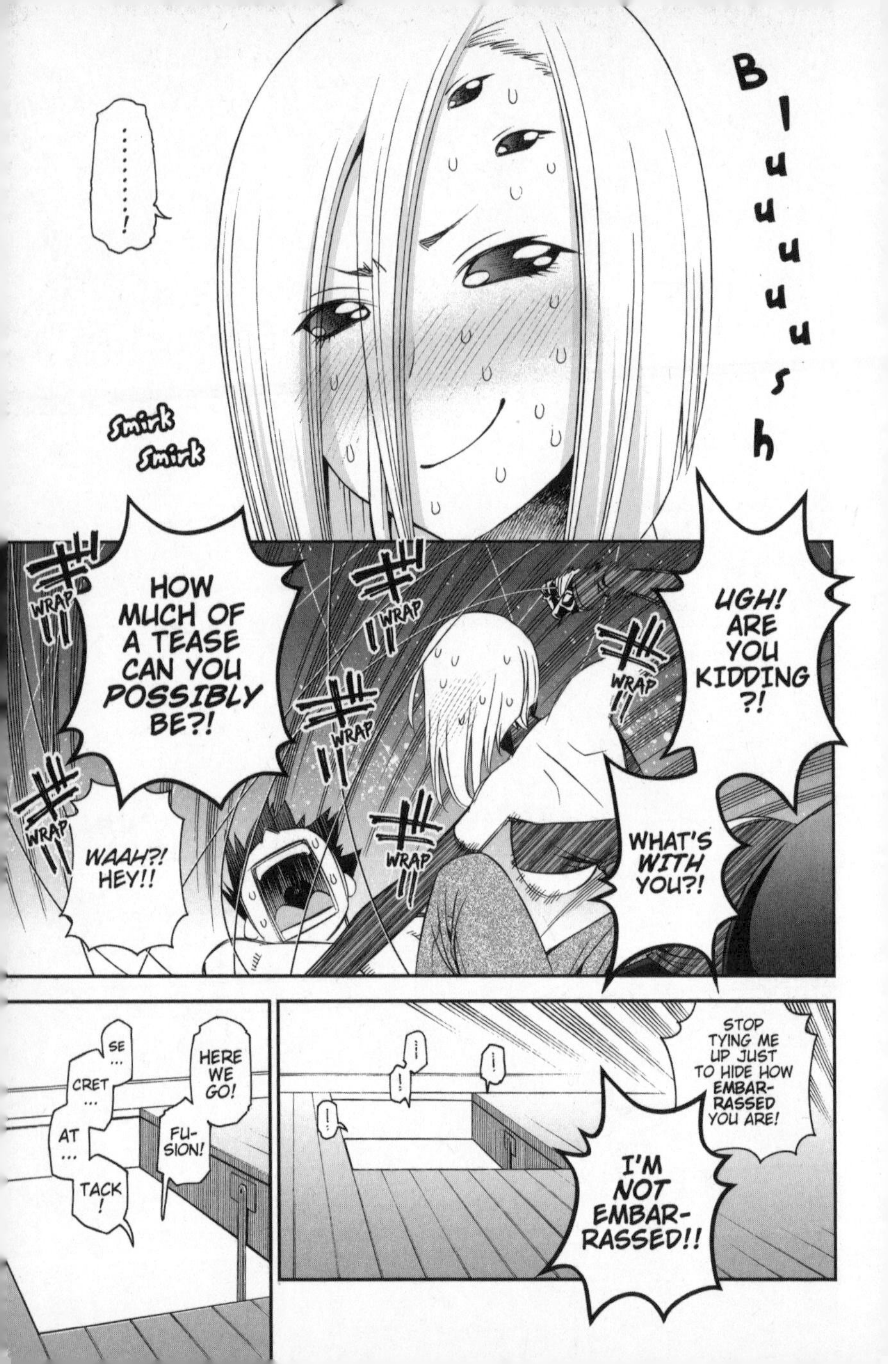
Bluuuuush
......!
Smirk Smirk
UGH! ARE YOU KIDDING?!
WRAP
WHAT'S WITH YOU?!
WRAP
WRAP
WRAP
HOW MUCH OF A TEASE CAN YOU POSSIBLY BE?!
WRAP
WRAP
WAAH?! HEY!!
STOP TYING ME UP JUST TO HIDE HOW EMBARRASSED YOU ARE!
I'M NOT EMBARRASSED!!
...!
...!
...!
HERE WE GO!
FUSION!
SE... CRET... AT... TACK!

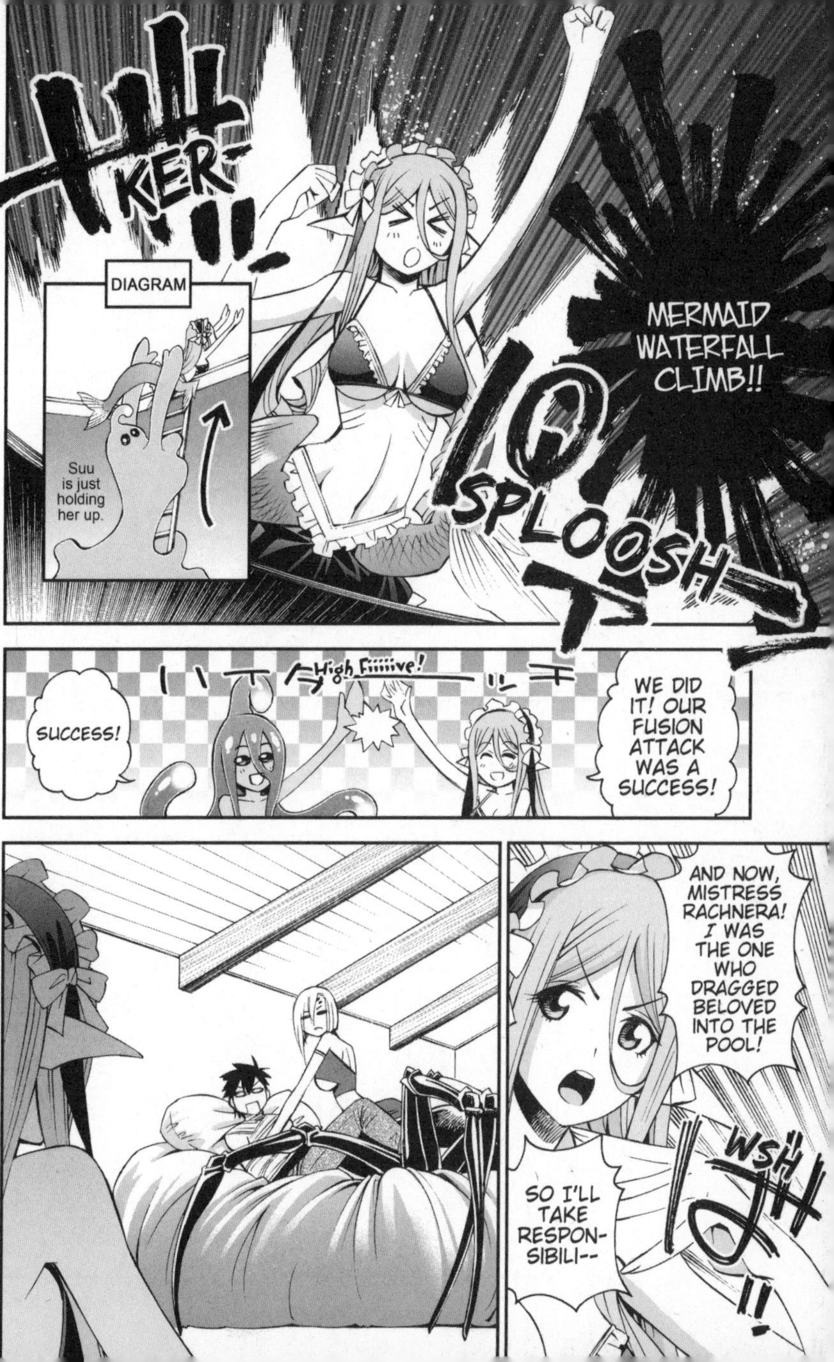
MERMAID WATERFALL CLIMB!!
KER-!!
SPLOOSH
DIAGRAM
Suu is just holding her up.
WE DID IT! OUR FUSION ATTACK WAS A SUCCESS!
High Fiiiiive!
SUCCESS!
AND NOW, MISTRESS RACHNERA! I WAS THE ONE WHO DRAGGED BELOVED INTO THE POOL!
WSH!!
SO I'LL TAKE RESPONSIBILI--

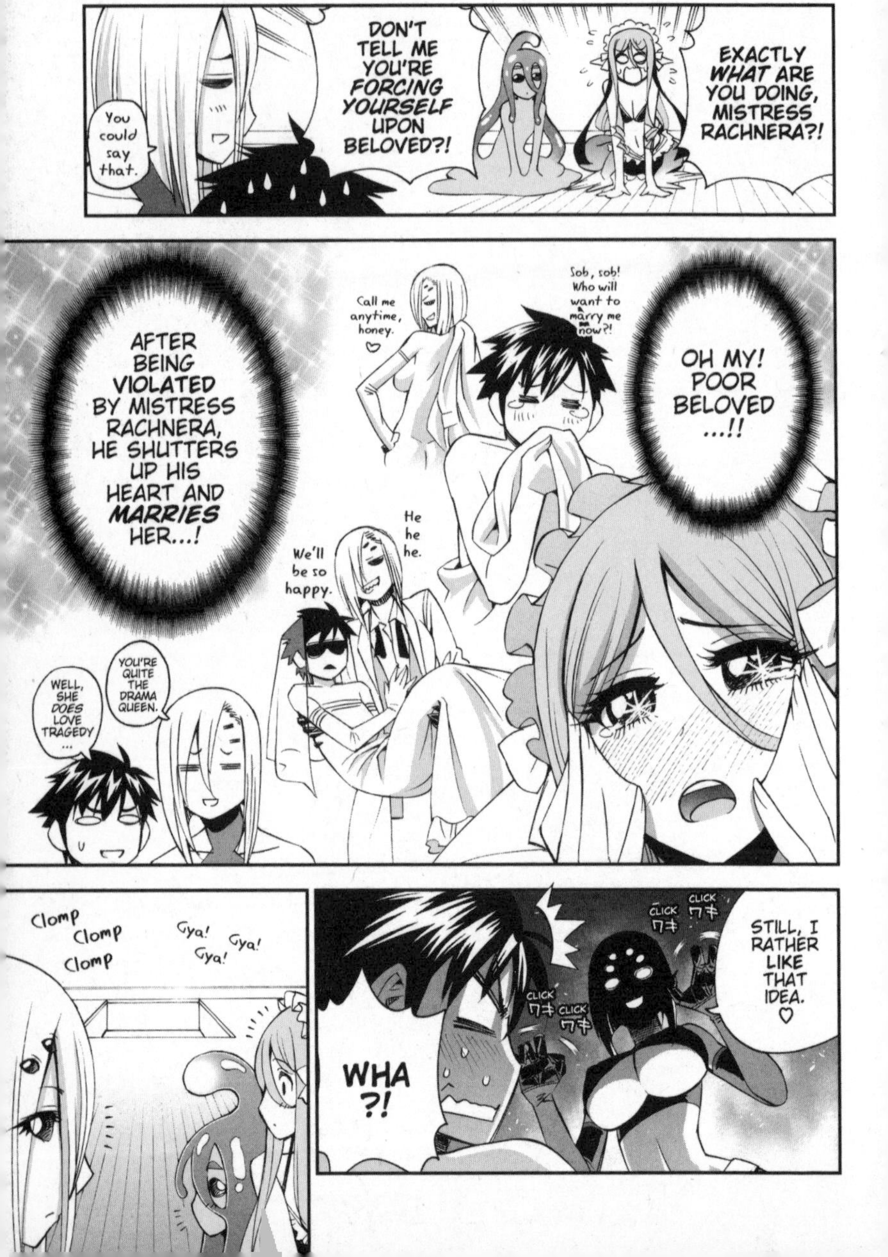
EXACTLY WHAT ARE YOU DOING, MISTRESS RACHNERA?!
DON'T TELL ME YOU'RE FORCING YOURSELF UPON BELOVED?!
You could say that.
OH MY! POOR BELOVED ...!!
Sob, sob! Who will want to marry me now?!
Call me anytime, honey. ♡
AFTER BEING VIOLATED BY MISTRESS RACHNERA, HE SHUTTERS UP HIS HEART AND MARRIES HER...!
He he he.
We'll be so happy.
YOU'RE QUITE THE DRAMA QUEEN.
WELL, SHE DOES LOVE TRAGEDY ...
STILL, I RATHER LIKE THAT IDEA. ♡
CLICK ワキ CLICK ワキ
CLICK ワキ CLICK ワキ
WHA ?!
Gya! Gya! Gya!
Clomp Clomp Clomp

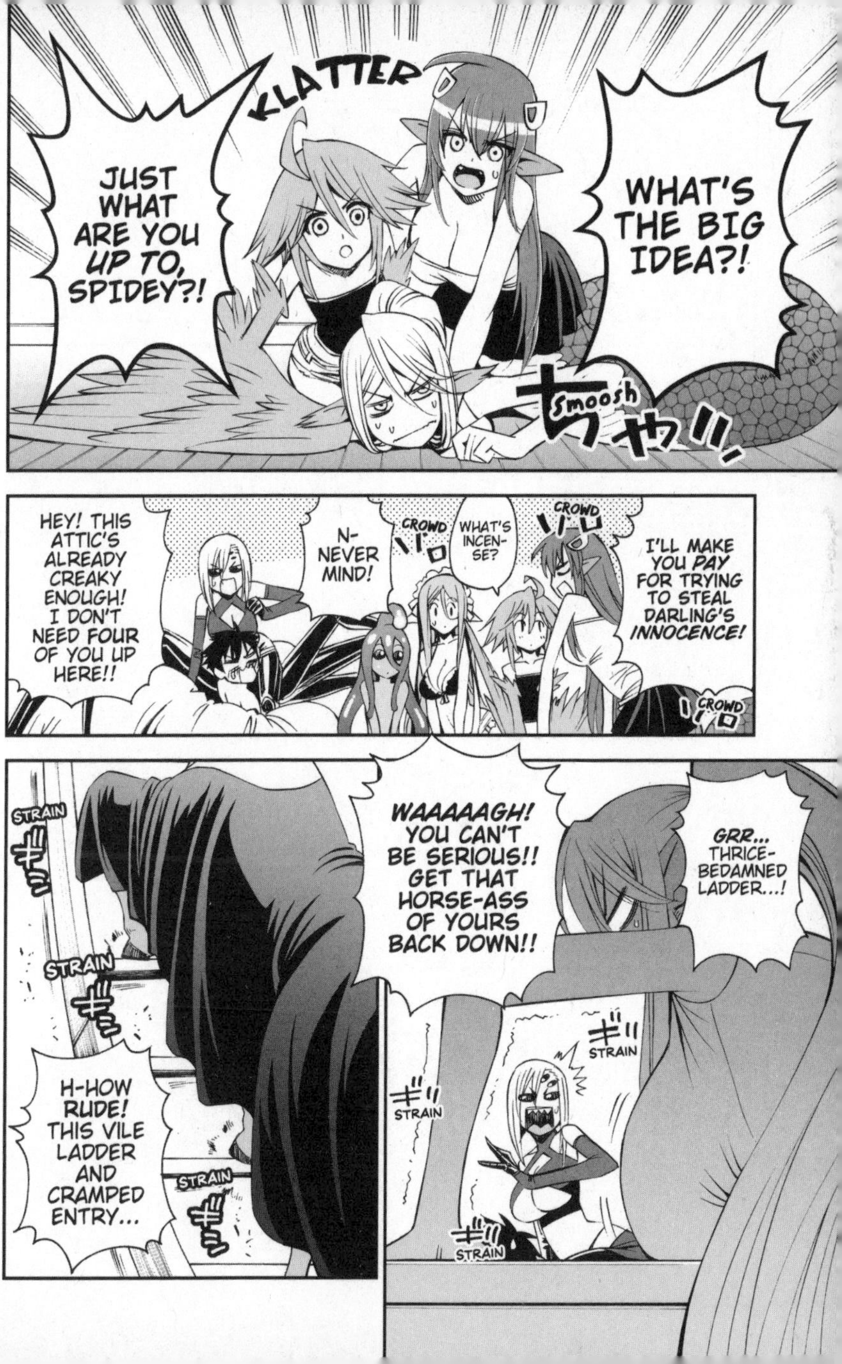
WHAT'S THE BIG IDEA?!
KLATTER
JUST WHAT ARE YOU UP TO, SPIDEY?!
smoosh
I'LL MAKE YOU PAY FOR TRYING TO STEAL DARLING'S INNOCENCE!
CROWD
WHAT'S INCENSE?
CROWD
N-NEVER MIND!
HEY! THIS ATTIC'S ALREADY CREAKY ENOUGH! I DON'T NEED FOUR OF YOU UP HERE!!
CROWD
GRR... THRICE-BEDAMNED LADDER...!
STRAIN
WAAAAAGH! YOU CAN'T BE SERIOUS!! GET THAT HORSE-ASS OF YOURS BACK DOWN!!
STRAIN
STRAIN
STRAIN
STRAIN
STRAIN
H-HOW RUDE! THIS VILE LADDER AND CRAMPED ENTRY...

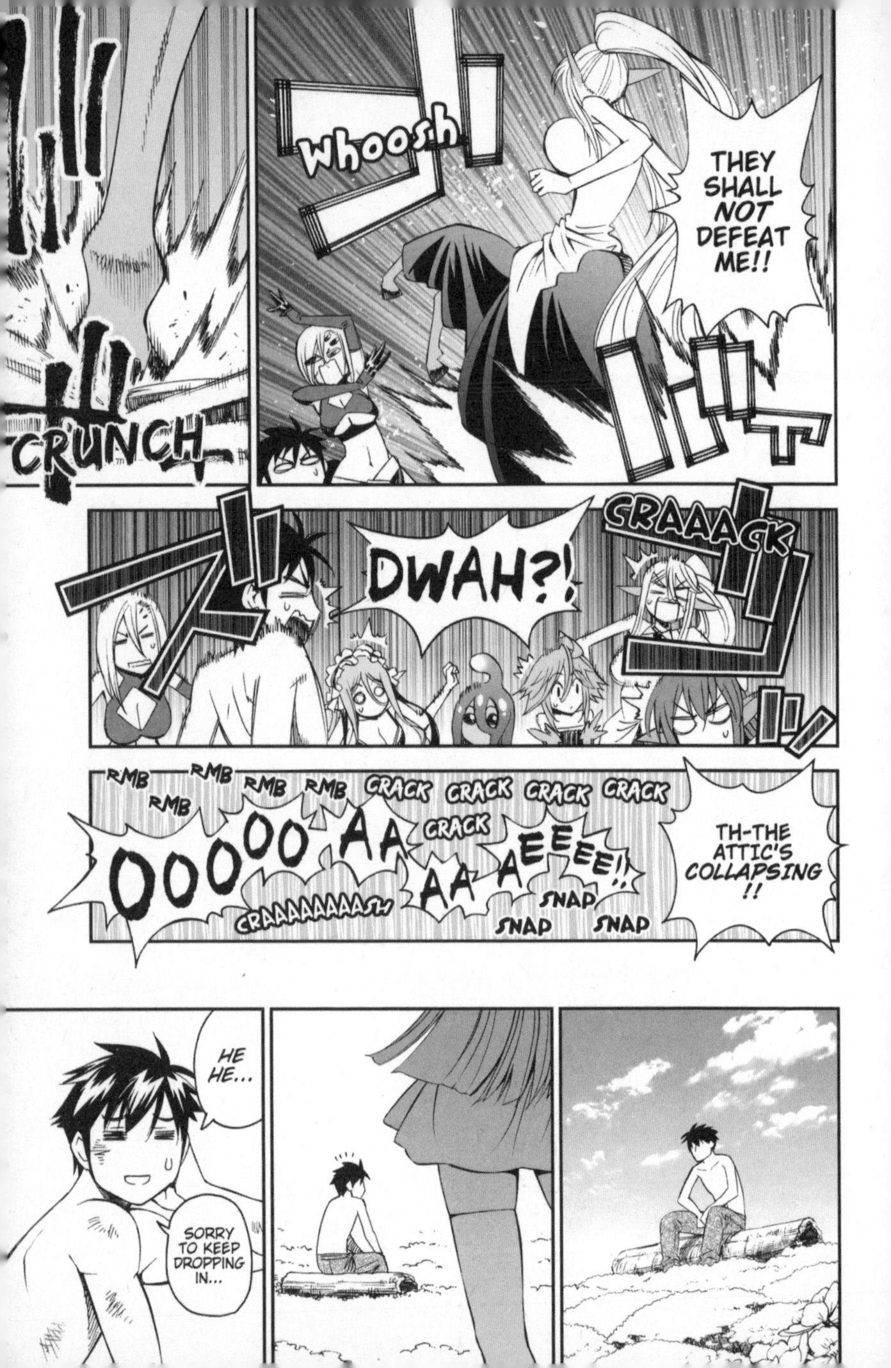
whoosh
THEY SHALL *NOT* DEFEAT ME!!
CRUNCH
CRAAACK
DWAH?!
TH-THE ATTIC'S COLLAPSING!!
RMB RMB RMB RMB RMB
CRACK CRACK CRACK CRACK CRACK
OOOOO AA AA AEEEEE!!
CRAAAAAAAASH
SNAP SNAP SNAP
HE HE...
SORRY TO KEEP DROPPING IN...

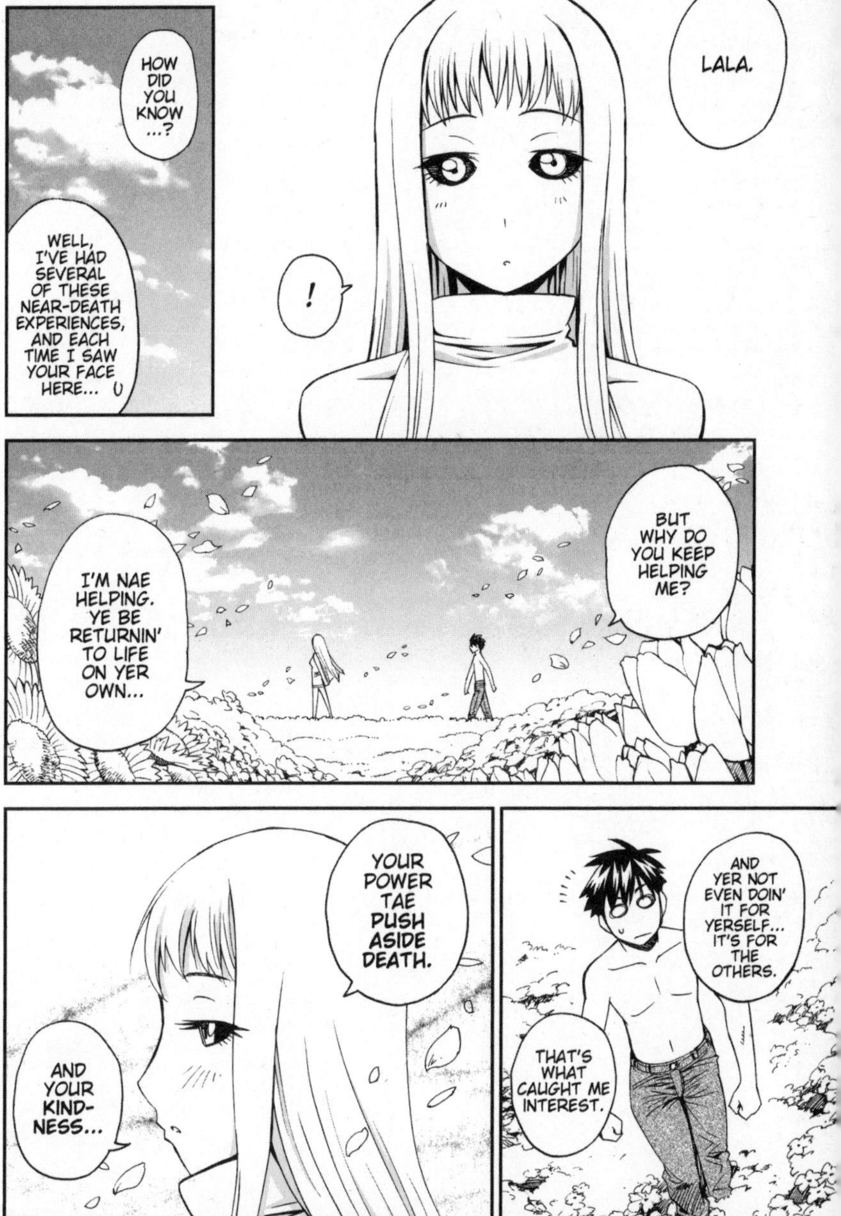
LALA.
!
HOW DID YOU KNOW ...?
WELL, I'VE HAD SEVERAL OF THESE NEAR-DEATH EXPERIENCES, AND EACH TIME I SAW YOUR FACE HERE...
BUT WHY DO YOU KEEP HELPING ME?
I'M NAE HELPING. YE BE RETURNIN' TO LIFE ON YER OWN...
AND YER NOT EVEN DOIN' IT FOR YERSELF... IT'S FOR THE OTHERS.
THAT'S WHAT CAUGHT ME INTEREST.
YOUR POWER TAE PUSH ASIDE DEATH.
AND YOUR KINDNESS...

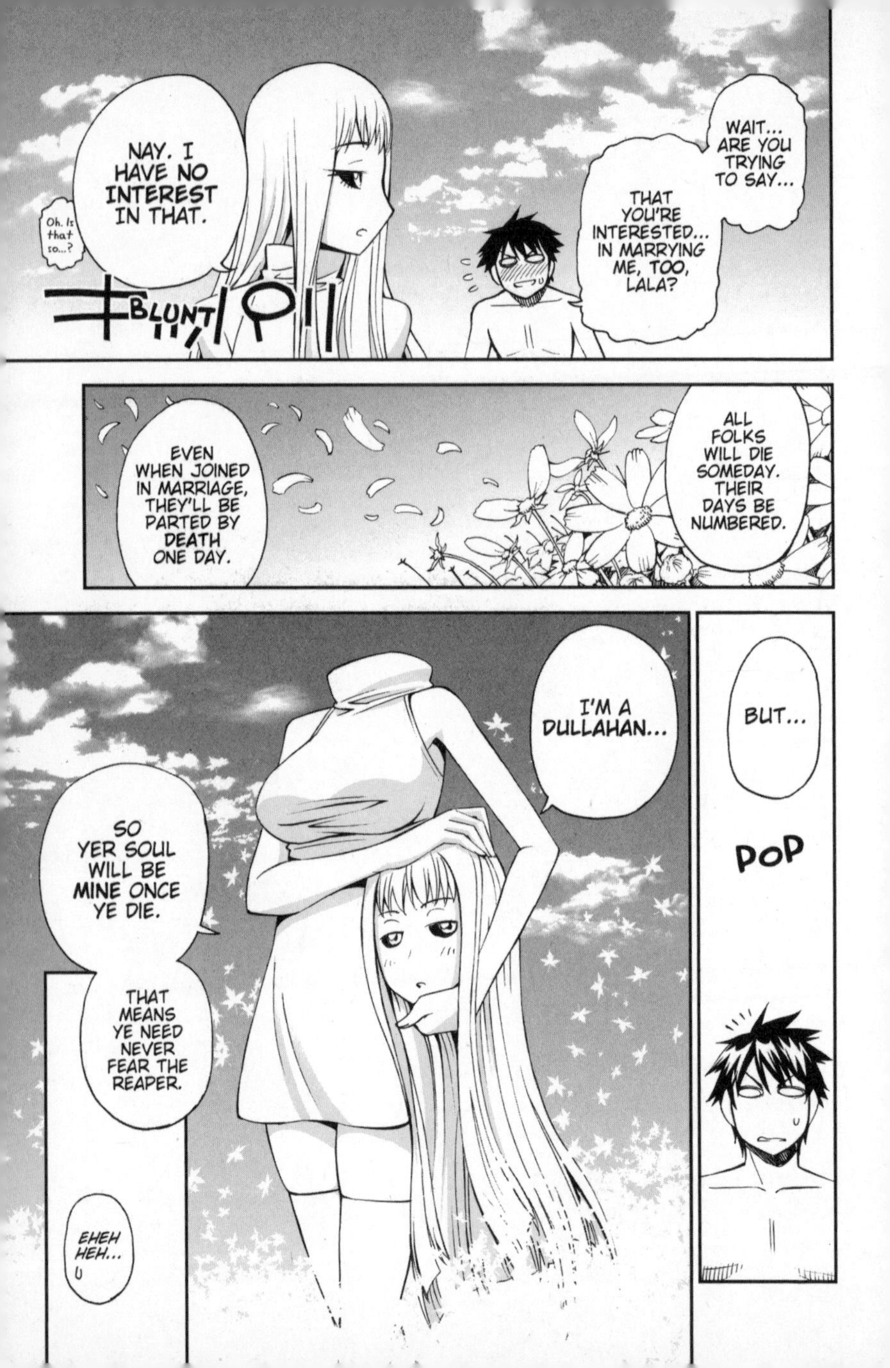
WAIT... ARE YOU TRYING TO SAY...
THAT YOU'RE INTERESTED... IN MARRYING ME, TOO, LALA?
NAY. I HAVE NO INTEREST IN THAT.
BLUNT
Oh. Is that so...?
ALL FOLKS WILL DIE SOMEDAY. THEIR DAYS BE NUMBERED.
EVEN WHEN JOINED IN MARRIAGE, THEY'LL BE PARTED BY DEATH ONE DAY.
BUT...
POP
I'M A DULLAHAN...
SO YER SOUL WILL BE MINE ONCE YE DIE.
THAT MEANS YE NEED NEVER FEAR THE REAPER.
EHEH HEH...

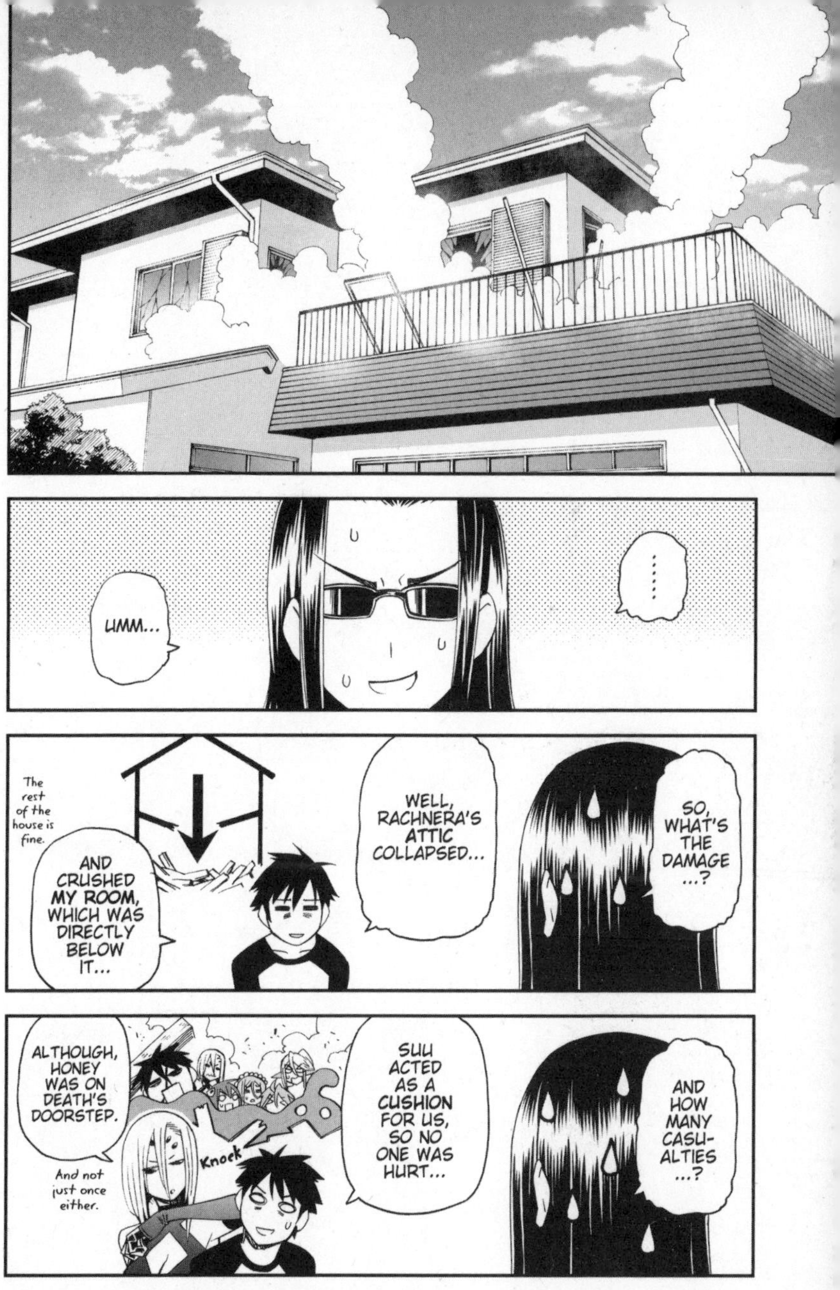
......
UMM...
SO, WHAT'S THE DAMAGE...?
WELL, RACHNERA'S ATTIC COLLAPSED...
AND CRUSHED MY ROOM, WHICH WAS DIRECTLY BELOW IT...
The rest of the house is fine.
AND HOW MANY CASUALTIES...?
SUU ACTED AS A CUSHION FOR US, SO NO ONE WAS HURT...
ALTHOUGH, HONEY WAS ON DEATH'S DOORSTEP.
Knock
And not just once either.

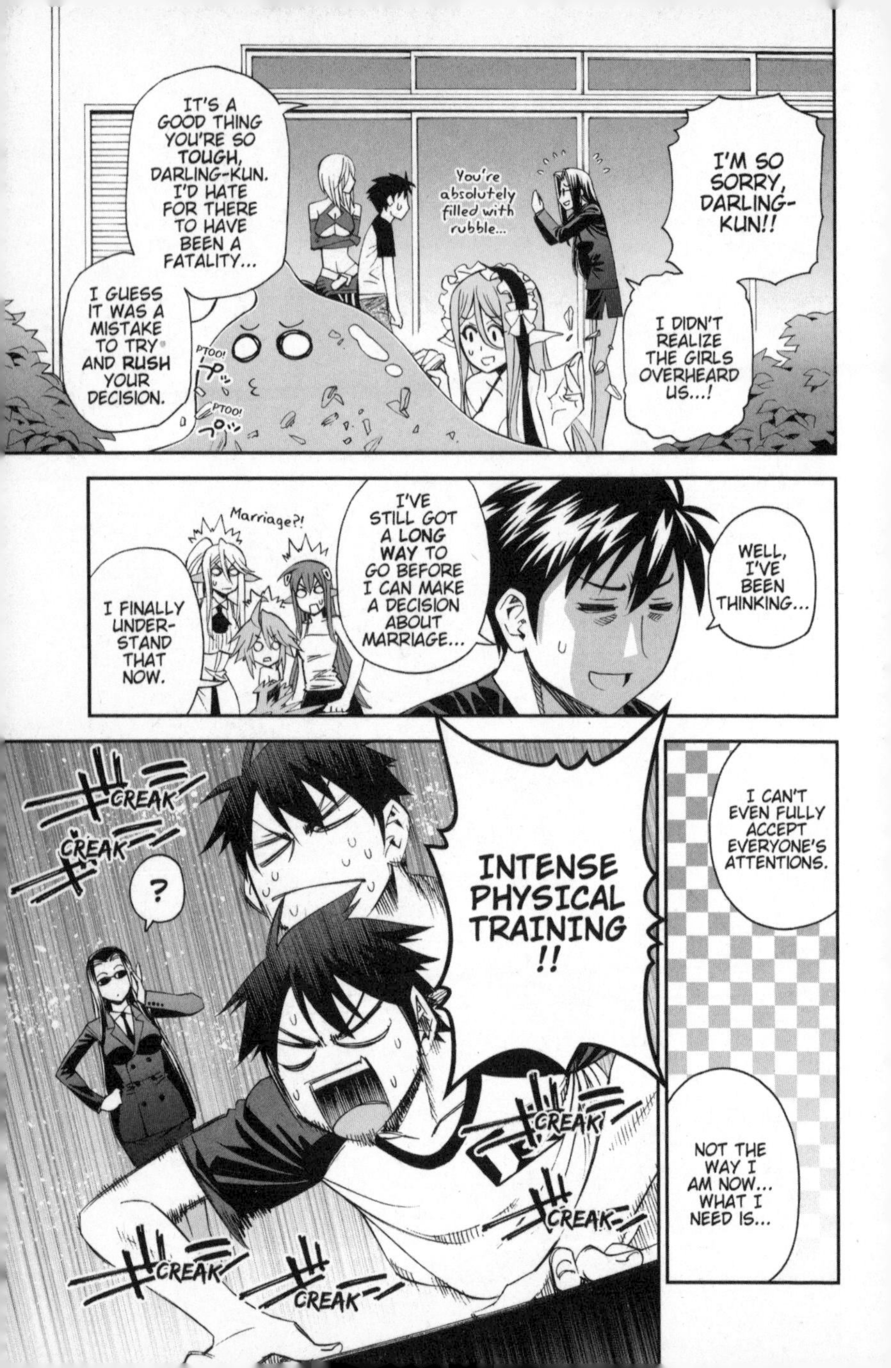
I'M SO SORRY, DARLING-KUN!!
I DIDN'T REALIZE THE GIRLS OVERHEARD US...!
You're absolutely filled with rubble...
IT'S A GOOD THING YOU'RE SO TOUGH, DARLING-KUN. I'D HATE FOR THERE TO HAVE BEEN A FATALITY...
I GUESS IT WAS A MISTAKE TO TRY AND RUSH YOUR DECISION.
PTOO!
PTOO!
WELL, I'VE BEEN THINKING...
I'VE STILL GOT A LONG WAY TO GO BEFORE I CAN MAKE A DECISION ABOUT MARRIAGE...
Marriage?!
I FINALLY UNDER-STAND THAT NOW.
I CAN'T EVEN FULLY ACCEPT EVERYONE'S ATTENTIONS.
NOT THE WAY I AM NOW... WHAT I NEED IS...
INTENSE PHYSICAL TRAINING !!
?
CREAK
CREAK
CREAK
CREAK
CREAK
CREAK

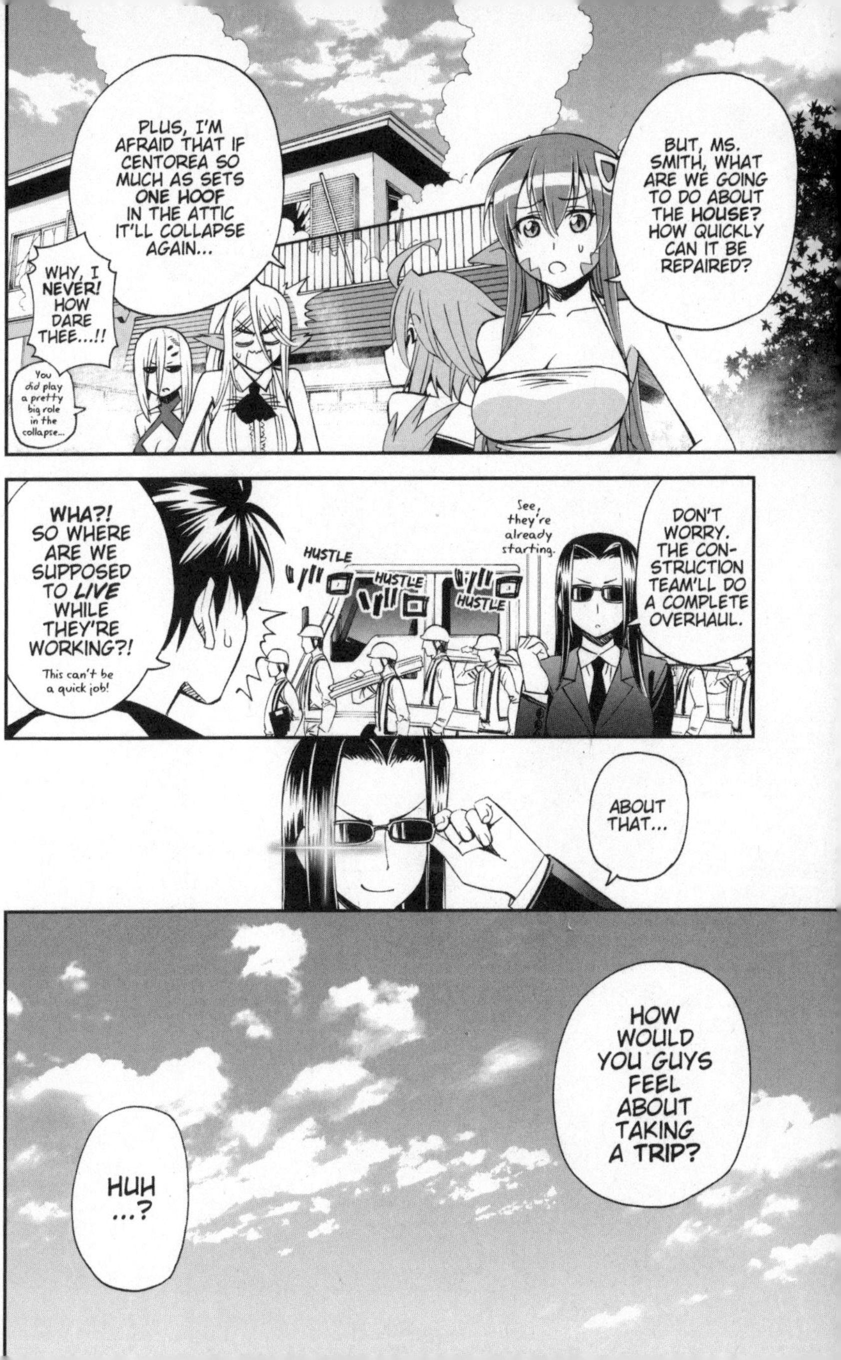
BUT, MS. SMITH, WHAT ARE WE GOING TO DO ABOUT THE HOUSE? HOW QUICKLY CAN IT BE REPAIRED?
PLUS, I'M AFRAID THAT IF CENTOREA SO MUCH AS SETS ONE HOOF IN THE ATTIC IT'LL COLLAPSE AGAIN...
WHY, I NEVER! HOW DARE THEE...!!
You did play a pretty big role in the collapse...
DON'T WORRY. THE CON-STRUCTION TEAM'LL DO A COMPLETE OVERHAUL.
See, they're already starting.
HUSTLE
HUSTLE
HUSTLE
WHA?! SO WHERE ARE WE SUPPOSED TO LIVE WHILE THEY'RE WORKING?!
This can't be a quick job!
ABOUT THAT...
HOW WOULD YOU GUYS FEEL ABOUT TAKING A TRIP?
HUH ...?

Monster Musume

Everyday Life with Monster Girls

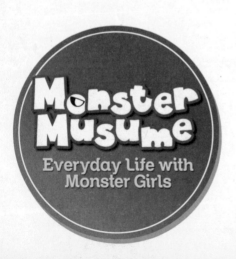

Meeting of the Mothers

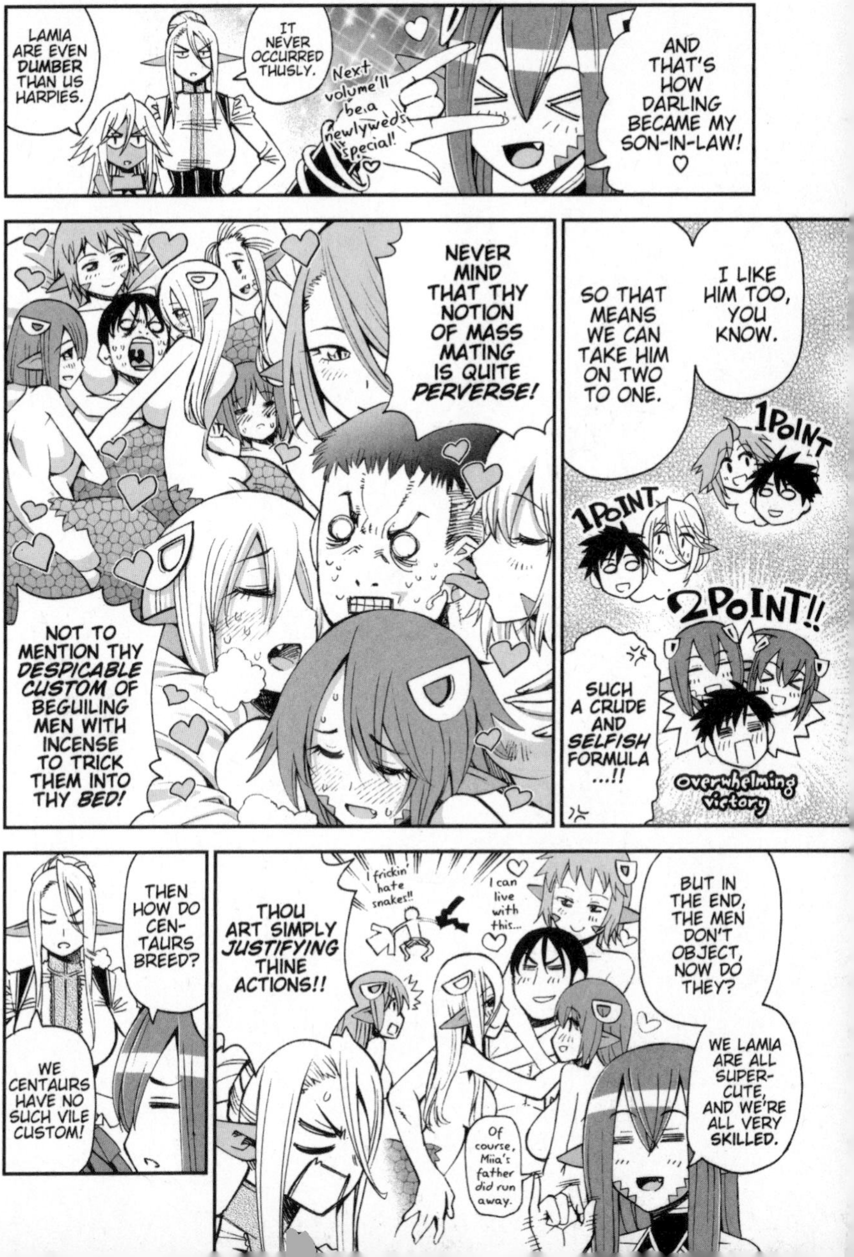

AND THAT'S HOW DARLING BECAME MY SON-IN-LAW! ♡
Next volume'll be a newlyweds special! ♡
IT NEVER OCCURRED THUSLY.
LAMIA ARE EVEN DUMBER THAN US HARPIES.
I LIKE HIM TOO, YOU KNOW.
SO THAT MEANS WE CAN TAKE HIM ON TWO TO ONE.
1POINT
1POINT
2POINT!!
SUCH A CRUDE AND SELFISH FORMULA ...!!
Overwhelming victory
NEVER MIND THAT THY NOTION OF MASS MATING IS QUITE PERVERSE!
NOT TO MENTION THY DESPICABLE CUSTOM OF BEGUILING MEN WITH INCENSE TO TRICK THEM INTO THY BED!
BUT IN THE END, THE MEN DON'T OBJECT, NOW DO THEY?
I can live with this...
I frickin' hate snakes!!
THOU ART SIMPLY JUSTIFYING THINE ACTIONS!!
WE LAMIA ARE ALL SUPER-CUTE, AND WE'RE ALL VERY SKILLED.
Of course, Miia's father did run away.
THEN HOW DO CENTAURS BREED?
WE CENTAURS HAVE NO SUCH VILE CUSTOM!

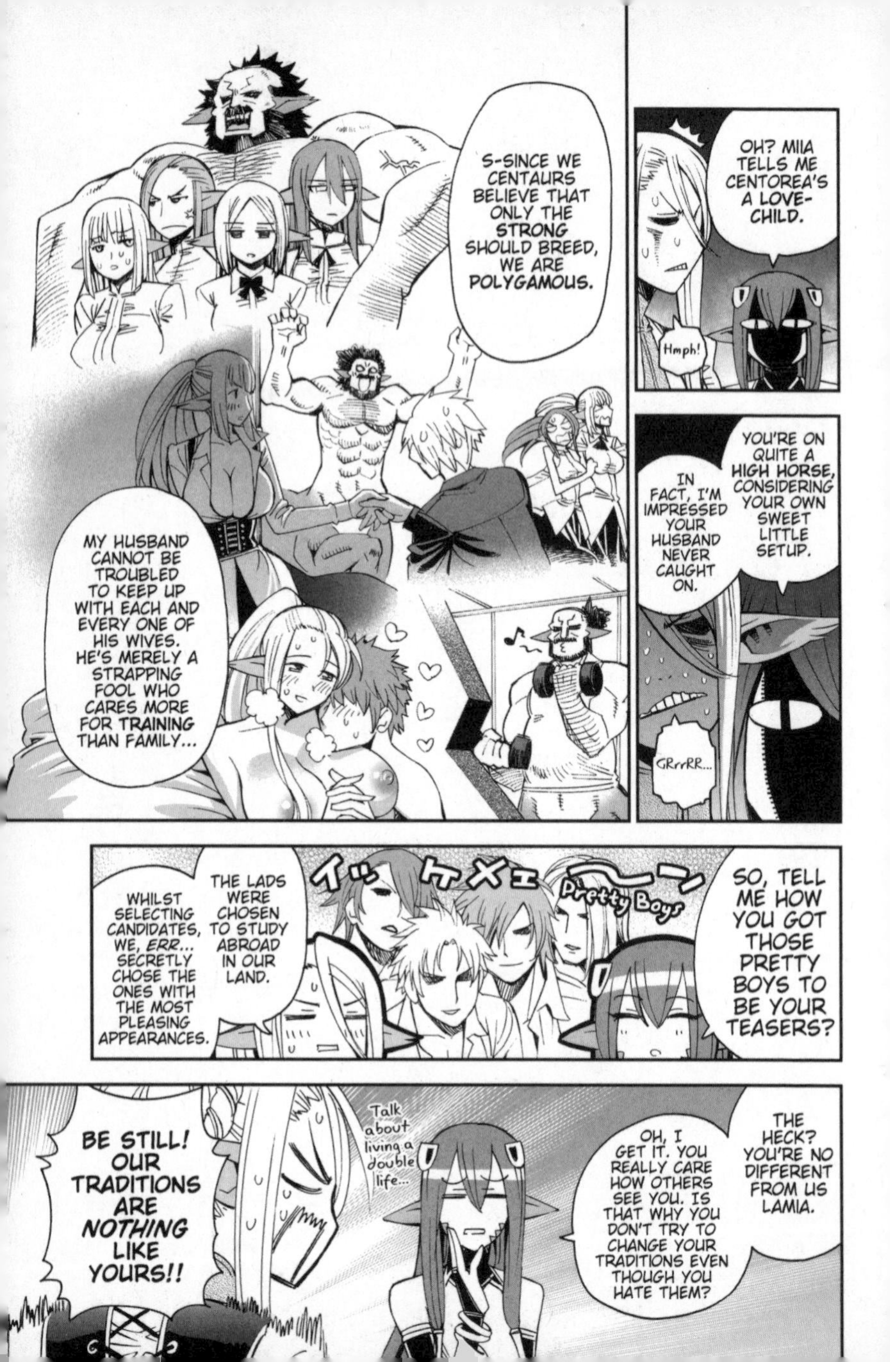

OH? MIIA TELLS ME CENTOREA'S A LOVE-CHILD.
Hmph!
YOU'RE ON QUITE A HIGH HORSE, CONSIDERING YOUR OWN SWEET LITTLE SETUP.
IN FACT, I'M IMPRESSED YOUR HUSBAND NEVER CAUGHT ON.
GRrrRR...
S-SINCE WE CENTAURS BELIEVE THAT ONLY THE STRONG SHOULD BREED, WE ARE POLYGAMOUS.
MY HUSBAND CANNOT BE TROUBLED TO KEEP UP WITH EACH AND EVERY ONE OF HIS WIVES. HE'S MERELY A STRAPPING FOOL WHO CARES MORE FOR TRAINING THAN FAMILY...
SO, TELL ME HOW YOU GOT THOSE PRETTY BOYS TO BE YOUR TEASERS?
イッケメェ〜〜ン
Pretty Boys
THE LADS WERE CHOSEN TO STUDY ABROAD IN OUR LAND.
WHILST SELECTING CANDIDATES, WE, *ERR*... SECRETLY CHOSE THE ONES WITH THE MOST PLEASING APPEARANCES.
THE HECK? YOU'RE NO DIFFERENT FROM US LAMIA.
OH, I GET IT. YOU REALLY CARE HOW OTHERS SEE YOU. IS THAT WHY YOU DON'T TRY TO CHANGE YOUR TRADITIONS EVEN THOUGH YOU HATE THEM?
Talk about living a double life...
BE STILL! OUR TRADITIONS ARE *NOTHING* LIKE YOURS!!

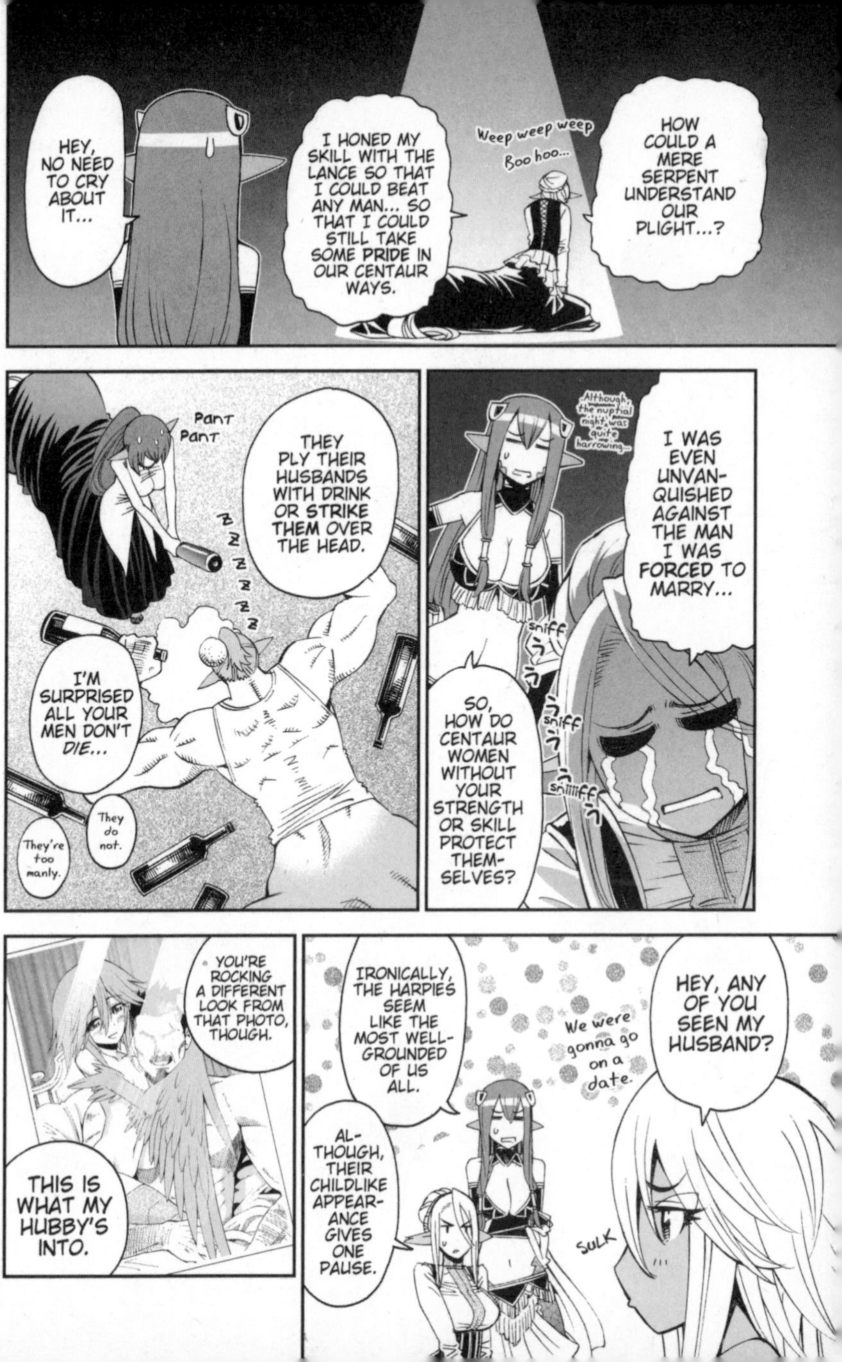
HOW COULD A MERE SERPENT UNDERSTAND OUR PLIGHT...?
Weep weep weep
Boo hoo...
I HONED MY SKILL WITH THE LANCE SO THAT I COULD BEAT ANY MAN... SO THAT I COULD STILL TAKE SOME PRIDE IN OUR CENTAUR WAYS.
HEY, NO NEED TO CRY ABOUT IT...
Although the nuptial night was quite harrowing...
I WAS EVEN UNVANQUISHED AGAINST THE MAN I WAS FORCED TO MARRY...
sniff
sniff
sniiiiff
SO, HOW DO CENTAUR WOMEN WITHOUT YOUR STRENGTH OR SKILL PROTECT THEMSELVES?
Pant Pant
THEY PLY THEIR HUSBANDS WITH DRINK OR STRIKE THEM OVER THE HEAD.
I'M SURPRISED ALL YOUR MEN DON'T DIE...
They do not.
They're too manly.
HEY, ANY OF YOU SEEN MY HUSBAND?
We were gonna go on a date.
IRONICALLY, THE HARPIES SEEM LIKE THE MOST WELL-GROUNDED OF US ALL.
ALTHOUGH, THEIR CHILDLIKE APPEARANCE GIVES ONE PAUSE.
SULK
YOU'RE ROCKING A DIFFERENT LOOK FROM THAT PHOTO, THOUGH.
THIS IS WHAT MY HUBBY'S INTO.

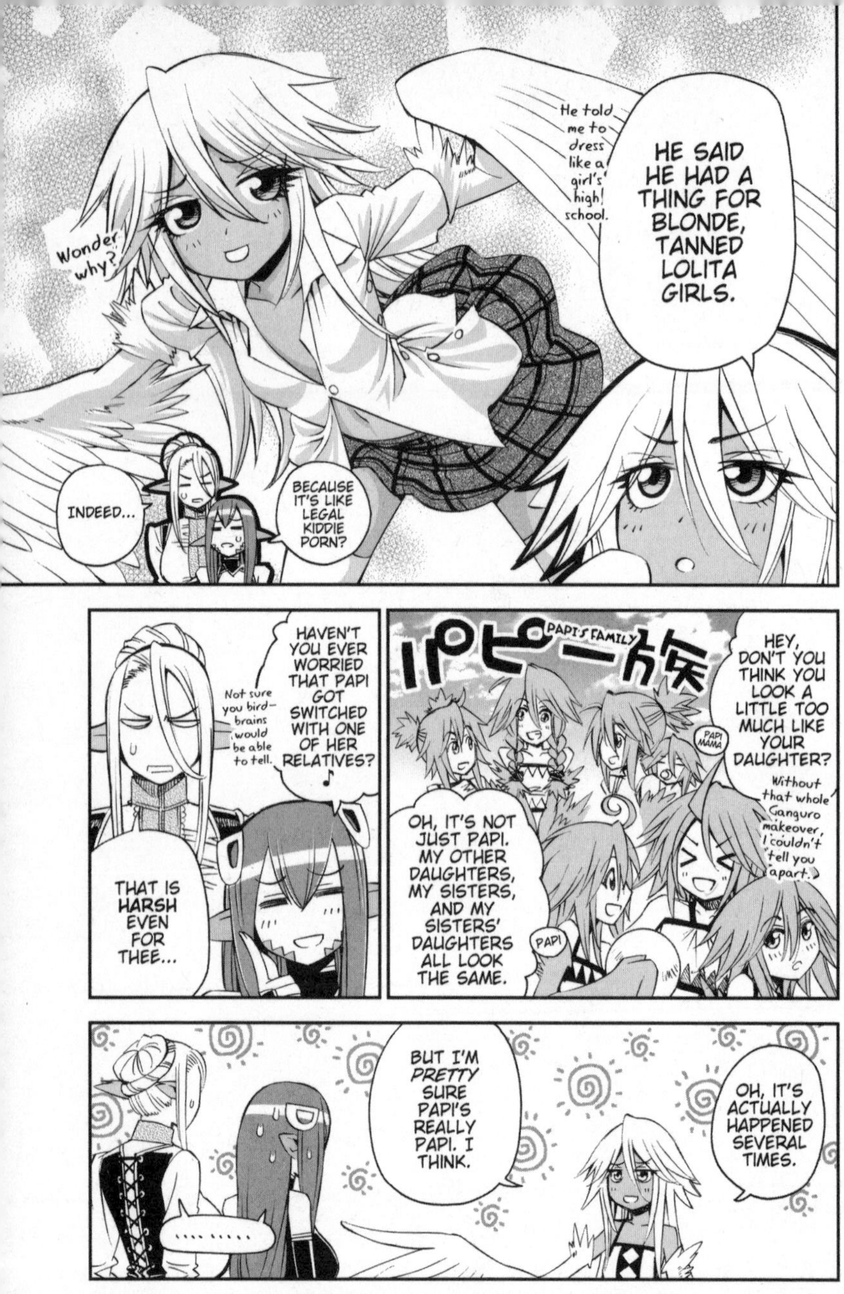
HE SAID HE HAD A THING FOR BLONDE, TANNED LOLITA GIRLS.
He told me to dress like a girl's high school.
Wonder why?
BECAUSE IT'S LIKE LEGAL KIDDIE PORN?
INDEED...
パピー一族
PAPI'S FAMILY
HEY, DON'T YOU THINK YOU LOOK A LITTLE TOO MUCH LIKE YOUR DAUGHTER?
Without that whole Ganguro makeover, I couldn't tell you apart.
PAPI MAMA
OH, IT'S NOT JUST PAPI. MY OTHER DAUGHTERS, MY SISTERS, AND MY SISTERS' DAUGHTERS ALL LOOK THE SAME.
PAPI
HAVEN'T YOU EVER WORRIED THAT PAPI GOT SWITCHED WITH ONE OF HER RELATIVES? ♪
Not sure you bird-brains would be able to tell.
THAT IS HARSH EVEN FOR THEE...
OH, IT'S ACTUALLY HAPPENED SEVERAL TIMES.
BUT I'M *PRETTY* SURE PAPI'S REALLY PAPI. I THINK.
......

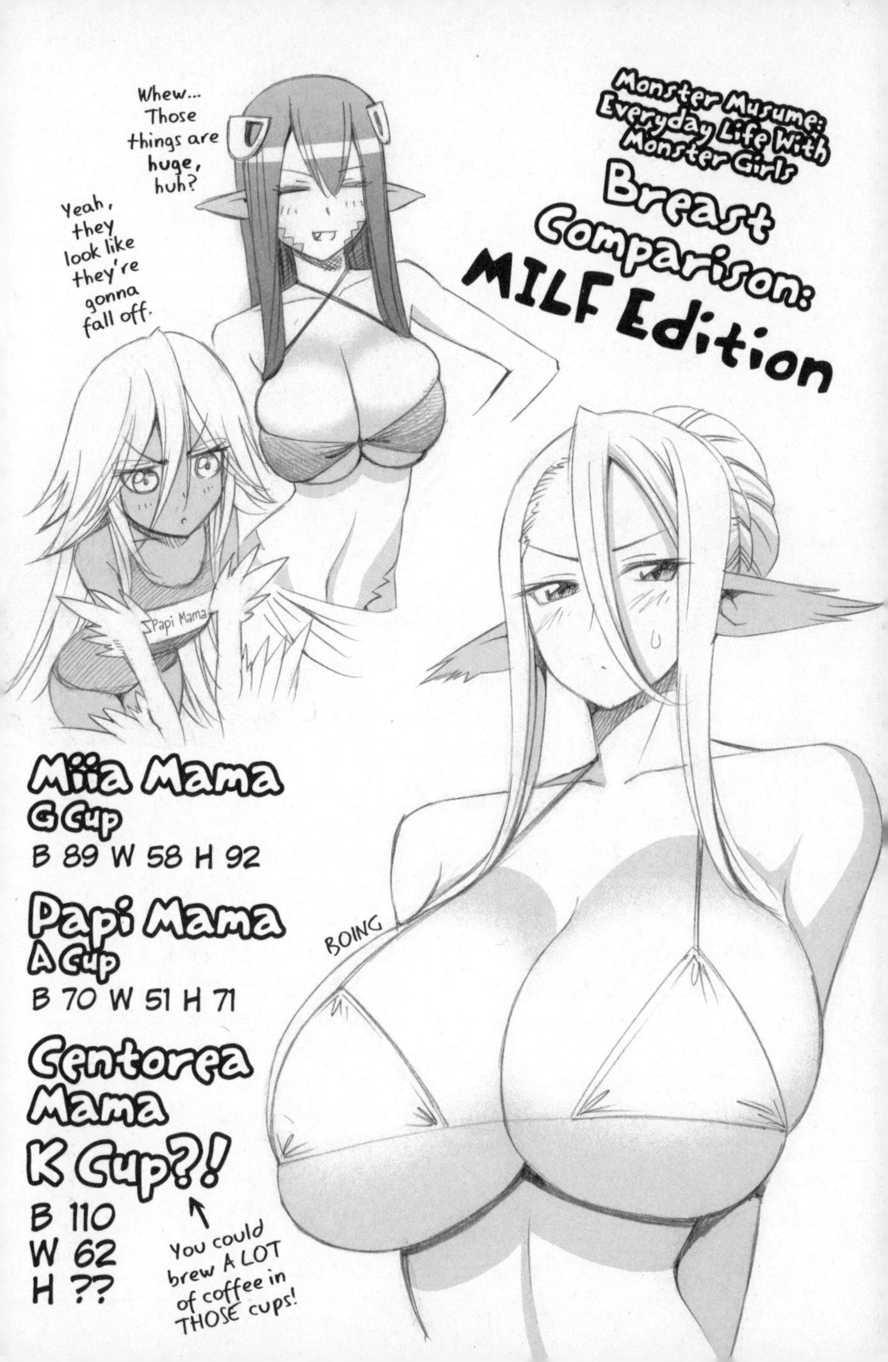
Monster Musume: Everyday Life With Monster Girls
Breast Comparison: MILF Edition
Whew... Those things are huge, huh?
Yeah, they look like they're gonna fall off.
Papi Mama
BOING
Miia Mama
G Cup
B 89 W 58 H 92
Papi Mama
A Cup
B 70 W 51 H 71
Centorea Mama
K Cup?!
B 110
W 62
H ??
You could brew A LOT of coffee in THOSE cups!

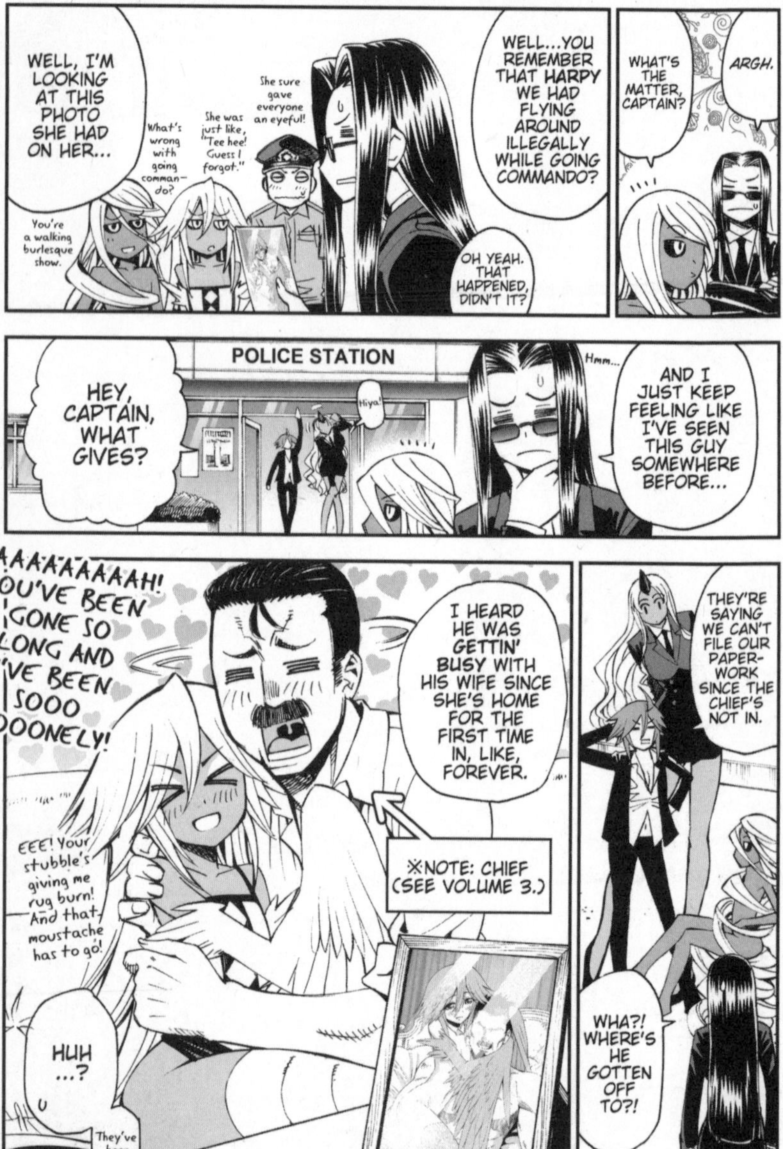
ARGH.
WHAT'S THE MATTER, CAPTAIN?
WELL...YOU REMEMBER THAT HARPY WE HAD FLYING AROUND ILLEGALLY WHILE GOING COMMANDO?
OH YEAH. THAT HAPPENED, DIDN'T IT?
She sure gave everyone an eyeful!
She was just like, "Tee hee! Guess I forgot."
What's wrong with going comman-do?
WELL, I'M LOOKING AT THIS PHOTO SHE HAD ON HER...
You're a walking burlesque show.
Hmm...
AND I JUST KEEP FEELING LIKE I'VE SEEN THIS GUY SOMEWHERE BEFORE...
Hiya!
POLICE STATION
HEY, CAPTAIN, WHAT GIVES?
THEY'RE SAYING WE CAN'T FILE OUR PAPER-WORK SINCE THE CHIEF'S NOT IN.
WHA?! WHERE'S HE GOTTEN OFF TO?!
I HEARD HE WAS GETTIN' BUSY WITH HIS WIFE SINCE SHE'S HOME FOR THE FIRST TIME IN, LIKE, FOREVER.
WAAAAAAAAAAH! YOU'VE BEEN GONE SO LONG AND I'VE BEEN SOOO LOOONELY!
※NOTE: CHIEF (SEE VOLUME 3.)
EEE! Your stubble's giving me rug burn! And that moustache has to go!
HUH ...?
They've been apart?

SEVEN SEAS ENTERTAINMENT PRESENTS

Monster Musume

story and art by OKAYADO

VOLUME 7

TRANSLATION
Ryan Peterson

ADAPTATION
Shanti Whitesides

LETTERING AND LAYOUT
Ma. Victoria Robado

LOGO DESIGN
Courtney Williams

COVER DESIGN
Nicky Lim

PROOFREADER
Janet Houck

ASSISTANT EDITOR
Lissa Pattillo

MANAGING EDITOR
Adam Arnold

PUBLISHER
Jason DeAngelis

Seven Seas books may be purchased in bulk for educational, business, or promotional use. For information on bulk purchases, please contact Macmillan Corporate & Premium Sales Department at 1-800-221-7945 (ext 5442) or write specialmarkets@macmillan.com.

ISBN: 978-1-626921-60-3

Printed in Canada

First Printing: August 2015

10 9 8 7 6 5 4 3 2 1

FOLLOW US ONLINE: ***www.gomanga.com***

READING DIRECTIONS

This book reads from ***right to left***, Japanese style. If this is your first time reading manga, you start reading from the top right panel on each page and take it from there. If you get lost, just follow the numbered diagram here. It may seem backwards at first, but you'll get the hang of it! Have fun!!

1
2
3
4
5
6
7
8
9

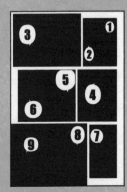